The Best of

SAN FRANCISCO

Editor
Colleen Dunn Bates

Contributing Editors
Owen Bubar, Wayne Karmitz, Pamela Mosher, Derk Richardson,
David Rubien, Rod Smith, David Timko, S. Irene Virbilia

Prentice Hall Press Editor
Edith Jarolim

Coordination
Alain Gayot

Directed by
André Gayot

Supervised by
Christian Millau

PRENTICE HALL PRESS ▪ NEW YORK

Other Gault Millau Guides Available
from Prentice Hall Press

The Best of Los Angeles
The Best of New York
The Best of Washington, D.C.

Published by Prentice Hall Press
A Division of Simon & Schuster, Inc.
Gulf + Western Building
One Gulf + Western Plaza
New York, New York 10023

Designed by Patricia Fabricant

Please address all comments regarding The Best of San Francisco to:
Gault Millau, Inc.
P.O. Box 361144
Los Angeles, CA 90036

Library of Congress Cataloging-in-Publication Data
The Best of San Francisco

Includes index
1. San Francisco (Calif.)—Description—Guide-books. 2. Restaurants, lunch rooms,
etc.—California—San Francisco—Guide-books. 3. Hotels, taverns,
etc.—California—San Francisco—Guide-books. I. Bates, Colleen Dunn.
F869.S33B465   1988   917.94'610453   87-29215
ISBN 0-13-076084-6

Special thanks to the staff of Prentice Hall Press for their help in producing this
Gault Millau guide.

Manufactured in the United States of America

CONTENTS

SHOPS

Where to find it and buy it, from gourmet groceries to California couture. Includes services usually known only to natives.

SIGHTS

There's more to San Francisco than cable cars. Walk the streets that Dashiell Hammett immortalized, wander the island that confined Al Capone, and explore the architectural gems that give this skyline such appeal.

ENVIRONS

You haven't seen the Bay Area if you haven't left the big city. We'll take you to Berkeley's best California-cuisine restaurants, Marin's best view spots and the wine country's best romantic inns.

BASICS

Everything you need to know about getting around in San Francisco like a true native. Includes late-night services, transportation facts and a calendar of interesting and unusual events.

MAPS

Finding your way around the city by the Bay.

INDEX

San Francisco

CITY ON THE MOVE

San Francisco is a city that could only have been founded and populated by dreamers and schemers. Its rich history is peopled with colorful characters—both fictional, like Dashiell Hammett's Sam Spade, and real, like Emperor Norton and Mayor Sunny Jim Rolph. And each is followed by new eccentrics from succeeding generations. It is a city constantly on the move, sometimes literally when the temblors roll through—a city always in the process of becoming something different. Like its unsettled earth below, San Francisco's image shifts with each historical era: it is a Gold Rush boomtown, a rollicking Barbary Coast seaport, Herb Caen's "Baghdad by the Bay," a solid union town, the Beat Generation's bohemia, a hippie haven for the '60s counterculture, the locus of gay and lesbian pride.

"No man is an island," claimed a little voice in an early song by the Jefferson Airplane, one of the rock bands that figured so prominently in making the city an acid-rock mecca in the '60s. But the band gave John Donne's dictum a uniquely San Franciscan twist by adding, "He's a peninsula." Surrounded by water on three sides, San Francisco is an often elegant, sometimes awkward compromise to its geography. It's so much more than "little cable cars" that "climb halfway to the stars," from the glorious bridges that link the city to the north and to the East Bay, to its challenging hills whose names—Russian, Potrero, Telegraph, Nob—echo the city's history of immigration and development. At any moment the fog could sweep in from the Pacific and shroud the hills in chilly mystery. Or the sun could break through the morning clouds and brighten the vivid hues on the faces of the restored Victorian row houses.

Above all, San Francisco is a city of neighborhoods, encompassing the pristine opulence of Pacific Heights, the working-class bustle of the Mission District, the chockablock frenzy of Chinatown, the sidewalk flair of the Castro, the lingering bohemianism of North Beach and the gentrified flower power of the Haight-Ashbury. And there is even room for new neighborhoods. In SOMA (South of Market), where ambitious entrepreneurs and conceptual artists compete for space, an architectural potpourri is still in the making. The best structures complement the city's natural beauty; there are nearly enough of these to counteract downtown's "Manhattanization," where ungainly masses of postmodern skyscrapers dwarf such landmarks as the Ferry Building and Coit Tower. Just blocks from the cold shadows of the glass-and-concrete Financial District, you can still walk down the Filbert Steps on Telegraph Hill, take in the exhilarating view of the Bay and step back a century in time by turning down picturesque Napier Lane.

Ultimately, San Francisco is animated by its people. The cultural contrasts shape its personality—from the society swells who subscribe to the symphony and opera to the Hispanics who dance to Afro-Cuban salsa and "son" in the Mission. On the borders of old Italian neighborhoods, Asian immigrants share sidewalk space with fourth-generation natives. Patrons of flashy gay discos coexist with the dart-throwing ale-quaffers of rowdy Irish pubs. San Francisco is a city inhabited and visited by those who have realized their dreams and those still struggling to see their dreams unfold. Even within its narrowing geographic and economic limits, San Francisco remains unfinished, a compelling site for international tourists and one of America's favorite homespun but exotic destinations.

RESTAURANTS

SAN FRANCISCO: A CULINARY FESTIVAL

That San Francisco is a restaurant town, nobody can deny. At last official count there were 4,200 restaurants in the city, or approximately one for every 98 people, which, if lined up kitchen-to-kitchen, would form a restaurant chain stretching roughly from Topeka, Kansas, to Bombay, with enough left over to change Bombay's image considerably.

The question is not whether San Francisco is a restaurant town, but what *kind* of restaurant town it is. The word "eclectic" is tempting, but there's more to it than that. The city is, after all, an international stew pot—a paella of peoples, a cassoulet of cultures, a social bouillabaisse. And every community—from Chinatown, Japantown, North Beach and the Mission to the sundry Asian, Pan-American and South-Seas enclaves—has its restaurants.

But San Francisco also has its own very special restaurant tradition, going clear back to the Gold Rush. The city's first restaurant was probably a room off the saloon in the long-gone Bella Union Hotel at Portsmouth Square, which was succeeded shortly thereafter by the original Poodle Dog, Maison Dorée and the fabulous Palace Hotel, where the legendary Lucien Heyraudt created a grand cuisine that routinely impressed visiting European royalty.

Today stalwart survivors of that tradition are scattered about town. Such places are often fondly described as "truly San Franciscan," that is, possessing a reassuring aura generated by dark polished wood, plenty of brass, frosted glass and mirrors, light fixtures designed with gas in mind, union waiters in starched jackets, espresso machines huffing like brass locomotives and well-heeled crowds clamoring for tables. Few if any of these joints serve truly distinguished food, though it's hard to go wrong with fresh Dungeness crab or that nearly eclipsed delicacy, Rex sole. One frequents such establishments not to worship the food but to cut the fog with a little whiskey and catch the spirit of the old days, good and otherwise, in "The City That Knows How."

In the past decade there has emerged a new kind of "truly San Franciscan" restaurant, one in which the ambience is merely a backdrop for the food. Places of this type do serve distinguished, often surprising and sometimes inspirational food (and, most likely, no whiskey). The chef's face may be familiar from magazine covers, talk shows or the inside flap of some heavily art-directed book. You know who they are.

Let it be said that Alice Waters is only (though quite deservedly) the most prominent member of a broad network of kitchen artists populating a culinary scene of international importance (her Chez Panisse is actually in Berkeley, but we broad-minded San Franciscans generously accept it as one of our own). Drawn by diverse factors—San Francisco's culinary tradition, the abundance of fine foods from land and sea, and the California wine industry's ascendancy, to name a few—many talented young chefs for years have chosen to make a go of it in the Bay Area instead of New York or Paris. The result is an ongoing culinary festival, a movable feast of great quality, diversity and imagination.

The third distinct group of San Francisco restaurants is a result of the city's international character. Designated loosely as ethnic places, these humble purveyors of cuisines from other lands often equal the superstars' efforts in brilliance and deft presentation. In fact, any number of Thai and Japanese houses thrive in relative anonymity year after year, while trendsetting new spots come and go like shooting stars.

Obviously, the answer to our opening question is that San Francisco is a *terrific* restaurant town. Always has been, always will be. Sure, it's possible to get a bad meal here—but you'd have to know where to go.

That's what this book is for.

SOME ADVICE AND COMMENTS

Reservations are a must in San Francisco's hottest restaurants. Call Masa's exactly three weeks before the day you wish to visit, call Chez Panisse a month in advance, and give Fog City, Campton Place and Stars plenty of notice as well.

California's laid-back image notwithstanding, San Franciscans like to dress up—they identify more with New Yorkers than Angelenos. Don't even think of going to L'Etoile, Fleur de Lys, Donatello, Masa's, Ernie's or the Carnelian Room without a coat and tie. The atmosphere is a little looser at such temples of California cuisine as Chez Panisse and Stars. And in trendy South of Market, anything goes.

Even if money is no object, don't limit your eating to the full-fledged restaurants reviewed in this chapter. As you'll discover in Quick Bites, San Francisco is also a great city for fun, inexpensive spots full of neighborhood and ethnic charm and some wonderful food: noodle houses, taquerias, coffeehouses, pasta cafés, barbecue joints and much more.

As is true across the country, San Francisco's most popular chefs tend to let success go to their heads and hop from one restaurant to the next, which of course is supremely frustrating to guidebook authors. If you visit a restaurant we tout, only to find the chef gone and the menu changed, forgive us—we've kept current as best we can.

ABOUT THE REVIEWS

Restaurants are ranked in the same manner that French students are graded, on a scale of one to twenty. The rankings reflect *only* the quality of the food; decor, service, wine lists and atmosphere are explicitly commented on within each review. Restaurants that are ranked thirteen and above are distinguished with toques (chef's hats), according to the following table:

4 toques, for 19/20
3 toques, for 17/20 or 18/20
2 toques, for 15/20 or 16/20
1 toque, for 13/20 or 14/20

Keep in mind that we are comparing San Francisco's restaurants to the best in the world, and that these ranks are *relative*. One toque for 13/20 is not a very good ranking for a highly reputed (and very expensive) restaurant, but it is quite complimentary for a small place without much culinary pretension.

Unless otherwise noted, the prices given are for a complete dinner for two, including an appetizer, main course and dessert per person, along with tax, tip and a bottle of wine. It is, naturally, hard to estimate the cost of wine; for our purposes we assume a modest bottle at a modest restaurant and a good California wine (usually $20 to $30 a bottle) at a more serious place. Lovers of the great Burgundies, Bordeaux or Champagnes will find their tabs higher than our estimates; conversely, those who like to eat lightly, sharing appetizers and desserts, will spend less. However, prices continue to creep up, so forgive us if a restaurant becomes more expensive by the time you visit it.

Toque Tally

18/20

Chez Panisse

17/20

Fleur de Lys   Masa's

16/20

Amelio's   Mount View Hotel
Café at Chez Panisse   Stars
Harry's Bar   Zola's

15/20

La Boucane   Hayes Street Grill
Campton Place   Miramonte Hotel
Donatello   Pierre
Ernie's   Le St. Tropez
L'Etoile   Square One
Fourth Street Grill   Zuni Café

14/20

Act IV   Dakota
Bon Temps Louisiana Restaurant   Fog City Diner
Caffe Sport   French Laundry
Chez Michel   Fuku-Sushi

The Grille (Sonoma Mission Inn)
Khan Toke Thai House
Modesto Lanzone Opera Plaza
Mustards

Narai
Royal Thai
Santa Fe Bar & Grill

13/20 ♗

Auberge du Soleil
Bay Wolf Café
Bridge Creek
Camargue
Christophe Restaurant
Elite Café
French Room
Garden House
Greens
Harbor Village Restaurant
Ironwood Café
Kabuto Sushi
Kinokawa
Madrona Manor

Mai's
Nikko Sushi
Nob Hill Restaurant
North China
Pacific Heights Bar & Grill
Peacock
Prego
Rings
Ristorante Milano
Rosalie's
Scott's Seafood Grill & Bar
Tadich Grill
Vanessi's
Yamato

12/20

Alejandro's Sociedad Gastronomica
Angor Wat
John Ash & Company
Augusta's
Buca Giovanni
Cadillac Bar
Café Majestic
Casa Madrona
Cendrillon
Le Central
China Moon Café
Ciao

Le Cyrano
De Paula's
Dixie Café
Gaylord's
Grifone Ristorante
Korea House
Melon's
Mitoya
Oliveto
Osome
Palm
Rodin

La Rondalla
Sanppo
The Shadows
Siam Cuisine
Swiss Alps

Taxi
El Tazumal
La Traviata
Yuet Lee

11/20

Billboard Café
Blue Light Café
Café Americain
Caprice
Le Castel
Circolo
Cuba
L'Entrecôte de Paris
Fior d'Italia
The German Cook
Haymarket Restaurant
Jackson Fillmore Trattoria
Janot's
Little Italy

Little Joe's
MacArthur Park
The Mandarin
Maxwell's Plum
Mountain Home Inn
Nakapan
Pat O'Shea's Mad Hatter
Paprikas Fono
Pavilion Room
Restaurant 101
Sam's Grill
Schroeder's
Trader Vic's

10/20

565 Clay
Jack's
Nicaragua
Original Joe's

Perry's
Savannah Grill
Travigne
Washington Street Restaurant

9/20

California Culinary Academy
Le Club
House of Prime Rib

Hunan
Lafayette on Pacific

8/20

The Big Four
Carnelian Room
Fournou's Ovens

Harris'
Tarantino's
Umberto

7/20

Doros

6/20

Café d'Arts

Kan's

The World's Cuisines

AMERICAN

Augusta's
The Big Four
Billboard Café
Blue Light Café
Bridge Creek
Campton Place
Fog City Diner
Harris'
House of Prime Rib
Ironwood Café
Jack's

MacArthur Park
Maxwell's Plum
Mountain Home Inn
Pat O'Shea's Mad Hatter
Perry's
Savannah Grill
Stars
Taxi
Vanessi's
Washington Street Restaurant

BRAZILIAN

De Paula's

CALIFORNIA

John Ash & Company
Bay Wolf Café
Café Americain
Café at Chez Panisse
Café Majestic
Casa Madrona
565 Clay
Fourth Street Grill
French Laundry
The Grille (Sonoma Mission Inn)
Haymarket Restaurant
Lafayette on Pacific

Madrona Manor
Melon's
Mount View Hotel
Nob Hill Restaurant
Pat O'Shea's Mad Hatter
Pacific Heights Bar & Grill
Pavilion Room
Rings
Santa Fe Bar & Grill
Taxi
Travigne
Zuni Café

CAMBODIAN

Angor Wat

CAJUN/CREOLE

Bon Temps Louisiana Restaurant
Dixie Café

Elite Café

CHINESE

China Moon Café
Harbor Village Restaurant

Hunan
Kan's

The Mandarin   Yuet Lee
North China

CONTINENTAL

Carnelian Room   Restaurant 101

CUBAN

Cuba

FRENCH

Act IV   Ernie's
Amelio's   L'Etoile
Auberge du Soleil   Fleur de Lys
The Big Four   Fournou's Ovens
La Boucane   French Room
Café d'Arts   The Grille (Sonoma Mission Inn)
California Culinary Academy   Janot's
Camargue   Masa's
Caprice   Miramonte Hotel
Le Castel   Oliveto
Cendrillon   Pierre
Le Central   Rodin
Chez Michel   Le St. Tropez
Christophe Restaurant   The Shadows
Le Club   Stars
Le Cyrano   Zola's
L'Entrecôte de Paris

GERMAN

The German Cook   Schroeder's

Swiss Alps

HUNGARIAN

Paprikas Fono

INDIAN

Gaylord's   Peacock

INTERNATIONAL

Café Americain   Zuni Café
Square One

ITALIAN

Buca Giovanni   Little Joe's
Caffe Sport   Modesto Lanzone Opera Plaza
Ciao   Oliveto
Circolo   Original Joe's
Donatello   Prego
Doros   Ristorante Milano
Fior d'Italia   La Traviata
Grifone Ristorante   Travigne
Harry's Bar   Umberto
Jackson Fillmore Trattoria   Vanessi's
Little Italy

JAPANESE

Fuku-Sushi   Kabuto Sushi

Kinokawa
Mitoya
Nikko Sushi

Osome
Sanppo
Yamato

KOREAN

Korea House

MEXICAN

Alejandro's Sociedad
  Gastronomica

Cadillac Bar
La Rondalla

NICARAGUAN

Nicaragua

POLYNESIAN

Trader Vic's

SALVADORAN

El Tazumal

SEAFOOD

Hayes Street Grill
Pacific Heights Bar & Grill

Sam's Grill
Scott's Seafood Grill & Bar

Tadich Grill   Tarantino's

SOUTHWESTERN

Dakota   Rosalie's
Fourth Street Grill   Santa Fe Bar & Grill

SPANISH

Alejandro's Sociedad Gastronomica

STEAKHOUSE

L'Entrecôte de Paris   Original Joe's
Harris'   Palm

SUSHI

Fuku-Sushi   Nikko Sushi
Kabuto Sushi   Osome
Kinokawa   Sanppo
Mitoya

THAI

Khan Toke Thai House   Royal Thai
Nakapan   Siam Cuisine
Narai

VEGETARIAN

Green's

VIETNAMESE

Garden House   Mai's

Restaurants

ACT IV

333 Fulton St., Civic Center - 863-8400

California/French

14

The buzz on this place is that it's the most romantic spot in town, and we have to agree. We were hooked from the moment we came in out of a sloppy San Francisco fog to find our table shimmering like a dream beside the merrily hissing fire (gas flame, but effective). This jewel box of a bar/lounge/dining room, at the back of the sweet little Inn at the Opera hotel, is luxurious and intimate, an Impressionist's version of a Victorian parlor. It's also quite small, but manages by the artful arrangement of velvet settees, low tables and foliage to create discreet spaces for couples and small groups. A tinkling piano covers the sound of beating hearts. In keeping with the romance, Deutz and Schramsberg are offered by the glass, and a bartender named Tim makes exquisite martinis, the kind William Powell and Myrna Loy pursued through several *Thin Man* movies (shot in San Francisco, by the way). A limited but excellent menu offers such lovers' fare as steak and salmon tartare, fluffy spanakopita (spinach encased in phyllo) and smoked trout with a heady horseradish cream. Rack of lamb is cooked as ordered, if infused with a little more garlic than love will bear. Keep in mind that Act IV is packed beyond enjoyment immediately before and after performances at the nearby Opera House and Symphony Hall, though it's fun to attend when ballerinas are holding court. Dinner for two, with wine, will run about $60.

Open daily 7:30 a.m.-10 a.m., 11:30 a.m.-2:30 p.m. & 5 p.m.-12:30 a.m. All major cards.

ALEJANDRO'S SOCIEDAD GASTRONOMICA

We aren't exactly sure what the "Sociedad Gastronomica" is or whether, in fact, it really exists, but we are told it is an association of Latin American gourmets and that Alejandro Espinosa is a member of it. At any rate, society or not, some

*1840 Clement St.,
Richmond District -
668-1184*

Spanish/Mexican

12/20

superb high Spanish dishes are served here, as well as some competent Mexican "common" fare to satisfy those who can only imagine ordering enchiladas and tacos in any Hispanic restaurant. The alejandrinos, little fried pastries filled with cheese, egg or peppers, make an excellent starter; the ceviche could be more vigorous, but it employs quality sea bass. The entrees—barring the competent but unexciting Mexican dishes—can be astonishingly good (the best paella Valenciana in San Francisco—fresh fish and shellfish, good chorizo, fresh vegetables, slightly overcooked chicken, and rice golden with saffron) or rather less successful (pan-fried trout topped with too-crisp serrano ham, tender rabbit in a too-sweet peanut sauce, overcooked snapper with delicious roasted garlic). The wine list is multinational and interesting, but unfortunately there are no riojas (though the bar knows how to prepare an excellent pitcher of sangria). Desserts are typically Spanish (i.e., flan), which is to say they should be avoided. The slightly kitsch decor (cheap ironwork and tile, heavy woods, heavy chandeliers) and the sometimes indifferent service detract from the experience, but we still think the paella is marvelous. About $50 for two, with wine.

Open Mon.-Thurs. 5 p.m.-11 p.m., Fri.-Sat. 5 p.m.-12 midnight, Sun. 4 p.m.-11 p.m. All major cards.

AMELIO'S

1630 Powell St., North Beach - 397-4339

French

16

We're not quite sure whether young chef Jacky Robert is a cuisinier or a magician. This gentleman has an uncanny knack for bringing lifeless dowager restaurants back into the full bloom of youth. Some eight years ago his rather nouvelle ideas put Ernie's, then in a sad state of culinary dilapidation, at the top of the city's restaurant ladder. Hungry for a restaurant of his own, Robert left Ernie's a few years ago to resurrect Amelio's, an Italian-Continental remnant of many decades past. With charming co-owner Chris Shearman, Robert has done the near-impossible: only a few months after he donned his toque, the raves came in and this tiny, elegant dining room (magnificent old woods, floral fabrics and dramatic flower arrangements, all skillfully and softly lit) was full once again. The food is an interesting blend of nouvelle cuisine and classic French, with a few Asian touches—Robert's lovely wife, Chong, is Korean, and he attributes much of his style to what he has learned from her. The best way to sample this eclectic cuisine is to order the often-changing dégustation menu. It may start with Robert's signature woven bi-color pasta with huge, barely cooked

Hawaiian prawns and sea scallops in a light cream sauce with caviar. Then it may progress to crisp little deep-fried quail in a ginger-soy-molasses marinade served atop snow peas, followed by an intermezzo of a grape and Champagne sorbet. You then have a choice of entrees; the best are the fine rack of lamb, again in an Oriental honey-and-soy marinade with incredible, thin Japanese noodles, the rare duck breast in an intense red wine sauce with ratatouille, and the lobster with a vegetable flan. The kitchen then takes charge of your meal again, sending out a lovely little salad—one night it included three delightful imported cheeses, another night an astounding Brie "pancake." Finally, you will be served dessert, perhaps a pyramid of exotic berries in a light pastry with English cream, or one of Robert's wonderful chocolate creations.

Ordering à la carte, one gets half the number of dishes for the same price (or more)—and it seems like most of Jacky Robert's attention is devoted to creating a fabulous dégustation menu. (He has recently started serving a simpler three-course menu that is also very fine.) The wine list includes every treasure imaginable, but we wish the recent California bottlings were priced lower. The service is mostly young, a tad pretentious and not always knowledgeable about what's going on in the kitchen, but they're trying harder each day. About $130 for an à la carte dinner for two, with wine; menus are $36 and $57 per person, without wine or tip.

Open nightly 5:30 p.m.-10:30 p.m. All major cards.

ANGOR WAT

4217 Geary Blvd.,
Richmond District -
221-7887

Cambodian

12/20

This restaurant has inspired some local restaurant critics to proclaim Cambodian cuisine the most exciting new cooking to hit these shores. But authenticity isn't one of Angor Wat's strong suits; to the best of our knowledge, poached salmon, Cornish game hen and vegetables sautéed in olive oil (all found on the menu here) have never been Cambodian staples. Nonetheless, the food here is expertly prepared and seasoned with such Southeast Asian basics as tamarind, ginger, lemon grass, coconut milk and chili peppers. It's all tailored to the American palate—meats and poultry are boned, fish are filleted and no innards are offered—but it's all delicious: stir-fried pork and prawns with winter melon sauce, five-spice broiled chicken, salmon with lemon-grass sauce and much more. Chef and owner Keav Ty has combined the cuisine of his heritage with his training as a

French chef, and the result is largely successful. The setting is pleasant, with pictures of Angor Wat (the temple) on all the walls, and the price is quite fair: $40 for dinner for two, with wine.

Open Mon.-Sat. 11 a.m.-3 p.m. & 5 p.m.-9:30 p.m. All major cards.

THE BIG FOUR

1075 California St. (Huntington Hotel), Nob Hill - 771-1140
French/American

8/20

The dining room off the lobby of the Huntington Hotel is one of the more attractive of San Francisco's grand hotel restaurants. With green leather banquettes and armchairs, mirrored walls and elegant brass candelabra, the room is immediately inviting. The restaurant is dedicated to the memories of the "Big Four" tycoons of nineteenth-century San Francisco: Hopkins, Huntington, Stanford and Crocker. Perhaps they would have received better service than we did. After standing in the foyer for ten minutes until the maître d' appeared, we then had to suffer intolerably long waits between courses. The food, alas, was hardly worth waiting for. Scottish smoked salmon, described to us by our cavalier young waiter as "the real McCoy," was satisfactory but would never set the world on fire. Similarly, the limestone lettuce salad with bay shrimp could not elicit any cries of excitement. Our waiter almost talked us into ordering as an entree the fillet of buffalo, a house specialty, until we saw someone at the next table trying to tear into it, unsuccessfully, with a steak knife. Instead, we chose an overdone quail marinated with chili, sweet peppers and walnut oil. We were promised roasted sweet garlic and brought inedible, almost raw cloves. Also served with it were fried wild rice fritters, delicious but very oily. From the uninviting dessert tray we chose a white chocolate mousse cake with a "surprise" filling: an insipid layer of raspberry jelly. About $100 for two, with wine.

Open daily 11:30 a.m.-3 p.m. & 5:30 p.m.-11 p.m. All major cards.

BILLBOARD CAFÉ

299 9th St., South of Market - 558-9500
American

11/20

It's garish, noisy and a lot of fun. The crowd ranges from account execs to artist types with green hair and acrylic paint on face and clothes (carefully applied for the occasion, no doubt), with mostly hip, young, hungry people in between. It's said that everyone looks good under neon, and this is the place to find out. The food is eclectic and solidly good, if unremarkable. We love the meatloaf and the chili, and have always found the fresh fish grilled just right—but we have to admit that it isn't the food that draws us, but the scene. If you don't meet someone you know here, you haven't been spending enough time on the social circuit. Two will spend a modest $35 for dinner with wine.

Open Mon.-Thurs. 11 a.m.-11 p.m., Fri.-Sat. 11 a.m.-12 midnight, Sun. 11:30 a.m.-4:30 p.m. Cards: MC, V.

BLUE LIGHT CAFÉ

1979 Union St., Marina District - 922-5510

American

11/20

We've heard more than one story of people arriving at the Blue Light with dinner reservations only to give away their table because they were having so much fun in the bar. But that's not the best way to do it; the best way is to make a reservation and show up early for a little preprandial tequila, raucous talk and rock 'n' roll. As is appropriate in a place owned by Boz Scaggs, there's a steady backbeat pulsing through the multilevel, industrial-tech restaurant. Galvanized aluminum, high ceilings and low light (abetted by skylights before dark) give the Blue Light a laid-back, Southern feel, as if it occupied an old warehouse on the bayou end of the Mississippi. On the other hand, it fits the upscale Union Street milieu as well—quite a trick. Steaks, chicken, spicy sausage and fresh fish are grilled over mesquite, sometimes just right, sometimes not quite right. At our last dinner here, we tried a good salad of fresh greens, tomatoes and roasted pecans and a special of grilled rockfish, which had been marinated in a spicy tamari-based mix and cooked on skewers. The fish had soaked too long and was overcooked, but it was tasty anyway, just the thing to wash down with a cold Corona. We love the slightly sweet cornbread and the tangy, creamy coleslaw that comes with most entrees. Mesquite-grilled steaks are arguably the most consistently good dishes, especially in the form of fajitas. Service is generally efficient, but on a busy evening it's wise to order some of Boz's patented buttermilk onion rings to keep hunger at bay while perusing the menu. Dinner for two, with beer, will run about $40.

Open Sun.-Wed. 6 p.m.-12 midnight, Thurs.-Sat. 6 p.m.-1 a.m. Cards: MC, V.

BON TEMPS LOUISIANA RESTAURANT

What a wonderful place! Chef Brad Borel—charming and ever attentive—and his lovely wife have created San Francisco's greatest outpost of this au courant cuisine, even though the city has several glitzier and more elaborate Cajun/Creole

1963 Sutter St.,
Japantown - 563-6300
Cajun/Creole

14

restaurants. What to order? Everything here is wonderful: such starters as Cajun popcorn (crayfish tails with aïoli) or soft-shell crab and shrimp rémoulade; such entrees as jambalaya with ham, chicken and shrimp, gumbos rich with shrimp, oysters, okra, crab, chicken and andouille sausage, and less traditional main courses, such as the chicken breast stuffed with cornbread, andouille sausage and crayfish; and such desserts as bread pudding and apple cobbler. The wine list is short but sweet, the service kind and efficient, and the owner/chef a joy—he even tours the dining room at the end of the night to see how his guests liked their meals, like a great chef in a French temple of gastronomy. About $50 for two, with wine.

Open Tues.-Thurs. 5:30 p.m.-9:30 p.m., Fri.-Sat. 6
p.m.-10:30 p.m., Sun. 5 p.m.-9 p.m. Cards: AE.

BUCA GIOVANNI

800 Greenwich St., North
Beach - 776-7766
Italian

12/20

Some time after leaving Vanessi's (a popular North Beach eatery), Giovanni Leoni resurfaced as owner of this most enjoyable restaurant, Buca Giovanni. As the name suggests, the dining room is below street level and was made to resemble a Toscana dungeon, with scoured brick substructures decorated with memorabilia and scenes from Lucca. The menu features many items from Tuscany rarely seen on San Francisco menus. An antipasto misto has a generous amount of aromatic bresaola and wonderfully sweet dried tomatoes with olive oil. Unfortunately, a disappointing green bean salad with chewy calamari does not measure up to the first starter—but the pastas are all a delight. We especially like the panzerotti salsa di noci, perfectly al dente ravioli pockets filled with seasoned veal and graced with a delicious, nutty sauce. Entrees are more uneven, ranging from the sweet, tender and flavorful lamb chops sautéed with herbs and butter to the fish of the day—on our last visit, overcooked sea bass, its flavor hidden by the otherwise fine sauce of vegetables, clams and mussels. To finish, try the ball of good chocolate gelato rolled in semi-sweet shavings. Buca Giovanni is also notable for its low-fat and low-salt daily specials for the health- and weight-conscious. A moderately priced wine list with good California selections makes for a pleasurable and affordable evening. About $70 for dinner for two, with wine.

Open Mon.-Thurs. 5:30 p.m.-10:30 p.m., Fri.-Sat. 5:30
p.m.-11:30 p.m. Cards: MC, V.

CADILLAC BAR

1 Holland Ct., South of Market - 543-8226

Mexican

12/20

The Cadillac Bar isn't exactly the most comfortable or relaxed restaurant in San Francisco, but it does serve some delicious Mexican food. This huge, glitzy, wood-and-glass warehouse of a restaurant features an open kitchen, a long bar, a crush of humanity and a din like Grand Central Station. It serves a different Mexican cuisine than can be encountered almost anywhere else in the city: a high, refined Mexican cuisine, unlike the street food—burritos, tacos, enchiladas—on most other menus. Here you'll find beautiful grilled red snapper in a tomato sauce with peppers and onions; fish and shellfish cooked in a paper bag; fabulous, tender goat; and shredded pork carnitas, tasty if too stewy. The Cadillac also serves combinations of many of its specialties (including an all-seafood combination) designed for *very* hungry groups. Desserts are uninviting, service is rushed but friendly, and the wonderful Mexican beers and tequila drinks are more interesting than the few wines. For those who lack creativity, the menu says that tacos and burritos are available upon request. About $40 for two, with beer or tequila.

Open Mon.-Thurs. 11 a.m.-11 p.m., Fri. 11 a.m.-12 midnight, Sat. 5 p.m.-12 midnight. All major cards.

CAFÉ AMERICAIN

317 Columbus Ave., North Beach - 981-8266

California/ International

11/20

All the clichés of the new California dining emporium are here in force: a rambling dining room with whitewashed walls, skylights, clear oak trim, odd knickknacks (in this case, sculptures fashioned from spent automobile parts) and the ubiquitous oak/mesquite grill open to the dining room for all to see (and smell). The eclectic menu borrows from French classic, French nouvelle, Italian modern and California cuisine, making use of good local ingredients. Unfortunately, the marriage of different cuisines here is not always successful. New potatoes stuffed with avocado and topped with lime and diced tomatoes are interesting as a starter, but the oak-fired pizzas are often charred and have dried-out toppings. An entree of lamb with a peppermint pesto sounds interesting, but when ordered rare it arrived cooked white throughout, with a pesto as thick as paste. However, the tomato pasta that occasionally accompanies entrees is wonderful—it merits its own place on the menu. The kitchen seems to put the best of its technique into the desserts: many tempting fresh blueberry (when in season) creations appear, and a caramelized walnut tart with crème fraîche truly satisfies. In keeping with au courant trends, the moderately priced wine list has many selections from small but good California vineyards. A reasonable $60 for dinner for two, with wine.

Open Mon.-Thurs. 7 a.m.-2:30 p.m. & 6 p.m.-10 p.m., Fri. 7 a.m.-2:30 p.m. & 6 p.m.-11 p.m., Sat. 6 p.m.-11 p.m. Cards: MC, V.

Café d'Arts

205 Oak St., Civic Center - 626-7100

French

6/20

A gruff, heavily accented voice greets us on the telephone with a recorded message. We are told we can only be seated at very specific times, we must be absolutely prompt or we will lose our table, and we must not smoke in the restaurant. We temporarily lose interest—this place doesn't sound like much fun—but next week drop in without a reservation and not at one of the specified times. We are seated immediately (well, not quite—they first insist on showing us the menu to see if the prices scare us off) in a small, half-empty room. We are immediately struck by the decor, or, rather, the lack of it. The restaurant has but twelve tables and is decorated tastefully but austerely. The uncushioned cane chairs are serviceable but not comfortable. Candle holders on the tables look like they came from a five-and-dime store. One lonely exotic orchid plant looks wilted. The tables are well set, however, with whimsical hand-painted plates. The expensive menu, divided into "arousers" (appetizers), "satisfiers" (entrees) and "delights" (desserts), is presented, along with a short, pricey wine list. Our waiter, a knowledgeable young man of some pretension, describes the specials from the eccentric chef, William Fragala. Two small breadsticks are brought; no other bread or butter is offered, ostensibly in the interest of health. Similarly, the chef uses precious few spoons of butter or cream in his "cuisine," and salt and pepper shakers are banished from the dining room. Although we heartily applaud health-oriented trends in nouvelle cuisine, any notions we have of Fragala being an American Senderens are quickly dispelled when the food arrives. Over the course of the evening, we are assaulted by his grand special appetizer, eggplant rolls stuffed with ricotta, Parmesan, chili and herbs in a tomato broth (a gooey, vile mess with no taste whatsoever); a "rare" breast of duck (overcooked beyond belief) with a sickening orange-bourbon marinade and a kumquat sauce, accompanied by coarse, almost raw vegetables and a horrid unidentifiable brown rice dish; and a white chocolate mousse with raspberry sauce. The best thing about the dessert is its microscopic portion. There may be worse places in San

Francisco, but, mercifully, we have yet to find them. About $90 for two, with wine.

Open Wed.-Sat. 6 p.m.-10:30 p.m. Cards: MC, V.

CAFÉ MAJESTIC
1500 Sutter St., Civic Center - 776-6400
California

12/20

Late in life, Stanley Eichelbaum left a career as a respected theater critic with a local tabloid to return to school (the California Culinary Academy) and pursue his fantasy of hosting and cooking in a theater/dinner club. Located in the Hotel Majestic (under another name the property was once reputed to be a brothel), the Café Majestic is a partial realization of his dream. The large, high-ceilinged room is divided into three dining areas, with small wall lamps and tall mirrors making the room seem even bigger, and a pianist making it seem even noisier. The entertainment has not been, by Eichelbaum's own admission, a sellout; the cooking is considerably more successful, though we'd give our last dinner here a mixed review. The prelude was admirable: a wild mushroom soup with minced scallions and red peppers and a cold avocado soup with red onion and a tomato salsa. The first act—a warm Chinese duck salad with a sherry-ginger-apple vinaigrette and a small pizza topped with goat cheese, sweet peppers, blanched garlic and prosciutto—had us ready to give the kitchen a standing ovation. But the second act flagged with a woefully overcooked sea bass en papillote and a tough (but tasty) roast leg of lamb au jus, perfumed with rosemary and garlic. The finale was composed of some particularly undramatic desserts. Eichelbaum shows considerable culinary promise; if he can extend his skill from the soups and starters to the rest of the meal, he will have a wonderful restaurant. Dinner for two, with wine, will run about $90.

Open Tues.-Sat. 7:30 a.m.-10:30 a.m., 11:30 a.m.-2:30 p.m. & 5:30 p.m.-11 p.m. Cards: AE, MC, V.

CAFFE SPORT
574 Green St., North Beach - 981-1251
Italian

14

This is a place of near-legendary status, often spoken of in hushed tones. When revered New York restaurant critic Mimi Sheraton was in town for a brief guest stint at the San Francisco *Examiner*, a time she spent shooting down more than a few local sacred cows, these were her words on Caffe Sport: "I wanted to try it, but I couldn't get in." That may be hard to believe, but anyone who's withstood the Caffe Sport ordeal knows two things: getting in can be a battle, and the management could care less about restaurant critics. Visit

Caffe Sport and you'll get an idea of what fraternity hazing is like—you'll be verbally roughed up and possibly humiliated by brusque and/or ribald Sicilian waiters, who know they serve soul-satisfying food and make you pay for it. Even if you're wise to the reservation system (begin calling at noon Tuesday for a spot that week; reservations are not accepted for parties of less than four), you'll have to wait outside for a half an hour or so. Once in, you may be crammed into a table designed to accommodate half your party, and you may turn gray before a hand-scrawled menu is made available. Pass the time by admiring the chaos of toys, knickknacks and Italian artifacts plastered to the walls and ceiling. The fun really begins when the waiter comes for your order. Let's say four of you have chosen four dishes. The waiter will tell you that you must order two single-size dishes and one double. If you have trouble deciding which item to order double size, he'll decide for you and will try to bully you into agreeing. But stand fast: Take as much time as you need, even if your waiter gets in a snit. He'll respect you for it later. During the ordering process you'll discover that there are no appetizers, not even salads. After ordering, you'll receive bread but no butter. Chances are you'll be too shell-shocked to make a decision about wine, so just take a carafe of white or red. But as soon as the large, colorful platters of food are brought out, all angst and confusion are washed away in a sea of garlic. You may be put off by the quantities of garlic at first bite, but it soon becomes clear that chef Antonio La Tona is working on a rarefied plane where high-impact flavors blend explosively. The pasta con pesto—a staple here and a perfect complement to practically everything on the menu—is laden with the traditional riches of olive oil, Parmesan (in mountainous quantity) and, of course, garlic, but it attains an ethereality that we can only attribute to the addition of stock. Caffe Sport's finest triumph, also stunningly rich, is the scampi—gigantic, tender prawns served in a creamless white sauce that defies explanation. The calamari all'Antonio comes with the same sauce, and we've seen people swoon over it. We've swooned ourselves over the langosto, an immense lobster spread-eagled on a platter and covered with a light tomato sauce, and the coziche, mussels bathed in a simple sauce of lemon, wine, garlic and olive oil. The only dish that has failed us is the pasta con funghi, which seems a bone tossed to the Chef Boy-ar-dee crowd. Desserts are uninteresting, which is just as well since you'll be full. Instead have an espresso, the perfect denouement to a sense-numbing evening—but don't dawdle too long or the waiter will start making faces. If you can't face the dinner crush, try Caffe Sport for lunch, unless you can't stomach food this rich in the middle of the day. Dinner for two, with wine, will run about $60.

Open Tues.-Sat. 12 noon-2 p.m. & 6:30 p.m.-10:30 p.m. No cards.

CALIFORNIA CULINARY ACADEMY

625 Polk St., Civic Center - 771-3500
French

9/20

Should we include this as a restaurant or as a listing in the Sights chapter? The Academy is a prestigious chef's school—a large fraternal hall of some sort that has been turned into glassed-in training kitchens, a large main dining room (rather elegant: fine carpets, huge skylights and gleaming tableware), a balcony café overlooking it all and a quite good bakery. After sampling one of the prix-fixe meals here, we still wonder how to categorize this place. The food these budding young chefs are taught to prepare is classical French, so classical that we have seen most of it only in old cookbooks in antiquarian bookstores. Perhaps we should list this place under Museums; it is, in fact, a museum dedicated to the preservation of ancient, banal, unhealthy, tedious cooking. And, to make matters worse, everything is served in *immense* portions! We have unhappy memories of an appetizer of dozens of canned-tasting snails in a leaden phyllo pastry in a pool of two vile sauces. An order of assorted pâtés, all heavy and inept, would feed six or seven trenchermen. Fish and shellfish dishes are complicated beyond belief—a recent plate of oysters, clams, mussels, lobster and halibut was served in a disgusting cream sauce and with all sorts of julienned vegetables, little squid's ink pastas and other complex knickknacks, all of which turned the whole inedible mess into a huge joke. Is this some madman's idea of French haute cuisine? The pastries (for example, a Swedish chocolate cake) are good, if too rich, and the wine list is decently priced. The kind and helpful service—all young chef students alternating as waiters—is overseen by rather gruff professionals with indistinguishable foreign accents. We wish these young chefs luck, and we hope they will rebel from this staid training and learn creativity. On Thursday and Friday nights and at lunch Friday, a "grand classical" buffet is served to gluttons for punishment. Prix-fixe menus are $13.75 and $16.50 at lunch and $23.50 at dinner, excluding wine and tip.

Seatings Mon.-Fri. 12 noon, 12:30 p.m., 6 p.m., 6:45 p.m. & 7:30 p.m. Cards: AE, MC, V.

CAMARGUE

*2316 Polk St., Russian
Hill - 776-5577*

French

13 🍳

Camargue is one of our favorite little neighborhood restaurants. The atmosphere in this storefront bistro is low-key and romantic (dim lights, flowers everywhere, wine casks), the service friendly, and the prices shockingly low—the four-course prix fixe dinner for $16 is the best bargain in the city. Soups are consistently good; cream of zucchini imparts the very essence of the vegetable. The starter of warm grilled eggplant and roasted red pepper with goat cheese is worth three times the $3 price tag, and the dish of monkfish, mussels and salmon à la nage presents each element at its best. Rack of lamb with a shiitake mushroom sauce and a nice little boneless rabbit in a flaky puff pastry are also excellent. And all entrees are accompanied by three lovely, al dente seasonal vegetables. Desserts are substantial: a floating island with a raspberry coulis and fresh berries; a poached peach stuffed with ice cream and served with a berry coulis and English cream; and fine homemade ice creams and sorbets. The short wine list is well chosen and well priced, and there are many fine offerings by the glass. Some very nice things are being done in this splendid little restaurant. About $50 for two, with wine; the prix fixe dinner of $16 per person does not include wine.

Open daily 5 p.m.-12 midnight. Cards: AE, MC, V.

CAMPTON PLACE

*340 Stockton St., Union
Square - 781-5155*

American

15 🍳

We were skeptical four years ago when young chef Bradley Ogden promised to redefine American cooking by creating an elegant, formal restaurant in a small, exclusive hotel, the Campton Place. He planned to use only American products, highlighting his personal notions of "American" techniques, and Ogden spent months hyping his ideas to the press and the public. Our initial impressions of his restaurant were that there was a commitment to quality in the kitchen and that the travelogue of a menu (Wisconsin this, Iowa that) sounded interesting, but that it was all defeated by sometimes sloppy technique, minuscule portions and absolutely gargantuan prices. Nonetheless, Campton Place remained very popular, and we began to hear of improvements in both the kitchen and the once-pretentious and sometimes inept service. So we returned for another look, and loved what we saw. It is still a shrine to American produce; Ogden searches the 50 states for the best of everything. The menu changes often; a recent meal started with an incredible duck sausage with spicy mustard and a little compote of preserved, candied vegetables. Another starter of Louisiana catfish cakes with deep-fried parsley was equally good. Soups—a high point since the restaurant's opening—often include a perfect crab chowder and an intense, velvety tomato soup with sage. Main courses are usually simple: sautéed Virginia veal steak (back to the travelogue) with a mountain of white truffles; perfectly poached salmon with a tomato-basil vinaigrette; and incredibly sweet lamb chops with potato pancakes and Blue Lake beans. Only a grilled quail with honey-cured bacon is dry from overcooking—and the shoestring potatoes that accompany it are soggy. Desserts are exquisite, from an American heartland apple-walnut crisp with homemade cinnamon ice cream to two pears, one poached in white wine, one in red, accompanied by pear sorbet. There's a great deal of attention to detail here; house-made bread and rolls are about the best in town, and service is now competent and pleasantly low-key for so formal a room. The dining room itself is lovely, with indirect lighting, comfortable (but too closely spaced) banquettes and tables in peach and earth tones, beautiful art deco mirrors and lavish sprays of flowers everywhere. There are two wine lists: a short one with some decent bottles at moderate prices, and a longer "cellar list," produced upon request, with exorbitantly priced treasures. Both Campton Place and its talented chef seem to be maturing with age; we look forward to more finesse in the years ahead. Thankfully, one no longer leaves Campton Place hungry, but one still leaves considerably poorer for the experience: about $150 for two, with wine.

Open Mon.-Fri. 11:30 a.m.-2:30 p.m. & 5:30 p.m.-10 p.m., Sat.-Sun. 5:30 p.m.-10:30 p.m. All major cards.

CARNELIAN ROOM

555 California St. (Bank of America Building), Financial District - 433-7500

Continental

8/20

It's too bad one can't eat scenery, because this place has a truly stunning view in one of America's best view cities. The ornate-to-gaudy room is banked with windows on the 52nd floor of the Bank of America building, San Francisco's tallest (at least for the moment). But is it worth a C-bill or so to watch the bright lights and fogtails, the bridges and ships, while suffering through food that has a pervasive musty character, with occasional notes of Sterno? Some may think so, no doubt depending on who's footing the bill. For those on expense accounts, this is an exhilarating place to do a power dinner (lunch is reserved for the private Banker's Club), especially considering the wine list, one of the most comprehensive in town. Alas, the food is dismal. You won't go too wrong with one of the simpler daily specials, such as fresh swordfish or salmon. And the steaks are well aged, if usually smothered in some kind of mess. Everything else is so pointlessly gussied up that it almost comes off as a spoof on Escoffier. Almost. With a moderate bottle of wine, about $120 for two.

Open nightly 6 p.m.-10:30 p.m. All major cards.

LE CASTEL

3235 Sacramento St., Presidio Heights - 921-7115
French

11/20

One of our most exalted colleagues considers this to be San Francisco's best restaurant; indeed, she claims it as one of her favorites in the United States. Although we love the setting (a comfortable converted Victorian townhouse in fashionable Presidio Heights) and the warm reception by owner Fritz Frankel and his lovely hostess, our enthusiasm dampens when we consider our only real criterion for rating a restaurant, the food. Seafood appetizers start with the best available ingredients (Norwegian salmon in a beurre blanc, Washington scallops on the half shell with ginger), but can be overcooked. Soups are either austere to the point of total blandness (cream of asparagus with not a tad of the vegetable's flavor) or gritty and ill-conceived (the house special, puréed oyster and spinach soup), and salads are decorative but banal. Entrees are either bland—leg of veal stuffed with veal mousse, leg of lamb in an indistinguishable sauce—or interesting but rather overcooked. The homemade desserts, however, are quite lovely, especially the chocolate cake with layers of meringue. The fashionable crowd that keeps Le Castel full has evidently not had our experiences with the cuisine, so perhaps we have just been unlucky. In any event, we will say that the atmosphere is relaxed and charming, and the wine list is comprehensive and, with the exception of the exorbitantly priced great French wines, quite moderate. Dinner for two, with wine, will run a reasonable $80.

Open Mon.-Sat. 6 p.m.-10 p.m. All major cards.

CENDRILLON

1132 Valencia St., Mission District - 826-7997
French

12/20

The chef's toque here recently passed from French to Vietnamese hands, though the cuisine remains French. We are quite fond of this little neighborhood bistro, which boasts both very high standards and very modest prices. Though inexpensively decorated, no expense is spared on the dramatically lit floral arrangement, the centerpiece of the room. The service is also noteworthy—it is welcoming and attentive, and reservations are honored immediately. The food has its ups and its downs, but there are many worthwhile dishes. We especially like the snails in puff pastry with a ginger sauce; the pasta with prawns; the provençal fish soup; the clam cream soup with puff pastry; the leg of chicken stuffed with veal mousse; and the marvelous swordfish in a light tarragon cream sauce. We prefer not to think about the bland cream of artichoke soup or the dry, over-cooked duck breast with green peppercorns. Desserts are all good: bread pudding with hot chocolate sauce, chocolate charlotte with a black currant sauce, and crêpes with an apple compote and Grand Marnier. The wine list is one of the city's better bargains—the 1982 Jordan Cabernet at $28 is a steal, even if it is still a bit young. And the food prices—a gift! About $40 for two, with wine.

Open Mon.-Sat. 5:30 p.m.-10 p.m. Cards: MC, V.

LE CENTRAL

453 Bush St., Union Square - 391-2233

French

12/20

More than most of San Francisco's "great" French restaurants, this simple bistro with its menu scrawled on blackboards and on mirrors reminds us of dining in France. Situated downtown, Le Central overflows at lunchtime, largely with business and political figures: it is a favorite of Mayor Diane Feinstein and other local dignitaries. Although they come here to do some political moving and shaking, they also come to nourish their bodies and souls with delicious and honest country French cooking. Starters include a good onion soup gratinée, an onion tart, leeks vinaigrette and, maybe best of all, a rich, spicy saucisson chaud in an abundant cream sauce. Sticking with the simplest entrees is best: a glorious herbed roast chicken, cold salmon sauce verte, rack of lamb. (Although the cassoulet is legendary, we are not among its enthusiasts.) The marinated sauerkraut with juniper berries in the choucroute à l'alsacienne is delicious, but the pork is lackluster. Desserts, if chosen carefully, are terrific, especially the tarte tatin with crème fraîche. With this food we would like (and expect) some wonderful fruity Alsatian wines, but none are to be had. The wine list—a weak spot—leans heavily toward California, and not the choicest selection. The service, though frenzied at lunch, is friendly and efficient to newcomers as well as to the famous clientele. About $70 for dinner for two, with wine.

Open Mon.-Sat. 11:45 a.m.-10:30 p.m. Cards: AE, MC, V.

CHEZ MICHEL

Michel Elkaim is the perfect host in this handsome bistro, an elegant combination of art deco and contemporary. The

804 North Point St., Fisherman's Wharf - 771-6077

French

14

competent and friendly French staff and the splendid (but, alas, overpriced) wine list put one immediately at ease, as does the heterogeneous menu, neither purely classical nor truly nouvelle. The cuisine is very competently prepared, with some superb surprises. Traditional lobster bisque is densely rich. The best appetizer is a quail salad—cold slices of the breast are fanned on a large plate, and the crisp legs are served separately atop a little lettuce and tomato salad. Snails are also, of course, available, and they are very good. Entrees tend to be simple, from the rack of lamb with red bell peppers to various grilled fresh fish. Request your fish just underdone; though the quality of the seafood is admirable, it sometimes emerges overcooked from the kitchen. Desserts are a high point of the meal: the chocolate soufflé served with a crème anglaise sauce is indescribably good. There are also fine chilled soufflés and splendid berries in puff pastry. Dear Michel, please be a little more gentle with the denizens of the deep and a second toque may come your way. This bistro hardly has bistro prices: about $100 for dinner for two, with wine.

Open Tues.-Sun. 6 p.m.-12 midnight. Cards: MC, V.

CHINA MOON CAFÉ

639 Post St., Union Square - 775-4789

Chinese

12/20

We had great hopes for this long-awaited restaurant owned by Chinese-cuisine scholar Barbara Tropp. At first, we were promised a quite grand establishment at another location; when that fell through, we were presented with this small, uncomfortable café with counter seating and tiny booths. Despite this, China Moon is always jumping with people, though there's nary an Asian in sight—not even among the waiters or the cooks in the closet-size kitchen, which is visible from the street. Nonetheless, we want to like this place, and we have, in fact, had some very good dishes here, but we have been disappointed too often to award Ms. Tropp a toque. We also find the prices excessive—main dishes hover around the $14 mark at lunch, a hefty tab given the atmosphere. At least your mealtime investment goes into high-quality ingredients; our last lunch included a generous and very good piece of Norwegian salmon steamed with a mustard sauce, and a spicy, very satisfying tangle of unusually tender lamb, sweet red peppers, onions and vegetables. We also have fond memories of some tasty appetizers: a cold calamari salad in a chili and ginger sauce, turnovers stuffed with spicy lamb, and ten-spice pork in Arabic bread. But we have been witness to several failures, including a very bland rice noodle stuffed with pork and minced fish; a cooked-to-death chicken breast in a "strange flavor" sauce (a name that does not exactly whet the appetite); and a plate of stir-fried clams and mussels, which had the taste and consistency of putty. Tropp's little café seems to get better with time, however, so perhaps by the time you read this she will have perfected her intriguing cuisine. About $75 for dinner for two, with a simple wine.

Open Mon.-Fri. 11:30 a.m.-2:30 p.m. & 5:30 p.m.-10:30 p.m., Sat. 5:30 p.m.-10:30 p.m. Cards: MC, V.

CHRISTOPHE RESTAURANT

320 Mason St., Union Square - 433-7560

French

13 🎩

A few years ago owner/hostess Lourdes Tarrat and chef Patrick Grepon sold their interest in a successful Sausalito restaurant to try their luck in the big city. First, they recognized that the heavy-handed classic cuisine that did well in Sausalito needed to be rethought. The transition has been slow; Grepon has not instantly become a disciple of the nouvelle, but prefers to experiment with his own blend of classic and contemporary on a daily menu, while keeping a standard menu of old workhorses for the unadventurous. Second, they wanted to keep prices moderate to encourage business. Finally, a pleasant atmosphere had to be supplied. In that venture Tarrat was almost successful; her dining room is done in purple and chrome with walls covered by art deco prints, but, though spacious, it feels unworkably cluttered. Case in point: a waiter bumped into and nearly tripped over a diner's chair while bringing wonderful fresh mussels in curry sauce and a ceviche featuring sea bass that tasted like it had been cooked. And, after clearing away the service for the rich, creamy lobster bisque and setting the table for the entrees (a slightly overdone chicken breast stuffed with a very good veal mousse and a fine boneless rabbit on a bed of onion confit), the incident was repeated. The salads (romaine lettuce topped with an excellent vinaigrette and minced walnuts, and halved heads of butter lettuce served with a very tasty warm goat cheese) arrived without incident. But we would have been fortunate had an obstacle larger than a chair greeted the waiter when he delivered the house dessert, coupe Christophe, fresh fruits with whipped cream served in a charred tulipe (the color the envy of any Dutch bulb grower breeding for intense brown or black). But then we would have missed the scrumptious profiteroles au chocolate. Our nerves, dazed from the haphazard (hazardous?) service, were calmed by the mellow jazz band, which plays every Friday and Saturday evening. All in all, we wish chef Grepon and hostess Tarrat well in their efforts to adapt to a new environment. About $60 or $65 for dinner for two, with wine.

Open Mon.-Sat. 11:30 a.m.-2:30 p.m. & 5:30 p.m.-11 p.m., Sun. 5:30 p.m.-10 p.m. All major cards.

CIAO

230 Jackson St., Financial District - 982-9500
Italian

12/20

Some restaurants are just too confounding! The dishes that Ciao does well are exquisite beyond words, but the dishes it does not do well are better left undiscussed. We have had dishes from the north of Italy that made us want to sing arias of praise, and others that made us want to say "ciao" to this Spectrum-owned restaurant and never return. Most of the antipasti are good, especially the antipasto misto. But the soups (a disastrous minestrone, for example) and the over-cooked pastas (such as the otherwise splendid fettuccine with shrimp, clams, squid and scallops) will disappoint. The best entrees will thrill: a huge and outstanding veal chop, charred and rare, and marvelous brochettes of quail stuffed with homemade sausage. If only the rest of the kitchen were up to this! The sorbets are original and outstanding—melon sorbet, for example, stuffed into a hollowed-out honeydew, or strawberry sorbet inside a fresh orange. The wine list contains both California and Italian bottlings at moderate prices, and a few good offerings are available by the glass. We wish this trendy haven (done in chrome, glass and wood, with an efficient staff) would iron out its problems and be deserving of the rating we would truly like to give it, but for now we must harden our hearts. About $70 for dinner for two, with wine.

Open Mon.-Sat. 11 a.m.-12 midnight, Sun. 4 p.m.-12 midnight. Cards: AE, MC, V.

CIRCOLO

161 Sutter St., Financial District - 362-0404
Italian

11/20

Fazol Poursohi spent $2.5 million rehabilitating this old restaurant site, and the money shows. The art deco setting is dramatic, with a marble entry, floor-to-ceiling marble bathrooms, 100 tables and, of course, an open kitchen with pizza ovens. Circolo means "disk" or "circle" in Italian; to carry out the theme, circular grinding stones serve as objets d'art. Circolo's subtitle is "Restaurant & Champagneria"; the pretentious "Champagneria" part of the title refers to the four sparkling wines served by the glass and nine by the bottle, all at eminently reasonable prices. In fact, everything here is reasonably priced, even inexpensive, a surprise when one considers Poursohi's investment and his determination to serve high-quality Italian food. Unfortunately, his cuisine lacks imagination and the kitchen lacks finesse. Our last meal included a calamari marinata that, despite the lemon juice and olive oil, featured dreadfully dry squid. Frutti di mare (mixed seafood) was a little better, though two of the mussels were rotten and all of them were tough. Agnolotti filled with fresh chard, ricotta and fresh sage was tasty but overly oily. Things looked up, however, with the fine complimentary foccacia and the generous piece of salmon served with properly cooked vegetables. But the meal took a turn for the worse with the commercial-tasting desserts. Still and all, the throngs of local office workers who lunch here daily know a bargain when they see one, and you could do worse than have a salad and a pizza or pasta here. About $30 for a simple lunch for two, with a glass of Shadow Creek Champagne; $70 for a generous dinner for two, with a bottle of Domaine Chandon.

Open Mon.-Thurs. 11:30 a.m.-3 p.m. & 5 p.m.-10 p.m., Fri. 11:30 a.m.-3 p.m. & 5 p.m.-12 midnight, Sat. 5 p.m.-12 midnight. Cards: AE, MC, V.

LE CLUB

*1250 Jones St., Nob Hill -
771-5400*
French

9/20

All across the city, exciting restaurants are flourishing, introducing their patrons to creative preparations of marvel-ous local and international products. We suppose that, to keep some kind of cosmic balance, a few places like Le Club must stay around, if only to remind us of how far the culinary world has come in a relatively short time. This place is so stuffy that it's silly: hovering waiters in ridiculous maroon tuxedoes, sedate rooms that are dark to the point of gloominess, a very overpriced wine list and menus without prices for the ladies. You'll even find matches embossed with your name upon arrival. Given all that, the choices on the menu should not be hard to guess: Caesar salad, poached salmon with hollandaise, tournedos Rossini and flambéed steak are just a few of the offerings. This kind of food, however, can be comforting and satisfying if well prepared, which is unfortunately not the case at Le Club. Even the onion soup gratinée, the kind of dish at which this sort of restaurant should excel, is bitter and unpleasant. We must admit that the quality of ingredients can be good, if mishandled—for instance, the tender, tasty sweetbreads that look like they are covered with melted plastic (actually a dreadful cream sauce). Desserts are predictably heavy-handed. About $130 for two, with one of the less expensive wines.

Open Mon.-Sat. 5:30 p.m.-12 midnight. All major cards.

CUBA

2886 16th St., Mission District - 864-9871

Cuban

11/20

Though Cuban cuisine is very popular on the East Coast, it is rarely seen in San Francisco—which is reason enough to visit this simple little Formica-and-linoleum eatery in the Latino Mission District. The most unusual and often quite good dishes are another reason. There are copious Cuban fish soups, with fish that is, alas, mercilessly overcooked, but the sea bass dishes are much better prepared. The meat dishes are all tasty, especially the Cuban roast pork and beef served with superb black beans. The service is—we'll be kind— relaxed; there are some good beers and only a few wines. A satisfying dinner with beer will cost two people $30.

Open Fri.-Wed. 11 a.m.-10 p.m. All major cards.

LE CYRANO

4134 Geary Blvd., Richmond District - 387-1090

French

12/20

Little neighborhood restaurants come and go, but Le Cyrano has been around for decades. The food is French ancien, the clientele merely ancient and the room a bit gloomy despite good lighting. Dinner is prix fixe only, starting with soup— good cream of leek or asparagus, mediocre onion—and continuing with a simple butter-lettuce vinaigrette. Main courses are the best part of the meal: a long-simmered stew of beef or veal, nice sautéed frogs' legs or a small individual rack of lamb. Choose any of those over the well-roasted duck with a too-cloying orange sauce. Desserts are pretty basic (crème caramel, fruit tarts), but the short wine list is reasonably priced—and the prix-fixe meals are downright cheap at $8.50 to $16 a person, without wine.

Open Mon.-Sat. 5 p.m.-10:30 p.m. No cards.

DE PAULA'S

2114 Fillmore St., Upper Fillmore - 346-9888

Brazilian

12/20

We visited Brazil recently and, we're sad to report, were hard-pressed to find a good meal. But upon returning to San Francisco, we were surprised to find this good little place tucked away in the newly trendy Upper Fillmore area. Appetizers are mostly pastry-like creations filled with cheese, meat or poultry, and they are not particularly good. The entrees, however, can be exciting: wonderful marinated pork, chicken marinated in dark beer and sautéed with peppers, onions and cream, and a fine feijoada, the black bean and pork stew that is Brazil's national dish. Entrees

35

have some remarkable—but not always delicious—accompaniments, such as refried beans with yucca flour; the flour itself is fried with bacon, olives and spices. Perhaps it's an acquired taste we have yet to acquire. There are some good beers, a few wines and delicious Brazilian soft drinks. The Brazilian desserts are too sweet by American standards, but the splendid chocolate from Cocolat ends the meal on a high note. About $40 for dinner for two, with beer.

Open Mon.-Thurs. 11:30 a.m.-2:30 p.m. & 5 p.m.-11 p.m., Fri. 11:30 a.m.-2:30 p.m. & 5 p.m.-12 midnight, Sat. 5 p.m.-12 midnight, Sun. 5 p.m.-11 p.m. All major cards.

DIXIE CAFÉ

532 Columbus Ave., North Beach - 397-1509

Cajun/Creole

12/20

One of the most pronounced trends in dining in the United States in the last five years has been a renewed interest in the regional cuisines of America, especially Cajun and Creole cuisines, which until recently had not reached far beyond Bourbon Street. Riding this wave of Louisianan popularity is the Dixie Café, a spin-off of the successful Elite Café, which shares the same menu. Though not terribly authentic, much of the food here is quite good. The gumbos and jambalaya lack their native fire, though they are flavorful. Blackened dishes are uneven; on the short menu is blackened "redfish," a wonderful Gulf treat, but a waiter confessed that the kitchen substitutes cod for this increasingly rare delicacy—and the cod does not hold up to blackening as well as redfish. But things look up considerably with the excellent filet mignon, blackened on the outside and blood-rare inside. Desserts are delicious: bread pudding, a rich cream cheese–pecan pie. The small wine list is reasonable, the strong Louisiana drinks are marvelous, and the service is low-key and efficient. The no-reservations policy may cause a wait, especially at peak times, but the extra wait for one of the cozy wood booths that seem so distanced from the bustling center of the room is worthwhile. About $50 for dinner for two, with wine.

Open Mon.-Sat. 5 p.m.-11 p.m., Sun. 5 p.m.-10 p.m. Cards: AE, MC, V.

DONATELLO

501 Post St. (Donatello Hotel), Union Square - 441-7182

Donatello continues to confound us. We have been avid followers of Cal Rossi's civilized, elegant bastion of northern Italian cooking for years, but the last year has seen much flux. First, after years of memorable dining here, we suffered through a disastrous evening in which not a single dish from the extensive menu was even passable. Admittedly, this was

Italian

right after the restaurant started a new policy of having a prix-fixe menu of four courses that would change every two days, and had we not been kept waiting an hour and fifteen minutes for our reserved table we may well have been able to order this menu before they ran out of it. Nonetheless, we assumed that ordering from the regular menu would be as reliable as always. How wrong we were! We left dejected, without a word of apology from the captain, to whom we expressed our displeasure. Why and when did we return? Only after some months and after hearing that the changing menu, with copious amounts of fine wines included in the price, was among the best meals in the city. After such an abysmal failure, we could hardly believe this, but Donatello spent the best part of three hours astonishing us with a dinner that was, to date, our best experience with Italian food outside Italy—a very extravagant claim to be sure! After the tortelli filled with homemade sausage in a sun-dried tomato sauce, monkfish sautéed in a beet cream sauce, the sweetest young lamb on the planet with fresh herbs and juniper berries, and a fig and walnut tart scented with orange, we were ready to make amends with Donatello. But then, as is too often the case these days, the chef up and left right at press time, denying us the opportunity to return and report on our findings. We can only hope that Cal Rossi's seasoning as a restaurateur will keep Donatello's cuisine as lovely and refined as his dining rooms, rich with marble, magnificent fabrics, amber crystal chandeliers and indirect lighting, and that the service will continue to be efficient and welcoming. The wine list is comprehensive, with some fine rare Italian bottles (at a price), but we highly recommend the set dinner, which includes well-chosen wines. Perhaps our next edition will award Donatello the three toques we had given it before the chef left. An elegant dinner for two, with wine, will set you back about $120.

Open daily 7 a.m.-11 a.m. & 6 p.m.-10:30 p.m. All major cards.

DOROS

714 Montgomery St., Financial District - 397-6822

Italian

7/20

As we approached this long-revered downtown institution for the first time, we almost walked right past it, so drab was its red brick exterior. After passing through the ornate foyer and entering Doros's salon, we experienced the sensation of having passed through a time warp. The cavernous dining room looks like some long-dead, twelfth-rate interior designer's idea of elegance. Impressionist and pre-Raphaelite paintings hang on paneled walls between tacky lamps. Huge red banquettes line the room's periphery, leaving the center to be filled with tables. The food is also from another era; certainly the food we sampled tasted as though it had been first put on the stove eons ago. None of the warm dishes had any texture or substance left. Cannelloni, the house specialty, could have been consumed through a straw. A gelatinous and fatty onion soup topped with a hard crust of bread and mozzarella was easily the worst we have ever had (including the canned varieties). Eggplant parmigiana had been cooked down to a mushy mass. A baby salmon stuffed with an unidentifiable mousse could be put into small jars and sold as baby food—that is, once the heavy and oily sauce had been removed. Desserts, however, are acceptable, though the waiter meekly confessed with a shrug of the shoulders that they are not house made. How we wish they would serve other dishes prepared elsewhere! It was with amazement that we overheard a patron boast about having been a loyal client for 34 years. But then the salon seems filled with people who somehow believe they are leading the good life. Perhaps one day they will learn that one's stomach is too high a price to pay for deferential service. $120 for dinner for two, with wine.

Open Mon.-Sat. 11 a.m.-2:30 p.m. & 6 p.m.-10:30 p.m. All major cards.

ELITE CAFÉ

2049 Fillmore St., Upper Fillmore - 346-8668

Cajun/Creole

13

It's said that since the Cajun craze hit, the noble redfish (apparently not blackened in its natural state) has become an endangered species. Don't blame the Elite. True, there are several redfish dishes on the menu—foremost among them, redfish Caroline, a fillet fried in a mélange of spices and covered with a creamy, piquant fresh crab sauce—but this Cajun/Creole menu makes good use of many other entree ingredients. For instance, filet mignon and fresh salmon are also blackened, and the thick, spicy gumbo alone is worth a visit. Reservations aren't taken, so there's usually a wait, but with fresh oysters, shrimp and crawfish and an excellent bar, nobody seems to mind hanging out. In fact, the wait at the Elite is part of the increasingly lively scene along Fillmore; Harry's Saloon, a preppy hangout, is just across the street, and the Pacific Heights Bar & Grill ("Pacbag" for short) is just beyond Rory's, one of the city's best ice cream parlors. Once the site of the Asia Café, a 1920s hot spot, the Elite has preserved much of the handsome dark wood paneling, deep booths, mirrors and fixtures from that era. Service is unfailingly efficient; the white-jacketed waiters are young and sharp. As if that weren't enough, the bartenders talk good baseball. Having gone on about all that, we must now admit that we (and many others) go to the Elite more for the Cajun martinis (made with pepper vodka), the bread pudding with bourbon sauce and the Creole cream cheese–pecan pie than for anything else. Dinner for two, with wine, will run about $75.

Open Mon.-Sat. 5 p.m.-11 p.m., Sun. 10 a.m.-3 p.m. & 5 p.m.-10 p.m. No cards.

L'ENTRECÔTE DE PARIS

2032 Union St., Cow Hollow - 931-5006
French/steakhouse

11/20

Americans, we are told, have been eating less beef in recent years. Aside from health reasons, we suspect this is partly due to the increasing unavailability of good beef. We have never thought of San Francisco as a great beef eater's town and were curious to see whether a French-style steakhouse could prosper here. Originally just serving sliced grilled New York steak with the "Café de Paris" shallot-mustard-butter sauce (a secret recipe, we are told), this restaurant has recently expanded to serve fish and other grilled meats and poultry. The real reason to come here, however, is still for the French steak dinner. It starts with a nice little butter lettuce salad with chopped walnuts and a tangy vinaigrette. The steak itself is tasty, though not particularly tender, and the sauce is unremarkable. French fries, in the true French style, are greaseless and delicious. Homemade desserts are beautiful to look at (profiteroles, tarte tatin) but unexceptional. The wine list, while not long, is well priced, with several premium wines available by the glass. The French and American serving staff is competent but, when rushed, somewhat less than efficient. We have had to pour our own wine all evening. About $60 for two, with wine.

Open Mon.-Sat. 11:30 a.m.-12 midnight, Sun. 11:30 a.m.-10 p.m. All major cards.

ERNIE'S

847 Montgomery St., Financial District - 397-5969
French

15

We were greatly saddened by the decline and fall of San Francisco's most famous restaurant some years ago, and thrilled at its resuscitation in the late '70s, when brilliant young Jacky Robert took over the kitchen and introduced nouvelle delights to this Continental dinosaur. When Robert left two years ago to co-own (and similarly resuscitate) Amelio's, we feared that Ernie's would slip back into a rut. Fortunately, our fears were unfounded. In fact, under Chapel-trained Bruno Tison, Ernie's is at its all-time best. Tison's Meridien Hotel training has made him comfortable with handling so large a restaurant, and all seems under control here for the first time. Although not every dish will delight (on our last visit, a rather tired John Dory suffered from a too-austere bell pepper sauce), most of them are very fine indeed. The pâté of sole and rockfish with a macédoine of vegetables in hazelnut oil is astounding; only slightly less astounding is the crab-filled ravioli in a coral-cream sauce. Tison's signature soup, cream of clam with a snowball of egg white and caviar, is a joy. Main courses, from roast tuna with eggplant and ginger to lamb breaded in parsley and served with an outstanding "pancake" of eggplant and zucchini, are uniformly good. But we still fear that not all the fish will be in immaculate condition on any given night. (This can be blamed in part on Ernie's obsession with getting the best ingredients from around the world, which is not always necessary given California's bounty, and not always desirable given the fragility of fish.) Desserts are among the best in town: our favorites are the wonderful chilled pear soufflé with strawberry sauce, the fantastic gratin of red fruit with crème brûlée, and some of the best ice creams and sorbets we've encountered. The wine list is extensive, well chosen and, shockingly, less expensive than in past years. As for the decor, some will argue that it only borders on good taste, but we find the Victorian bordello interior in this old townhouse charming, especially when contrasted with Tison's modern creations. Our only real hesitation in recommending Ernie's is the sometimes cold reception and aloof service, but this seems to be improving. As well it should at these prices: about $150 for two, with wine.

Open daily 6:30 p.m.-10:30 p.m. All major cards.

L'ETOILE

1075 California St.
(Huntington Hotel), Nob
Hill - 771-1529

French

15

This is San Francisco's greatest bastion of the filthy rich; hardly a day goes by without reference to L'Etoile in the local society columns. The decor is lavish but comfortable— plush, well-spaced banquettes, fabulous mirrors, huge ferns and exotic flower arrangements—and the service is among the best in the city. Recently, chef Claude Bougard has made a few detours from his classical training, and the menu is now all the more interesting. A salad of quail, goose foie gras and lobster with a terrine of chanterelles is an opulent starter; warm green beans with bay scallops is more down to earth, but equally fine. A traditional lobster bisque has too much sherry, but the cold tomato-and-bell-pepper soup is excellent. Bougard has a talent for preparing fish, as evidenced by the salmon in puff pastry, swimming perfectly in a light beurre blanc, and the wonderfully simple salmon scallops topped with caviar. Also outstanding is the very rare duck breast in a not-too-sweet berry and orange sauce— quite a daring dish for a basically traditional house. The lamb dishes, however, can be uneven: a simple rack is splendid, but a saddle stuffed with a vegetable mousse is dry and salty. Desserts (soufflés, pastries, sorbets) are lovely, and the wine list is astounding (as are the accompanying prices). L'Etoile is not for the faint of wallet: about $200 for two, with wine.

Open Mon.-Sat. 6 p.m.-10:30 p.m. All major cards.

FIOR D'ITALIA

601 Union St., North Beach - 986-1886

Italian

11/20

In May of 1986, San Francisco's oldest Italian restaurant made headlines when it celebrated its 100th birthday— people were lined up around the block to eat at century-old prices. This may well be the last time justifiable lines are seen until the bicentennial celebration, because this spacious and rather opulent place serves some of the most ordinary food, albeit with a few exceptions. Starters range from a gristly "home-cured" bresaola to a good dish of sautéed prawns, and main courses range from a flavorless calamari steak to a deftly prepared salmon. Desserts are chosen from a cart; the crostata and tiramisu are the lesser of the evils. The service is as inconsistent as the food—almost fawning at one visit, then unreachable and almost rude at the next. If you're lucky and you order well, you may have a pleasant meal here. About $70 for dinner for two, with wine.

Open daily 11:30 a.m.-10:30 p.m. All major cards.

565 CLAY

565 Clay St., Financial District - 434-2345

California

10/20

One of the major restaurants to open in 1986, 565 Clay is a comfortable, wood-paneled room with efficient service, an intriguing, well-priced wine list (including many by the glass) and some creative food that is, alas, more imaginative than good. It was originally planned as a vegetarian restaurant, but the founders decided that would be too risky a venture—so they waded into the murky waters of California cuisine. The starters with a Southern bent, such as corn fritters with chutney or pan-fried oysters with light-as-a-feather hollandaise, show promise. But all is lost when one is presented with overcooked ahi tuna topped with a compote of exotic fruits (which would have made a halfway decent dessert), or a nouvelle jambalaya with sandy clams and cooked-to-death chicken. The wheat bread from the Tassa-jara Zen Society bakery is splendid, and the desserts (wonderful bread pudding, fresh pear pie and very dense chocolate mousse) provide a nice finish for a meal that starts off well, veers disastrously off course and ends on a positive note. Some improvements in the entree department, and this place could have real potential. Dinner for two, with wine, runs about $65.

Open Mon.-Fri. 11:30 a.m.-2:30 p.m. & 5:30 p.m.-9:30 p.m., Sat. for private parties only. All major cards.

FLEUR DE LYS

777 Sutter St., Union Square - 673-7779

French

17

This is San Francisco's best restaurant. There! We've said it, we've taken a stand, so now we must justify it. If just last year we had made the above comment about Fleur de Lys, the city would have thought us mad—for until last year, this was just another one of San Francisco's stuffy, ancien régime French restaurants with routine food, a pretty but too dimly lit draped tent of a room—lush but not inviting—and a charming, dapper owner, Maurice Rouas. Rouas proved himself shrewd as well when he brought Hubert Keller, a brilliant young protégé of Roger Vergé, in as both partner and chef de cuisine. Keller, in addition to working under Vergé at Moulin de Mougins, opened two restaurants for him, in São Paulo, Brazil, and in San Francisco (the financially troubled Sutter 500). He was much influenced by Vergé's "cuisine of the sun," as well as by his training at a tender age at some of the other best houses in France, including Haeberlin and Bocuse.

After joining Fleur de Lys, Keller wisely turned up the lights to spotlight his magnificent food and added lovely floral arrangements to the room to give it a new vibrance. But why do we bother discussing such mundane matters as decor, when the real matter to discuss is the food? In the tradition of a great French chef, Keller offers a lengthy but not unmanageable menu and two prix-fixe meals each evening, usually of five or six very small courses. We highly recommend one of these daily-changing prix-fixe menus, because Keller consigns his greatest dishes to them. The six-course menu might start with a "garden" of vegetables and snails in a broth of wine, garlic and herbs; go on to gently sautéed American foie gras with a stew of endive and ginger in Sauternes; then offer lobster wrapped in a spinach "package," followed by a lemon and Champagne sorbet; then present *two* entrees: veal atop artichoke hearts and wild mushrooms in an intense demi-glace, followed by breast of squab in a red wine sauce served inside a hollowed-out baked potato. But surely the meal doesn't end now! Keller would be unfulfilled were he not to send out some of his fabulous desserts, never less than three different ones on a large plate: perhaps a warm raspberry sabayon in a berry coulis, a chocolate soufflé cake in a pool of green mint sauce, and a terrine of grapefruit sorbet with exotic fruits—incredible! Fear not, those who prefer to order à la carte: each dish will be perfect—skillfully undercooked roast salmon in a ginger butter; a "double-duck" dish of foie gras and rare duck breast atop spinach; an incredible grilled swordfish salad with French beans; and much, much more. The service, too, is flawless, with Rouas nearly always on hand, and shy young Hubert sometimes touring the room at the end of the evening. The wine list is a volume, with many fine, affordable selections. Yes, we dare say this is San Francisco's best restaurant, indeed one of the nation's best. About $150 for dinner for two, with wine (prix-fixe menus are $42 and $47 per person, without wine).

Open Mon.-Sat. 6 p.m.-10 p.m. All major cards.

FOG CITY DINER

1300 Battery St., North Beach - 982-2000

American

14

Part Empire Diner, part Dashiell Hammett and part yuppie grazeteria, the Fog City Diner gets our vote for the most fun restaurant in town. For one thing, it's great looking—a gleaming, low-slung, romantic cross between a '30s roadside diner and a '40s big-city bar and grill. For another, the dressed-up clientele is as handsome and lively as the restaurant. Add to this a well-staffed and well-stocked bar, a counter from which you can watch the intricate but frenzied ballet in the kitchen, and an irresistible, reasonably priced menu of contemporary American food, and you'll understand why you need dinner reservations days (even weeks) in advance. Seemingly all of San Francisco is willing to put up with long waits, a cool welcome and sometimes perfunctory service to hang out in one of the classic wooden booths and sample from the menu of "small" and "large" plates. (Everything, even the herb-scented bread, is à la carte, so before long you'll have a table full of little plates.) Co-owner and chef Cindy Pawlcyn, also the owner of the wine country's Mustards, has created a menu with something for everyone, from the trendy to the traditional: crisp Caesar salad with homemade croutons, fried mozzarella with a vibrant tomato sauce, a grilled pasilla pepper stuffed with jack cheese, a strange but tasty garlic custard with shiitake mushrooms and walnuts, the best crabcakes on earth, savory Italian sausage with polenta, ordinary onion rings, satisfying burgers, juicy grilled skirt steak and various grilled fish with lively sauces. The fruit pies are all-American and marvelous, with perfectly flaky crusts, but our favorite dessert is the smooth-as-silk crème brûlée. If you can't get in for dinner, visit for a late-afternoon snack, when the pace and atmosphere are more relaxed—but the food is just as good. The size of your tab depends on your appetite: two can have a snack and a glass of wine each for $20 or a feast with a bottle of wine for $60 or so.

Open Sun.-Thurs. 11:30 a.m.-11 p.m., Fri.-Sat. 11:30 a.m.-12 midnight. Cards: MC, V.

FOURNOU'S OVENS

905 California St. (Stanford Court Hotel), Nob Hill - 989-1910

French

8/20

Some people must think we enjoy writing bad reviews. Not so—no sane person wishes to make enemies or see honest businesses suffer. We especially dislike giving bad reviews to places that are otherwise (other than the food, that is) quite deserving. And that brings us to Fournou's Ovens. The reception is warmth itself; the dining room, with its magnificent tiles, immense working ovens and adjoining glassed-in terrace, is one of the loveliest restaurant settings in the city, and the service is always superb, attentive yet unobtrusive. We would love to stop right here, but go on we must. Was the food *really* as bad as we recall from our last visit? Did they really brutally overcook the delicate domestic foie gras and serve it with an artichoke "mousse" that tasted like moistened breakfast cereal? Was there any crab in the crab bisque, which left an aftertaste that nauseated us? Why was the grand specialty from those aforesaid huge ovens, rack of lamb, overcooked and served with an immense knife that resembled a murder weapon? Were the accompanying vegetables served completely raw—and where did they find young carrots that bitter? Was the dacquoise (clearly homemade—no bakery would dare send out the likes of this) as insipid as we recall? Perhaps this was all part of a bad dream. The wine list is long and well-priced, and perhaps after a few bottles your mind will no longer be on this wretched food. We have to look long and hard to find a major restaurant quite this disappointing. About $120 for dinner for two, with wine.

Open nightly 5:30 p.m.-11 p.m. All major cards.

FRENCH ROOM

495 Geary St. (Four Seasons Clift Hotel), Union Square - 775-4700

Like dining in a luxury salon on a steamship in a bygone era, an evening at the French Room provides lots of nostalgic comfort, with its elegant patterned chairs and chaises, plush carpets, giant chandeliers and huge potted palms. The service, too, is always efficient and welcoming, though roles

French

sometimes get confused, with busboys serving and waiters clearing. And the food, happily, is nearly as soothing to the palate as the setting is to the spirit. True, some of the more complicated dishes are not always skillfully prepared (over-cooking being the primary fault), but one can dine well here. The Norwegian salmon is always of exceptional quality, and there are some intriguing seafood soups. But we prefer to be as old-fashioned as the room and order the delightful roast prime rib served from a gigantic silver cart, prefaced by the good oysters Rockefeller or the Caesar salad and concluded by one of the fine desserts from the cart. The wine list is fabulous and surprisingly well priced—perhaps the best wine list in town. About $120 for dinner for two, with wine.

Open daily 7 a.m.-11 a.m., 12 noon-2 p.m. & 6:30 p.m.-10:30 p.m. All major cards.

FUKU-SUSHI

1581 Webster St. (Japan Center West), Japantown - 346-3030

Japanese/sushi

The sushi here is perhaps the best in town, but what doubly attracts us is the place's gestalt. From the moment you step into the dim, romantic interior you are treated like an emperor (or an emperor's mistress), with full attention lavished on you by the waitress and the sushi chef. The latter is a true master, gracefully assembling his creations out of the freshest of ingredients. After you start feeling your sake and get bolder in your ordering, the chef may offer you his finest creation: a piece of uni (sea urchin) topped with a raw quail egg. The merry atmosphere and great food are conducive to prodigious ordering, so the bill can add up fast. Expect to pay from $45 to $70 for two, with sake.

Open Wed.-Mon. 5:30 p.m.-10:45 p.m. Cards: AE, MC, V.

GARDEN HOUSE

133 Clement St., Richmond District - 221-3655

Vietnamese

Precious few good things have resulted from the troubles in Southeast Asia, but this gem of a regional restaurant in the inner Clement Street shopping district is one of them. Owner Nguyen Ngoc Ut fled Vietnam with his family during the war, bringing with him a marriage of cuisines that goes back to the time when Vietnam was part of French Indochina. The Vietnamese sensibility is seen in the emphasis on the freshest seafood and vegetables—including, naturally, hot chili peppers—while the French influence shows in what might be termed the conceptual sophistication: clever, often amazing flavor combinations and gorgeous presentations. The dining room leans toward a European aesthetic with wood-paneled walls and pristine linen tablecloths. One major quibble is the music, invidious nonstop middle-of-the-road drivel. Shut out the sound, however, and focus on the goi cuon, shrimp and pork rolls wrapped in paper-thin rice skins and served with a savory-sweet dipping sauce. Cilantro is the key flavor in this and many other dishes. Banh mi chien cua is a wonderful appetizer of crab beignets, rounds of French bread slathered with a scrumptious crab mixture and deep-fried ever so briefly. The flavors of the lemon beef salad, thin slices of beef in a lemon-mint dressing, telescope outward in a hot pepper glow. Entrees tend not to be as deft or enthralling, but the curries are very good. It's also worth noting that Garden House does a great job of packing food to go, making it one of our favorite stops on the way out to Golden Gate Park. About $30 for two, with drinks.

Open Mon.-Thurs. 5 p.m.-10 p.m., Fri.-Sun. 10:30 a.m.-10 p.m. All major cards.

GAYLORD'S

900 North Point St. (Ghirardelli Square), Fisherman's Wharf - 771-8822

Indian

12/20

Originally started in New Delhi, this worldwide chain now has representatives in Bombay, London, New York and Los Angeles, as well as several Bay Area locations. Though the individual restaurants are privately owned, the chefs are trained in India; each has a specialty, such as masalas. This Gaylord's is elegantly and comfortably appointed, with bay windows overlooking the harbor. The food is as reliable and respectable as Gaylord's reputation, though none of it will dazzle you. Starters include vegetable samosas (deep-fried pastry pockets stuffed with curried tomatoes, potatoes and peas) and a classic mulligatawny, a mild chicken and rice soup. The best entree is the chicken tandoori, which is cooked in the tandoor oven after marinating for hours in a curry sauce. Indian desserts can be over-rich; try the delicious farmer's cheese instead. About $50 for two, with beer.

Open Mon.-Sat. 12 noon-2 p.m. & 5 p.m.-11 p.m., Sun. 12 noon-3 p.m. & 6 p.m.-10:45 p.m. All major cards.

THE GERMAN COOK

612 O'Farrell St., Union Square - 776-9022

German

11/20

The people who run this tiny neighborhood restaurant will probably be shocked to see their establishment in this guide—but good food is good food, no matter how unpretentious the surroundings. This minuscule place has perhaps eight tables and a counter that seats four—and this capacity is due to an expansion several years ago that doubled the size of the restaurant! Although San Francisco is not a city noted for German food, the German Cook serves admirable wursts, sauerbraten, wiener schnitzel and a nice (if slightly greasy) roast duck. Such off-the-menu specials as German meatloaf and stuffed roast chicken are also quite good, though the soups and salads are banal. There are but few wines (at a reasonable cost), but we prefer to accompany this hearty food with a great German beer. Only the uncomfortable chairs and the mural on the wall (apparently a child's conception of a pastoral scene from the German Alps) mar an otherwise enjoyable dining experience. About $25 for two, with beer.

Open Mon.-Sat. 4:30 p.m.-9:30 p.m. Cards: MC, V.

GREENS

Building A, Fort Mason - 771-6222
Vegetarian

13 🎩

This is probably the most talked-about upscale vegetarian restaurant in the nation, and in the past we have wondered why, having found the cuisine to be very uneven. But we are pleased to report that the new general manager, Rick Jones, one of the original Ricks behind Café Americain in North Beach, has brought a considerable measure of consistency to this attractive, view-struck converted warehouse. The menu changes weekly, reflecting the season and the availability of fresh, local foods. Our favorite time to visit Greens is in the fall, when the kitchen does some marvelous things with mushrooms. All year long pizza is offered, and it is always exceptional, as are (appropriately enough) the salads; we recall a particularly delightful salad of lettuces, mango and pecans in a balsamic-shallot vinaigrette. Homemade desserts (apricot and cherry cobbler, sorbets, chocolate hazelnut cake) will quickly rid you of any virtuous feeling you may have after a meatless Greens meal. You'll feel even less virtuous if you succumb to the temptations of Bruce MacAllister's wine list, one of the best in town. On à la carte weeknights, expect to spend $60 for two, with wine; the weekend prix fixe is $25 a person, without wine.

Open Tues.-Sat. 11:30 a.m.-2:30 p.m. & 6 p.m.-9 p.m., Sun. 11 a.m.-2 p.m. Cards: MC, V.

GRIFONE RISTORANTE

1609 Powell St., Russian Hill - 397-8458
Italian

12/20

Opened not long ago by Bruno Pella, who grew weary of retirement, Grifone owes some of its recent reputation to having become the darling of a noted San Francisco journalist. But it owes the rest of its reputation to itself, for offering good northern Italian food at moderate prices. The setting is rather formal, yet comforting—a plum-colored dining room with a timbered ceiling and porcelain chandeliers, kept busy by the attentive staff. The menu offers both hot and cold antipasti, including frutti di mare in conchiglia (warm prawns and crab in a shell) and a combinazione di antipasto (cold meats and calamari); both are very good. The minestrone has a thick, tangy bacon-and-garlic base, though its vegetables can be overcooked. Much better is the light and fluffy gnocchi in a creamy pesto, among the finest we have had in San Francisco, and the calamari alla livornese (squid stew served with black olives), a fine change from the usual fried or sautéed preparations. Veal dishes—saltimbocca and lombata di vitello capriccio (tomato gratin and mushroom sauce on polenta)—can be a little overcooked and oversauced; without that flaw, Grifone would surely deserve a toque. The desserts, including zuppa inglese and zabaglione, are competently done, and many regional and premium Italian wines are offered on the moderately priced wine list. About $60 for dinner for two, with wine.

Open nightly 5 p.m.-11 p.m. Cards: AE, MC, V.

HARBOR VILLAGE RESTAURANT

4 Embarcadero Center, Financial District - 781-8833

Chinese

13 🍳

Harbor Village is the first American outpost of the Harbor View Group, which owns hotels and restaurants in Hong Kong. Its interior—teak, rosewood, crystal, carpeting, bar, piano and perhaps even the hostesses in slinky gowns—was shipped across the Pacific in three huge cargo containers and plopped down in the middle of the Financial District. The result is a sort of Chinese nouveau opulence that only borders on the tasteful. Harbor Village was carefully thought out and is skillfully run—service is quietly attentive, the kitchen is efficient and the food is consistently very good. Everything we've tried has been tasty and fresh, but we can especially recommend anything with bones or shells: squab, duck, whole catfish, rock cod and crab netted from an immaculately maintained aquarium. Soups are also exceptional, especially the shark's fin and the conpoy, which contains pricey dried scallop shreds. A regal Chinese dinner for two, with wine, will cost about $70.

Open Mon.-Fri. 11 a.m.-2:30 p.m. & 5:30 p.m.-9:30 p.m., Sat.-Sun. 10:30 a.m.-2:30 p.m. & 5:30 p.m.-9:30 p.m. All major cards.

HARRIS'

2100 Van Ness Ave., Van Ness - 673-1888

The Harris Ranch is a civilized, much-welcome oasis in the long, dreary journey between San Francisco and Los Angeles on Interstate 5. Every time we undertake this tedious trek, we look forward to a rest stop at the Ranch for excellent steaks, chops and ranch-grown produce. When we learned that Ann Harris was planning to open a city restaurant, we

American/steakhouse

8/20

greatly looked forward to having her wonderful ranch fare so close to home. Unfortunately, several meals at her elaborate new restaurant turned eager anticipation to shock and dismay. Yes, the beef is from the Harris Ranch, and yes, if the chef deigns to send it out of the kitchen properly rare, the Harris' steak will be very good (the bone-in New York is by far the best steak). But everything else is dismally disappointing. Did the chef drop the salt shaker in the onion soup by accident? If so, he did it on two successive visits. And what of the sweetbread pâté, which resembled dog food? And what about the special appetizer, which was presented with pride—over- and under-ripe figs with prosciutto of distressingly low quality, which came with blueberries and little swirls of near-frozen butter and packaged Melba toast? We could go on and on. The dining room is modeled after a steamship's, with huge potted palms, frosted glass and plush banquettes. After our last regrettable dinner here, we felt as if we were indeed on a steamship—perhaps the *Titanic* or the *Andrea Doria*. Only the steak and the excellent homemade desserts (presented on a lovely pastry cart) prevent Harris' from being a total disaster. And the prices! About $90 for dinner for two, with wine.

Open Mon.-Fri. 11:30 a.m.-2 p.m. & 5 p.m.-11 p.m., Sat. 5 p.m.-11 p.m., Sun. 4 p.m.-10 p.m. Cards: AE, MC, V.

HARRY'S BAR

500 Van Ness Ave., Civic Center - 864-2779

Italian

16

We tend to distrust restaurants with cute ideas. Here, the conceit was to open a restaurant modeled after the world-famous Harry's Bar in Florence (owner Spectrum Foods has many restaurants, including another Harry's in Los Angeles and several Pregos). The artful little menu has a beautiful litho of Firenze on the cover, and prices are listed in lire as well as dollars—just one more cute idea, it seemed. But a closer inspection of the menu led us through northern Italian and Florentine dishes that, we surmised, the kitchen could not possibly pull off. Three hours and a number of courses later, we sat in a state of shock—we had been magically transported to Italy. Everything was truly magnificent. We wanted to leap up and kiss the chef, but, alas, he quit before we could get to the kitchen. Harry's then limped along for a time, becoming just another nice Italian restaurant—but now, we are happy to report, an extremely talented young Italian has taken over the kitchen, and the food once again sings. The Italian classics are still in place—from incomparable paglia e fieno to inspired tiramisu —but now a French touch can be perceived in the lightly cooked fresh foie gras served with a glass of Madeira, the lovely wild mushrooms (chanterelles, porcini, etc.) in phyllo dough, and the oysters with basil butter. And Harry's succeeds outside the kitchen as well, with its comprehensive, reasonably priced collection of Italian wines, its witty Italian waiters, as friendly as they are efficient, and its elegantly plush red dining rooms, whose high ceilings and decently spaced tables are conducive to the long, leisurely evenings at the table that one has in Italy. Dinner for two, with wine, will run about $80.

Open Mon.-Thurs. 11 a.m.-3 p.m. & 5 p.m.-11 p.m., Fri. 11:30 a.m.-3 p.m. & 5 p.m.-12 midnight, Sat. 5 p.m.-12 midnight, Sun. 5 p.m.-11 p.m. All major cards.

HAYES STREET GRILL

320 Hayes St., Civic Center - 863-5545

Seafood

15

In a city that should have some of the best fish in the world, it is criminal that the vast majority of San Francisco's seafood restaurants are ghastly (especially the ones at Fisherman's Wharf). This dreary situation inspired young Patricia Unterman, a fellow restaurant critic, and some of her friends to open a decent fish restaurant. At first, Hayes Street served only grilled fish and a few composed salads, but how this place has grown! The appetizers are among the best in the city: marinated warm mozzarella with roasted eggplant and onion, a smoked chicken and mango salad, a quail salad, a winter salad of beets, walnuts and Stilton, the world's best marinated herring . . . the list is endless. The entrees are mostly from the blackboard and depend on what fresh fish are available. On any given day there may be more than a dozen varieties: angler, swordfish, salmon of two types, sea bass, flounder, glorious Washington bay scallops, Maryland soft-shell crabs . . . a seafood lover will be in seventh heaven. Best of all, not only is it all perfectly fresh, but it also leaves the mesquite grill or sauté pan moist and properly cooked, an absolute rarity among San Francisco's fish restaurants. The non–fish lover is catered to with such dishes as a large grilled veal chop with porcini mushrooms, a simple grilled steak or homemade sausages. Pasta of the highest quality is often paired with shellfish in ways that recall Venice. And the desserts, all homemade, just get better: crème brûlée that is unequaled in town, homey fruit cobblers that are simplicity and perfection itself, and opulently rich tortes. The well-priced wine list offers an intelligent selection of both imports and Californians, and the young, capable staff is dedicated, though often rushed, especially at the popular and hard-to-reserve pre-theater or opera seatings. A seafaring dinner for two, with wine, will run about $65.

Open Mon.-Fri. 11:30 a.m.-3 p.m. & 5 p.m.-10 p.m., Sat. 6 p.m.-11 p.m. Cards: MC, V.

HAYMARKET RESTAURANT
3011 Steiner St., Pacific Heights - 921-2141
California

11/20

This simple restaurant is as cute as can be: two country farmhouse–style rooms complete with beamed ceilings, Mexican paver tile floors, whitewashed walls and a crackling fireplace. The small, regularly changing menu is also inviting: a few salads, a pasta or two, and such entrees as grilled mahi mahi with blood orange sauce, grilled chicken with an apple-Calvados sauce and a New York steak with herb butter. But the Haymarket has more than a few problems. At our last visit, we were served by a frenetic waiter who looked at us blankly when we asked for food recommendations; when we chose a bottle from the small list, he abruptly said, "It's all gone," then could not recommend a substitute. And food was inexcusably slow coming from the kitchen, especially considering the sparse crowd that night. Sadly, not much of it was worth waiting for. The Caesar salad was ho-hum, and the penne with mushrooms had a bland sauce; in fact, the sauces on all the entrees were poorly conceived and prepared. But there were a few successes, notably the salad of endive, delicate smoked chicken and thinly sliced pears. The quality and the preparations of the meats and poultry also showed that the kitchen has potential. Desserts are a mixed bag: satisfying bread pudding with vanilla sauce, unpleasant-tasting apple crumb pie and deliciously nutty hazelnut ice cream that does not need the overabundance of raspberry sauce. We want to like this charming spot, and we hope the bugs are worked out soon. Dinner for two, with wine, will run $75.

Open Tues.-Sat. 6 p.m.-10 p.m., Sun. 10 a.m.-2 p.m. Cards: MC, V.

HOUSE OF PRIME RIB
1906 Van Ness Ave., Van Ness - 885-4605
American

9/20

We had just written a very critical review of this one-entree restaurant, based on several meals a few months prior, when we learned that it had changed hands. The new owner invested $650,000 in renovating the place and proclaimed that the food was "better than ever." This meager goal didn't seem too hard to accomplish, but we still didn't relish returning. But return we did, and we are pleased to announce that the dishes that were so pitiful under the ancien régime (the rib itself, the mashed potatoes, the Yorkshire pudding) were quite good—not exciting, but decent. That is the good news; the bad news is that the dishes that used to be decent (the lettuce, beet and egg salad with "French" dressing, the creamed spinach, the desserts) were awful. The salad literally swam in a sickeningly sweet dressing; the spinach tasted like it had come from a can; and, to finish, the waiter proudly brought us pecan pie with a crust as thick as an accountant's ledger and ten times less interesting. And the changes in decor! Once tomb-dark, with faded leather banquettes, it now has some kind of Oriental modern/floral look—surely the most criminal waste of money ever for a decorator's service. The grandmotherly waitresses who had ruled here since creation have given way to a corps of kind but hilariously inept youngsters. About $60 for dinner for two, with wine.

Open Mon.-Sat. 5:30 p.m.-10 p.m., Sun. 4 p.m.-10 p.m. Cards: AE, MC, V.

HUNAN

924 Sansome St., North Beach - 956-7727

853 Kearny St., Chinatown - 788-2234

5723 Geary Blvd., Richmond District - 221-3388

Chinese

9/20

Hunan's humble Kearny Street restaurant deserves (and has) a place in contemporary culinary lore, because this is where Americans were first treated to the red-pepper delights of the hot cuisine of China's Hunan province. But in the last few years, the spicy cooking of Hunan, Szechwan and Thailand has flourished in cities across the country, and these pioneers now seem banal. Perhaps this is because, despite the heavy use of hot peppers, the cooking here is fundamentally bland. The beef tastes like the chicken, which tastes like the fish—and they all taste only of hotness. Main dishes are all cooked the same way—stir-fried with green peppers, onion and lots of chilis. The dishes containing smoked meats (ham, chicken) add one extra flavor: intense saltiness. These failings are most noticeable at the Geary restaurant, the least popular of the three; the best of the lot is the tiny original on Kearny. At the newer barn of a restaurant on Sansome, expect noise and crowds. Dinner for two, with beer, will cost about $25.

Open Mon.-Sat. 11:30 a.m.-9:30 p.m. Cards: AE, MC, V.
Open Mon.-Sat. 11:30 a.m.-9:30 p.m. No cards.
Open daily 11:30 a.m.-9:30 p.m. Cards: AE, MC, V.

IRONWOOD CAFÉ

Named after a town on Michigan's northern peninsula, the Ironwood Café was designed to look like a northwoods lumber-town café. The high-ceilinged, two-level dining

*901 Cole St.,
Haight-Ashbury -
664-0224*

American

13

room is filled with old-time touches—antique oil lamps, a wooden mannequin, knotty pine booths—that give it a warm, cozy feel. If only the same could be said of the service, which lacks the cheery, informal attention one would expect of a small-town café. On the other hand, much attention is given to the food, as evidenced in all the details: spiced breads that are baked on the premises, homemade ice creams, well-chosen wines and so on. The kitchen has a deft hand with seafood; the daily-changing menu offers such dishes as lightly baked ehu (Hawaiian sea bass), broiled parrot fish and broiled oysters with ginger. The only dishes that have disappointed us are soups and salads—not bad, just lackluster. The dessert selection changes frequently and is always worth sampling. About $50 for a tasty dinner for two, with wine.

Open Mon.-Fri. 11 a.m.-2:30 p.m. & 5:30 p.m.-10:30 p.m., Sat. 5:30 p.m.-10:30 p.m. Cards: AE, MC, V.

JACK'S

*615 Sacramento St.,
Financial District -
986-9854*

American

10/20

In business at one location or another since 1864, Jack's is an "old San Francisco" restaurant that is the darling of the Montgomery Street financial community. The room is austere, with linoleum floors, bright lights and downright tacky table service; the waiters can be rather rude to unknowns; and the food ranges from the sublime to the dreadful. Best bets are the incredible fresh cracked crab with the world's best homemade mayonnaise, the fried eggplant and the superb au gratin potatoes. But avoid the charred (inside and out) lamb chop stuffed with a ghastly lamb kidney, the overcooked chicken with artichokes and the desserts. Don't let the cheesy decor fool you—men will not be seated if they are not wearing ties. About $80 for dinner for two, with wine.

Open Mon.-Fri. 11:30 a.m.-9:30 p.m., Sat.-Sun. 5 p.m.-9:30 p.m. No cards.

JACKSON FILLMORE TRATTORIA

2506 Fillmore St., Upper Fillmore - 346-5288

Italian

11/20

Owner Jack Kreitzman covers most of the bases in this rollicking trattoria. We've never had a bad time here, though on occasion we've had trouble getting in and have never found the food inspired, just good. Anchoring the northern boundary of the Upper Fillmore neighborhood, within easy walking distance of such popular watering holes as Harry's Saloon and Alta Plaza, Jackson Fillmore has been packed virtually from the minute it opened. The cuisine is southern

Italian with a bullet—which isn't always for the best, given that region's overdependence on olive oil. It's pretty authentic, as witnessed by the number of times we've overheard parties reminiscing about Roman holidays past. Especially good are the antipasti, which can make for a nice light meal. In particular, try the delicious eggplant saltimbocca and the insalata di pomodori, a salad of tomatoes, tiny zucchini, red onion and garlic marinated in olive oil and vinegar—the essence of late summer, even if it is foggy outside. We have experienced curt, even rude service, but that, too, is authentically Roman. The large portions, reasonable prices and festive atmosphere keep packing them in. Two can eat well for $30, with a glass of wine each.

Open Tues.-Thurs. 5:30 p.m.-10:30 p.m., Fri.-Sat. 5:30 p.m.-11 p.m., Sun. 5 p.m.-10 p.m. Cards: MC, V.

JANOT'S

44 Campton Pl., Union Square - 392-5373
French

11/20

This cramped, noisy bistro was hailed by the press as the most authentically French casual restaurant in San Francisco —but after a recent meal here we have severe reservations about this claim. The service is not particularly attentive and the reception can be downright rude, especially to solitary diners. Does the food make up for this? Hardly. Onion soup is bland, snails in garlic butter are oily, and a seafood sauté in a fennel butter sauce is a failure. But there are some respectable dishes, and a few very good ones. Try the cream of celery soup, one of the well-presented salads with a fine Roquefort, and one of the tempting entrees: leg of veal with homemade noodles, wonderful little lamb chops or paupiettes of sole with a spinach mousse. Less distinguished, though decent, are the desserts: cheesecakes, fruit tarts and a white-and-dark-chocolate mousse. The wine list is quite extensive and fairly moderate in price. There are good things about Janot's, but not enough to justify the lack of comfort. Dinner for two, with wine, will run about $80.

Open Mon.-Sat. 11:30 a.m.-2:30 p.m. & 6 p.m.-10 p.m. All major cards.

KABUTO SUSHI

5116 Geary Blvd., Richmond District - 752-5652

Although the star chef at this small, fashionable sushi joint was long a prime attraction at Kinokawa, Kabuto still has its little problems. One great ringmaster does not a circus make, or something like that. The inestimable Sachio Kojima, from Hokkaido, is a true sushi samurai, and a consummate showman to boot. Knives seem to sprout from his hands as

Japanese/sushi

he slices, shapes, wraps and presents pelagic morsels. His ceremonial cries are from the heart, as are occasional outbursts of applause from awestruck patrons (fine young cannibals, mostly), many of whom followed him from the Financial District and all of whom accept their tidbits with profound delight. Although he makes no personal claims, Sachio is credited by his fans with having invented the California maki—maguro, crab and avocado surrounded by rice and wrapped in seaweed. His tiger eye, a psychedelic treasure of smoked salmon and poached squid, is hypnotic. Watching Sachio's herky-jerky routine, one can't help but picture David Byrne with a sword. Unfortunately, as we've seen on several occasions, the show needs direction. Service in the tiny storefront–cum–country inn can be somnolent and, on occasion, snappish. Best to skip the dinner menu and stick to sushi. About $50 for two, with sake.

Open Mon.-Tues. & Thurs.-Sat. 5 p.m.-3 a.m., Sun. 5 p.m.-11 p.m. Cards: AE, MC, V.

KAN'S

708 Grant Ave.,
Chinatown - 982-2388
Chinese

6/20

Kan't! This establishment sadly typifies those restaurants that rest exclusively on past laurels. In the '40s and '50s, John Kan introduced gourmet Chinese cooking to San Francisco. Many well-earned dining awards grace the walls of the still-elegant dining room; a gallery of autographed photos boasts of the many celebrity guests. Perhaps celebrities are still accorded deference—and a fine meal—but not so the anonymous visitor. You will understand why the room is kept so dim when the food begins to arrive. An appetizer combination consists of greasy, nearly meatless chicken wings, fried won tons that taste like lava with a texture to match, and shrivelled, overcooked prawns. But we should have been happy with this course, since it turns out to be the highlight of the meal. The winter melon soup is tasteless, but it is a vast improvement over the sizzling rice soup, which is nasty. Sesame chicken is coated with a flour "plaster" of an inedible consistency. The "tumble" (grated beef and water chestnuts) suffers from meat that does not taste prime and vegetables that taste canned. Lobster à la Kan completes the assault by turning out to look and taste like muckish gruel. A full bar and our waiter's repeated offerings of wine or cocktails are clues to the best way to enjoy this place. About $70 for dinner for two, with wine.

Open Mon.-Fri. 12 noon-10 p.m., Sat. 12 noon-11 p.m., Sun. 4:30 p.m.-10 p.m. All major cards.

KHAN TOKE THAI HOUSE

*5937 Geary Blvd.,
Richmond District -
668-6654*

Thai

 14

Wear slip-on shoes and clean socks to Khan Toke, because the first thing you'll do is hand your footwear over to be checked until after dinner. That disconcerts some people, but we look forward to padding into the lushly carpeted, candlelit labyrinth of dining rooms in our stocking feet to begin what has never failed to be a resplendent feast. Diners are seated on floor cushions at low tables (some have wells for feet) with padded back supports. Appetizers are generally the best part of an outstanding menu; one could make a memorable meal with several openers and an order of exquisite pad Thai noodles. One must is the green papaya salad, a piquant dish laced with fresh chilis. The artfully layered flavors that give each dish a special character induce us to drink wine with our Khan Toke meals, rather than beer as at most Thai restaurants. And the wine list is up to it—delicate Sauvignon Blancs and perfumed Gewurztraminers are just right to boost the dynamics, point up the subtleties and, not least, extinguish the flames just short of causing any serious mental damage. A special treat on Sunday evenings is provided by temple dancers, who perform sinuously against the backdrop of intricate hardwood wall carvings and windows overlooking as tropical a garden as one will find in San Francisco. About $40 for two, with a modest wine.

Open nightly 5 p.m.-11 p.m. All major cards.

KINOKAWA

*347 Grant Ave., Union
Square - 956-6085*

Japanese/sushi

13

The sushi bar in this exemplary Japanese restaurant has the virtue of staying open late most nights, but that joy is tempered by the presence of Ono No Shiro, the adjacent, very popular piano bar—so one faces the unhappy prospect of being regaled in the midst of wasabe bliss with a loud, drunken, multilingual version of "Bad, Bad Leroy Brown" from next door. But no matter: This is some of the best sushi in town, vying with Nikko and Kabuto in the skilled-chef department and beating both in ambience. The decor is as stylish as traditional Japanese motifs get, without crossing over into the fashionable neon madness inspired by Gobots and Godzilla. We've traipsed in here at all hours and have always found the hamachi fine and the uni sweet. Elsewhere in the house are many small, grass-matted niches, each with its own gas hibachi. A waitress deftly lights the flame, then brings the raw or marinated meat, seafood and vegetables of choice, and the rest is up to you. To our way of thinking, mesquite's more fun in the privacy of your own backyard, but then there was one rainy evening downtown when

Kinokawa's hibachis beckoned and worked a lasting magic. Sushi can run to $60 for two, with sake; a hibachi dinner will run about $45.

Restaurant open Mon.-Fri. 11:30 a.m.-2:30 p.m. & 5 p.m.-11 p.m., Sat.-Sun. 5 p.m.-11 p.m.; sushi bar open Sun.-Thurs. 5 p.m.-12 midnight, Fri.-Sat. 5 p.m.-2 a.m. All major cards.

KOREA HOUSE

1640 Post St., Japantown - 563-1388

Korean

12/20

This is Asian soul food, with enough heat to blow both Thailand and Hunan Province right off the map, and some delicacy of flavor to boot. The pale wood decor of the large upstairs room (a nightclub is downstairs) is beautiful in a stark, mountainish way, though there's little to stare at but other patrons, a reassuring number of whom look Korean. Each of the many tables has its own gas barbecue for personal immolation of various marinated meats and fish. Squid, in a sweet-hot marinade, is particularly satisfying to grill. It puffs up and turns purple, echoing the reaction of some Westerners to the fierce spiciness of most of these dishes. Aside from the barbecue selections (all served with pickled vegetables and a peppery broth), there are such magnificent traditional dishes as sang sum chi gaw, a stew of fish, greens, mushrooms, noodles and tofu that is guaranteed to clear blocked sinuses. And don't neglect mun aw hwe, defined on the menu as "steamed ugliest fresh octopus with hot sauce." Gnarly, perhaps, but ugly? No way—it tastes too good. Service is lickety-split. Best of all, Korea House is open until 3 a.m. Two can have dinner and plenty of cold Korean beer and still get out for $35.

Open daily 11 a.m.-3 a.m. Cards: MC, V.

LAFAYETTE ON PACIFIC

290 Pacific Ave., North Beach - 986-3366

California

9/20

The history here—it was once a Barbary Coast blacksmith's shop—is not lost on the diner. The pianist pounds on her instrument as if it were an anvil. Restrooms are not always clean. And the chef treats his grill as if it were a blacksmith's forge, overcooking dishes almost to the point of inedibility. There are a few good things here, especially the wonderfully flaky and juicy strawberry tart and the tasty (if overcooked) beef fillet in a properly understated red wine sauce. But the bacon, spinach and curly endive salad, the artichoke soup and the veal chop in a wild mushroom sauce are better left undiscussed. Wines are modestly priced, and there are several selections served by the glass, but this does little to redeem. About $60 for dinner for two, with wine.

Open Mon.-Thurs. 11 a.m.-10 p.m., Fri. 11 a.m.-10:30 p.m., Sat. 5 p.m.-10:30 p.m. Cards: AE, MC, V.

LITTLE ITALY

4109 24th St., Noe Valley - 821-1515
Italian

11/20

Nestled in one of the city's yuppie enclaves, Little Italy is immensely popular with both neighborhood residents and outsiders. They love the generous portions, affordable prices, homey atmosphere and country-style ("contadina") cooking. The food is simple; winners include a prosciutto and cheese–stuffed artichoke and a dish of chicken broiled with bell peppers, garlic, potatoes and mushrooms. There are disappointments (such as the Italian onion soup), but it's all authentic and hearty. Dessert is, predictably, limited to zabaglione, though it is given interest with good fresh fruit. About $50 for dinner for two, with wine.

Open nightly 6 p.m.-10:30 p.m. Cards: MC, V.

LITTLE JOE'S

523 Broadway, North Beach - 433-4343
Italian

11/20

Just as there are cult films, so there are cult restaurants. Little Joe's many followers swear this is the best restaurant in San Francisco, nay, the best in the country. But though one can have a very nice meal here, it just isn't worth the potential two-hour wait for a table. The restaurant's motto, "Rain or shine, there's always a line," is unfortunately all too true. The no-reservations policy and the refusal to provide any kind of waiting area (instead, customers form a long, snaky line around the bar, getting entirely sloshed before finally being seated) considerably mar our enjoyment of a meal here, though we suspect that the loyalists consider the wait half the fun, akin to paying one's dues. Pastas are always correctly al dente, and any of the pastas with mussels or clams are memorable. The veal dishes, the best of which are the saltimbocca and a big, saucy parmigiana, are all admirable. Surprisingly, the Italian fish stews are made to order, though the timing is sometimes off—the shellfish may be perfectly done but the fish may be cooked to gruel. Vegetables are always well prepared and abundant. In fact, all the portions are abundant, making dessert unnecessary—a blessing, since they are mundane. The young waitresses (many of Italian origin) are friendly but dreadfully hurried; the whole mood of Little Joe's is too frantic for those who enjoy relaxed meals. Still, there's little point in being critical—no matter what we say, there will always be an interminable line here. A very reasonable $20 per person for dinner with wine.

Open Mon.-Thurs. 11 a.m.-10:30 p.m., Fri.-Sat. 11 a.m.-11 p.m., Sun. 2 p.m.-10 p.m. No cards.

MacArthur Park

607 Front St., Financial District - 398-5700

American

11/20

There is no park in San Francisco named MacArthur, but there is a large converted warehouse named MacArthur Park in North Beach that serves fashionable American cuisine. Although the small front dining room faces a lovely wooded square, the three back dining areas are more elegant. On a bright summer day, the preferred seating is a delightful little patio at the very rear of the restaurant, sheltered by a greenhouse roof. First-rate ingredients are clearly used, but the cooking techniques can be sloppy. For instance, an appetizer of grilled pasilla peppers filled with three cheeses is marred by too-charred surfaces, and a fine salad of romaine with Roquefort and walnuts contains an errant walnut shell. The best entrees are from the oakwood smoker—a superb chicken in a barbecue sauce, a delicious spicy sausage—but two are to be avoided: the smoked Petaluma duck, which has an unpleasant layer of unrendered fat and a cloyingly sweet lingonberry sauce, and the grand specialty, baby-back ribs, which are so meatless that they could be served to a vegetarian. From the mesquite grill emanates a parade of honest steaks, chops and fresh fish. Whatever you order, make sure to accompany it with the best dish in the house, the side of crisply fried Bermuda onion "strings." Desserts are homemade and satisfying (apple pie, shortcake), and the service is amicable and well meaning, if rushed. Dinner for two, with wine, will be about $60.

Open Mon.-Thurs. 7 a.m.-10 a.m., 11:30 a.m.-2:30 p.m. & 5:30 p.m.-10:30 p.m., Fri. 7 a.m.-10 a.m., 11:30 a.m.-2:30 p.m. & 5:30 p.m.-11 p.m., Sat. 4:30 p.m.-11 p.m., Sun. 10 a.m.-2:30 p.m. & 4:30 p.m.-10 p.m. Cards: AE, MC, V.

Mai's

1838 Union St., Cow Hollow - 921-2861

Vietnamese

13

When you've had enough of the trendy shops along Union Street, seek respite in this charming little hideout. The sign might not attract you, but the handsome bistro setting (burnished wood, copper fixtures, a few outdoor tables) will. This decor might lead you to expect provincial French fare, but the kitchen produces a remarkably skilled Vietnamese cuisine. Everything here is wonderful: crisp rolls stuffed with shrimp, pork, noodles and bean sprouts; fresh salads dressed with Vietnamese fish sauce and rice wine vinegar; aromatic soups poured over rice noodles; la lot beef, a marvelous blend of ground beef and spices wrapped in la lot leaves and charbroiled; and lemon-grass chicken sautéed with onions. If you're in the do-it-yourself mood, try the Vietnamese-style shabu, a bubbling chicken broth in which you cook morsels of meat, fish, tofu and vegetables, then dip them in soy sauce. The Vietnamese waiters may not speak fluent English, but they are full of smiles and are most attentive. Dinner for two, with beer, will run about $30.

Open daily 10 a.m.-10 p.m. All major cards.

THE MANDARIN

900 North Point St. (Ghirardelli Square), Fisherman's Wharf - 474-5438

Chinese

11/20

Cecilia Chiang has been delighting tourists and gastronomes alike for nearly twenty years here in Ghirardelli Square, and more recently in Beverly Hills. So it is especially sad for us to have to report the Mandarin's recent decline. We have long loved the Mandarin for its intelligent offerings of the finest from China's various provinces, for its discreet service and for its handsome setting in the rafters of the old warehouse building. The house specialties had always been reliably delicious—incomparable potstickers, pungent tangerine beef, moist tea-smoked duck, minced squab served in crisp lettuce leaves and so on. But our last meal here, a lunch, confirmed the word around town—the Mandarin seems to have lost its spirit. Lunch began with an egg flower soup no better than that found at cheap Chinese lunch counters all over town. Next came the acclaimed tea-smoked duck, which needed more smoke and less grease. Things picked up with the kung-pao scallops, which featured a good, fiery sauce and properly cooked scallops. But the Mongolian lamb was stringy and off tasting, and the beef in the tangerine beef was tough and gristly. We can only hope that Ms. Chiang will light a fire under her kitchen and return the Mandarin to its former status. About $35 for lunch for two, with a glass of wine, and $70 for dinner for two, with wine.

Open daily 12 noon-11 p.m. All major cards.

MASA'S

648 Bush St. (Vintage Court Hotel), Union Square - 989-7154

French

17

Masa's is second only to Washington, D.C.'s Jean-Louis for having the highest ugly-decor-to-sublime-food ratio. When we settled in for our first meal at this nationally famous temple of gastronomy, we immediately disliked Masa's. The room looks like a dressed-up motel lobby, the wines are shockingly overpriced, and the service is thoroughly pretentious and unprofessional. In fact, we were ready to leave without trying a bite. But then a little plate of remarkably delicious amuse-gueules arrived: tiny pastry cups filled with a mushroom mixture, which set the stage for the marvelous meal to come. We sampled a great many dishes that night, and every single one of them was good. Many, in fact, were ethereal. Despite the decor, despite the service, despite the prices, Masa's is an exceptional restaurant.

It's a consistent restaurant, too. Many predicted that Masa's would decline after the original chef and co-owner, Masa Kobayashi, died in 1984—after all, he *was* the restaurant. But he had wisely chosen Bill Galloway, a man of considerable talent, as his sous-chef, and owner Bill Kimpton was smart enough to promote from within. Galloway preserved Masa's refined classic French menu, but it was no mere imitation; he became as much a master as Masa. Then, quite recently, Galloway left, once again causing concern. But Kimpton went with a winning formula and promoted from within again, and we are happy to report that Galloway's former sous-chef, Julian Serrano, is just as skilled as his predecessors.

Everything here is good, but there is one dish you must not miss: the incredibly tender and delicious foie gras from New York, which is very lightly sautéed and served with a veal demi-glace and black truffles. It has no equal in California. Other exceptional starters are the thick, chunky sausage of shrimp, scallops and lobster—a marvelous blend of taste and texture—and the supremely satisfying bisque of Sacramento crayfish, rich with the taste of crayfish and saffron. At our last dinner here, the entrees weren't quite up to the exceptional appetizers, but they were still very good. Medallions of lamb was a simple dish, the lamb flavorful and rare as ordered, if too chewy. A tiny breast of squab was precious but tasty, served with a delightful chestnut purée and marrow mousse. Given the relatively small entree portions, we were taken aback when the Maine lobster arrived— a monstrous lobster served in its shell, the tender, perfectly cooked meat buttery but not oily. Desserts are all heavenly, especially the blood orange sorbet, the chocolate mousse cake and the white- and dark-chocolate mousses. The wine list is rich with Bordeaux and Burgundies, but you have to be rich yourself to try any of them. In fact, you need a positive cash flow to dine here at all, even with a California wine: with the prix-fixe dinners at $60 a head, plus surcharges, an aperitif, a moderate bottle of wine and tip, two of you will spend from $200 to $230.

Open Tues.-Sat. 6 p.m.-9:30 p.m. All major cards.

MAXWELL'S PLUM

The Bay Room—Maxwell's Plum's main dining room—is aptly named: its view of San Francisco Bay is dramatic

*900 North Point St.
(Ghirardelli Square),
Fisherman's Wharf -
441-4140*

American

11/20

indeed. But the rest of Warner LeRoy's multimillion-dollar monument to bad taste is garish beyond belief, with tons of stained glass, immense chandeliers and a decor featuring every color of the rainbow. The service is young and attentive (but not terribly competent), and, fortunately, the food is by no means as ghastly as the surroundings. The kitchen's concern for using the best available ingredients shows in the seafood pâté in a tomato coulis, the gazpacho that evokes Andalusia and the perfect rack of lamb. However, the long, unwieldy menu (like the too-lavish decor) is evidence that the restaurant is trying too hard to do too much for too many people. So along with the good there are such horrors as the salmon on a bed of spinach with a sauce of mussels and bay shrimp, one of the worst fish dishes we've had in a long time. Desserts, such as a chocolate mousse cake, are competent, and the wine list is pricey and unexciting. About $75 for dinner for two, with wine.

Open Mon.-Sat. 11:30 a.m.-11 p.m., Sun. 10:30 a.m.-11 p.m. All major cards.

MELON'S

*246 McAllister St. (Abigail
Hotel), Civic Center -
626-5675*

California

12/20

There is both creativity and confusion at work here. The Civic Center location, just a few blocks from City Hall, the Opera House, Symphony Hall and the judicial courts, invites success. Indeed, the lunchtime clientele includes a good number of the state's high court judges. At lunch, the menu is quite varied, with nice salads (a niçoise, for example), homemade pot pies, good fish dishes (grilled bass in beurre blanc, blackened redfish) and splendid desserts. At night, however, when the kitchen tries to do complex nouvelle cuisine dishes, confusion reigns. Pâtés, made by Marcel et Henri, California's best pâté maker, are splendid. Soups are generally puréed vegetables (cauliflower on a recent visit) in cream; their coarseness makes them seem more like vegetable dishes than soup. On our last visit, the very short photocopied menu described a rare, nouvelle-style duck breast with three mushrooms in a brandy-Port sauce. Instead, we were brought a delightfully crisp middle-European half duck with brandy-soaked mushrooms— clearly not what the menu described, but still quite good. The kitchen, alas, seems to have a heavy hand with fish: the halibut poached in orange juice, lime juice and ginger and topped with mango was both overcooked and ill-conceived, a concession to trendiness without gastronomic substance. As at lunchtime, desserts are homemade and good. But again confusion reigns. We were promised a blueberry, blackberry and apricot cobbler and instead were served a delicious compote with good (but not house-made) ice cream. Why is there such a communication gap between the kitchen and the dining room? Perhaps these able youngsters are merely overextending themselves. Dinner for two, with wine, will run about $50.

Open Tues.-Sat. 7 a.m.-10:30 a.m., 11:30 a.m.-2:30 p.m. & 5:30 p.m.-9 p.m., Sun. 8 a.m.-2 p.m. & 5:30 p.m.-9 p.m. All major cards.

MITOYA

1855 Post St. (Japan Center), Japantown - 563-2156

Japanese/sushi

12/20

This is a slice from Tokyo's fast lane, the Ginza, where eating as entertainment is taken seriously. Mitoya occupies two rooms on the second level of Japan Center; the larger room does double duty as a coffeehouse by day and sing-along disco by night. The smaller, more attractive room is a robata-yaki bar, similar to a sushi bar but offering, in addition to sushi and sashimi, a range of meats, vegetables and what have you that are grilled to order over open flames and served in bite-size portions. Even a bite at a time, the most eclectic eaters are sated long before running out of dishes to try. But a warning: Sophisticated as you may be, East is East and West is West. Avoid fermented bean curd unless you've had it before and know you like it. One delicious tidbit is a thin slice of lean beef wrapped around a young asparagus spear and briefly fired. Slices of sweet yam, cooked quickly and served with butter melting over them, are divine. The robata-yaki master can recommend the evening's most propitious choices, which are also posted on a board overhead. Shoes are removed before entering, and guests sit before the bar with feet dangling in a well. There's one table in the corner for large parties. The decor resembles a set from a Kurosawa epic about the Shogunate; as in a sushi bar, the foods are displayed in a glass case betwixt diners and chefs. Feel free to point and gesture—the universal language, where food is concerned. About $35 for two, with beer.

Open Sun.-Thurs. 6 p.m.-2 a.m., Fri.-Sat. 6 p.m.-2:30 a.m. All major cards.

MODESTO LANZONE OPERA PLAZA

Most San Franciscans feel that Modesto Lanzone provides the most satisfying Italian dining experience in a city filled with innumerable Italian restaurants, and for the most part we agree. We have certainly had better Italian meals, and

601 Van Ness Ave., Civic Center - 928-0400

Italian

14

other places (Donatello's, Harry's) have had more skilled chefs in the kitchen. But charming Modesto, a longtime San Francisco maître d' and restaurateur, has created a wonderful environment and a consistently rewarding cuisine. He first opened his doors in Ghirardelli Square; though the original still stands, we much prefer this new Opera offshoot, which serves as a showcase for Modesto's immense collection of modern art and sculpture. The food, like the decor, is often artful. Starters can be quite good—such things as a warm roasted breast of rabbit on a bed of hearts of endive, a cold stuffed breast of veal, and the best marinated mozzarella with tomatoes we have had outside Italy. The pastas—some very creative—are always properly al dente, and the entrees are consistently good. A fantastic lobster is taken from the shell, sautéed with brandy, sherry and tomatoes, and returned to its shell. Perfectly done roast chicken is served with artichokes and sour cream, plump capon is stuffed with prosciutto and Fontina, and lamb medallions are sweet and flavorful, if not as rare as ordered. Desserts are the weakest part of the meal; only a cold zabaglione cake is at all interesting. The wine list is long—California, French and, of course, Italian —but is for the most part dreadfully overpriced. If Modesto himself is present, the service can be efficient and almost chummy; if he is not, it can be slow. About $90 for dinner for two, with wine.

Open Mon.-Fri. 11:30 a.m.-12 midnight, Sat. 5 p.m.-12 midnight. All major cards.

NARAI

2229 Clement St., Richmond District - 751-6363

Thai

14

Run by a family of Chiu Chow Chinese, Narai is one of the very best Thai restaurants in San Francisco, and one of the few patronized by Asians. It is also the only Bay Area restaurant that dares serve the notorious durian fruit. Banned from public transportation and hotels in Thailand because of its awful odor, durian nonetheless has many addicts; eating it is said to be like eating custard in a sewer. Narai's menu offers both Thai and Chinese dishes; we prefer the Thai, though everything here is fresh tasting and well prepared. No one cooks better squid: still translucent, yet tender and warm, it is poached for a matter of seconds before being tossed in a piquant salad or into the hot and sour seafood soup, surely one of the best seafood soups in town. The soup is loaded with clams, shrimp, shark's fin and scallops and is rich with the fragrance of kaffir lime, lemon grass and coriander. (If only the kitchen would omit the mock crab!)

Start your meal with an order of fried crab cakes, creating your own dipping sauce from the table condiments, or the plump roast quail served with seasoned salt. Skip the overly sweet mee krob and try one of the good curries, made with pastes of fresh seasonings instead of Indian-style spices. If you want to sample one of the Chinese offerings, have the delicious Chiu Chow pan-fried oysters, served as a kind of omelet over bean sprouts. Besides the exotic durian, which is served with glutinous rice flavored with sweetened coconut milk, Narai's warm taro, gingko nut and red date pudding is one of the city's most unusual desserts. Since there are only twelve tables in this clean, friendly restaurant, you may have to wait. About $40 for dinner for two, with Thai beer.

Open Tues.-Sun. 11 a.m.-10 p.m. Cards: MC, V.

NICARAGUA

3015 Mission St., Mission District - 826-3672
Nicaraguan

10/20

A steady fixture in one of the outer Mission District's banana belts, Nicaragua has that no-frills cantina feel of a regional family restaurant—that is to say, greasy but friendly, even if you don't speak Spanish. We stop in frequently for an afternoon beer with ceviche, a tasty mixture of marinated rockfish and salsa, with plenty of cilantro and, on the side, freshly made corn chips. Tamales are tops, in two varieties: nacatamal (beef) and yoltamal, the purist's tamale (all cornmeal). We've also enjoyed vigoron, a combination of tender steamed yucca and crispy fried pork. The fried bananas served with most dishes are terrific when eaten with a side order of sour cream. If there's any fresh, whole-fried snapper offered, accept; likewise the staple, indio viejo con arroz y maduro (spiced beef with rice and fried bananas), which is hearty and cheap. The jukebox is terrific—salsa pleases the ear as well as the palate. Two can eat and drink quite well for $20.

Open Mon.-Thurs. 11 a.m.-10 p.m., Fri.-Sat. 11 a.m.-12 midnight. No cards.

NIKKO SUSHI

1450 Van Ness Ave., Van Ness - 474-7722
Japanese/sushi

13

This was the city's first sushi bar, and it remains one of the foremost—for a certain crowd, mainly mature business types on expense accounts. There are other Japanese restaurants that are more fun, but few that are better. The fish displayed before a trio of sushi samurai at the blond pine bar is unspeakably fresh, and the formal dining rooms, with both traditional floor seating and Western tables, manage to provide the calm of a mountain inn without sacrificing the urban edge of excitement. For those who are temporarily sushied out (it happens) there are three ways to go. Dinners cooked to order include straightforward renditions of teriyaki and tempura. Some tables are equipped with gas hibachis for such nabemono dishes as shabu shabu (hot pot), yosenabe (mixed grill) and the well-known sukiyaki, an old favorite that is too often overlooked in these times of rampant exotica. Finally, the à la carte menu offers most of the above plus such specialties as salmon isobe age, a salmon steak wrapped in crisp seaweed and deep-fried in egg batter, then served with a tangy soy-based sauce. All the while, the murmur of genteel voices in several languages is punctuated by the peacefully discordant notes of a samisen. As might be expected, there is usually a wait at the sushi bar, where it's not unusual to spot young chefs from other houses intently observing their colleagues' techniques. Sushi can run to $60 for two, with sake; dinner will be about the same.

Open Tues.-Fri. 11:30 a.m.-3 p.m. & 5 p.m.-11:45 p.m., Sat.-Sun. 5 p.m.-11:45 p.m. All major cards.

NOB HILL RESTAURANT

California St. & Mason St. (Mark Hopkins Hotel), Nob Hill - 392-3434

California

13

Peter Morency, a graduate of the Culinary Institute of America in upstate New York and a former employee of Berkeley's Santa Fe Bar & Grill, has taken over this kitchen as part of the Mark Hopkins's effort to create a showcase for contemporary California and American cuisine. They are serious about their work, as evidenced by the exceptional breadth of the wine cellar and the Cruvinet machine, which allows Nob Hill to offer many fine wines by the glass (at, we must add, very high markups). Another clue to the intent here is the restaurant's vegetable and herb garden on the hotel's grounds. We are happy to report that the efforts are proving successful—the menu shows inventiveness and the kitchen shows skill. We have sampled many good dishes here, including two starters: squash blossoms stuffed with roast veal and goat cheese and the lobster-avocado won tons with an orange-ginger sauce. Entrees change frequently; we recommend ordering one of the daily specials, such as the dish that combined succulent, lightly breaded sweetbreads with a superbly cooked prime filet mignon in a red bell pepper sauce (only the accompanying vegetables were ho-hum). Desserts are not exceptionally creative, but you'll be more than pleased with the crème brûlée. Of interest are the regularly scheduled "visiting chef" dinners hosted by vintner Robert Mondavi. A restaurant to watch—if it continues to improve, it will help propel American cuisine beyond the triteness of the mesquite grill. Dinner for two, with wine, will run about $115.

Open nightly 6 p.m.-10:30 p.m. All major cards.

NORTH CHINA

2315 Van Ness Ave., Van Ness - 673-8201

Chinese

13

North China's location on north Van Ness Avenue, which doubles as Highway 101 along that stretch, is the worst thing about it. We love the place, but, frankly, that busy drag is a drag. There's nowhere to stroll after dinner, even though the neighborhood is safe at any hour. Even the restaurant's tasteful, soothing interior provides only a temporary respite from the lurching traffic outside. But we keep returning because the food is so wonderful. The mandarin crêpes are the best we've encountered. They're offered with an unprecedented range of fillings—served warm with hoisin sauce and a choice of chicken, shrimp, mushrooms or mushu pork, or stir-fried with egg and bean curd. Like the crêpes, steamed buns are made on the premises daily and are served with such entrees as smoked tea duck, which is perfectly crisp on the outside and tenderly moist inside. A cold plate, North China's equivalent of antipasti, offers delectable glazed short ribs, spiced beef, smoked fish and sesame chicken salad. All in all, the meticulous use of fresh and first-quality ingredients makes the food consistently pleasing. Service is extremely efficient, and the price is right at about $35 for dinner for two, with a moderate bottle from the superb wine list.

Open Mon.-Sat. 11 a.m.-2 p.m. & 4 p.m.-10 p.m. Cards: V.

ORIGINAL JOE'S

144 Taylor St., Union Square - 775-4877

Italian/steakhouse

10/20

Located on one of the sleaziest blocks in San Francisco, just steps from several of the city's busiest porno theaters, this landmark has been serving generally fine grills and generally wretched Italian food for over half a century. On our last visit we were pleased to find the veal preparations and sautés considerably improved: the chicken sauté sec and the veal cacciatore were both eminently respectable. Alas, the pastas were as overcooked as ever, reassuring us that some things never change. We were sad to see a change (albeit slight) for the worse in the quality of the steaks, though they are still huge and very reasonably priced. As always, the fish dishes are to be carefully avoided, except for the greaseless and quite lovely deep-fried calamari. Entrees are served with your choice of four accompaniments; skip the greasy fried potatoes, mushy vegetables and ravioli filled with something akin to sawdust, and have the spaghetti—it's overcooked, of course, but the meat sauce is delicious. The waiters, many of whom have been here for eons, range from friendly to amusingly gruff. The room itself is rather grim, with lots of red vinyl and a '50s cocktail-lounge look. There is no wine list to speak of, but the drinks are strong and cheap. This place is not bad at all if you order properly, and the price is certainly right. About $35 to $40 for dinner for two, with drinks.

Open daily 10:30 a.m.-1:15 a.m. Cards: MC, V.

PAT O'SHEA'S MAD HATTER

*3848 Geary Blvd., Richmond District -
752-3148*

American/California

11/20

"We cheat tourists and drunks," says the sign over the door, but don't believe it. They do not discriminate at the Mad Hatter. What they do, more than anything, is deliver fair value in food and libations, not to mention nonstop sports on several prominent, high-resolution TV monitors fed by satellite. If the Giants or the 49ers are in the playoffs, this is the next best place after Candlestick to watch them. Come to think of it, the Mad Hatter may be better than the stadium, because the food is so good. Daily specials, like the daily sports roster, are listed on a blackboard. Offerings typically include fresh, honestly prepared fish, meat and pasta creations, along with good salads. This is a hungry person's pub in the true Irish tradition, offering just about everything you'd expect to find in a yupped-up bar and grill except attitude and high prices. We've had superb rack of lamb, excellent anglerfish and salmon, and a good salad of tender greens with sun-dried tomatoes, sweet red onions and peppery nasturtiums (edible flowers being a delightful incongruity here). Roasting potatoes is a high art, particularly when the tasty tubers are set off by succulent slices of roast beef. The waitresses are formidable in their green Mad Hatter T-shirts, but if you don't give them any trouble they won't have to slap you around much. Good California wines are available, as well as such fresh, creamy draft beers as Guinness, Bass and San Francisco's own Anchor Steam. After dark the tables are folded away, a cover charge is instituted, and, presumably, the posted motto goes into effect for the evening. About $25 for two, with a beer.

Open Mon.-Sat. 11:30 a.m.-9 p.m., Sun. 11 a.m.-3 p.m. No cards.

OSOME

The austere surroundings may be uninviting and the service may be indifferent, but this is some very fine sushi. Order an

1923 Fillmore St., Upper Fillmore - 346-2311

Japanese/sushi

12/20

assorted sushi or sashimi dinner and you'll get a sampling of the extremely fresh tuna, octopus, salmon, shrimp and mackerel accompanied by pungent sliced ginger and fiery wasabe. Sushi lovers should stay at the bar, the better to appreciate chef Toshi's considerable talents; others should take one of the tables and try the traditional eight-course kaiseki meal. About $45 for a sushi-and-sake dinner for two.

Open Wed.-Mon. 5 p.m.-11 p.m. All major cards.

PACIFIC HEIGHTS BAR & GRILL

2001 Fillmore St., Upper Fillmore - 567-3337

Seafood/California

13

The Pacbag, as it's known to habitués, was a hit from the moment the first perfectly crisp local oyster was opened at the bar just inside the front doors. It's a restaurant with something for everyone, assuming everyone is a yuppie. Beyond the oyster bar, with its unprecedented array of fresh bivalves and crustaceans from several oceans, there's an elegant and intimate upstairs dining room, as well as a see-and-be-seen salon fronting the sidewalk. The upper room has some design problems; the track lighting, meant to be intimate, makes diners facing the banquette feel as if there's a pickup truck with its brights on parked behind them. And some of the various upholsteries clash. Seafood is the big deal here, and it has always been stellar on our visits, mesquite grilled and offered with a choice of interesting sauces, from dill butter to salsa to red-pepper cream. The appetizers make great light entrees. A good range of wines, including Champagne and dessert wine by the glass, is available. About $70 for two, with wine.

Open daily 11 a.m.-3 p.m. & 5 p.m.-10 p.m. Cards: AE, MC, V.

PALM

586 Bush St., Union Square - 981-1222

Steakhouse

12/20

We like the old New York Palm, with its sawdust-covered floors, insolent waiters and interminable waits for a table. As we see more and more Palms across the country, however, we question the wisdom of turning this New York landmark into a chain. This branch is perfectly fine, but it doesn't have the same cachet as the original. Oh, there's the same menu, sawdust and caricatures, but the steaks and lobsters aren't quite as good, the dining rooms are far more elegant (New York's Palm is anything but elegant), and the waiters are inauthentically friendly and helpful. They will suggest an excellent starter of romaine with a fine imported bleu cheese or a fresh prawn cocktail; skip the vile cocktail sauce and enjoy the exquisite prawns au naturel. Your entree, of course, will be either a steak or a lobster, the two dishes that have made the Palm famous. Steaks are all prime (though prime isn't what it once was) and all good, though we prefer the New York strip to the filet mignon. The immense Nova Scotia lobsters are sometimes flavorful, sometimes not, and the price tags are obscene. Avoid the Palm's famous "half and half," a half order of greasy onion rings and a half order of cottage fries that are somehow bone-dry and greasy at the same time. Instead, accompany your meal with a good baked potato or fresh seasonal vegetables, properly al dente. Desserts are banal, especially the New York–style cheesecake, which should never have come West. About $90 for a steak dinner for two, with wine; the sky's the limit for a lobster dinner.

Open daily 11:30 a.m.-10:30 p.m. All major cards.

PAPRIKAS FONO

900 North Point St. (Ghirardelli Square), Fisherman's Wharf - 441-1223

Hungarian

11/20

A friendly, comfortable spot that makes for a restful lunch stop while shopping Ghirardelli Square. Request a table on the balcony, which has a fine view of the Bay, and enjoy the attentive service. But don't expect too much of the Hungarian cuisine—it is simple and good, but it is neither remarkable nor terribly authentic. Best bets are the langos, the garlicky fried peasant bread; the bay shrimp marinated in a dill-mustard sauce; the flavorful (if a little overcooked) mixed grill of beef, lamb, sausage and a pork steak; and the simple strudels. The pastas tend to be too heavy and oily. About $25 for lunch for two, with a glass of wine.

Open daily 11 a.m.-11 p.m. All major cards.

PEACOCK

2800 Van Ness Ave., Van Ness - 928-7001

Indian

13 🍳

Located in a restored Victorian mansion, the Peacock sets a standard for Continental formality not often found in ethnic restaurants. The second-floor dining room is quite posh, with floor-length drapes, thick carpets, commodious chairs and fresh flowers, all in shades of peach and pink. Expect to be kept waiting for at least a short while in the first-floor anteroom; this wait will give you time to peruse the voluminous wine list. Once seated, let the waiter know how sturdy your palate is, since the kitchen is very good about keeping hotness to a minimum upon request. Nearly everything is good: masala kulcha, the tandoor-baked bread stuffed with herbs and onion; juicy, tandoor-cooked chicken that has been marinated for hours in yogurt and spices; rogan josh Kashmiri, an aromatic, flavorful dish of lamb with nutmeg; and murgh sagwala, a wondrous combination of chicken and spinach. Side dishes are the only disappointments: baked eggplant and saffron rice can be too mushy. The Indian desserts are typically very sweet. About $60 for a delicious dinner for two, with wine, in a lovely setting.

Open Sun.-Fri. 11:30 a.m.-2:30 p.m. & 5:30 p.m.-10:30 p.m., Sat. 5:30 p.m.-10:30 p.m. All major cards.

PERRY'S

1944 Union St., Cow Hollow - 922-9022

American

10/20

During the wild and crazy '70s, Perry's was known for having the most salacious cruising scene on Union Street (quite an achievement). That is to say, few patrons admitted to going there just for the victuals. Now that things have cooled down in the bar, one hears more raves about the food. Admittedly, Perry's hamburger is perhaps the best bar burger in town, a generous one-third pound of prime beef on a poppyseed egg roll, appropriately messy with the traditional burger trimmings and cheese on request. The cottage fries are great, too. But the rest of the menu is hit-or-miss. On the miss side, we've had bland, greasy fried chicken, on the order of a Swanson's TV dinner, and pasty desserts. On the hit side, we've enjoyed the robust, scintillating Chinese chicken salad, garlicky fettuccine with white clam sauce, good, crisp salads and well-aged steaks, which are usually cooked more or less to order. Sample from the good California wine list, but skip dessert and head out onto Union Street to satiate your sweet tooth elsewhere. Anywhere from $30 to $50 for two, with wine.

Open daily 9 a.m.-12 midnight. Cards: AE, MC, V.

PIERRE

15 3rd St. (Meridien Hotel), South of Market - 974-6400

French

15 🍴

The Meridien hotel chain is trying to spread the good cheer of fine French cuisine to each of its outposts, from Saudi Arabia to Rio. Someone in the chain had the brainstorm of sending a top French chef to each locale to create a menu, install a protégé in the kitchen and go about his merry way, perhaps returning now and then to update the menu and see how the young chef is doing. To San Francisco they sent the distinguished Alain Chapel, who created—quite unsuccessfully—a little Mionnay in San Francisco. The food was always brilliantly conceived—could Chapel do less?—but just not in line with the best local produce. Some dishes were too precious and too complex, while others simply failed for lack of proper ingredients.

Well, M. Chapel is scarce at the Pierre these days, and we

must commit a sacrilege and say that he is not missed. Now in the capable hands of the Meridien's new food and beverage manager, Jean-Pierre Moullé, the Pierre has reached new heights. Appetizers, once a weak point, are now excellent. Sautéed fresh duck foie gras is brilliantly partnered with caramelized apples. A lively snail and crayfish salad in a garlic-herb dressing features California-raised snails, not canned imports. A cold lobster "gazpacho," with zesty tomatoes, zucchini and chunks of lobster, is truly splendid. The chef has a talent for cooking fish, as witnessed by the beautiful fresh local salmon with a caviar and lettuce butter, bass with a coral butter and turbot with a crayfish fumet. And the talent goes further, to the crisp leg and rare breast of pheasant with a compote of leeks and truffles, the tender young lamb in a lime sauce with a vegetable flan, and more such delights. Disappointment only comes at the end of the meal, when one is presented with tarts and cakes of average-to-mediocre quality and a dismal cheese tray, though we understand an effort is being made to improve the situation. The service is flawless, among the best in the city; the room elegant and quiet, with well-spaced banquettes and tables; and the wine list inspired—and since Moullé took over, wine prices have actually gone down! As much as we admire M. Chapel, we suggest he stay away and let this California operation run itself. Dinner for two, with wine, will run about $120.

Open Mon.-Fri. 11:30 a.m.-2 p.m. & 6 p.m.-10 p.m., Sat. 6 p.m.-10 p.m. All major cards.

PREGO

2000 Union St., Cow Hollow - 563-3305

Italian

13 🍳

Part of a consortium that runs several San Francisco and Los Angeles establishments (Ciao, MacArthur Park, Harry's Bar), Prego is known as a singles' bar and a place to have good open-fired pizza or calzone. But it should be known for its fine meals served in several smartly styled dining rooms. These bright, art-filled spaces are a most pleasant setting in which to sample some of the best pasta creations to be found in San Francisco. The agnolotti d'aragosta, half-moon pockets filled with lobster and prosciutto in a light, lemony cream sauce, is exquisite. The trittico di gnocchi (a dish fashioned after the Italian flag) combines fluffy potato dumplings with three tasty sauces: tomato, pesto and a creamy gorgonzola. The mussel and tagliolini starter is a treasure. Among the antipasti, choose the mozzarella, fontina and prosciutto roll served with a sweet basil and olive oil dressing. Less exciting than the pastas, though still very good, are the entrees; one of the best is the Petaluma duck breast topped with an herb butter and accompanied by wonderful baby vegetables (sweet carrots, zucchini and cherry tomatoes). The best of the desserts is the tiramisu, the Italian classic that combines ladyfingers, espresso, chocolate and mascarpone cheese. An inexpensive wine list has a good selection from both Italy and California. A reasonable $50 for dinner for two, with wine.

Open daily 11:30 a.m.-12 midnight. Cards: AE, MC, V.

RESTAURANT 101

101 California St., Financial District -
788-4104

Continental

11/20

Looking good matters here. The dramatic design is both handsome and intimate, with cool colors and faux marble. The tables are beautifully set. The diners look like middle-aged models for Polo ads. The waiters are well-groomed and discreet. And the food is colorfully and artfully arranged. But beauty goes only skin deep at Restaurant 101. The most lasting impressions from our last meal were a small dish of Santa Barbara shrimp with lobster sauce that was made nasty by far too much fennel; a properly cooked but bland grilled chicken breast with two small plantains; and a dismal white-and-dark-chocolate checkerboard mousse. But we know chef Fred Halpert has it in him to do better, having enjoyed his former restaurant in Los Angeles, the now-defunct Mangia. Perhaps this ambitious nouvelle cuisine exceeds his reach, or perhaps he simply needs more time to perfect his menu. In any event, you will certainly enjoy the inspired setting and the attentive service, if not the prices: $110 for dinner for two, with wine.

Open Mon.-Fri. 11:30 a.m.-2:30 p.m. & 6:15 p.m.-10 p.m., Sat. 6 p.m.-10 p.m. Cards: AE, MC, V.

RINGS

1131 Folsom St., South of Market - 621-2111

California

13

Young chef Julie Ring and her family have created a very nice place to be on a warm night or lazy afternoon. The open-air, open-kitchen restaurant has a lovely garden room in back with a roof that is rolled back when the weather permits. The Southwest-influenced California cuisine is as well conceived and satisfying as the decor, thanks to the very fresh ingredients and simple style of cooking. Black beans and blue-corn tortillas show up regularly, as do beautiful roasted peppers; thankfully, these fashionable ingredients are not abused. We have especially fond memories of the salad of baby greens, the spinach and Asiago frittata, the black bean and salmon chili and the various grilled fish. This handsome, art-filled restaurant also boasts a counter that's popular with solitary diners. About $60 for dinner for two, with wine.

Open Mon. 11:30 a.m.-3 p.m., Tues.-Thurs. 11:30 a.m.-3 p.m. & 6 p.m.-10 p.m., Fri. 11:30 a.m.-3 p.m. & 6 p.m.-11 p.m., Sat. 6 p.m.-11 p.m. Cards: MC, V.

Ristorante Milano

1448 Pacific Ave., Russian Hill - 673-2961

Italian

13

You won't find a kitschy canopy laden with hanging grape clusters and Chianti bottles in this small neighborhood restaurant. Instead, you'll find a chic split-level dining room with clear woods, gray banquettes and framed scenes of Milan—and you'll find very good northern Italian cooking. The dishes are simple, honest and very satisfying: a mixed antipasto with marinated cheeses and cured meats (including carpaccio); a mixed grill with tender veal, juicy marinated chicken, wonderfully spiced Italian sausages and several vegetables, some of which take well to grilling and some of which don't; and delicious pastas (try the heavenly tortellini alla panna). Desserts are better than the Italian norm, especially the zabaglione cake and the light but rich-tasting mascarpone cheesecake. The wine list is brief but well chosen. Dinner for two, with wine, will run about $50.

Open Tues.-Sat. 5:30 p.m.-11 p.m. Cards: MC, V.

Rodin

1779 Lombard St., Marina District - 563-8566

French

12/20

Shortly after it opened, this new restaurant drew rave reviews from local critics, all of whom overlooked the glaring inconveniences to patrons. We were greatly disappointed by the cluttered feel (a single small room with eleven tables) and starkly drab interior, with just an occasional touch of brass to break up all the beige. The acoustics were also distressing; despite piped-in music, we could hear conversations from across the room. And the service was dreadfully slow and inattentive. All these problems, however, are surmountable, and we hope the management addresses them promptly, because we would like to return—Rodin has plenty of potential. Though it has a long way to go, the short menu is promising. We were quite pleased with the visually stunning and wonderful-tasting veal medallions with a mushroom purée and a tomato-wine sauce, accompanied by beautiful vegetables. Some dishes were less impressive, but could be lovely with a little more finesse, especially the gratinée of oysters, mussels and scallops with Parmesan, which suffered only from a slightly charred pastry cup, and the lightly poached baby trout stuffed with a mushroom purée, which needed just a bit more flavor. Dessert was the highlight of the meal. Baked Alaska in a sunburst sauce of strawberry, apricot and cream was a tribute to the aesthetic ability of the chef, and a chocolate cake in a pool of raspberry purée was a wonderful contrast between tart and sweet. The wine list is well chosen and moderately priced, with several nice wines served by the glass. Time will tell whether this restaurant will deserve its premature kudos—whether the kitchen's skills will grow even stronger and will not be compromised by an inattentive staff. About $90 for dinner for two, with wine; prix-fixe tasting menus are $32 and $35 without wine.

Open Mon.-Sat. 5:30 p.m.-10:30 p.m. All major cards.

LA RONDALLA

901 Valencia St., Mission District - 647-7474

Mexican

12/20

This mad, crazy quilt of a restaurant, open into the morning, serves some of the best Mexican food in town. The atmosphere is zany: a long counter in the front room facing the open kitchen and three back rooms decorated with Christmas-tree lights, balloons, stuffed birds, cheap fake Tiffany lamps and other assorted junk. La Rondalla consistently puts out fine dishes: one of the best guacamoles north of the border, glorious asado (thin rare grilled steak smothered with fresh onions, potatoes and tomatoes) and equally good adobada, marinated pork fillets topped with the same combination. The strolling and not-too-competent mariachi band and the confused waitresses attired in red blouses and tight black skirts add to the fun. The Mexican beers are fine and cheap and the noise level only mildly excruciating. A wonderful place for a late-night meal. A mere $25 for dinner for two, with beer.

Open Wed.-Mon. 11:30 a.m.-4 a.m. No cards.

ROSALIE'S

1415 Van Ness Ave., Van Ness - 928-7188

Southwestern

13

Our first visit to this place dissolved into hysteria, and it wasn't just the wine. By the time we'd spent a long lunch hour in the midst of canvas dummies, aluminum palm trees and furniture that looked like it was designed by the Flintstones, it was all we could do to discuss the food without hooting. It had resembled something from a futuristic archaeological museum, but it had been good. Or had it? We returned for dinner a week later, and the food really was good. Delicious, even. But weird. The Southwestern influence is apparent in such ingredients as cactus and jalapeño chiles. The duck burrito we'd slopped and giggled through at lunch wasn't available for dinner, nor was the oddly tasty chicken Tschopitoulas, a kind of creamed chicken dish with plenty of basil, corn and green beans in the sauce, served tostada style on a fried tortilla. Instead, we found ourselves sampling such off-the-adobe creations as breast of pheasant with pancetta and cabbage; venison with gooseberries and sweet-potato chips; lamb sausage with goat cheese polenta; and filet mignon with three different fire-roasted peppers (all hot). In retrospect, the best dishes were the appetizers: French fries with rosemary butter, warm asparagus tips with black-bean vinaigrette and the like. By the time we'd worked our way through dinner in the unnerving shade of those sheet-metal palms, it was all we could do to choke down some fresh strawberries and cream chantilly in puff pastry with a rhubarb and Elysium wine sauce, accompanied by a glass of '72 Leopold Gourmel l'age des epices Cognac. But we managed all right. About $80 for dinner for two, with wine.

Open Mon.-Fri. 11:30 a.m.-2:30 p.m. & 5:30 p.m.-10:30 p.m., Sat.-Sun. 5:30 p.m.-10:30 p.m. Cards: AE, MC, V.

LE ST. TROPEZ

126 Clement St., Richmond District - 387-0408

French

15

What a find! Tucked away on a commercial street chock-full of ethnic (mostly Oriental) restaurants and singles' bars, this little French country inn with its gas-log fireplace and copper utensils on the walls is a homey setting for some of the most creative French cooking in San Francisco. Young Basque chef Gerald Hirigoyen, new at the helm after his predecessor was snatched up by New York's Le Grenouille, is offering a new cuisine at ridiculously low prices. The regular menu is lovely, but the "menu gastronomique" (which changes every few days) is extraordinary. On a recent visit, our meal started with a rich, perfect cream of celery soup, followed by three small salads of smoked salmon, eel and sturgeon on mâche lettuce with tiny beet slices. After a bizarre but refreshing lingonberry and green peppercorn sorbet, we were brought an astonishing pheasant dish: the very rare breast was served in a light, not-too-sweet black-berry sauce, and the thigh and leg meat were removed from the skin, cooked with the bird's sweet liver and marinated cabbage, and stuffed back into the skin. This dish deserved a 19! With this menu gastronomique, a choice of any of the house desserts is offered, and the choosing is difficult. The plate of homemade ice creams (kiwi, strawberry, honey) and sorbets (pineapple, raspberry) with fresh berries in a pool of crème anglaise is astounding; no less virtuoso are the marquise au chocolat and the hot apple tart. If you order from the menu, try the roast squab with honey and saffron or the fillet of beef with juniper berries and a confit of shallots. Though not comprehensive, the wine list is intelligent, and there are several good wines by the glass. The service is very kind, but there are sometimes long waits between courses. Happily, the food is well worth the wait. The menu gastronomique is $25 per person, without wine (one of the best bargains in town); an à la carte dinner for two, with wine, will run about $65.

Open Mon.-Sat. 5:30 p.m.-10 p.m. Cards: MC, V.

SAM'S GRILL

374 Bush St., Financial District - 421-0594

Seafood

11/20

In business at various locations since 1867, Sam's Grill has established itself as one of the revered old–San Francisco seafood restaurants. With reasonable prices, unpretentious and efficient service and a commitment to using quality fresh fish, Sam's has a regular following among the denizens of the Financial District. These business-wise regulars know the secret to enjoying Sam's: always ask what is fresh, ask for it rare and, above all, avoid all sauces. Generous portions of sautéed rex sole, sand dabs or broiled swordfish will delight, but woe unto he who orders anything with a complex sauce. Start with East Coast oysters or the fresh asparagus in a mustard sauce, order your fish carefully and finish with the exceptionally good cheesecake, and you will leave Sam's very contented. A reasonable $50 for dinner for two, with wine.

Open Mon.-Fri. 11 a.m.-8:30 p.m. Cards: MC, V.

SANPPO

1702 Post St., Japantown - 346-3486

Japanese/sushi

12/20

Who says fine Japanese food has to cost a fortune? Lately it seems that modestly indulging oneself at a San Francisco sushi bar will bring a check that may cause heart failure. Not so at Sanppo. Although the decor is modified Formica and the presentation is not as elaborate as at more elegant Japanese restaurants, there is artistry in the kitchen combined with very low prices. Sushi and sashimi are perfectly fresh and quite fine, but Sanppo's real forte is tempura. It makes some of the best in town: lobster tempura is a fabulous indulgence, and the more standard prawn and vegetable tempuras are a delight. Also showcasing the kitchen's exceptional talent for frying are the amazing fried oysters, which have not a trace of grease. Recommended too are the traditional long-simmered noodle dishes. Expect friendly if

77

somewhat rushed service, a wait at peak times and a low tab: $30 for two, with sake or beer.

Open Tues.-Sat. 11:45 a.m.-10 p.m., Sun. 3 p.m.-10 p.m. No cards.

SCOTT'S SEAFOOD GRILL & BAR

2400 Lombard St., Marina District - 563-8988

Seafood

13

Incredible as it may seem, there aren't many good seafood places in the City by the Bay. In fact, the rule of thumb is that the farther a seafood restaurant is from Fisherman's Wharf, the better it will be—and Scott's is a good distance from the wharf. This Cape Cod house is somewhere between kitschy and comfortable, the service is friendly but rushed, and the wait at peak hours (no dinner reservations are taken) can be very, very long. The food, however, justifies the wait. To start, have the fine varietal oysters on ice, the wonderful clam chowder or (when in season) the glorious baked mussels or boiled cracked crab. The fried seafood dishes (oysters, calamari), a disaster at most places, are greaseless and wonderful. But the stars of this show are the seafood sautés: the sauté of scallops and prawns with marvelous saffroned rice is sheer perfection. There are some nice but overpriced California wines and a few uninteresting desserts. About $60 for dinner for two, with wine.

Open Sun.-Thurs. 11:30 a.m.-10:30 p.m., Fri.-Sat. 11 a.m.-11 p.m. All major cards.

SCHROEDER'S

240 Front St., Financial District - 421-4778

German

11/20

Schroeder's should thank its lucky stars that we rate a place solely on food, because we've encountered the most intolerably rude service on the planet in this brusque Teutonic haven for the businessman on the go. Asking for a glass of water is considered a venial sin; changing your order ten seconds after giving it is a mortal sin. Were the waiters not so intimidating, they would doubtless starve for lack of tips, but no one in their right mind would dare stiff these men of steel. If you can tolerate the rudeness and the lack of comfort from the hard wooden chairs and long communal tables, you may actually get some good, if heavy, German food: wursts, schnitzels and the best sauerbraten in San Francisco. The pig's knuckles, roulade of beef and roast chicken are also very traditional, filling and good. Desserts are fine: a rich chocolate cake and a light apple strudel are two of the best. German beers, both draft and bottled, are available, and there are a few good, well-priced German wines. If only someone would take a whip and chair to those tuxedoed tigers! Dinner for two, with beer, will run about $50.

Open Mon.-Fri. 11 a.m.-9 p.m. Cards: AE.

THE SHADOWS

1349 Montgomery St.,
North Beach - 982-5536
French

12/20

The beauty of the garden and the picturesque view of the Bay Bridge, Treasure Island and the Oakland-Berkeley hills are entrancing. Converted in late 1985 from a mediocre German restaurant, the Shadows offers a warm welcome and attentive service under the competent direction of maître d' Jean Dupret (who also excels in making suggestions from the extensive and modestly priced wine list). The menu's scope and the creativity of certain combinations are intriguing, but the kitchen is uneven. The duck terrine with pistachios and truffles has plenty of robust duck flavor but barely a hint of the nuts and truffles. Pasta with bay scallops and snails in a puff pastry with basil butter can both be lovely if they aren't overcooked. A mixed green salad composed of the freshest ingredients is lightly dressed in a good red wine vinaigrette. The venison in a Cassis sauce is a bit overcooked, but the meat is tender and perfectly complemented by the sweet but almost pungent flavor of black currants. And its accompanying dishes—pasta in a butter sauce, a zucchini flan and al dente vegetables—are quite remarkable. However, the medallions of veal are overcooked and unimproved by the creamy but tasteless red bell pepper sauce. Desserts, however, are consistently good; try the marquise of dense, unsweetened chocolate in a raspberry coulis or the lemon mousse in a strawberry sauce. There is obvious creative potential in the kitchen, but it is sometimes stymied by an occasional ill-conceived combination, inferior ingredients or erratic preparation. We hope that in time the cuisine here matches the lovely ambience and service. Dinner for two, with wine, will run about $90.

Open nightly 5 p.m.-10 p.m. All major cards.

SQUARE ONE

190 Pacific Ave., North
Beach - 788-1110
International

15

In chef-owner Joyce Goldstein's early days at Square One (not so long ago), she presented an eclectic international cuisine that intentionally defied categorization. It was always interesting, if not always cohesive and successful, but she has gradually drifted away from the internationalism and focused on her strong suit: the regional cuisines of Italy. In the process, she has developed a consistent, well-researched collection of superb dishes from all over Italy. The menu changes nightly, so at one visit you may be offered Tuscan specialties and at another, Ligurian. Salads are always inspired (broccoli with an anchovy and garlic vinaigrette; arugula, mustard greens and watercress served with a focaccia made with walnuts, Gorgonzola and onions), and the grilled dishes (a veal chop with pappardelle; poussin in a garlic-oil marinade) are always precisely cooked. If you are offered fresh berries covered with a moscato-amaretto mousse for dessert, immediately accept. And by all means take advantage of the tremendous wine list, which boasts moderate prices and some very good choices by the glass. Dinner for two, with wine, will run about $75.

Open Mon.-Thurs. 11:30 a.m.-2:30 p.m. & 5:30 p.m.-10 p.m., Fri. 11:30 a.m.-2:30 p.m. & 5:30 p.m.-10:30 p.m., Sat. 5:30 p.m.-10:30 p.m., Sun. 5 p.m.-9:30 p.m. Cards: AE, MC, V.

STARS

150 Redwood Alley, Civic Center - 861-7827

American/French

16

No one could ever accuse Jeremiah Tower of humility—he makes it abundantly clear that *he* is the star behind Stars, though in recent times he is seen with increasing infrequency at this flagship of his culinary fleet. Though not always (or even often, these days) behind a stove in his immense, magnificent open kitchen, every dish is produced by remarkably dedicated Tower trainees and carries the master's signature. We've visited Stars many times, with Tower both in residence and away, and we've yet to have a bad dish, let alone a bad meal. But we do have bad news: the room is a huge, extraordinarily noisy barn—Tower's concept of a brasserie, with a long bar, several adjoining dining rooms, a glassed-in wine storage room and the aforementioned huge open kitchen. The back dining area isn't too loud, but in most of the restaurant quiet conversation is impossible; your waiter or waitress, a charming and efficient youngster, may have to shout to describe the dishes on the daily-changing menu.

Happily, the food compensates for the din. Tower, who is largely self-taught and was one of the forces behind the success of Chez Panisse, is a man of much talent. Though he describes his cuisine as "New American Classic" (the title, in fact, of his successful cookbook), it seems to us to be a hybrid of French nouvelle cuisine and its younger brother, so-called California cuisine. Since the menu changes daily, we cannot predict your selections, but we can report on past successes. For an appetizer you may have a fish "paillard" (cooked on the plate); two examples are salmon with garlic, ginger, Italian parsley and tomatoes and tuna with a tomato coulis. Or perhaps you will be offered one of the creative, astounding pastas: pasta shells stuffed with veal brains and duxelles in a pesto sauce or warm pasta salad with smoked duck or smoked lamb. Sometimes the kitchen makes wonderful brochettes; we sampled a memorable one composed of snails, artichoke and prosciutto with a garlic-sage aïoli. And there are always salads and soups: splendid mussel chowder with bacon, onion and saffron, marvelously dense Cuban black bean soup with sour cream, garlic soup with herb and ham profiteroles, smoked trout salad with golden caviar and basil cream, sweet pepper salad with herbed goat cheese. The entrees, whether simple (very rare grilled swordfish with mixed squash and a dill beurre blanc, fillet of beef in an anchovy-pepper sauce) or complex (grilled smoked duck breast in a roast shallot sauce with an eggplant purée, risotto with sweetbreads, truffles and leeks, sautéed chicken breast with a white-root purée and basil hollandaise), are remarkable. And oh, those desserts: the best apple pie on earth, warm berry cobblers with vanilla-bean ice cream and dense chocolate creations. Only the overly eggy and bland soufflés are disappointing. The wine list is long and on the expensive side, though there are many good selections by the glass and some good half bottles, a rarity in these parts. Dinner for two, with wine, will run $100 or more.

Open Mon.-Fri. 11:30 a.m.-2:30 p.m. & 5:30 p.m.-11 p.m., Sat.-Sun. 5:30 p.m.-11 p.m. All major cards.

SWISS ALPS

605 Post St., Union Square - 885-0947

German

12/20

Lucerne native Heinz Oetiker's cozy little restaurant in the theater district is as stable as the Matterhorn itself. The service is very friendly (they clearly anticipate and expect a tourist trade and will probably ask you where you're from), and the ambience is decidedly alpine: inside, the walls of the tiny dining room are decorated with murals proclaiming folksy Swiss maxims, and outside, the marquee boasts of the "Fondue Specialties," which are not bad at all. However, as often happens in the nearby theaters, the real stars don't get top billing—the veal, not the fondue, is the reason to visit Swiss Alps. Oetiker is clearly comfortable with both the French and Germanic aspects of Swiss cuisine, as evidenced by two fine veal dishes: on the French side, a superb veal Cordon Bleu (stuffed with the thinnest, most delightful ham and a nice Gruyère), and, on the German side, the delicious Geschnetzeltes Kalbfleisch (veal in a rich cream sauce). Oetiker also prepares admirable sweetbreads (which can be so often ruined by a heavy hand) and fine lightened versions of such old German warhorses as sauerbraten. Starters are less interesting—simple salads and adequate homemade soups—and the desserts (crème caramel, poire belle Hélène) will never set the world on fire. On the other hand, neither will the check: dinner fmr twm, with beer or wine, will run about $40.

Open Tues.-Sat. 5 p.m.-10 p.m. Cards: MC, V.

TADICH GRILL

240 California St., Financial District - 391-2373

Seafood

13

Tadich Grill has been around in one incarnation or another since the Gold Rush of 1849, and it is much revered by its legion of fans, both locals and regular visitors to the city, for whom Tadich epitomizes San Francisco. Count us among those fans, despite the very disappointing meal we suffered through recently. But we won't dwell on that lapse—every other meal before and since has been terrific. And we will always love the charming, old–San Francisco ambience: the private wooden booths, the chummy counters, the Financial-District lunchtime chaos and the very professional waiters. Fond gustatory memories from this menu of honestly pre-pared, high-quality seafood include robust, incredibly deli-cious cioppino, flavorful calamari steak and juicy grilled swordfish. Great French bread is served in abundance, and wine is poured Italian-style in small tumblers. Our bad meal may have boded ominously of inconsistency, but we can assure you that we'll be back, waiting happily with a drink for one of the booths to open up. Expect to spend about $50 for dinner for two, with a modest wine, and about $30 for lunch, with a glass of wine.

Open Mon.-Fri. 11 a.m.-9 p.m. No cards.

TARANTINO'S

206 Jefferson St., Fisherman's Wharf - 775-5600

Seafood

8/20

Restaurants in the Fisherman's Wharf area all seem to fit into a common mold. All have lovely views of the inner Bay, all are pricey, and all cater to the one-time tourist trade. Despite San Francisco's abundance of good fresh seafood, these places—Tarantino's among them—serve mediocre fish that is sometimes not at peak freshness and sometimes admittedly frozen, which is why locals stay away from these Wharf tourist traps and try their damnedest to keep their out-of-town guests away as well. But it would hardly matter if Tarantino's served the freshest fish in the world—the heavy hands in the kitchen could destroy any delicate morsel from the deep. Take, for instance, the special seafood cocktail, which was so vinegary that in a blind tasting we could never have guessed which seafood was used. Or consider the ghastly cioppino in a lemonade-like broth. It is possible, however, to get a piece of decent grilled fish (a nice swordfish, for example), but we suspect this is an anomaly. The desserts—ice cream sundaes and the like—are the sort found in grade school cafeterias. Dinner for two, with wine, will cost about $60.

Open daily 11:30 a.m.-11 p.m. Cards: AE, MC, V.

TAXI

374 11th St., South of Market - 558-8294

California/American

12/20

Sometimes you stagger off the dance floor, pull up your socks and say, "I'm hungry." But you don't feel like sweating in some dive. That's why Taxi is where it is, within easy bopping distance of four big dance clubs and half a dozen crowded bars. It's upscale, it's trendy, and the food is pretty good. Set up like a cross between a warehouse and an artist's loft, with traditional, elegant table settings and loud, punky music, the room effectively maintains the club mood, or creates a little of it for those who may have dropped in after work. We tried grilled swordfish with a peppercorn sauce, a cheeseburger and grilled chicken with a spicy pepper sauce. It all tasted just fine. We had divine blackberry cobbler for dessert, and we sampled from the cool wine list. All in all, we had a good time, then went back up the street and worked it all off under the strobe lights. Two will spend about $50 for dinner with wine.

Open Mon.-Wed. 11 a.m.-4 p.m. & 5 p.m.-11 p.m., Thurs.-Sat. 11 a.m.-4 p.m. & 5 p.m.-12 midnight, Sun. 5 p.m.-11 p.m. All major cards.

EL TAZUMAL

3522 20th St., Mission District - 550-0935

Salvadoran

12/20

This little neighborhood restaurant in the Mission District serves the cuisine of El Salvador, which is not too common in San Francisco. The dining room is homey and nicely decorated, a nice change from the omnipresent Formica and linoleum. For those not accustomed to (or curious about) Salvadoran cooking, El Tazumal also serves some very good Mexican food (for example, superb enchiladas). But it would be foolish to pass over such wonderful Salvadoran specialties as beef tongue in a garlicky red tomato sauce. Ice-cold beer is the best accompaniment to this cuisine. About $30 for dinner for two, with beer; you can sample some of these dishes for less at the neighboring taqueria.

Open daily 10 a.m.-10:45 p.m. AE, MC, V.

TRADER VIC'S

*20 Cosmo Pl., Nob Hill -
776-2232*

Polynesian/Asian

11/20

The first page of Trader Vic's lengthy menu tells the story—not a very interesting one—of founder Vic Bergeron, a French Canadian entrepreneur who died not long ago. The menu explains Vic's philosophy of life, why he chose the hokey South-Seas motif for his restaurants, his dedication to quality, his belief in a polyglot society and on and on ad nauseum. This pontificating didn't help our appetite, but we forged ahead and ordered copiously—and how surprised we were! We sampled many good dishes, starting with the "pupus" (snacks): wonderful spareribs, fried prawns, crab puffs and sliced pork, which are best accompanied by one of the deadly but delicious tropical drinks. We then moved on to a diverse array of appetizers, including crab crêpes, prawns stuffed with lobster mousse and a fantastic "Bongo Bongo" cream soup of puréed oysters and spinach. Among the entrees we tried was roast Indonesian lamb, rare as ordered and well marinated, with a too-sweet peanut sauce that was mercifully served on the side. A simple poached salmon with a mousseline sauce and whitefish roe was beautifully done, the sauce delicate and the fish still translucent at the center. Chinese and other Asian dishes are also offered, ranging from the good to the adequate. Desserts are tasty, if heavy; the mud pie will be ambrosial for chocoholics. The costly wine list is well chosen, but we prefer to stick with the exotic drinks—they're expensive, but one is usually enough. Unfortunately, the service can be condescending or even rude to unknowns, and the chance of a nobody being seated in the very social and crowded Captain's Cabin is virtually nil. If you don't dine here, at least visit the terrific bar for a rum concoction and some pupus—but be forewarned that men must wear jackets and ties. Dinner for two, with drinks, will run about $90 (or more).

Open Mon.-Fri. 11:30 a.m.-2:30 p.m. & 5 p.m.-12 midnight, Sat.-Sun. 5 p.m.-12 midnight. All major cards.

LA TRAVIATA

*2854 Mission St., Mission
District - 282-0500*

Italian

12/20

A longtime mainstay of the opera crowd, La Traviata is an amusing restaurant that manages, unlike many of its North Beach counterparts, to offer both a congenial atmosphere and good food. Located in what is now the city's Hispanic district, La Traviata's long, barrel-vaulted dining room has walls plastered with pictures of opera personalities. Piped-in opera music will help amuse you while you wait for a table. You can also watch those already seated devour such excellent seafood preparations as polpo Traviata (an appetizer of baby octopus) or an entree of sautéed squid with mushrooms and capers. Also watch the looks of amazement as diners bite into the wondrous veal Traviata, a dish of thinly sliced veal topped with layers of melted Parmesan and paper-thin prosciutto in a tangy oil and sherry sauce. And during the long wait for your table, note the number of times people say "Beverly Sills"—they are ordering a delicious stuffed chicken breast named in her honor. When you are finally seated, you'll have a choice of accompaniments for your entree; be sure to choose the heavenly tortellini in cream sauce. And select one of the entrees mentioned above, not the good-quality sweetbreads that are ruined by a heavy, oily sauce. As for dessert, any choice you make will be satisfying. The wine list offers Italian bottles rarely seen in the United States (because they are at times not deemed good enough for export). Dinner for two, with wine, will run a reasonable $50.

Open Tues.-Sun. 4 p.m.-10:30 p.m. All major cards.

UMBERTO

141 Steuart St., Financial District - 543-8021

Italian

8/20

Umberto is part of an international chain started by Umberto Menghi in Canada, where on his television program, *The Elegant Appetite*, he has been called "the James Bond of cooking." The reference to the man with the license to kill was not lost on us after a meal at Umberto—the food here is completely lifeless. Descending the stairway from the street into the waiting lounge, one feels like one has just stepped into the slick pages of *Casa Vogue*. All the elegant and fashionable components of a chic Mediterranean villa are here: huge terra cotta floor tiles, arched doorways, white-washed walls and alcoves showcasing spotlighted art and artifacts. From this visual beginning we had hopes for a sophisticated form of nuovo cucina, but our hopes were immediately dashed. From Umberto's kitchen comes fare that does injustice to both the classical and new cuisines of Italy. Calamari fritti is moist but has a soggy, oily breading. Pastas are of singularly low quality: our last meal included fettuccine with porcini mushrooms, whose sauce was so pasty we were tempted to shred our menus and use the sauce to make papier-mâché figurines. Lasagne di mare is made with a traditional béchamel and with a nod to trendiness—noodles blackened with squid's ink—but it can be mercilessly overcooked. The only starter that has been even remotely satisfying is the rich and flavorful zuppa di ostriche. But we have found nothing to recommend from the entree list. Veal scaloppine resurrects the pasty mushroom sauce, and lamb chops, though properly pink, are banal and tasteless. The dessert cart is no better. The real saving grace of this place is the extensive wine list, which offers well over a hundred regional and premium Italian wines. Perhaps Umberto should be transformed into a soup kitchen and/or wine bar. Dinner for two, with wine, will run about $90.

Open Mon.-Fri. 11:30 a.m.-2:30 p.m. & 5:30 p.m.-11 p.m., Sat. 5:30 p.m.-11 p.m. All major cards.

VANESSI'S

498 Broadway, North Beach - 421-0890

Italian/American

13

This isn't exactly the world's friendliest restaurant: we've had brusque, unaccommodating waiters and captains on more than one occasion. But Vanessi's is one place where the food really does compensate. The mixed antipasto—Italian meats, cheeses, cold prawns, scallions, olives—is a little mundane, and the pastas, a tortellini Alfredo for example, are competent but not creative (though the carbonara is one of the best we've had). But the main courses are quite remarkable. Fish and shellfish are handled beautifully. A sauté of scallops and shrimp "agrodolce" in garlic butter is perfectly prepared and of the very highest quality. The meats—prime steaks and sweet young lamb chops—are expertly grilled and are among the best in the city. And those little new potatoes fried with onion, garlic, peppers and parsley—we dream of them! Most desserts, though not made in-house, are delicious, especially the chocolate cake from the nearby Victoria Bakery. Don't miss the warm zabaglione, the best in the city, which is for once not over-liquored. The Italian offerings on the wine list are only moderately overpriced; the California wines, more so. Dinner for two, with a simple wine, will run about $70.

Open Mon.-Thurs. 11:30 a.m.-11 p.m., Fri. 11:30 a.m.-12 midnight, Sat. 4:30 p.m.-12 midnight. All major cards.

YAMATO

717 California St., Nob Hill - 397-3456

Japanese

13

Yamato has been San Francisco's best Japanese restaurant for decades and has been honored with many awards—though lately, with more fashionable (and expensive) competitors on the scene, Yamato is overlooked, at least by reviewers. But its adoring fans, both Oriental and Occidental, know the truth—Yamato is still a very fine restaurant. We are among the fans of this elegant house atop Nob Hill, with its lovely Japanese decor, remarkably gracious service and traditional but very well-prepared cuisine. Sushi and sashimi are admirable, and the quality of the tempuras, teriyakis and sukiyakis are all beyond reproach. Seafood fans must have the appetizer of steamed clams, a huge pot of just-barely cooked, exceptionally fine clams. Wines are reasonably priced, but we prefer to accompany our meals with a good sake or Japanese beer. Fixed-price meals range from $12.50 to $19.50 per person, without drinks; an à la carte dinner for two, with sake, will run about $55.

Open Tues.-Fri. 11:45 a.m.-2 p.m., Tues.-Sun. 5 p.m.-10 p.m. All major cards.

YUET LEE

*1300 Stockton St.,
Chinatown - 982-6020*

Chinese

12/20

When Michael Yu was murdered not long ago in a Chinatown bar, the followers of his quirky restaurant felt concern as well as sorrow—concern that Yuet Lee's quality would slip, since, of the three brother/owners, he was the master chef. Fortunately, Yuet Lee still serves several near-flawless Hong Kong–style Cantonese seafood dishes, albeit in an ambience best described as grim: a dank downstairs dungeon outfitted with tables, an upstairs room next to the open kitchen (definitely the preferred seating, but you'll wait forever for a table here) and a garish green and orange Formica dining room. But the dinginess is quickly forgiven after a taste of the Maine lobster or Dungeness crab, two of Yuet Lee's best dishes. Either crustacean is netted from a murky fish tank and quickly stir-fried to a gleaming perfection with black beans and chilis or with ginger. The best dishes are those that are expensive or odd; anything whole is also good—poached chicken, steamed sand dab or catfish. But avoid the inexpensive noodle and combination dishes, which can be as vile as the atmosphere. Everyone orders the crunchy, fried "salt and pepper" squid, one of the best squid dishes we have tasted. Vegetable dishes, particularly a water spinach called "long green" cooked with either garlic or fermented bean curd, are also a good bet. To add to the physical discomfort, no beer or wine is served, but both can be brought in from a narrow grocery two doors north on Stockton Street, which apparently makes a living off thirsty Yuet Lee customers. A seafood dinner for two, with tea, will run about $40.

Open Wed.-Mon. 11 a.m.-3 a.m. No cards.

ZOLA'S

It took us two years to discover Zola's, long after several rave reviews appeared. Zola's was just too easy to miss, a mere

1722 Sacramento St., Polk Gulch - 775-3311

French

16

dozen or so tables in an unfashionable district far from any other decent restaurant. And the cuisine—we wondered how anyone would have the patience to replicate the often complicated and time-consuming recipes we love so dearly from Provence. But our first visit was a revelation, and we felt guilty for having ignored lovely little Zola's for so long. Catherine Pantsios has brought to her tiny, personal paradise a loving re-creation of her favorite dishes from a traditional country French kitchen, modifying them with touches of creative genius that make her one of California's leading young French chefs. Though the dining room is small, it is elegance itself: white stucco walls, an open-beam cathedral ceiling and a central floral display of breathtaking beauty. The true beauty, though, is in the wonderful dishes dispensed from the kitchen. The menu is seasonal, emphasizing the best available ingredients. A warm tart is usually offered as an appetizer, perhaps one of tomatoes and herbs. Or you may be offered a splendid caponata served with toast rounds and goat cheese. Asparagus lovers will delight in the cold asparagus in an orange vinaigrette. If Catherine has made a duck confit, order it—it will be of a quality seldom seen outside France. The little stuffed quail on a bed of polenta with homemade sausage brought tears to our eyes. Long-simmered stews, perhaps a blanquette de veau, show the patience and skill of the kitchen. And Catherine has mastered more than country cooking—she can also prepare a modern cuisine that is perfection, such as a rare duck breast with its grilled leg in an olive purée. But these modern dishes you can have elsewhere; you won't find Catherine's style of country cooking anywhere else in town. End your meal with a sampling from the fine cheese tray and one of the thrilling desserts. Consider a bread pudding with pre-served strawberries, the likes of which you have never tasted, a light-as-air chocolate torte or a polenta pound cake with fresh berries and a berry crème anglaise. Several premium wines are offered each night by the glass, and the wine list, while short, shows good taste and a dedication to serving fine wines reasonably. The service is young, friendly and extremely efficient. Dinner for two, with wine, is a veritable gift at $70.

Open Tues.-Sat. 6 p.m.-11 p.m. All major cards.

ZUNI CAFÉ

No one is neutral when it comes to the Zuni: they either love it or hate it. The restaurant is extraordinarily uncomfortable

1658 Market St., Civic Center - 552-2522

California/ International

15

—seating is on stone benches (albeit cushioned) and the noise level approaches that of a circus. On top of that, portions are often small to the point of being unsatisfactory, and the service is erratic: sometimes lovely, sometimes arrogant and unaccommodating. Further, no one has ever accused the Zuni of giving away its food; in fact, if you don't order what it considers to be enough food, it reserves the right to charge for extra bread (delicious sourdough wheat). Though the food isn't really Southwestern, the decor is: strange desert flowers and cacti, rustic desert colors, live succulents on each of the rough tables, and so on. It's attractive but stark, providing little of the comfort one usually seeks at dinner time.

This all being said, you might wonder why we have awarded Zuni two toques. The answer is that we rank on food only, and this place serves some remarkably creative and accomplished food. The kitchen has been rightly accused of inconsistency in the past—we recall a dinner one night of terrible jambalaya and dismal lamb—but in the last year or so Zuni has done nothing but improve. Starters range from the simple (several varietal fresh oysters from the seafood bar, a green salad with Oregon blue cheese and walnuts) to the complex (fried soft-shell crab with a caponata and parsley salad, crab and shrimp rémoulade with a wonderful aïoli and levain toast). Soups are superb; we recall an especially remarkable pumpkin with chile and a purée of zucchini and escarole. Entrees are divided into light entrees and main courses, though the small portions make them all seem light. Light entrees may include risotto with duck, andouille sausage and vegetables or baked polenta with shiitake mushrooms. The more substantial main courses lean to wonderful fresh fish, served rarer here than any other San Francisco restaurant dares serve (which is a source of many complaints from the uninitiated). Only the desserts can disappoint, though occasionally there is a spectacular pie made with some exotic berry. But the wine list makes up for this failing—the selection of domestic and imported bottles is outstanding and extremely low priced. Zuni's eclectic cuisine combines elements from northern Italy, French nouvelle and chef Judy Rodgers's clever imagination, and it's all made with the finest local produce. They call it "California cuisine"; we call it a melting pot for the best of the old and the new world. Dinner for two, with wine, will run about

$75. There's also a new, less expensive "café menu" for those who want a light meal or snack.

Open Tues.-Fri. 11:30 a.m.-2:30 p.m. & 6 p.m.-11 p.m., Sun. 11 a.m.-3 p.m. & 6 p.m.-10 p.m.; café hours: Tues.-Sat. 11:30 a.m.-12 midnight, Sun. 11 a.m.-11 p.m. Cards: AE, MC, V.

QUICK BITES

Asian

B & M MEI SING

62 2nd St., South of Market - 777-9530

This is no place for intimacy. You place your order at the counter, take a numbered plastic disk, join strangers at a huge table and wait until a caterwauling waitress walks by with your plate. The sumptuous noodle dishes make the ordeal well worth it, though, which is why thousands of downtown businesspeople flock here daily for lunch. Delectable mein or fun noodles serve as a base for beef, pork, duck, shrimp, chicken or fish balls, and you can ask that won tons—incredibly delicate and smashingly seasoned—be thrown in as well. Our favorite is the gon lo mein with duck, a gigantic platter of thin noodles with tender duck in a rich, satiny sauce. To avoid crowds, arrive before noon or after 1:30 p.m. Lunch for two, with a beer each, will run just $10.

Open Mon.-Fri. 10:30 a.m.-3:30 p.m., Sat. 10:30 a.m.-2:30 p.m. No cards.

CHARCOAL BARBECUE HOUSE

2123 Irving St., Sunset District - 665-0966

Nestled away in the Sunset District, this little Korean establishment reeks of authenticity. The clientele is largely Korean, and some of the many condiments served here are truly intimidating. There are plenty of others, however, to successfully season your main course, which should comprise two meat orders, either beef, pork or chicken, which you grill yourself on a hibachi placed on your table. Waitresses ensure that you don't burn your dinner, and the finished product—sandwiched into lettuce leaves with hot sauces, marinated radishes and pickled bean concoctions—is magnificent. If your appetite is boundless, also try the dae dok, a platter of crispy bean and clam pancakes. Dinner for two, with sake, will run about $30.

Open daily 11 a.m.-10 p.m. Cards: MC, V.

HONG KONG TEA HOUSE

835 Pacific Ave., Chinatown - 391-6365

For traditional no-frills dim sum, the Hong Kong Tea House sets the standard. Crowds form early outside this huge dining hall to sample the many "little hearts"—everything from sweet black bean paste dumplings to braised fried chicken feet, which is not for the faint of palate. What we can unreservedly recommend are the rice flour balls filled with pork, but there's really nothing here you'll regret ordering. Two will feast for $17.

Open daily 9 a.m.-3 p.m. No cards.

MIFUNE

1737 Post St., Japantown - 922-0337

This pleasant and comfortable café serves comfort food, Japanese-style: wonderful bowls of steaming soup noodles that will take the chill out of the foggiest day. Though Mifune offers adequate, inexpensive and well-presented sashimi and tempura dinners, noodles are the thing to get: soba, thin buckwheat-flour noodles, or udon, thick white noodles, typically served with miso soup and different combinations of meat and vegetables. We prefer the soba noodles served with either the marvelously crisp and light shrimp and vegetable tempura or the beef and egg. On warm days, the cold noodle dishes are deliciously satisfying. Service is exceptionally prompt. About $16 for a noodle lunch for two, with sake.

Open daily 11 a.m.-9:30 p.m. All major cards.

GOLDEN DRAGON

816 Washington St., Chinatown - 398-3920

Sheer heaven for carbo-loaders, Golden Dragon serves every variation of Chinese noodle dish. Tangles of mein and fun noodles are topped with all manner of savory sauces, meats, fish and vegetables, and they're all good. Try the mein noodles with tomato and beef, the braised noodles with barbecued pork and cabbage or the mein with shrimp and Chinese greens. The Formica-clad dining room is authentically chaotic. A mere $12 for two, with beer.

Open daily 8 a.m.-11 p.m. All major cards.

YANK SING

53 Stevenson St., South of Market - 495-4510

427 Battery St., Financial District - 362-1560

Yank Sing's shrewd owners saw the potential in marketing dim sum to a largely non-Asian business-lunch crowd, and they have realized that potential. Both downtown branches are crowded, but less so than the typical dim sum house (and less frenzied as well). Attention is paid to service and presentation, and the quality is uniformly good. True, you'll have less choice and a higher tab than at a Chinatown teahouse, but the tables are set with linen and flowers, and the dumplings and steamed sweet and savory dishes are all delicious. Lunch for two, with beer, will run as much as $25.

Open daily 11 a.m.-3 p.m. Cards: MC, V.

Barbecue

BLACKBURN'S PIT BARBEQUE

1338 Ocean Ave., Ingleside - 239-7115

What makes trekking out to this relatively remote neighborhood unquestionably worthwhile is the oak-burning stove, which yields magnificently smoked meats and chicken. When topped with one of Blackburn's sauces (the hot is not quite hot enough), the barbecue boasts a certain *je ne sais quoi* that puts this place in a league with the Bay Area's heavy hitters (Flint's and Everett & Jones). The hot links are superb, and the baked beans—redolent of smoky bacon—are like none we've ever tasted. A slab of beef or pork ribs, some beans and beer will send two people on their merry way for under $20.

Open Mon.-Thurs. 3 p.m.-10 p.m., Fri.-Sat. 12 noon-12 midnight. Cards: MC, V.

EVERETT & JONES BARBEQUE

5130 3rd St., Bayview - 822-7728

This rather seedy branch of the acclaimed Berkeley barbecue house is almost as good as Oakland's Flint's, which is saying a lot. Out of the brick oven emerge outstanding chicken and hot links bathed in a fiery, soul-satisfying sauce. Only the overly chewy ribs keep Everett & Jones from stealing Flint's barbecue crown. Eat here or, better yet, take a heap of chicken and links home for less than $15 for two.

Open Sun.-Thurs. 11 a.m.-12 midnight, Fri.-Sat. 11 a.m.-2 a.m. No cards.

HOG HEAVEN

770 Stanyan St., Haight-Ashbury - 668-2038

Not exactly your typical rib joint, Hog Heaven boasts a rather elegant decor of glass, chrome and woodwork, with a long bar and amusing cartoons of happy pigs. Despite the inauthentic decor, it also boasts some fine Memphis-style barbecue, especially the delicious pork shoulder and the savory beef and pork ribs. However, the barbecued chicken, sausage and duck can be too dry, though they are compensated for by the terrific coleslaw and cornbread and the good, if greasy, onion rings. And the homemade desserts—apple cobbler with dense whipped cream, Key lime pie, Boston cream pie—will indeed put you in hog heaven. About $25 for two, with beer.

Open Mon.-Tues. 5 p.m.-9 p.m., Wed.-Sun. 11 a.m.-10 p.m. Cards: AE, MC, V.

LEON'S BAR-B-Q
1911 Fillmore St., Upper Fillmore - 922-2436

In a city not known for good barbecue, Leon's serves unusually tender and juicy ribs and chicken and fiery hot links. The rich sauce isn't the best in town, but it tastes just fine when you've a craving for spicy and authentic Southern barbecue. Accompaniments (cornbread, coleslaw, potato salad, baked beans) are ordinary—neither good nor bad. Skip the homemade desserts, which can be dreadful, and instead wander up Fillmore Street for an ice cream cone. The atmosphere is everything a true barbecue joint should have and less. About $20 for two, with beer.

Open Mon.-Sat. 11 a.m.-10 p.m., Sun. 1 p.m.-9 p.m. No cards.

SAN FRANCISCO BAR-B-Q
1328 18th St., Potrero Hill - 431-8956

Thai cuisine, with its fresh, vivacious tastes, has rapidly become dear to the hearts of many gourmands. But few realize that the Thais have also mastered the art of barbecue. Once you've sampled the grilled ribs or chicken—imbued with garlic and Thai spices—at San Francisco Bar-B-Q, you may never go back to American barbecue. The meats here are cooked to perfection, and the flavors literally explode in your mouth. (They're so well spiced, in fact, that you can feel free to skip the treacly dipping sauce.) The food is as inexpensive as it is exquisite: a whole chicken is just $7. And though we couldn't possibly envision a better complement to the food than an ice-cold bottle of Singha Thai beer, the owners are now offering a small but tasteful selection of California wines. Crowds gather quickly to fill the small, unappointed dining room, so arrive early or order takeout— or bring your food next door to Bloom's Tavern. Dinner for two, with beer, will run about $15.

Open Tues.-Sat. 11 a.m.-2 p.m. & 4:30 p.m.-9:30 p.m. No cards.

Cafés & Diners

CAFÉ LATTE

With its fresh ingredients, Italian basics and California-cuisine influence, Café Latte is one of the stars of the

100 Bush St. (2nd Floor), Financial District - 989-2233

downtown lunch scene. Homemade pastas hang drying in view, soon to be incorporated into splendid salads with grilled marinated chicken, prawns or other fresh seafood. Other courses, ranging from marinated eggplant to fruit-and-cheese platters, are inspired, as are the homemade cakes and tarts. Expect a line during the lunch rush, but also expect gracious service once seated. Lunch for two, with house wine, will run about $26.

Open Mon.-Fri. 7 a.m.-10:30 a.m. & 11:30 a.m.-3 p.m. All major cards.

CAFFE TRIESTE

609 Vallejo St., North Beach - 392-6739

A North Beach survivor of the Beat Era, Caffe Trieste was the espresso bar of choice for Jack Kerouac and Allen Ginsberg. Not much has changed since then—Trieste is still a good, quiet spot for conversation and a cappuccino or an aperitif. Come here on a Saturday night to hear opera or on a lazy weekday afternoon to wax philosophical with a friend. About $16 for a sandwich and a glass of Chianti for two.

Open Mon.-Fri. 7 a.m.-12 midnight, Sat. 7 a.m.-12:30 a.m., Sun. 7 a.m.-10:30 p.m. No cards.

CHA CHA CHA

1805 Haight St., Haight-Ashbury - 386-5758

For the first few months of its short life, this eclectic, noisy little café was undiscovered and sleepy. But then the critics descended, and the lines have been long ever since. Thankfully, the sudden popularity didn't cause a drop in Cha Cha Cha's quality, and the American/Latin/trendy food is as tasty as ever. There are nice pastas with seafood, good grills (a choice New York steak with roasted sweet peppers is a bargain at $9) and a remarkable Cuban black bean soup. While you wait for one of the few tables, amuse yourself by watching the crowd, a happy mix of diehard flower children and clean-cut yuppies. Dinner for two, with wine, will run about $25.

Open Mon.-Thurs. 5 p.m.-11 p.m., Fri.-Sat. 5:30 p.m.-11:30 p.m. No cards.

DOIDGE'S

Poached-egg fanciers are fussy people. They like them just so, and consequently are usually disappointed when they

*2217 Union St., Cow
Hollow - 921-2149*

order them out. This is why Doidge's has such a loyal following—its fans know their poached eggs, whether plain or Benedict style, will be cooked with precision, arriving on the table with just the right amount of runniness. The same goes for the delicious baked eggs. This attention to eggy detail is evidence enough of the quality in this all-American café, which is charmingly decorated in an urban farmhouse sort of style. Though lunches and dinners are fresh and good, breakfast is the time to visit Doidge's (so many do that you should make reservations a few days in advance). Omelets are fluffy and perfectly cooked, French toast is heavenly, and fruit is vibrantly fresh. Bring your own wine at lunch or dinner, and expect to pay about $15 for breakfast for two.

*Open Mon.-Wed. 8:30 a.m.-2:30 p.m., Thurs.-Sun. 8:30
a.m.-9 p.m. Cards: MC, V.*

EAGLE CAFÉ

*The Embarcadero &
Stockton St. (Pier 39),
Fisherman's Wharf -
433-3689*

Although Pier 39 has rapidly become a tourist trap and teen hangout, the venerable Eagle Café is a refreshing breath of old San Francisco, serving hearty breakfasts and robust lunches to fishermen and dock workers. In an oaky, salty, manly setting, regulars put away fluffy, buttery hotcakes and eggs and the Eagle's signature corned beef hash. Lunch is similarly proletarian and satisfying, with he-man-size steaks and dense soups thick with meat. The drinks are strong, the bar honest and the Bay view sweeping. About $8 or $9 for breakfast and $12 for lunch for two, without drinks.

*Open Mon.-Fri. 6:30 a.m.-2:30 p.m., Sat.-Sun. 6:30 a.m.-3
p.m. No cards.*

LORI'S DINER

*336 Mason St., Union
Square - 392-8646*

Riding the neo-diner wave that is sweeping the country, Lori's successfully evokes memories of a '50s urban diner. In this era of mesquite, the burgers are fried, the French fries authentically greasy and the salads appropriately drab. The milk shakes, however, are wonderful, and we've found a few nice dishes on the menu, especially the omelets. Beware of the strange "fried chicken steak" —don't get confused, as we did, and think it's chicken-fried steak (there's a big difference). The atmosphere is high-camp '50s—waiters and waitresses in full diner costume, Elvis posters, vinyl booths and chrome every-

97

where—and the crowd is upscale '80s. About $15 for two.

Open daily 7 a.m.-11 p.m. No cards.

MARCO'S PIZZA

1535 Haight St.,
Haight-Ashbury -
552-4200

Marco's makes far and away the best thin-crust New York-style pizza in San Francisco. The great calzone will also appease homesick New Yorkers. If you're in the Haight area and don't want to deal with the bizarre skinheads and street people who frequent Marco's, have your pizza delivered. About $10 for two.

Open daily 11 a.m.-1 a.m. No cards.

MARIO'S BOHEMIAN CIGAR STORE

556 Columbus Ave., North
Beach - 362-0536

Don't you believe it when cynics proclaim the death of North Beach. It may not be as unspoiled as it was in the '50s, but as long as the Bohemian Cigar Store survives, the spirit of North Beach will carry on. Just across the street from Washington Square, Mario's is a true locals' hangout and the quintessential North Beach coffeehouse. Wonderful cappuccinos, delicious focaccia sandwiches and a lemony ricotta cheesecake (made by the owner's wife) are served at the bar or at one of the small tables in this homey hole-in-the-wall. About $7 for a sandwich and a cappuccino.

Open Mon.-Sat. 10 a.m.-1 a.m., Sun. 10 a.m.-6 p.m. No cards.

PORK STORE CAFÉ

1451 Haight St.,
Haight-Ashbury -
864-6981

The hearty American breakfast is raised to an art form in this crowded little coffee shop. Everything is wonderful, from the coffee to the grits, but we have our favorites: the perfect corned beef hash with poached eggs, the homemade biscuits and the incredible record-album-size pancakes cooked with berries, bananas or apples. About $12 for breakfast for two.

Open Mon.-Fri. 7 a.m.-3 p.m., Sat.-Sun. 8 a.m.-4 p.m. No cards.

SPUNTINO ITALIAN EXPRESS

524 Van Ness Ave., Civic
Center - 861-7772

Spectrum Foods has done it again with Spuntino, a bustling café and bakery next to Harry's Bar, the jewel in Spectrum's crown. Spuntino was designed to attract local office workers, Civic Center employees and patrons of the opera, symphony and theater, and attract them it does. The bright, attractive café offers irresistible Italian fast food: antipasti salads, sandwiches made on freshly baked Italian breads (including focaccia), beautiful little pizzas, homemade pastries and rich gelati. It's all fresh, simple, tasty and reasonably priced: about $15 for lunch for two, with a glass of wine.

Open Mon.-Fri. 7 a.m.-12 midnight, Sat. 11 a.m.-12 midnight. No cards.

SQUID'S CAFÉ

96 McAllister St., Civic Center - 861-0100

When it opened a few years ago, Squid's seemed like an idea that couldn't go wrong, at least for calamari fanciers, with squid prepared expertly in a variety of cross-ethnic ways and served in a loud, new wave environment. But since new wave became old and new owners took over, Squid's seems to have lost some of its spark, and some of its once-great dishes are now merely good. But there is still some fine food here, especially the soul-satisfying calamari Elena—squid drowned in a bowl of spicy tomato sauce—and the frangione —a sandwich of grilled squid, superb Italian sausages (from Danny's), melted cheese and marinara sauce. Start with the deep-fried artichoke hearts, accompanied by house-made aioli, and wash it all down with an Anchor Steam beer. The daily fresh fish and pasta specials are hit or miss, but on request the spunky, punk waitpeople will steer you away from the failures. Dinner for two, with beer or wine, is about $25.

Open Mon.-Sat. 11:30 a.m.-12 midnight, Sun. 5 p.m.-10 p.m. Cards: MC, V.

STOYANOF'S

1240 9th Ave., Sunset District - 664-3664

This lively, noisy, family-run café near Golden Gate Park is well known for its very good Greek dinners, but we especially like it for lunch, when you may order (self-service) delicious phyllo pastries filled with spinach, tender lamb or one of several cheeses, and sit in the lovely garden patio in back. The phyllo is especially fine and flaky. There are also good stuffed grape leaves and an interesting assortment of homemade desserts (apple strudel, Sacher tortes). On a warm day, a Greek salad, a glass of wine and a plate of fresh fruit make for a lovely lunch. At dinner, expect aromatic roast leg of lamb, perfect moussaka, baked chicken with a tomato-herb sauce, and baklava, all served in the hectic but charmingly decorated dining room. About $12 for a light lunch for two, with a glass of wine.

Open Tues.-Thurs. & Sun. 10 a.m.-9 p.m., Fri.-Sat. 10 a.m.-10 p.m. AE, MC, V at dinner only.

99

SWAN OYSTER DEPOT
1517 Polk St., Polk Gulch - 673-1101

Let the tourists line up at Fisherman's Wharf for overpriced, banal seafood cocktails—we'll be here at Swan's, pulling a stool up to the marble counter and reveling in the combination seafood salad (bay shrimp, prawns, crab, sometimes a bit of lobster), a different-every-day concoction that is one of our favorite San Francisco lunches. Also terrific are the rich New England–style clam chowder, the oysters and the freshly smoked salmon, especially when washed down with a glass of good, reasonably priced white wine. Swan's is first and foremost a retail fishmonger, so seating is limited to the counter and the amenities are basic—but the fish is heavenly. About $30 for a seafood lunch for two, with wine.

Open Mon.-Sat. 8 a.m.-5:50 p.m. No cards.

TAD'S STEAK
120 Powell St., Union Square - 982-1718

The steaks are probably the worst reason to come here, though if you are desperate for a complete steak dinner for about five dollars, there is none better. A much better reason to visit Tad's is the outstanding marinated roast chicken and the good homemade bleu cheese dressing on the crisp green salads. Beer and a quite good house wine are inexpensive, and charming host Don Levin's madcap sense of humor lightens the atmosphere. This place is wildly popular with locals and tourists, both those on a tight budget and those who can afford to eat wherever they please but love a bargain. A mere $16 for dinner for two, with a glass of wine.

Open daily 7 a.m.-11:30 p.m. No cards.

TOMMY'S JOYNT
1101 Geary Blvd., Van Ness - 775-4216

This garish sports-lovers' pub is to be commended for three things: its collection of more than 90 great beers from around the world; its hefty, tasty sandwiches of beef brisket, turkey and the like; and the fact that you can be fed here after midnight. The more ambitious dishes (usually Italian or Mexican) and the acclaimed buffalo stew look better than they taste. About $12 for a sandwich-and-beer meal for two.

Open daily 11 a.m.-2 a.m. No cards.

TRIO CAFÉ

No proper Upper Fillmore shopping/browsing trip should begin without breakfast at Trio, a most civilized café owned

1870 Fillmore St., Upper Fillmore - 563-2248

by three enthusiastic, cheerful women. Have a bowl of caffe latte at the stand-up counter, or take one of the few tables in this pretty little white room and indulge in the lovely scones, the crisp toast with homemade jam, and the fresh-squeezed juices. Lunch runs to beautiful fruit-and-cheese platters, simple sandwiches and creative salads. From $9 to $15 for breakfast or lunch for two, with a caffe latte or a glass of wine.

Open Tues.-Sat. 8 a.m.-6 p.m., Sun. 10 a.m.-6 p.m. No cards.

VICOLO PIZZERIA

201 Ivy St., Civic Center - 863-2382

Ever since the tiny, recherché Vicolo opened in this hidden alley, ravenous opera and symphony patrons have had to stop complaining about the lack of good neighborhood cafés. Cynics call this type of fare "yuppie pizza," meaning that the crust is puffy and the toppings include such things as capers, Gorgonzola and sun-dried tomatoes. But we find the pizza to be delicious and more Italian than most, as do the many who line up here daily. About $22 for a pizza meal for two, with wine.

Open Mon.-Sat. 11:30 a.m.-11:30 p.m. No cards.

VIVANDE PORTA VIA

2125 Fillmore St., Upper Fillmore - 346-4430

Our favorite café in town, Vivande is a gourmand's paradise. Slick shelving and glass deli cases are packed with vegetable and pasta salads, tortas, pâtés, cheeses, sausages, pastries, wines and gourmet groceries, and in the open kitchen behind the counters the industrious staff sautés pasta sauces, steams cappuccinos and arranges lovely plates of antipasti. That owner Carlo Middione, a cooking teacher and caterer, loves food is evident; that you will love his food will be evident with your first bite. To start, try the assorted cold plate, which can include such delights as caponata; wonderful whole roasted onions in balsamic vinegar; a salad of cannelli beans, caviar and onion and another of celery, mushrooms and sweet red peppers; and any of several rich pâtés. The homemade pastas—with steamed mussels, savory sausage, carbonara or pesto sauces, and more—are all delicious, and the desserts, especially the lemon tart and the exquisite chocolate-nut roll, are incomparable. To avoid the lines that invariably form at lunch, arrive before 12:15. And make sure to stop here when you're stocking your next picnic basket. About $38 for a pasta-and-pastry lunch for two, with a glass of good wine.

Open Mon.-Fri. 11 a.m.-7 p.m., Sat. 11 a.m.-6 p.m., Sunday 11 a.m.-5 p.m. Cards: MC, V.

Delis

ACROPOLIS BAKERY AND DELICATESSEN
*5217 Geary Blvd.,
Richmond District -
751-9661*

The ethnicity of the Acropolis is a bit confusing. Though its name is Greek, the current owners are Chinese and the clientele and the cooks are Russian. The food, however, shares none of this confusion—it's all Russian and it's all exquisite. Everything is freshly made and delicious: home-made breads, meat pastries and pies, stuffed cabbage, splen-did chicken cutlets, myriad salads and hearty desserts. Since Acropolis has been "discovered," the old Russian ladies who have been coming to this off-the-beaten-path (and mundane) section of the city for years now have to share their corner of the world with food-wise tourists and locals. Expect leisurely service, expect to share a table, and expect to pay about $12 for lunch for two, with a glass of wine.

Open Tues.-Sat. 8 a.m.-7 p.m., Sun. 8 a.m.-4 p.m. No cards.

MAX'S OPERA CAFÉ
*601 Van Ness Ave., Civic
Center - 771-7300*

Max's looks about as much like a real deli as Madonna looks like the Virgin Mary. In a room filled with a slick bar and stylish furniture, Broadway-bound waiters and waitresses, all smiles and good cheer, leave their serving stations at the drop of a matzo ball to hop on the piano and belt out a show tune or an aria. It's all great fun, but is it deli? As a Catskills comedian would say, "Take the food—*Please.*" Max's serves huge portions of food that is either inedible (the worst lox on earth), barely edible (gigantic sandwiches of poor-quality meats) or rather decent (a fine smoked chicken breast and some nice salads). The desserts (cheesecake, chocolate cake, fruit cobblers) cover entire platters, but while their size is Gargantuan, their quality is Lilliputian. Nonetheless, long lines form every night to sample the indignities. About $30 for two, with wine.

Open Mon. 11:30 a.m.-10 p.m., Tues.-Thurs. 11:30 a.m.-12 midnight, Fri.-Sat. 11:30 a.m.-1 a.m., Sun. 11:30 a.m.-11 p.m. All major cards.

Hamburgers

BILL'S PLACE

2315 Clement St., Richmond District - 221-5262

There is usually a long wait here for a table or a counter seat, but the people-watching on eclectic Clement Street (lined with singles' bars, ethnic restaurants and interesting shops) will keep you amused. Not a place for the health-conscious, Bill's fries hamburgers that are among the messiest in town, a grease-lover's dream come true. Also greasy, but much less edible, are the French fries. But the milkshakes are great, the service is friendly and prompt, and the atmosphere is pleasant. About $20 for two, with beer or milkshakes.

Open daily 11 a.m.-9 p.m. No cards.

CLOWN ALLEY

42 Columbus Ave., North Beach - 421-2540

This classic burger stand serves the best stand hamburger in town. Open until 3 a.m., Clown Alley is a favorite late-night stop for cabbies and partiers and a favorite lunch spot for local businesspeople. The fries and shakes are no more than ordinary, but the juicy grilled burgers are great, especially when accompanied by a bottle of beer, something rarely found at burger stands. A burger and a beer will run about $6.

Open daily 6 a.m.-3 a.m. No cards.

THE GRUBSTAKE

1525 Pine St., Polk Gulch - 673-8268

The burgers here are no more than decent, but they taste just fine at 4 a.m., when San Francisco's dining options are limited in the extreme. The Grubstake's house burger is large and cooked as ordered, topped with bacon and cheese, and the fries are among the best in town. Also worthwhile are the salads and breakfasts. This place is just off the most decadent part of Polk Street, which means the clientele ranges from prostitutes of various sexes to cabdrivers and bank presidents. About $15 for two.

Open daily 7 a.m.-5 a.m. No cards.

HAMBURGER MARY'S ORGANIC GRILL

Hamburger Mary's is an absolute madhouse. At any given moment, the clientele may include yuppies casually attired, yuppies in business attire, transvestites, men in black leather

1528 Folsom St., South of Market - 626-5767

and a suburban housewife or two, all suffering interminable waits for a table or a seat at the counter. Popular for years, this mental asylum serves some very good hamburgers (the Meaty Mushroom is especially tasty), salads and omelets. Heartier fare—steaks, grilled fresh fish and a daily special or two—is also offered. The noise level is excruciating, and the waiters (young men in skin-tight clothing) often seem to be from another planet, but all in the name of fun. Not a place for Aunt Fanny from Des Moines! About $20 for two.

Open daily 10 a.m.-1:15 a.m. Cards: AE, MC, V.

HARD ROCK CAFÉ

1699 Van Ness Ave., Van Ness - 885-1699

Although this immense junk food emporium was fashioned from an old automobile showroom, it is actually more reminiscent of another sort of transportation: a huge train station at rush hour. The noise level is so torturous that you'll have to carry on conversations in sign language, and only high school yell leaders will be able to transmit their orders to the young, attractive, free-as-a-breeze (but efficient) waitresses. As evidenced by the huge bar, the loud classic rock, the wild rock-memorabilia decor, the finned Cadillac emerging from a wall and the constant crush of trendy teens, the scene is the thing, not the food. That's just as well, because the hamburgers are usually overcooked on the too-hot mesquite grill, and the barbecued chicken and ribs are cloyingly sweet. But the chili isn't bad and the desserts (strawberry shortcake, hot fudge sundaes, apple pie and chocolate cake) are all excellent. There's always a wait, much to the benefit of the bar's income. About $20 for two, with beer.

Open Sun.-Thurs. 10:30 a.m.-11:30 p.m., Fri.-Sat. 11:30 a.m.-12 midnight. Cards: AE, MC, V.

Mexican & Central American

LA CUMBRE

515 Valencia St., Mission District - 863-8205

In the heart of San Francisco's Hispanic district, La Cumbre serves the best carne asada (marinated grilled beef) burritos in town. With guacamole and sour cream added, these huge burritos will satisfy the biggest hunger—but then you'd have to pass up the incredible quesadillas. The assortment of good

Mexican beers is very reasonably priced. About $10 for two, with beer.

Open Mon.-Sat. 11 a.m.-9 p.m., Sun. 12 noon-8 p.m. No cards.

LOS PANCHOS

3206 Mission St., Mission District - 285-1033

Aficionados of the quesadilla should consider graduating to its Salvadoran counterpart, the pupusa. A seasoned flour patty that is literally pumped up with cheese and grilled, then (optionally) topped with a spicy coleslaw, the pupusa can serve as a wonderful meal in itself, especially when complemented with a side order of fried plantanos (plantains) and sour cream. Or try a pupusa as an appetizer to preface a dish from Los Panchos's comprehensive and excellent menu of Mexican and Salvadoran food. A couple of pupusas per person, some plantanos and beer will cost about $13 for two.

Open daily 11 a.m.-3 a.m. No cards.

TAQUERIA SAN JOSE

2830 Mission St., Mission District - 558-8549
2282 Mission St., Mission District - 558-8549

Several Mission District joints vie for the title of best burrito house, but for our money this place is the all-around winner. The atmosphere may be strictly plastic and fluorescence, but you can sample burritos stuffed with whole beans, fresh salsa and such unusual but authentic ingredients as lengua (tongue) and cabeza (head). For the less adventurous, there are burritos filled with beef, chicken and pork, copiously stuffed and as good as you'll find anywhere. Also delicious are the small meat sandwiches called tortas. Burritos and beer for two will run about $9.

Open daily 8 a.m.-2 a.m. No cards.

EL TAZUMAL TAQUERIA

3530 20th St., Mission District - 550-1928

Many of the fine Salvadoran and Mexican dishes served at El Tazumal Restaurant next door can be sampled at this great little taqueria. Each of the many regulars has his or her own passionate favorite—ours is the robustly delicious chile relleno burrito. About $9 for two, with a beer.

Open Mon.-Sat. 8 a.m.-8:45 p.m. No cards.

LA VICTORIA

2937 24th St., Mission District - 550-9292

Walk on past the marvelous bakery to the dining room in back and settle in for a bargain-basement feast. La Victoria's Mexican classics are unusually well prepared: perfectly steamed tamales stuffed with savory pork; huge, fresh chicken or beef tostadas; and exceptionally moist chicken braised in a robust red sauce. The menu is entirely in Spanish, but the friendly staff will be happy to translate. Bring your own beer, and on your way out, stop at the bakery counter for a bag of delicious Mexican cookies. Two can stuff themselves silly for $9.

Open daily 10:30 a.m.-10 p.m. No cards.

NIGHTLIFE

THE CITY AT NIGHT

"The city that knows how" knows above all how to have a good time at night. Concentrated in vibrant pockets throughout the many ethnically, culturally and economically diverse neighborhoods, from the Marina to the outer Mission, the waterfront to the Sunset, San Francisco's nightlife is as rich and eclectic as the city's population. As one of the world's great bar towns, San Francisco has more classy saloons, cozy pubs, boisterous taverns, colorful watering holes and seedy dives than even the natives can fully appreciate. Similarly, a wide variety of nightclubs spans both the hilly geography and the spectrums of music and comedy. But the entertainment clubs don't have an exclusive hold on rock, jazz or humor: many of the city's bars offer live performances. For specific monthly and weekly listings, consult the *Bay Guardian*, *Calendar* magazine, the *San Francisco Chronicle*'s Datebook, the *Oakland Tribune*'s Calendar and *San Francisco* and *Focus* magazines.

Bars

ABBEY TAVERN

*4100 Geary Blvd.,
Richmond District -
221-7767*

On any given weekend night, the Abbey Tavern is bursting with a young and boisterous crowd bellying up to the horseshoe-shaped bar for frothy pints of Guinness on tap (kept at basement temperature in true Irish fashion). One of the most popular Irish pubs in the city, the Abbey calms down to a friendly neighborhood pace during the week, when you can actually make conversation or play a casual game of darts. But prepare to stand in line on St. Patrick's Day.

Open daily 11 a.m.-2 a.m. No cards.

THE ALBION CLUB

*3139 16th St., Mission
District - 621-9213*

As with many of San Francisco's classic neighborhood watering holes, the Albion maintains a low profile during the week, with locals splitting time between the bar, the pool table and the jukebox in the corner. This is a perfect place to stop into while roaming the Mission. On weekends, expect to see hordes of young, collegiate-looking swells.

Open daily 2 p.m.-2 a.m. No cards.

BALBOA CAFÉ

3199 Fillmore St., Marina District - 921-3944

Everything at the Balboa oozes calculation, from the deliberately nostalgic exterior to the classic fern-bar interior and the yupped-out, late-night cruisers in designer clothes. Tourists can't resist this narrow café and bar, which specializes in hamburgers, nouvelle lunches and coffee and snow-cone drinks. Nor can shoppers from the upscale Union Street boutiques. It's worth the wait for tongue-in-chic people-watching.

Open daily 11 a.m.-2 a.m. All major cards.

THE BOONDOCKS

The Embarcadero & Spear St. (Pier 28), South of Market - 777-1588

When the new wave of socially conscious journalists deserted the long-standing Press Club for, among other things, its sexist membership policies, it swept into the Boondocks, elbowing in next to the declining population of longshoremen from the nearby docks. The mix at this alternative press club and working-class bar is as refreshing as the salty, foggy breeze blowing in off the Bay.

Open Mon.-Fri. 11 a.m.-9 p.m., Sat. 10:30 a.m.-6 p.m. Cards: MC, V.

BUENA VISTA

2765 Hyde St., North Beach - 474-5044

Legend has it that the ever-crowded "Bee Vee" introduced Irish coffee to San Francisco in 1953. Now it serves 1,700 a day to the tourists who jam the round oak tables and crowd up to the old mahogany bar. Overlooking the Bay, close to Ghirardelli Square, the Cannery and Fisherman's Wharf, this plainly decorated, turn-of-the-century café is as much a tourist attraction as it is a bar, so expect the resultant hubbub.

Open Mon.-Fri 9 a.m.-2 p.m., Sat.-Sun. 8 a.m.-2 a.m. No cards.

CARNELIAN ROOM

555 California St. (Bank of America Building), Financial District - 433-7500

As long as height limits are maintained on new construction, no bar will challenge the panoramic view from the Carnelian Room. From an elevation of 780 feet (52 floors), the sights are so breathtaking that it might take you a while to notice the spectacular interior decor of European art and antiques. The prices of everything, especially the food, are as sky-high as the setting, and dress codes (jackets and ties for men) are enforced in the evening. But there's no better way to see the Golden Gate Bridge, the Pacific Ocean, the Marin hills and the city itself while sipping a cocktail.

Mon.-Fri. 3 p.m.-12:30 a.m., Sat. 4 p.m.-1:30 a.m., Sun 10 a.m.-12:30 a.m. Cards: AE, MC, V.

DELUXE

1511 Haight St.,
Haight-Ashbury -
552-6949

The gentrification of Haight-Ashbury might be symbolized by the sleek, sculpted metal doors of the Deluxe. Deco-consciousness abounds, from the streamlined exterior to the black and silver interior. And the clientele is dominated by the most recent émigrés to the former hippie haven—young, well-heeled trend followers. It adds up to a visually intriguing alternative to the run-of-the-gin-mill neighborhood bar.

Open daily 2 p.m.-2 a.m. No cards.

DOVRE CLUB

3541 18th St., Mission
District - 552-0074

Without losing its neighborhood flavor, the Dovre offers a heady brew of politics—Irish Republican, feminist, local radical—and a forgettable decor. Journalist Warren Hinckle said of the Dovre, "It smells the way a bar ought to smell—like a toilet." You don't have to raise your glass to "Patrick's Irish Toast" posted above the door ("Let's drink to the final defeat of the British army in Northern Ireland") to enjoy this unpretentious hangout. Not everyone talks politics; you can shoot pool with friendly folks or take a turn at Irish step dancing. Drinks are good and reasonably priced.

Open daily 8 a.m.-2 a.m. No cards.

EAGLE CAFÉ

The Embarcadero &
Stockton St. (Pier 39),
Fisherman's Wharf -
433-3689

A small miracle of redevelopment along the Embarcadero was the preservation of the Eagle Café, since 1928 the best real saloon on the waterfront. Sure, they had to move it across the street and replant it amid the plastic tourist schlock of Pier 39, but the interior remains unchanged, the prices are shockingly fair, and the Barbary Coast atmosphere is thicker than the fog that rolls in off the water. Among the cafeteria-style breakfast and lunch dishes, the corned beef hash is legendary. Outdoor seating brings the Bay view into your lap, and there are still plenty of old salts around to bend your ear with tall tales from the sea.

Open daily 6:30 a.m.-1:30 a.m. No cards.

EDINBURGH CASTLE

950 Geary St., Polk
Gulch - 885-4074

Delicious fish and chips that the waiter orders for you from the Old Chelsea around the corner arrive wrapped in newspaper. Malt vinegar stands in bottles on the tables. Darts are thrown perpetually on the back mezzanine. Bartenders pull rich drafts of Bass, Watney's, John Courage, Guinness and the local favorite, half & half (ale and stout). Unblended single malt whiskeys are available. The convivial, country-side pub atmosphere is accented by old, heavy wooden tables, beamed ceilings, intimate balconies, Scottish knickknacks and British memorabilia. The jukebox is thick with music from the British Isles. And the tavern is large enough to accommodate hearty crowds without the shoulder-to-shoulder hassle of the trendier holes. It all adds up to one of the most delightful and relatively untouristed establishments in the Bay Area.

Open Mon.-Fri. 5 p.m.-2 a.m., Sat. 4:30 p.m.-2 a.m., Sun. 4:30 p.m.-1 a.m. No cards.

ENRICO'S
504 Broadway, North Beach - 392-6220

You won't escape the tourists here, in the city's most famous sidewalk café, but if you manage to grab a table on a sunny afternoon or temperate evening, you'll enjoy watching the amazingly diverse array of characters parade up and down Broadway. The al fresco drinking and dining is almost beside the point when you gaze out on the tourists, punks, sailors, business folk, leftover beats and hippies, and dancers from the nearby flesh parlors. John and Yoko used to hang out here in their San Francisco days. And while the bohemian days are but a memory, the spirit is palpable under Enrico's awning, diluted perhaps by the celebrity status of the place but easily revived with an espresso or a shot of brandy.

Open daily 11:30 a.m.-3 a.m. Cards: AE, MC, V.

L'ETOILE
1075 California St. (Huntington Hotel), Nob Hill - 771-1529

A meeting place for the rich and famous, this subterranean bar in the posh Huntington Hotel is an extension of the equally famous and social restaurant. The safari motif and the stiff prices are a bit much, but the music of brilliant cocktail pianist Peter Mintun and the chance to hobnob with high society more than compensate. One could not overdress for L'Etoile.

Open Mon.-Sat. 5:30 p.m.-12 midnight. All major cards.

HARRINGTON'S BAR & GRILL
245 Front St., Financial District - 392-7595

Not to be confused with similarly named Irish bars (Herrington's on Jones and Harrington's Harry Pub on Larkin), this large, two-room, two-bar watering hole is mobbed at five o'clock, and the singles action is heavy in the early evening. Despite the Financial District location, the clientele includes plenty of casually dressed folk, and when the after-work crowd thins, Harrington's becomes an easygoing hangout where the Irish whiskey flows generously.

Open Mon.-Tues. 9 a.m.-10 p.m., Wed.-Thurs. 9 a.m.-11 p.m., Fri. 9 a.m.-1 a.m., Sat. 11:30 a.m.-7:30 p.m. No cards.

HOUSE OF SHIELDS

39 New Montgomery St., Financial District - 392-7732

When director Wim Wenders wanted to shoot a bar that would pass as John's Grill in the film *Hammett*, he eschewed the original, which still exists, in favor of the House of Shields. Indeed, you get the feeling that you are stepping back into the 1920s or '30s, or even earlier, when you toddle into this classic drinking spot. The setting is comfortingly reminiscent of a bygone golden era: large curved booths and ornate light fixtures, waiters in formal wear who don't introduce themselves with, "Hi, I'm Chuck and I'll be serving you tonight," stuffed big-game heads, a replica of the old Comstock Bar from the nearby Palace Hotel, even spittoons. One comes here to sip and sit leisurely (but not on bar stools, as there are none) and to chat amicably (not to watch TV, as there is none).

Open Mon.-Fri. 9 a.m.-10 p.m. Cards: AE, MC, V.

IRELAND'S 32

3920 Geary Blvd., Richmond District - 386-6173

If northern and southern Ireland were reunited, there would be 32 counties, which explains the name of this popular Irish pub and gives a good indication of the strong IRA tilt. It also indicates that the crowd is a no-frills assemblage of neighborhood folk and Irish devotees who will cross the city for a pint of Guinness and good conversation.

Open daily 11 a.m.-2 a.m. Cards: AE, DC.

JAY N BEE

2736 20th St., Mission District - 648-0518

Looking for a slice of down-to-earth neighborhood life in a San Francisco bar? You'll find it at this bustling, unadorned tavern—in its crowded, narrow tables, ample breakfasts and brunches, hearty lunches and boisterous crowd of neighborhood workers, cops on the beat and journalists from the alternative weekly newspaper, the *Bay Guardian*, around the corner. Once people start hanging out here, they tend to remain loyal, but the atmosphere welcomes newcomers.

Open Mon.-Fri. 6 a.m.-10 p.m., Sat. 7 a.m.-9 p.m., Sun. 8 a.m.-7 p.m. No cards.

LA ROCCA'S CORNER TAVERN

957 Columbus Ave., North Beach - 441-9260

While the original charm of North Beach corrodes under new coats of pastel paint, while old Italian family businesses are displaced by franchise ice cream, cookie and pizza joints, and while the characters who are the human face of that charm lose ground to lawyers, accountants and real estate developers, La Rocca's remains a holdout for neighborhood integrity. Art Institute students clad in black hang out with old North Beachers, and tourists weave through without upsetting the balance. The delicate equilibrium is maintained by an earnest atmosphere, timeworn decor and a jukebox that appeals to all ages and tastes. People have even been seen dancing cheek-to-cheek here.

Open Sun.-Thurs. 12 noon-12 midnight, Fri.-Sat. 12 noon-2 a.m. No cards.

THE LITTLE SHAMROCK

807 Lincoln Way, Sunset District - 661-0600

The great earthquake of 1906 took down walls here in the Sunset District, but the Little Shamrock cashed in a bit of its Irish luck and remained standing. This genuine survivor has been in the same location since 1893. The old-time decor includes a clock that stopped ticking during the earthquake and the original bar and back bar. On weekend afternoons, athletic types spill in from the softball fields and bicycle paths in Golden Gate Park, but it's still easy to find a quiet nook to play backgammon, dice or darts, or to simply sink into a reverie on one of the living room couches in the alcove.

Open daily 3 p.m.-2 a.m. No cards.

MISSION ROCK RESORT

817 China Basin St., China Basin - 621-5538

Hardly a bar that you would run across by accident, the Mission Rock is tucked among the piers and dry docks south of the Bay Bridge, far removed from the tourist traps of Fisherman's Wharf and Pier 39. Here you'll find an assortment of fishermen, longshoremen, shipbuilders and anyone with a good nose for a great waterfront hangout. From the two outdoor decks, better sheltered from the breezes than points north, you can look out across the Bay or down along the docks and watch a working waterfront, not a Disneylandish replica.

Downstairs bar: open daily 7 a.m.-7 p.m. (closing time varies depending on the crowd); upstairs bar: open daily 8 a.m.-2 a.m. Cards: AE, MC, V.

LE MONTMARTRE

2125 Lombard St., Marina District - 563-4618

This attractive Marina bistro combines a romantically French environment with seductive Brazilian music played live by several of the Bay Area's splendid Latin jazz and pop bands. Attracting a wonderfully international crowd of Europeans and South Americans—and, of course, French sailors when their ships are in port—Le Montmartre is decorated with Parisian dioramas and features a jukebox stocked with the dreamy vocals of Edith Piaf, Charles Aznavour and others.

Open nightly 4 p.m.-2 a.m. No cards.

LEFTY O'DOUL'S
333 Geary St., Union Square - 982-8900

Before the Giants moved here from New York, the home-town baseball team was the minor league Seals, and Frank J. "Lefty" O'Doul was one of the city's great sports heroes. This old-fashioned bar and cafeteria, suitable for the entire family, is rife with baseball lore and memorabilia, including fascinating photographs of Lefty—with Dizzy Dean, Joe DiMaggio, General Douglas MacArthur and more—and other legends. Hofbrau-style sandwiches and generous hot dishes complete the homey atmosphere.

Open daily 8 a.m.-2 a.m. No cards.

PARADISE LOUNGE
11th & Folsom, South of Market - 861-6906

As the South of Market area (SOMA) remakes itself into a self-important haven of hipness, the folks at the Paradise refuse to take the scene too seriously. The young crowd, spinning off the neighborhood's burgeoning new music scene, sport ultra-cool fashions and geometric haircuts. But the nightly no-cover-charge entertainment—including jazz, pop cabaret and tap dancing—adds an offbeat lounge-lizard touch. The hors d'oeuvres are free and the drinks come in chilled glasses.

Open nightly 4 p.m.-2 a.m. No cards.

PAT O'SHEA'S MAD HATTER
3754 Geary Blvd., Richmond District - 752-3148

With three satellite dishes, nine 25-inch televisions and sports memorabilia galore, Pat O'Shea's is one of San Francisco's premier sports bars, impossibly crowded when the 49ers are on the tube. But football jocks aren't the only patrons. In the evening, University of San Francisco students make this a regular hangout; at lunch time, it fills up with neighborhood workers drawn by the cheap pints of brew and outstanding corned beef sandwiches; and several nights a week local blues and rock bands play for dancing.

Open daily 10 a.m.-1:30 a.m. No cards.

PAUL'S SALOON

A cozy and unpretentious bar with a fireplace and a friendly, casually dressed clientele, Paul's is the only bluegrass bar in the city. Banjos, guitars, mandolins and fiddles send their

3251 Scott St., Marina
District - 922-2456

jittery, swinging sounds into the air, inspiring infectious grins and uninhibited foot stomping. There's no need to dress up—just come ready to absorb some of the best locally produced "high lonesome" harmonies and down-home pickin'.

Open daily 3 p.m.-2 a.m. Shows nightly 9 p.m.-12:30 a.m.
No cards.

PERRY'S

1944 Union St., Cow
Hollow - 922-9022

Because it is famous for several reasons, this bar and restaurant is always jammed. Recommended in the original *Preppy Handbook* as a premier pickup spot, Perry's is crawling with upscale singles in the evening, some of whom come to spot the politicos and celebrities in action. Others are drawn by the rather expensive but reliably good American food—breakfasts and brunches, burgers, chicken, soups—in the back dining room. Unlike most of the city's fern bars, Perry's has a broadbased appeal—thus the constant crush.

Open daily 9 a.m.-12 midnight. Cards: AE, MC, V.

PERSIAN AUB ZAM ZAM

1633 Haight St.,
Haight-Ashbury -
861-2545

Don't tell Bruno that you heard about his splendid oasis from a guidebook. Don't be in a rush, and don't flop down on the couches in the cozy back alcove and expect gracious service. But appreciate the Persian Aub Zam Zam for what it is, and you'll experience one of the most perfect bars in San Francisco. His father opened the place more than 40 years ago, and, as he will tell you in his curmudgeonly commentaries, Bruno has seen the Haight-Ashbury neighborhood evolve (or disintegrate) around him ever since. His specialty is the martini (although he can't get his favorite British Plymouth gin anymore), and he looks down on "Madison Avenue" brands and frilly concoctions. The dimly lit decor is soft and soothing, and the jukebox full of sweet, swinging music from the big band era. The entire windowless bar, from the arched doorways and tiered liquor shelves to the romantic mural behind the bar and Bruno himself, is a classic.

Open Mon.-Wed. & Fri.-Sat. 4 p.m.-on (closing time varies).
No cards.

THE PLOUGH AND STARS

No Irish pub crawl would be complete without a stop at this no-frills, no-nonsense, music-oriented bar. The crowd is an unpretentious mix of Irish nationalists, serious drinkers from

116 Clement St., Richmond District - 751-1122

the old country and blue-jeaned young folk from the neighborhood. The biggest attraction is the evocative live and recorded Irish music—the best airs, reels and jigs in the city, for listening or dancing.

Open daily 12 noon-2 a.m. No cards.

REDWOOD ROOM

495 Geary (Four Seasons Clift Hotel), Union Square - 775-4700

Located in the grand old Clift Hotel, this elegantly appointed room is a classic. The high ceilings, the gorgeous dark wood, the art deco lighting fixtures and furnishings, the majestic paintings, the brass railings and the beveled glass all come together to create an aura of impeccable class. Union Square conventioneers, elderly women dressed up for the afternoon, hotel guests and tourists fill up the comfortable chairs and soak in the grand style.

Open daily 11 a.m.-3 p.m. & 4:30 p.m.-1 a.m. All major cards.

THE RITE SPOT

2099 Folsom, Mission District - 552-6066

Ask around and you'll find that the Rite Spot is one of the favorite bars of the most unlikely people, and thus the clientele is diverse and unpredictable. The afternoon regulars play liars' dice with the bartender. The weeknight crowd includes folks dispersing from the Mission District clubs and theaters. On weekends, the few designer-attired suburbanoids who've discovered this art bar come by, hoping to absorb some of its bohemian flavor. But the Rite Spot's hipness is its lack of deliberate hipness. Now and then the jukebox yields to live music at the piano.

Open Mon.-Fri. 1:30 p.m.-2 a.m., Sat.-Sun. 7 p.m.-2 a.m. No cards.

ROLAND'S

3309 Fillmore St., Marina District - 921-7774

Something more than a bar and yet not quite a full-fledged jazz club, Roland's fills a unique niche in the city. The music is always live, played by an array of Bay Area artists accompanied by versatile saxophonist Jule Broussard. From bebop to pop fusion, salsa to soul, the music is always bright and swinging, occasionally spelled by stand-up comedy. The crowd is lively. No cover charge on Saturday afternoon, Sunday, Monday and Tuesday.

Open Mon.-Fri. 8 p.m.-2 a.m., Sat. 2 p.m.-2 a.m., Sun. 4 p.m.-2 a.m. Cards: AE.

SALOON

1232 Grant Ave., North Beach - 989-7666

Sometimes called the 1232, this venerable North Beach institution has become a haven for hippie holdovers, where musicians from the golden era of San Francisco rock bands (Quicksilver Messenger Service, Country Joe and the Fish, Big Brother and the Holding Company) can work out with new bands in front of fans who knew them when. The musical mainstay is blues, just as gritty and raw as the setting dictates. The bar itself is even more of a survivor than the clientele, having been around since 1861. It doesn't quite look every year of its age, but it has a distinct Beat and pre-Beat character.

Open Mon.-Sat. 9 p.m.-2 a.m., Sun. 4 p.m.-2 a.m. No cards.

SPECS' TWELVE ADLER MUSEUM CAFÉ

12 Adler St., North Beach - 421-4112

In recent years, a few stalwarts have attempted to re-create the golden age of jazz in North Beach, and Specs' has been one of the most successful attempts. Not that this colorful little off-Columbus bar needs bebop jam sessions to add any character—the locals and regulars supply plenty of that. Brick walls slanting narrowly in off the alley are practically hidden beneath humorous signs and arcane memorabilia from Barbary Coast days, and old black-and-white photographs capture the images of the neighborhood's heyday. Once you've settled into this comfortable, salty, sometimes loud and rowdy dive, you'll feel the modern era fade away.

Open Mon.-Fri. 4:30 p.m.-2 a.m., Sat.-Sun. 5 p.m.-2 a.m. No cards.

TOMMY'S JOYNT

1101 Geary Blvd., Van Ness - 775-4216

You can spot Tommy's Joynt from three blocks away, so bold and tasteless is the giant lettering splashed across the outside walls. But for all its tourist-trap trappings and precious bric-a-brac, Tommy's is a funky and genuine hofbrau with a terrific selection of beers (over 90 at last count) and a hearty menu famous for buffalo stew, bean 'n' beer soup and thick sandwiches.

Open daily 10 a.m.-2 a.m. No cards.

TOSCA CAFÉ

242 Columbus Ave., North Beach - 986-9651

Sometimes on weekends, when the place is hopping, the dance-beat thumps from the disco downstairs obliterate the grand sounds from Tosca's famous jukebox. The opera records add one more element of old-world charm to this classic North Beach hangout. Weeknights are quieter and therefore better for a casual drop-in. Slide into one of the old leather booths and settle in for a legendary cappuccino, made here with chocolate, steamed milk and brandy. Or design your own coffee drink and see what name the friendly waiter gives it. The giant espresso machine at the end of the long bar is an impressive sight.

Open nightly 7 p.m.-2 a.m. No cards.

VESUVIO CAFÉ

255 Columbus Ave., North Beach - 362-3370

Although North Beach boasts preciously few reminders of the Beat era, when Kerouac, Ginsberg, Corso and others scrawled or read their poetry in the bookstores and cafés, the Vesuvio has hardly changed since it opened in 1949. Located near Lawrence Ferlinghetti's City Lights Bookstore, this delightfully casual bar is appropriately dark and cozy, with a balcony for people watchers and an abundance of nooks where you can settle in for a long, comfortable stay. Poets and chess players are always in evidence, and tourist fascination with the authentic bohemianism seems to have subsided.

Open daily 6 a.m.-2 a.m. No cards.

WASHINGTON SQUARE BAR & GRILL

1707 Powell St., North Beach - 982-8123

Ed Moose's famed restaurant, just off picturesque Washington Square, is notable for its solid and dependable Italian menu, but the bar is legendary for the steady clientele of writers, reporters, lawyers and politicians. The "Washbag" is typically packed with this neatly attired professional crowd, standing around the long bar—hosted by especially friendly barkeeps—and gazing over the nearby diners. But even more rewarding than the celebrity-gazing is the music supplied by a rotating crew of superb pianists, particularly Harlem stride specialist Mike Lipskin, the city's finest saloon pianist, who re-creates the sounds and aura of the 1920s and '30s through music inspired by Fats Waller and James P. Johnson.

Open Mon.-Fri. 11:30 a.m.-12 midnight, Sat. 11:30 a.m.-2 a.m., Sun. 10 a.m.-12 midnight. All major cards.

Cabaret

CITY CABARET

401 Mason St., Union Square - 441-7787

A recent addition to San Francisco's small cabaret scene, this attractive downtown spot has tenuously carved out a niche by presenting two or three different revues during the week, each in extended runs. Entertainment ranges from light-hearted looks at modern life via witty songs to musical parodies by classically trained musicians.

Showtimes and cover charge vary. Cards: MC, V.

CLUB FUGAZI

678 Green St., North Beach - 421-4222

In its fourteenth year and its umpteenth incarnation, Steve Silver's "Beach Blanket Babylon" is still wowing the tourists and the local repeats who can't get enough of the high-camp song-and-dance routines. First it went "Bananas," then "To the Moon," and now BBB "Goes Around the World," featuring zany tunes, outrageous costumes and world-record-breaking hats. The Fugazi is an old North Beach Italian music hall that has retained its cozy charm amid the frenetic off-off-off-Broadway antics of the talented Babylon cast. Minors are admitted to the Sunday matinee only.

Shows Wed.-Thurs. 8 p.m., Fri.-Sat. 8 p.m. & 10:30 p.m, Sun. 3 p.m. & 7:30 p.m. Tickets $12-$25. Cards: MC, V.

FINOCCHIO'S

506 Broadway, North Beach - 982-9388

Long before San Francisco's gay population burst out of the closet, the female impersonators at Finocchio's were all the rage. And even though the novelty of cross-dressing has worn off the jaded citizenry, and campy stage drag has been raised to the level of art by Charles Pierce, Finocchio's is still a prime nightlife attraction, especially for busloads of voyeuristic tourists. Don't expect to be ignored when the "ladies" start flapping through the house. There's no drink minimum.

Open Tues. & Thurs.-Sun. 8 p.m.-1:30 a.m. Shows Tues. & Thurs.-Sun. 9 p.m., 10:20 p.m. & 11:40 p.m. Cover charge $8. No cards.

PLUSH ROOM

940 Sutter St. (York Hotel), Union Square - 885-6800

For all of San Francisco's vaunted sophistication, cabaret is a risky business here. Just look at the checkered career of the lovely and appropriately named Plush Room. Tucked into the small, understatedly elegant York Hotel, this true cabaret has been up and down in the '80s but holds onto the belief that an audience exists for the type of cool, intelligent entertainment it presents. While the Plush Room gives an occasional break to a fine local chanteuse, it specializes in importing New York singers who in turn specialize in Gershwin, Porter, Coward, Berlin, Sondheim et al. There's a two-drink minimum.

Shows Tues.-Thurs. 8:30 p.m., Fri.-Sat. 8 p.m. & 10:30 p.m., Sun. 8 p.m. Cover charge varies. All major cards.

Comedy

San Francisco has long been a hotbed of stand-up comedy, from the North Beach days of Lenny Bruce, Mort Sahl, the Smothers Brothers and others through the meteoric rise of Robin Williams. Although there are only a few pure comedy clubs, many bars and music clubs include comics in their bookings. Also, the annual San Francisco Comedy Competition, a springboard to national attention, runs for several months at various venues throughout the summer and fall season; check newspaper listings for details.

HOLY CITY ZOO

408 Clement St., Richmond District - 386-4242

In the guise of a homey neighborhood bar, woody and informal, the Zoo functions as a breeding and training ground for the city's immense brood of stand-up comics. You can't expect Robin Williams to show up unannounced and improvise for half an hour (although it's not out of the realm of possibility), but you can count on witty material being worked out by a variety of crazy characters. In addition to regular showcases, the Zoo hosts the Tuesday open-mike night, the Monday night "Talk Show" and the best students from its own stand-up workshop. There's usually a two-drink minimum.

Shows Sun.-Thurs. 9 p.m., Fri.-Sat. 9 p.m. & 11 p.m. Cover charge $2-$7. Cards: MC, V.

OTHER CAFÉ

100 Carl St., Haight-Ashbury - 681-0748

With the resurgence of stand-up comedy in the '80s, this cozy Haight-Ashbury neighborhood watering hole has developed into a regular stop on the busy local circuit. Now the still-freewheeling Other takes dinner reservations for priority seating and specializes in the top names emerging from the Bay Area, such as Will Durst and Paula Poundstone. Monday and Tuesday are audition nights. Minors are welcome.

Open nightly 9 p.m.-1 a.m. Showtimes vary. Cover charge $6-$8. Card: AE.

PUNCH LINE

444 Battery St., Financial District - 397-7573

As local comics climb the ladder of success, they pass through the Punch Line, San Francisco's most "professional" comedy club. Part of entertainment baron Bill Graham's nightlife empire, the slick, brick-walled, comfortable club presents some of San Francisco's most polished performers, along with amateur showcases, an open-mike night on Sundays and a "comedy underground night." It is also one of the regular sites for the annual Comedy Competition. Mexican food and sandwiches are available, and there is a two-drink minimum.

Open Tues.-Sun. 7:45 p.m.-1:30 a.m. Shows Tues.-Thurs. & Sun. 9 p.m., Fri.-Sat. 9 p.m. & 11 p.m. Cover charge $3-$8. Cards: MC, V.

Dancing

CESAR'S PALACE

3140 Mission St., Mission District - 648-6611

This large, lively club in the city's predominantly Hispanic outer Mission District offers a spacious dance floor, a colorfully mixed crowd and the best Latin music in the Bay Area. Cesar's Latin All-Stars, the brassy house band of master musicians, churns out a variety of Afro-Cuban polyrhythmic dance beats. Once in a while, great salsa and Latin jazz artists from New York appear.

Open Thurs. 8 p.m.-2 a.m., Fri.-Sun. 9 p.m.-6 a.m. Cover charge $6. No cards.

CLUB METROPOLIS

1484 Market St., Civic Center - 621-5001

A recent addition to the uncontrollably burgeoning South of Market scene, this large complex is aimed slightly above the middle of the road—"casually elegant attire required"—but does not aspire to being a clone of the hipper-than-thou arty nightspots that triggered the SOMA movement. It features a very big dance floor, large booths for kicking back, excellent loud sound and a young crowd that follows the dress code.

Open Mon.-Fri. 11 a.m.-2 a.m., Sat. 8 p.m.-2 a.m. No cover charge Mon.-Thurs., $5 Fri.-Sat. Cards: MC, V.

I-BEAM

1748 Haight St., Haight-Ashbury - 668-6006

When it's not the live showcase for cutting-edge rock bands from around the world (see "Music Clubs" entry), the Beam is San Francisco's premier new-wave dance club, with the emphasis on *new*. Deejays throughout the city thrive on one-upmanship, and here they pride themselves on playing the latest discs from the underground. The sound is loud and steely, consistent with the dizzying laser and light shows, flashing videos and silver-and-black industrial decor. The crowd is young, hip, dressed in black and sometimes as concerned with haircuts as with music.

Open Tues.-Sat. 9 p.m.-2 a.m., Sun. 5 p.m.-2 a.m. Cover charge varies; students admitted free Wed.-Thurs. No cards.

NEW ORLEANS ROOM
California St. & Mason St. (Fairmont Hotel), Nob Hill - 772-5259

Once home to the legendary San Francisco trombonist and bandleader Turk Murphy, the New Orleans Room now showcases Don Neely's Royal Society Sextet, which swings its way through classic dance arrangements of old-time Crescent City jazz from the 1920s and '30s. Patronized by upscale tourists who can afford the steep Nob Hill drink tabs and the unrepentant fans of pre-Depression sounds, the New Orleans Room is a class joint for Prohibition-era hoofers.

Open Tues.-Sat. 6 p.m.-2 a.m. Shows 9:30 p.m.-1:30 a.m. Cover charge $3 after 9:30 p.m. All major cards.

OASIS
11th St. & Folsom St., South of Market - 621-8119

One of the pioneering ventures of the SOMA renaissance, the Oasis is a former motel transformed into a new wave entertainment and dining complex. During the warm season, the Plexiglas dance floor is taken off the swimming pool for Friday afternoon "weekend warm-ups." At night, the fairly funky (with aspirations toward industrial chic) multi-room club hosts a young, hip dancing and drinking crowd, with a soundtrack of new rock, urban funk and Top-100 dance hits. Wednesday nights are especially worthwhile: roots rock and blues bands shake the sliding glass doors for free. There's a two-drink minimum.

Open for dancing Tues.-Sun. 8 p.m.-3 a.m., for lunch Mon.-Fri. 11 a.m.-3 p.m. Cover charge free-$3. No cards.

PALLADIUM
1031 Kearny St., North Beach - 434-1308

When the urge to dance strikes you late at night in North Beach, head for the Palladium, which offers loud Top-40 tunes until dawn. A holdover from the disco era, this garish, thumping club attracts young suburbanites and tourists and feeds them a constant diet of mainstream rock hits and videos.

Open Wed.-Sun. 9 p.m.-6 a.m. Cover charge $7. No cards.

ROCKIN' ROBIN'S

*1840 Haight
St., Haight-Ashbury -
221-1960*

Especially popular with the Big Children of the baby-boom era, this casual and funky Haight-Ashbury club has live deejays spinning old platters from the golden age of rock and roll. Specializing in '50s and '60s oldies, they play rockabilly, Motown, R & B, soul and vintage rock. In addition to videos, pinball machines, free shuffleboard and tequila nights on Sundays, the amusements include dancing bartenders.

Open daily 12 noon-2 a.m. Cover charge $1-$3 (after 9 p.m.). No cards.

THE STONE

*412 Broadway, North
Beach - 391-8282*

After the live heavy metal, hard rock and new wave shows are over, young devotees of all of the above head for the Stone, an after-hours dance club that showcases very loud deejay rock and a bright panorama of videos. Its once-seedy decor has been transformed by lots of black paint, and there's a small bar in the back corner, tiered tables for taking a breather and a large dance floor for bouncing around to the latest sounds.

Open for dancing Fri.-Sat. 12 midnight-6 a.m. Cover charge $8. No cards.

TROCADERO TRANSFER

*520 4th St., South of
Market - 495-6620*

The Troc is an up-to-the-minute fashion statement in music, dress and lifestyle, with a clientele that is there to make the scene as much as to dance to the late-breaking hits selected by deejays for whom being in the know is a life-and-death matter. Though predominately young, the crowd doesn't lean toward any particular ethnic or sexual persuasion. The Troc is a SOMA pioneer from the days of disco, remaining hip at all costs.

*Open Thurs 9 p.m.-2 a.m. (usually for private parties),
Fri.-Sat. 10 p.m.-dawn. Cover charge $5-$7, plus $5 fee for
6-month membership. No cards.*

WOLFGANG'S

*901 Columbus Ave., North
Beach - 474-2995*

On most Saturday nights, Bill Graham's rock-solid live music club becomes a mecca for young, clean-cut, preppy urbanites and suburbanites. "Dance Dance" is piloted by a couple of the Bay Area's best mainstream deejays, spinning a mixture of Top 40, new wave and golden oldies. Downstairs at NOMA (as in "North of Market") on Friday nights, "Rock of the '90s" caters to a slightly more current-trend-conscious crowd. A disastrous fire closed Wolfgang's last summer, and it was still closed when we went to press, but it should be back in action by the time you read this. Minors are welcome.

Open nightly 9 p.m.-2 a.m. Cover varies. Cards: AE, MC, V.

Jazz

BAJONES
1062 Valencia St., Mission District - 282-2522

John Bajones has made his popular neighborhood bar something of a chameleon on the local jazz scene by vacillating in his booking policy between pop-oriented dance bands and straight-ahead acoustic jazz. Located just a heartbeat away from the center of the city's Mission District, Bajones is roomy and neighborly, with good sound and a vibrant, ethnically mixed clientele. Live Latin music, rock and roll, blues and funk are the commercial mainstays, but top-flight jazz musicians appear on an irregular basis.

Open nightly 6 p.m.-2 a.m. Shows 9:30 p.m. on. Cover charge $4-$5. No cards.

JAZZ WORKSHOP
473 Broadway, North Beach - 398-9700

In the 1950s and '60s, North Beach was the jazz mecca of San Francisco, but the incursion of live flesh shows and the demise of Keystone Korner left the old bohemian neighborhood virtually saxless. It's too early to herald a renaissance, but the reemergence of the Jazz Workshop, in an appropriately dingy but homey setting, has been a boon for the city's jazz folk. Fine local artists hold forth throughout the week, hosting open jam sessions every night at 5 p.m. The mainstream sounds favor piano, vocals and vibes and offer a hip and soothing escape from the frantic scene out on the street.

Open nightly 5 p.m.-2 a.m. Shows Mon.-Thurs. 9 p.m., 10:30 p.m. & 12 midnight, Fri.-Sat. 9:30 p.m., 11 p.m. & 12:30 a.m., Sun. jam session 5 p.m.-2 a.m. Cover charge $5. All major cards.

KIMBALL'S
300 Grove St., Civic Center - 861-5555

When the near-legendary Keystone Korner closed in the early '80s, Jane and Kimball Allen turned their restaurant into the city's premier jazz club. But the woeful economics of jazz took their toll, and Kimball's pared back its schedule, bringing in big-name acts for occasional two- or three-night runs. Hoping to draw in the jazz crowd while not alienating the toney clientele that drops in after the opera, ballet or symphony around the corner, Kimball's offers mostly mainstream jazz in a California-cuisine setting of blond wood and pricey drinks. Artfully presented dinners and snacks from the oyster bar are available. If you're going for the music, arrive early to be sure you can see the small stage.

Open daily 11:30 a.m.-2:30 p.m. & 6 p.m.-2 a.m. Shows nightly 9:30 p.m. & 11 p.m. Cover varies. Cards: AE, MC, V.

MILESTONES
376 5th St., South of Market - 777-9997

Sonny Buxton is the most urbane and gracious club host in the Bay Area, introducing acts in a suave and mellifluous radio announcer's voice and radiating the natty elegance that he wants his nightspot to represent. He turned this SOMA hole-in-the-wall into a classy bar, with polished brass gleaming against muted earth tones and pastels, and an intimate (read undersized) listening area for first-rate jazz. The drinks are overpriced and the service sometimes intrusive, but the sound system is excellent and the music—emphasizing vocalists, big bands and swinging small acoustic groups—is dependably superb. Along with hosting the occasional big name on tour, Milestones showcases local talent. The crowd comprises black and white business folk stopping in after work, journalists (including columnist Herb Caen) from the newspaper buildings down the street and jazzophiles hungry for a bebop fix.

Open Mon.-Fri. 4 p.m.-2 a.m., Sat. 6 p.m.-2 a.m., Sun. 5 p.m.-1 a.m. Showtimes vary. Cover charge $5-$10. No cards.

PASAND RESTAURANT AND LOUNGE
1875 Union St., Marina District - 922-4498

By day, Pasand is a fine restaurant serving South Indian cuisine. By night, the pace picks up as one of three fine house bands fills the lounge with pleasant jazz. A half-dozen of the city's many jazz vocalists rotate with the bands, singing bebop, blues, pop and Latin standards to a casually dapper crowd. Dinner is served until 10 p.m., but good burgers and delicious appetizers are available until 1 a.m.

Open daily 11:30 a.m.-2 a.m. Shows nightly 8:30 p.m.-12:30 a.m. No cover charge. Cards: AE, MC, V.

YOSHI'S

Gertrude Stein's dictum that "there is no there there" aside, San Francisco's best jazz club is in Oakland. Just a 25-

*6030 Claremont Ave.,
Oakland - 652-9200*

minute ride from the city (by BART or by car across the Bay Bridge), Yoshi's boasts the loveliest listening space and the best jazz bookings in the Bay Area. The 200-plus-seat room adjoins a fine Japanese restaurant and shares the same tasteful, airy decor. The high, slanted ceiling creates a refreshingly open feeling and bounces the sound neatly into the upstairs balcony. Hosts graciously turn off the blenders and espresso machines and discourage audiences from talking during the music. Since the restaurant's liquor license doesn't apply to the showroom, only non-alcoholic drinks are served, but you can slip out to the "real" bar upstairs in between sets. Two or three nights a week, local pianists, vocalists and combos hold forth in the relaxed fashion of an upscale neighborhood bar. But the rest of the time, large, racially and generationally diverse crowds pack in for the fine, internationally famous jazz artists who play four- and five-night runs.

Open nightly 7 p.m.-1 a.m. Shows Sun.-Thurs. 8 p.m. & 10 p.m., Fri.-Sat. 9 p.m. & 11 p.m. Cover charge varies. Cards: AE, MC, V.

Music Clubs

There has never been a shortage of rock and roll in San Francisco. Since the heyday of the great acid-rock bands that played for free in Golden Gate Park, a vital underground rock scene has been part of the city's rich cultural character. Sometimes the struggling local bands are overshadowed by such mega-groups as Journey, the Starship and Santana, and a lot of attention is given to major touring bands playing such concert venues as the Warfield Theatre, the Cow Palace, Shoreline Amphitheatre, the suburban Concord Pavilion or the Greek Theatre in Berkeley. But the best grass-roots music, peppered with hot out-of-town acts, can be found at the clubs listed below.

CLUB DV8

*55 Natoma St., South of
Market - 957-1730*

As you approach DV8, through back alleys and deserted parking lots beneath the concrete maze of criss-crossing freeways and Bay Bridge on- and off-ramps, you might instinctively start snapping your fingers, like some refugee from *West Side Story*. Once inside the forboding, bouncer-guarded warehouse door, you could cut the hipper-than-thou atmosphere with a switchblade. Faux marble columns and other ultra-cool Greco-Roman decorations abound. "Underground dancing" and art installations—iguanas in sand pits, pop sculptures—are mainstays of this trendy South of Market club, along with the young, posing crowd dressed in black. Punk chic notwithstanding, the crowds for the live rock shows, featuring the latest new wave band from Minneapolis or synth-pop pretenders from Europe, can be tamely middle-of-the-road, like the celluloid heroes of *West Side Story*.

Hours, showtimes and cover charge vary. Cards: AE, V inside the club; no cards at the door.

DNA LOUNGE
375 11th St., South of Market - 626-1409

Warehouse chic is the predominant theme in San Francisco's burgeoning South of Market area, where industrial buildings are remodeled with postmodern disregard for stylistic coherence. Although the clubgoers sometimes wear the detached look of fashion models, they are twitching with the underlying anxiety common to scenemakers. With its large bar, planted smack in the middle of the main floor, and its room-circling balcony, DNA is an ideal club for observing the genetic code of the evolving SOMA subspecies. The music is loud and booming, and bookings favor the up-and-coming local bands that play original, offbeat rock and roll, which makes DNA one of the best spots to hear early rumblings of the Bay Area's next big thing in pop.

Open Mon.-Sat. 9 p.m.-2 a.m. Showtimes and cover charge vary. No cards.

FULL MOON SALOON
1725 Haight St., Haight-Ashbury - 668-6190

If you aren't concerned with the latest trends in synth-pop, hard-core punk, hairstyles and attitudes, the Full Moon offers a down-home alternative to the cutting edginess of the hip SOMA nightspots. The decor is funky, the dress casual and the clientele relaxed, befitting the lingering post-hippie ethos that the club preserves in the legendary Haight-Ashbury. Summer of Love holdouts and baby boomers on a bender hang out to hear dinosaurs from the acid-rock era. But the main fare is a revolving schedule of local reggae, rhythm and blues and good ol' rock and roll intended for dancing. Occasional headliners include visiting Chicago blues musicians and Motown-era revival acts.

Open nightly 8:30 p.m.-2 a.m. Shows nightly 9:30 p.m. No cover charge Sun.-Wed.; cover charge varies Thurs.-Sat. Cards: MC, V.

I-BEAM

*1748 Haight St.,
Haight-Ashbury -
668-6006*

You won't want to frequent the Beam if you're allergic to styling mousse or if you develop a nervous reaction to the color black. You'll have to put your aversions aside if you want to see the hottest underground rock bands from the U.S. and the U.K. Before they break through to mainstream audiences or sign with major record labels, or during their noncommercial careers as cult bands played only on college radio, "new music" groups play this venerable neo-industrial nightclub. If the wave is new—whether it's punk, garage-band thrash, neo-psychedelic, nouveau-folk or electric noise —it's bound to break at the Beam. Amid giant I-beams and drill bits, strobe lights and lasers flash while avant-garde videos are projected on the walls and incredibly loud music batters the crowd. You can retreat to the lobby or one of the two bars for a respite before hurling yourself back into the throng. Headliners don't usually take the stage before midnight on Mondays (the Tuesday sets are earlier), and the shows are standing-, dancing- or slamming-room only.

Open Mon.-Sat. 9 p.m.-2 a.m., Sun. 5 p.m.-2 a.m. Live shows Mon.-Tues. Showtimes vary. Cover charge $3-$5. No cards.

GREAT AMERICAN MUSIC HALL

859 O'Farrell St., Union Square - 880-0750

San Francisco's most eclectic music club is indeed a beautifully maintained turn-of-the-century music hall, complete with Corinthian pillars, ornate red-and-gold rococo trim and a U-shaped balcony overlooking the stage and main floor. Although it has the standard nightclub small round tables and cane-back chairs jammed together for maximum seating, the Great American Music Hall is the most comfortable spot in town to see the greatest variety of music. The most popular Bay Area dance bands hold forth on nights when out-of-town headliners aren't booked. The music swings from straight-ahead jazz through country, bluegrass, folk, new age, Latin jazz, blues, soul, funk and fusion, and the promoters aren't afraid to take a commercial risk when they know the music is of a high artistic and adventurous quality. Everybody should be able to find something of interest any given week. Good sandwiches, burgers and salads are available from the kitchen at relatively reasonable prices.

Open one hour before early show (usually 8 p.m. or 8:30 p.m.). Closing time and cover charge vary. No cards.

LAST DAY SALOON

*406 Clement St., Richmond
District - 387-6343*

One of the least pretentious rock clubs in the city, the Last Day is an old standby. Pop styles may come and go, but as long as there are audiences for earnest rock, blues and reggae, this solid nightspot will be packing them in. The dance floor is small, surrounded by tables, with a walk-up bar and a rear room for overflow seating. In addition to local favorites who churn out a multitude of boogie grooves, often for no cover, the Last Day books top blues, rock and R & B artists from around the country. The club appeals to the rowdier side of the Big Chill generation, and is frequented by rough-hewn regulars from the Sunset and Richmond districts.

Open daily 2 p.m.-2 a.m. Showtimes and cover charge vary. No cards.

NIGHTBREAK

*1821 Haight St.,
Haight-Ashbury -
221-9008*

The decor, dress and clientele are casual funk, the scene is '80s eclectic, and the bands are among the best local offbeat rockers who haven't yet broken into the bigger clubs. Thrashing garage pop with idiosyncratic twists is the specialty several nights a week; when bands aren't booked, rock deejays get the crowd moving.

Open daily 1 p.m.-2 a.m. Showtimes and cover charge vary. No cards.

THE STONE

*412 Broadway, North
Beach - 391-8282*

The Broadway strip has been beleaguered for years by topless joints and more recently by antagonism between teen cruisers and the cops, but the Stone has held its ground as a mainstream rock showcase and after-hours dance club. The broad, spacious room features a large dance floor and table seating on two terraced levels. Security folk can be brusque with overindulgent patrons, and the drink service is sometimes spotty, but the atmosphere is fairly loose. The college-age crowd changes according to the music being performed, which runs from heavy metal and hard rock staples to underground pop, trendy new wave and '60s throwbacks.

*Open Sun.-Thurs. 8 p.m.-2 a.m., Fri.-Sat. 7 p.m.-6 a.m.
Showtimes Sun.-Thurs. 9 p.m., Fri.-Sat. 8 p.m. Cover charge
varies. No cards.*

VENETIAN ROOM

*California St. & Mason St.
(Fairmont Hotel),
Nob Hill - 772-5226*

This elegant Nob Hill supper club showroom was once the exclusive province of middle-of-the-road pop singers and well-heeled audiences raised on Glenn Miller, Frank Sinatra and Dean Martin. The cover charge and drink prices are still

129

steep, the tables are still set with linen and silver, and the Venetian Room Orchestra still plays romantic standards for dancing before the shows. But maestro Dick Bright injects a quirky contemporary sensibility into the house band, and the bookings now reflect the baby-boomer generation's coming of age: Jack Jones, John Gary and Englebert Humperdinck are now the exceptions, while such jazz greats as McCoy Tyner and Wynton Marsalis, such soul giants as James Brown, and such rock survivors as Donovan and the Mamas and the Papas are not unusual.

Open Tues.-Sun. 7:30 p.m.-1 a.m. Shows Tues.-Sun. 9 p.m. & 11 p.m. Cover charge $17-$25. All major cards.

WOLFGANG'S

901 Columbus Ave., North Beach - 474-2995

When rock acts are touring to promote a new record and they aren't big enough for the concert halls or amphitheaters, they play Wolfgang's, an odd-shaped 400- to 700-seat (depending on whether they put tables on the dance floor and how many tables they pack in) North Beach club not far from Fisherman's Wharf. The club boasts a terrific sound system, a highly professional staff and good views from almost everywhere, except the back tables on the narrow balcony. Most of the acts are established draws that aren't too far off the mainstream of contemporary rock, although Wolfgang's is known for its excellent Wednesday night reggae dance parties featuring major Jamaican performers, and occasional jazz and blues shows of exceptional quality. Advance dinner reservations, which will ensure the best available seating, are taken for some shows, and deejays spin hit records for dancing downstairs at NOMA (see "Dancing" entry).

Hours, showtimes and cover charge vary. Cards: AE, MC, V.

HOTELS

Luxurious

CAMPTON PLACE HOTEL

340 Stockton St., Union Square - 781-5555

Campton Place was a hit from the beginning, as much for its acclaimed restaurant as for its very elegant and very expensive rooms. Opened just a few years ago after $18 million in renovations, Campton Place doesn't have the old San Francisco aura of some of the city's other great hotels, such as the St. Francis or the Clift, but it has a great location just off Union Square and a quiet, discreet ambience. Its size also commends it: with just 126 rooms, Campton Place is never overrun with conventioneers and large tour groups. (The stratospheric prices also keep the riffraff at bay.) The lobby, lounges, guest rooms and large suites are all exceptionally attractive and comfortable, with a skillful mix of rich colors, antique and contemporary furnishings, plush carpets and fresh flowers. Service is stressed: intelligent concierges, prompt valet and room services, business and secretarial services, and so on. The restaurant is almost as good as its incredible reputation, and the small bar is a great spot for a quiet drink. Valet parking is $19 a day.

Singles & doubles: $170-$230; suites: $475-$775.

THE DONATELLO

501 Post St., Union Square - 441-7100

Just apart from the chaos of Union Square sits the Donatello, a most refined hotel that recently changed hands (it had been the Pacific Plaza) and became a member of the prestigious Relais et Châteaux chain. The affiliation is deserved—this is a very attractive, friendly and discreet hostelry. The lobby and bar lounge areas are opulent without being fussy and cluttered; everything, with the exception of the highball-glass chandelier (which smacks of a Holiday Inn), is in very good taste. Rooms are spacious and quiet; some are a bit frumpy, but they are more than comfortable. Amenities include a quiet bar, an acclaimed Italian restaurant, valet parking (for $14 a day), afternoon tea and complimentary *Wall Street Journals* and terry robes. Reception, valet and concierge services are all exceptionally helpful.

Singles & doubles: $150-$210; suites: $295-$415.

FAIRMONT HOTEL

This Nob Hill oldtimer is now all the more famous—it stars as the St. Gregory on the TV series *Hotel*. This alone is

*950 Mason St., Nob Hill -
772-5000*

reason enough not to stay at the Fairmont, unless you don't mind large (albeit relatively prosperous) tour groups. The massive lobby is dramatically ornate but fairly ugly, and one tends to feel lost. However, the views from the tower addition (notable for its horrid exterior) are spectacular, the rooms are large and well appointed, and the service is good. There are seven restaurants, including one atop the tower with wonderful views and one open 24 hours a day. Another of the restaurants, the Venetian Room, is a supper club that headlines big-name singers.

Singles: $140-$205; doubles: $170-$235; suites: $450-$1,600. Weekend packages available.

FOUR SEASONS CLIFT HOTEL

*495 Geary St., Union
Square - 775-4700*

One of the finest of the old San Francisco hotels, the Clift is perhaps best known for its wonderful Redwood Room, an impressive bar featuring polished redwood paneling and beautiful art deco light fixtures. The adjoining restaurant, the French Room, is an old-fashioned delight, with gleaming chandeliers and painted woodwork, and the lobby is appropriately dramatic. Rooms are good-sized and quiet, especially the upper rooms, which can also have fine views. The Four Seasons management is making a concerted (and apparently successful) effort to woo the business traveler who is tired of the sterility and impersonality of the glass tower hotels; there is a full-time business concierge and every kind of business service, from secretarial services to conference rooms to such high-tech amenities as computer modems and fax machines. The intelligence and helpfulness of the staff is on a par with the high prices.

Singles: $145-$205; doubles: $145-$225; suites: $375-$700. Weekend and theater packages also available.

THE MARK HOPKINS INTER-CONTINENTAL

*One Nob Hill (California
& Mason), Nob Hill -
392-3434*

The Mark Hopkins is a longtime favorite of conservative, middle-aged couples who favor Lincoln Continentals and Cadillacs over Porsches and BMWs. The lobby is elegant in an outdated way: crystal chandeliers, lots of mirrored walls, '70s-style contemporary furniture (tufted leather couches, glass-and-brass coffee tables) and sweeping drapes. The large rooms and suites are done in a similar manner, except that the furnishings lean more to antiques. Service is bright and friendly. The upper rooms have great views, as does the Top of the Mark, the rooftop bar that is a must-visit on a clear night.

Singles: $145-$205; doubles: $175-$235; suites: $300-$1,000. Weekend packages available.

HUNTINGTON HOTEL
1075 California St., Nob Hill - 474-5400

The Huntington's exceptional refinement makes it our favorite Nob Hill hotel. Its regulars include such prosperous people as Calvin Klein, Robert Redford, Leontyne Price and Baron Guy de Rothschild, all of whom care more about the quality of their rooms than about passing through a gigantic, dramatic lobby. Though very attractive (white woodwork, deep red carpets and upholstery), the Huntington's tiny lobby is anything but ostentatious. The rooms, however, are unequaled for their level of comfort and opulent but tasteful decor. Personal service is stressed, as is the individuality of the rooms, which are furnished with lovely antiques, objets and paintings. With only 143 rooms, the Huntington gives one the feeling of staying in one of Europe's fine old hotels. The complete range of business services are provided, and the concierge is excellent. There are two restaurants: L'Etoile, an admirable (and expensive) classical French restaurant, and the Big Four, an extremely handsome tribute to San Francisco's Victorian-era railroad magnates.

Singles: $130-$200; doubles: $150-$240; suites: $260-$590.

SHERATON-PALACE HOTEL
639 Market St., Union Square - 392-8600

Even if you don't stay at this grand old dowager, you must come for a look, a drink and perhaps a meal. Don't miss the Pied Piper Room, a clubby, wood-paneled restaurant and bar with the wonderful Maxfield Parrish mural of the same name. Then head for the Garden Court, a breathtaking room of marble columns, crystal chandeliers and rich carpeting, all underneath a remarkable leaded glass dome. (Once the hotel's carriage entrance, the Garden Court is now a restaurant best known for Sunday brunch.) The hotel itself is large (526 rooms) and rather formal, with spacious rooms decorated in an ordinary, if comfortable, manner. Parking is $12 a day *without* in and out privileges.

Singles: $95-$150; doubles: $110-$165; suites: $225-$1,000.

THE SHERMAN HOUSE
2160 Green St., Pacific Heights - 563-3600

Northern California is full of enterprising people who are converting charming old houses into homey inns—but none has created an inn as luxurious and opulent as the Sherman House. Built in 1876 by Leander Sherman, the owner of the Sherman Clay Music Company and a devoted opera buff, the house boasts a three-story recital hall where turn-of-the-century musicians performed. In 1980 Manou Mobedshahi and his young wife bought the old mansion and spent four years and a considerable fortune restoring the buildings and extensive gardens. The main house has twelve rooms and the carriage house, six; all are straight out of the pages of *Architectural Digest*. Every one is large and furnished with exceptionally fine antiques and rugs, and most have canopied beds, down comforters, marble fireplaces, modernized black-granite bathrooms, wet bars, whirlpool tubs, color TVs and stereo systems. Some have such extras as a private garden or rooftop deck; a few rooms and the restaurant have views of the Bay. The personal service is exemplary: maids will unpack luggage, chauffeurs will pick you up from the airport in a Rolls or a '62 Jaguar, and the skilled Swiss chef will prepare a refined snack or full-blown feast any time of the day or night. The Sherman House is located away from all the other top hotels in Union Square, Nob Hill and the Financial District, which does not recommend it to those who like to be where the action is. But it is a perfect stop for those who value quiet and old-world refinement, those who want a taste of cultured San Francisco 100 years ago, and those who have plenty of money.

Singles & doubles: $190-$275; suites: $300-$600.

SIR FRANCIS DRAKE

450 Powell St., Union Square - 392-7755

Though not exactly luxurious, the Sir Francis Drake is one of the better known of the old San Francisco hotels. The less-than-chic middle-American clientele loves the doormen dressed up like Renaissance artisans, the Union Square location and the ornate lobby and lounges. We, however, find it to be too touristy and crowded, with ordinary rooms and disappointing restaurants (the Starlite Roof and Crusty's Sourdough Café, a place no local would ever visit). Still, the staff is friendly, the location is good, and the prices aren't too bad.

Singles: $95-$145; doubles: $115-$165; suites: $250-$550. Weekend package: $88.

THE STANFORD COURT

905 California St., Nob Hill - 989-3500

The Stanford Court eschews the more vulgar ostentation of the neighboring Fairmont, opting instead to project an image of refined luxury. The "court" in the name refers to the courtyard automobile entrance, which features a large stained-glass dome over a fountain. The smallish lobby is homey and inviting, and the rooms are large and quite comfortable, though the furnishings are a bit dated. Make sure to request a room with a view; not all have them. Long a favorite of ours for its elegance and attention to detail, we confess displeasure at our last visit, when the service level (including housekeeping) had slipped a bit. We can only hope this was a temporary lapse. Public facilities include a beautiful ballroom, a lovely bar and several restaurants, including the famed (but disappointing) Fournou's Ovens. Valet parking is $15 a day, with in and out privileges.

Singles: $145-$205; doubles: $175-$260; suites: $370-$700.

WESTIN ST. FRANCIS

335 Powell St., Union Square - 397-7000

We do love visiting the St. Francis, one of San Francisco's most famous grand old hotels, just to see the exceptional rosewood-paneled lobby and to have a drink in the lovely lobby bar. But we have not enjoyed staying here since the construction of the modern tower some years ago, which brought the room total up to an excessive 1,166 and made the place seem overrun with tourists. The location is in some ways ideal—facing Union Square—but it is a little *too* close to the action; lower-level rooms can be noisy.

Singles: $120-$205; doubles: $150-$235; suites: $250-$1,500.

Small & Charming

THE ABIGAIL

246 McAllister St., Civic Center - 861-9728

If you're looking for a bargain and don't mind being away from Union Square and downtown—or want to be near the Civic Center and the Opera—call up the Abigail immediately to make a reservation. You can't beat the charm, friendliness and comfort for the price. "Haute hunt" might describe the decor at this British-owned hotel: moose heads peer over the small lobby, with its black-and-white tile floors and homey clutter; prints of sporting dogs and hunting scenes line the walls. The rooms are small and not completely immune to street noise, but they are very comfortable. Each is equipped with surprisingly handsome antiques, an aging color TV, a phone and a private bath that is clean and large enough, if not especially modernized. Just off the lobby is an attractive restaurant/bar, where you can have Continental breakfast as well as lunch and dinner. There's no parking, so you'll have to use a local garage.

Singles: $55; doubles: $65-$70; suite: $140.

THE ALBION HOUSE

135 Gough St., Civic Center - 621-0896

A small (eight-room) bed-and-breakfast that is neither especially cheap nor especially luxurious, in a neighborhood that is neither chic nor shabby. Not far from the Opera House and Symphony Hall, the Albion counts many small cafés and galleries as its neighbors. It lacks the fussy charm of the city's more Victorian-style inns, but the large, redwood-beamed living room and the small, comfortable rooms (seven with private bath) are attractively decorated nonetheless. If you are sensitive to street noise, ask for a room towards the back. No hotel parking, but spaces are easy to find in the neighborhood and lots are inexpensive.

Singles & doubles: $63-$89; suites: $95-$105.

THE AMSTERDAM

749 Taylor St., Nob Hill - 673-3277

There are few amenities—no valet parking, no concierge, no restaurant, no room service, no elevator—but this frumpy little hotel is a find for the frugal. Well located just above the Sutter Street shops and galleries on the south slope of Nob Hill, the Amsterdam has 27 small, plain rooms on three floors, some with private baths. The accommodations are clean and comfortable; all are equipped with phones and small black-and-white TVs. Complimentary coffee and tea are served in the morning in the folksy lobby.

Singles: $31-$36 (sharing bath), $45 (private bath); doubles: $36-$41 (sharing bath), $48 (private bath).

THE ARCHBISHOP'S MANSION

1000 Fulton St., Civic Center - 563-7872

No ordinary parson's quarters are these. Built in 1904, this bed-and-breakfast is a resplendent example of old San Francisco wealth—though it was built not for some captain of industry, but for the Archbishop of San Francisco. The three-story mansion facing historic Alamo Square (near the Opera and the Civic Center) has been lovingly restored to its original beauty: rich, polished woodwork, thick carpets, vaulted ceilings, crystal chandeliers and a lovely stained-glass dome over the staircase. Rooms feature queen-size beds, nineteenth-century French antiques, fine linens and silks and private baths; many have fireplaces. Amenities include a good breakfast served in your room, limousine service to the nearby Opera and Symphony Hall, and an accommodating staff. Another plus: free parking.

Rooms & suites: $95-$185.

GALLERIA PARK HOTEL

*191 Sutter St., Union
Square - 781-3060*

A creation of developer Bill Kimpton and interior designer Nan Rosenblatt, the Galleria Park originally opened in 1911 and was restored and reopened a few years ago. The lobby is an art nouveau vision, with a crystal skylight, etched glass and a sculpted fireplace. There are 177 rooms and suites; rooms are small but exceptionally attractive, and suites are lovely and well-designed, with soothing colors, fireplaces, stereos and large TVs. Like the Bedford, this hotel stresses comfort, style and economy over service; though the staff is more than friendly, there is neither a doorman nor a concierge (though the bellman can be trusted for advice). Amenities include an outdoor jogging track, well-appointed conference rooms and two restaurants: Bentley's Oyster Bar, modeled after the Oyster Bar in New York, and Brasserie Chambord. Parking is a reasonable $10 a day, with in and out privileges.

Singles & doubles: $99; suites: $125-$325.

HOTEL BEDFORD

*761 Post St., Union
Square - 673-6040*

The Bedford, another Kimpton-Rosenblatt hotel, offers one of the best deals in the area. All singles and doubles, even those with king-size beds and good views, are just $79; reserve early to get one of the more desirable rooms. The old hotel was renovated skillfully and tastefully, if not opulently (though it's quite elegant for the price). The good-sized lobby is cheerful; it opens onto the walnut-paneled Wedgwood Bar and the pretty, skylit Café Bedford, which serves simple California cuisine. Rooms are compact, clean and comfortable, with minirefrigerators, small color TVs, white walls and floral fabrics; bathrooms are old-fashioned but not rickety. The small staff is very friendly. Located a few blocks west of Union Square, the Bedford is close enough for convenience but far enough away to be relatively quiet. Valet parking is $10.50 a night.

Singles & doubles: $79; suites: $120-$130.

HOTEL DIVA

*440 Geary St., Union
Square - 885-0200*

If Eurostyle is your style, you'll feel right at home at Hotel Diva, one of the newest additions to the moderately sized and priced Union Square hotels. True, the entrance and tiny lobby (stainless steel and glass, with four large TV monitors tuned to the same movie) make the Diva look a bit like a bank. But the small rooms are as well-equipped and cleverly designed as can be, featuring high-tech TVs with VCRs, minibars, comfortable beds with down comforters and tasteful contemporary Italian furniture. Unfortunately, the views are mostly of neighboring brick walls, but that helps ensure quiet. There is neither a restaurant nor room service, but there are some very slick conference and meeting rooms and an accommodating staff. If you can't abide noise, request a room on an upper floor.

Singles: $95; doubles: $105. Weekend packages available.

HOTEL UNION SQUARE

114 Powell St., Union Square - 397-3000

Tremendously popular, no doubt because of its good location and its very low prices, the Union Square is not especially service oriented. Nor is it as sophisticated as its sister hotels, Hotel Diva and Kensington Park; rooms are old and vaguely musty, and the Continental breakfast includes coffee served in Styrofoam cups. Most doubles are just $68, however, so one can't be too fussy given the price (though we'd rather spend $11 more and stay at the Bedford). Avoid the rooms facing the street; the location at the base of the Powell Street cable car line ensures constant noise. The small bar, Dashiell's, is named for mystery writer Dashiell Hammett, who lived and wrote in the hotel for a while.

Singles & doubles: $68-$88; suites: $118.

HOTEL VINTAGE COURT

650 Bush St., Union Square - 392-4666

Designer Nan Rosenblatt has left her distinctive touch on yet another reasonably priced San Francisco hotel, the Vintage Court—perhaps the best-looking hotel she has designed. Located just far enough away from Union Square to avoid excessive noise, the Vintage Court is a very good value: just $89 for any room. All the rooms are quiet and homey, with good king-size beds, stocked minibars, cable TV, comfortable furnishings and Rosenblatt's trademark floral fabrics. (Reserve early to get one of the larger rooms.) The lobby is welcoming and calm and the staff is charming, if minimal (like others in this small chain, the Vintage Court puts economy over service, so there is neither valet parking nor a concierge). Curiously, this attractive, well-priced hotel is home to Masa's, the tacky, incredibly expensive (but quite good) French restaurant with a national reputation.

Singles & doubles: $89.

INN AT THE OPERA

333 Fulton St., Civic Center - 863-8400

This inn has many things going for it: history (built in 1927 to house opera stars), location (a few steps from the Opera House and Symphony Hall), decor (shades of peach, lots of fresh flowers, tasteful artworks and objets d'art) and ambience (discreetly luxurious, yet casually friendly). There are, however, a few drawbacks, particularly the noise from the nearby freeway. The rooms are quite small, though attractive and well-equipped (wet bars, minirefrigerators, microwaves, terry robes); all have queen-size beds. On the ground floor, the handsome Act IV Lounge is notable for its pianist in the evening and its late supper, served until 1:30 a.m. The nearest parking lot is shockingly expensive, but street parking can usually be found.

Singles & doubles: $95-$115; suites: $125-$165.

THE INN AT UNION SQUARE

440 Post St., Union Square - 397-3510

A small, European-style hotel, the Inn at Union Square could almost be considered a bed-and-breakfast. There are just 30 rooms, no lobby to speak of, and no services; Continental breakfast and afternoon tea are served in the small parlors on each floor. The rooms are a bit fussy, with lots of florals and Georgian furniture; most have king-size beds and down pillows, and there's a penthouse suite with a fireplace, bar, sauna and whirlpool tub. The suites face busy Post Street, and can therefore be noisy; the rooms look out onto neighboring brick walls, and hence are quieter, if less aesthetic. All rooms are equipped with color TVs, but the reception isn't great. Comfort is not in short supply here, but we find our money better spent at the Orchard, the Petite Auberge, the Vintage Court and the Bedford.

Singles & doubles: $95-$160; suites: $260-$300.

KENSINGTON PARK HOTEL

450 Post St., Union Square - 788-6400

A handsome but eccentric little hotel near Union Square, the Kensington Park has adopted a British style. The small, very attractive lobby (shared with neighbor Theater on the Square) is on the ground floor, but the hotel's rooms don't start until the fifth floor—the Elks Club's dining, meeting and exercise rooms occupy the interim floors. Rooms are small but not cramped, with English furnishings and shades of blue, green and rose. Complimentary coffee, tea and crumpets are served each morning in the foyers on each floor, and guests gather around the piano in the lobby in the afternoon for tea and sherry. The staff makes an effort to make each guest feel welcome. Valet parking is $14 a day.

Singles & doubles: $98-$108; suites: $140-$350.

THE MANSION HOTEL

Those who expect cable TV, coffee shops and convention facilities from a hostelry will not enjoy the Mansion, a posh

2220 Sacramento St., Pacific Heights - 929-9444

bed-and-breakfast that reeks of refinement and old-world charm. The 1887 Queen Anne house near Lafayette Park has nineteen guest rooms, none with TVs, but some with marble fireplaces or private terraces. All are furnished with beautiful antiques. Breakfast is served in bed, and nightly performances of classical music are given in the parlor. Tennis players will enjoy the proximity to Lafayette Park's courts. Parking is available nearby for $7 a day.

Singles & doubles: $89-$200.

THE ORCHARD HOTEL

562 Sutter St., Union Square - 433-4434

A choice stop for Union Square shoppers who expect comfort but would rather spend their money at Gump's or Saks than on a pretentious hotel. The Orchard sits on relatively quiet Sutter Street, which houses such shops as Williams-Sonoma, La Ville du Soleil and Jessica McClintock. The lobby, done in shades of rose and green, is as inviting and comfortable as it is attractive. Guests and visitors alike may enjoy a drink in the lobby bar or good French food in the adjacent restaurant, Annabel's. The compact rooms are homey and comfortable, with aging but spotless bathrooms and the increasingly common minibars.

Singles & doubles: $85-$105; suites: $170.

PETITE AUBERGE

863 Bush St., Union Square - 928-6000

There is no more cozy inn in all of San Francisco (except for the neighboring White Swan, owned by the same good people). A romanticized interpretation of the French country look has been skillfully put together here: earthy paver tile floors, delicately flowered wallpaper, country furnishings and French windows and doors. "Darling" is probably the best word for this place. (We must take exception, however, to the overabundance of cutesy stuffed teddy bears.) The basement level comprises a breakfast room with French doors opening onto a small garden, and a lounge/bar area where good California wines and tea are served in the afternoon. The upper floors are taken up by 26 small and adorable rooms, all with private bath and queen-size beds, many with fireplaces. The Bush Street location is a short walk to Union Square, yet away from the throng of tourists. Parking is $15 a day.

Singles & doubles: $95-$145; suites: $185.

THE QUEEN ANNE

1590 Sutter St., Civic Center - 441-2828

This large (49-room) bed-and-breakfast sits in the north of the Civic Center, not far from prestigious Pacific Heights. The authentically restored Queen Anne–style mansion has a plush parlor, a majestic mahogany staircase, two conference rooms and that San Francisco rarity, free parking. Rooms range in size from small to spacious; they all have high ceilings, antique furnishings, telephones and remote-control TVs. The better rooms have fireplaces, wet bars and bay windows. Wake up to Continental breakfast served in your room; relax with afternoon tea and sherry in the parlor. A good bet for those who like the personality of old bed-and-breakfasts but want modern conveniences.

Singles & doubles: $89-$109; suites: $139.

STANYAN PARK HOTEL

750 Stanyan St., Golden Gate Park - 751-1000

Built in 1905 and restored in 1983, the Stanyan Park is on the National Register of Historic Places. Just across the street from Golden Gate Park and around the corner from funky Haight Street, its location attracts fans of the great park and doctors visiting nearby U.C. Medical Center. Both comfort and period ambience are maintained here: bath-rooms have been reasonably modernized and antique fur-nishings are simple and homey. The best bet for a larger group or an extended stay is one of the two-bedroom suites, which sleep six and include kitchens, dining rooms and four-poster beds. The room rate includes a decent Continental breakfast and friendly service. Weekend visitors should be prepared for daytime noise from the many park visitors.

Singles: $62-$88; doubles: $72-$88; suites: $105-$145.

TLC SUITES

655 Powell St., Nob Hill - 477-4600

Nob Hill's newest addition has set out to woo business travelers, and it certainly deserves their patronage. These well-designed small suites have office areas with two-line phones and computer plugs, complete kitchens with such necessities as coffee beans and grinders, and entertainment systems that include stereo TVs, VCRs and compact disc players. Service is stressed—the bright staff will get you anything and everything you need. (There is neither restaurant nor bar, but someone will run out and get you supplies from nearby vendors.) The surprising thing about TLC is the price—it is more than competitive with the huge glass towers that usually attract business people. True, these minisuites aren't exactly oversized, but every comfort is provided, and the location is very good.

Studios: $99; suites: $125-$145.

VILLA FLORENCE

Another old hotel that has been skillfully spruced up for a clientele that doesn't want to spend more than $100 for a

225 Powell St., Union
Square - 397-7700

Union Square location. This particular location is a little tawdry—gaudy electronics stores line the block—but it is very well situated for a Union Square shopping spree. The Italianate lobby is unusually attractive, with a fireplace, plush seating and a lovely fresco of Florence. The rooms combine simple, modern dressers and armoires (which, of course, hide TVs) with flowery chintz bedspreads, drapes and overstuffed chairs. A good home-away-from-home for the price.

Singles & doubles: $92; suites: $109-$149.

THE WASHINGTON SQUARE INN

1660 Stockton St., North
Beach - 981-4220

Those enamored with the old-world charm of North Beach and Washington Square will be pleased to find this very friendly and pleasant hideaway. The fifteen-room bed-and-breakfast faces onto the park; the two most expensive rooms have bay windows overlooking the square. The rooms are predictably small, homey and cozy, and they are as quiet as can be expected of a Washington Square location. Most have private baths and some have king-size beds. Prices include breakfast as well as the tea and very nice scones served in the afternoon by the personable staff.

Singles: $55-$150; doubles: $65-$160.

WHITE SWAN INN

845 Bush St., Union
Square - 775-1755

Without a doubt our favorite inn in San Francisco. The White Swan, owned by the same people who brought the city the ultra-sweet Petite Auberge, makes large and modern hotels seem like gulags. Though officially a bed-and-breakfast, the White Swan has none of the problems that keep some people away from B & Bs. Each of the 27 rooms is exceptionally large, with a king- or queen-size bed, fireplace, refrigerator, phone, color TV and ample bathroom, and the inn offers such big-hotel amenities as valet parking, shoe shining and concierge, turn-down and secretarial services. The English-country look has been created with remarkable skill; every inch of the place is attractive and inviting. The lower level houses the communal rooms: a large breakfast room (with doors opening onto a small garden), a lounge and a very cozy library, all with fireplaces. The breakfast is more than generous, as are the afternoon hors d'oeuvres, tea and wine. The location is outstanding for Union Square shopping.

Singles & doubles: $115-$145; suites: $225.

Large & Modern

CATHEDRAL HILL HOTEL

1101 Van Ness Ave., Civic Center - 776-8200

This newish hotel may not have the most attractive interior in town (too much green for our taste), but it is not without advantages. For one, it has free parking, a big bonus in car-clogged San Francisco. It also frequently offers a very reasonable weekend package at $79 a night. You won't get a Bay view, but you'll get all the big-hotel amenities, including a swimming pool, in-room movies, conference and banquet facilities and the Hilltop Club, the hotel's full-service concierge floor with deluxe rooms. The standard rooms are average in size and equipped with comfortable but generic hotel furniture.

Singles: $90-$120; doubles: $100-$160; triples: $145; suites: $160-$475. Weekend packages available.

HOLIDAY INN AT CHINATOWN

750 Kearny St., Chinatown - 433-6600

An especially unattractive concrete tower on the border of Chinatown and the Financial District, the Holiday Inn is usually packed with conventioneers, airline employees, business people and unimaginative tourists. The ambience and decor are as plastic and impersonal as one would imagine of a Holiday Inn. However, parking is free, there's a rooftop pool (open April through October only), and the location is convenient to the Financial District, the Embarcadero, Chinatown and Union Square. Many rooms have good views.

Singles: $99-$129; doubles: $114-$144; suites: $450.

HOLIDAY INN AT UNION SQUARE

480 Sutter St., Union Square - 398-8900

This 400-room, 30-story hotel was built in 1971 and looks it. The concrete-and-glass exterior is dreadful, the lobby is boring and the atmosphere is sterile. Predictably, the place is popular with tour groups and convention planners. We are fond, however, of the charming little bar on the top floor dedicated to the memory of Sherlock Holmes. The rooms are reasonably spacious and reasonably comfortable, with good views all around, and the hotel is well-located for Union Square shopping.

Singles: $102-$126; doubles: $117-$141; suites: $275.

HYATT ON UNION SQUARE

345 Stockton St., Union Square - 398-1234

Business travelers are the primary clientele of this 700-room Hyatt in the heart of the Union Square district. The modern tower has a modern decor to match—done up in lots of neutrals and pastels, the rooms, lobby and public spaces are easy on the eye. If you want a large, well-situated, comfortable business hotel, you will be pleased with the Hyatt. The conference and meeting facilities are good, and the Regency Club takes care of executives who are used to a little pampering. The upper floors boast lovely views.

Singles: $159-$189; doubles: $184-$214; suites: $300-$900; Regency Club: $214-$700. Weekend packages available.

HYATT REGENCY SAN FRANCISCO

5 Embarcadero Center, Financial District - 788-1234

This Financial District monster sits at one end of the sprawling Embarcadero Center, which makes it a good location for visiting business people. There are more than 800 rooms and large meeting facilities, so expect to see a lot of people milling around the huge, very dramatic atrium-style lobby, which soars twenty stories overhead. Rooms are spacious and tastefully furnished, though rather bland and corporate; upper rooms can have fine vistas. The view-struck should visit the revolving rooftop bar (avoid the restaurant) for a dizzying sight.

Singles: $159-$228; doubles: $184-$258; suites: $545-$690.

THE MERIDIEN HOTEL

50 Third St., Union Square - 974-6400

This sterile tower is located just south of Market Street, not far from Union Square and the Moscone Center. Part of the international chain owned by the French government, the Meridien is to be commended for its personal attention, its attractive, comfortable rooms and its very good restaurant, Pierre. The rooms feature well-stocked minibars (good wines, mineral waters, European chocolates and biscuits), dramatic windows and comfortable beds. Everyone, from the concierge to the maids, is unusually friendly and helpful.

Singles: $140-$195; doubles: $170-$225; suites: $275-$1,000. Weekend packages available.

MIYAKO HOTEL

1625 Post St., Japantown - 922-3200

With 205 rooms, the Miyako is one of the smallest of San Francisco's modern hotels, and certainly one of the most pleasant. We prefer the simple, handsome Japanese-style rooms (tatami mats, futon-style beds and deep soaking tubs) over the Western-style rooms, though they still have such Oriental touches as shoji screens and wood-block prints.

Overstressed business people should request one of the twelve rooms or suites with private redwood saunas. The service is lovely, the Garden Bar is a peaceful spot, and the Miyako's location is great for sushi-bar-hopping in Japantown. Parking is $10 a day.

Singles: $93-$135; doubles: $113-$175; suites: $175-$300.

RAMADA RENAISSANCE HOTEL
55 Cyril Magnin St., Union Square - 392-5000

This massive new hotel has it all: over 1,000 rooms, a health club, several restaurants and bars, plenty of meeting and banquet rooms and the Renaissance Club, a service-oriented hotel-within-a-hotel. This Ramada will change your perception of the chain, if you're used to seeing the cookie-cutter motels across the country. The valets wear top hats and tails, the lobby is an expanse of marble, palms, statuary and ugly contemporary chandeliers, and the rooms can be quite attractive. Located midway between Union Square and the Moscone Center, the hotel attracts both tourists and conventioneering business people. Not for those who hate being lost in the crowd.

Singles: $115-$165; doubles: $130-$180; suites: $165-$500.

SAN FRANCISCO HILTON & TOWER
333 O'Farrell St., Union Square - 771-1400

Business must be booming at the Hilton, because it continues to expand like mad. The current room count is a staggering 1,700, and *another* addition is in the works that will bring the total up to 2,100—which will make this the largest hotel in Northern California. If you don't mind staying in a hotel bigger than most farm towns, you'll enjoy the Hilton. The tower rooms are large, quiet and comfortable, the location is convenient to Union Square shopping and downtown office buildings, and the views can be wonderful. Expect to see stampeding hordes of conventioneers and expect to get lost now and then.

Singles: $105-$180; doubles: $125-$200; suites: $335-$590.

SAN FRANCISCO MARRIOTT FISHERMAN'S WHARF
1250 Columbus Ave., Fisherman's Wharf - 775-7555

Although it aggressively woos the business traveler, the Marriott is not exactly convenient to downtown and the Financial District. Nor is it convenient to good restaurants, since Fisherman's Wharf is an enclave of overpriced tourist traps. But it is an attractive, quiet hotel with 256 well-appointed rooms and friendly service. Business travelers can take advantage of the complimentary morning limousine to the Financial District, and they can take a room on the top-floor Executive Level, a private-club floor that features Continental breakfast, complimentary newspapers and other bonuses. Valet parking is a reasonable $8 a day, with in and out privileges.

Singles: $135-$143; doubles: $150-$158; suites: $195-$350.

SHERATON AT FISHERMAN'S WHARF

*2500 Mason St.,
Fisherman's Wharf -
362-5500*

A tourist hotel in the heart of San Francisco's tourist mecca, Fisherman's Wharf. But the business traveler is not neglected: There's a shuttle service to downtown and an in-house Business Center. The 525 rooms are standard-issue Sheraton, which is to say modern, quiet and comfortably appointed, if less than inspirational in decor. The hotel's several restaurants are no better than the nearby Fisherman's Wharf seafood houses. Parking is just $7.50 a day, with in and out privileges.

Singles: $115-$150; doubles: $135-$170; suites: $300.

Airport

SAN FRANCISCO AIRPORT HILTON

*San Francisco International
Airport - 589-0770*

It may look like another terminal, but it's the Airport Hilton, the only hotel with the dubious distinction of being located on the airport's grounds. The decor is dreadful and there's nothing to do but sit by the pool and watch planes roar by overhead—but if you need to be right at the airport (perhaps for an early-morning departure) you will be reasonably comfortable here. Buses run every ten minutes to all the airline terminals, and parking is free.

Singles: $104-$120; doubles: $119-$135; suites: $340-$430.

SHOPS

TO MARKET, TO MARKET

Like all great cities, San Francisco is a classic market town. Even with the proliferation of suburban shopping malls, the city continues to draw shoppers from all over the Bay Area, even from all over the West (we know many Angelenos who come to San Francisco every December to do their Christmas shopping). The lure of San Francisco's shops is irresistible. You can pamper yourself on a Magnin's or Neiman's spree (facial, lunch, shopping), you can admire Union Square's jewels and designer clothes, you can wander such great neighborhood shopping streets as Union and Sacramento, where mixed in with the upscale chains and lively restaurants are terrific one-of-a-kind boutiques. Oh, the malls have struck the city too—such touristy places as Ghirardelli Square and Pier 39 and such chain-store collections as Embarcadero Center and Crocker Center Galleria—but these places have little to do with San Francisco's standing as a great shopping town. It's the city's creative mix that makes it such a powerful credit-card magnet. Since its founding, San Francisco has been an eccentric town, a strange collaboration between the conservative and the crazy. It's this mix that gives San Francisco's shopping scene its character. No matter what you're seeking—from the trendy to the staid, the classic to the bizarre—you'll find it here.

San Francisco's best shops, with a few exceptions, are clustered together in several great neighborhood shopping districts. Here are our favorites:

The most famous is Union Square, the downtown region that centers on a one-block spot of greenery of the same name. Aside from the department stores and big-money boutiques adjacent to the square, make sure to wander Sutter Street and Maiden Lane.

If words like Chippendale, Regency and French Provincial are music to your ears, head for the Jackson Square area of the Financial District. Roughly bordered by Pacific, Montgomery, Washington and Sansome, Jackson Square is home to many fine antiques dealers.

The young and the upscale have made Union Street in historic old Cow Hollow the city's premier shopping street. Start at Van Ness and head west about ten blocks or so, and you'll pass through a shopper's paradise. There are plenty of cafés and bars along the way to keep your spirits up.

One of the city's newest shopping districts is on upper Fillmore Street, from Sutter to Pacific. Vivande and Trio, two of our favorite city cafés, can be found here, along with a couple of dozen unique and worthwhile shops.

Further west in prosperous Presidio Heights is a several-block-long stretch of Sacramento Street lined with shops that would also be at home on trendy Union Street.

For a look at how the times have been a changin', head over to Haight Street in the Haight-Ashbury, the locus of flower power in the '60s. The baby boomers have moved up in the world, and mixed in among the remaining street people and diehard hippies are smartly dressed yuppies taking time out from restoring their Victorian houses to spend some money in the very '80s shops springing up here.

In general, we have limited our reporting on San Francisco's best shops to those found within city limits. However, a few exceptions were made, most notably in the "Food" section—several food shops in the East Bay and Marin are among the best in the country and are worth a trip from San Francisco.

Antiques

Along with poking into the scattered, idiosyncratic collection of shops listed in this section, antiques aficionados should make a pilgrimage to the Jackson Square area of the Financial District, on Jackson Street near Montgomery. This officially declared Historic District is rife with such fine antiques merchants as Norman Shepherd and John Doughty, both of whom sell seventeenth-, eighteenth- and nineteenth-century French and English pieces; Hunt Antiques, dealers of Regency, Jacobean and Georgian furniture and art; Carpets of the Inner Circle, which sells, appraises and restores antique rugs; and Robert Domergue, who specializes in French Provincial and Italian furniture.

ARGENTUM

1750 Union St., Cow Hollow - 673-7509

Glass cases of fine silver of the eighteenth and nineteenth centuries, including silverware, candlesticks, vases, some American arts and crafts pieces and affordable silver seals, line the walls of this lovely store, located at the back of an alley off Union Street.

Open Mon.-Sat. 11 a.m.-5 p.m.

ARTIQUES

2167 Union St., Cow
Hollow - 929-6969

Billing itself as "affordable art," Artiques is a major dealer of Icart and Maxfield Parrish vintage lithographs. There's also a varied assemblage of seventeenth- to early-twentieth-century etchings, lithographs and oils. Neither the art nor the prices are blue chip, but there are some very good pieces. If you poke around a bit, you're sure to find something you not only love but can afford.

Open Mon.-Sat. 10 a.m.-6 p.m., Sun. 10:30 a.m.-5:30 p.m.

BAUER ANTIQUES

1878 Union St., Cow
Hollow - 921-7656

Eighteenth-century French antiques are sold at reasonable prices. Downstairs is a bargain basement with English and French country furniture and some prints; these pieces pale beside what's available upstairs, but the occasional deal surfaces.

Open Mon.-Sat. 11 a.m.-5 p.m.

BIZEN

3314 Sacramento St.,
Presidio Heights - 346-3933

Although just large enough to step inside and turn around, this tiny shop is floor-to-ceiling with antique Japanese treasures. Among them is a respectable collection of Imari ware, both the handpainted sometsuke and the stenciled inban. Especially elegant and affordable are the eighteenth-century woven and lacquered flower baskets from Kyoto.

Open Tues.-Sat. 11 a.m.-4 p.m.

HAWLEY BRAGG

3364 Sacramento St.,
Presidio Heights - 363-8122

Hawley Bragg specializes in French antiques, but it certainly keeps an eye out for other interesting objects, and sells quality items in a good range of prices—from $3,000 for a spectacular pair of nickel silver chairs crowned with rams' heads, made in India for the English during the Raj, to $85 for framed hand-colored etchings and $75 for carved English lawn-bowling balls. Interior design services are also available.

Open Mon.-Sat. 10 a.m.-5:30 p.m.

WILLIAM B. MEYER

1714 Union St., Cow
Hollow - 673-3770

Some of the most arresting items in William B. Meyer's collection of silver and antiques are the antique military medals. The stern countenances of kings and queens suspended from ribbons and bars make wonderful and unusual gifts, ranging in price from $50 to $300. The silver napkin rings fall into the same category. The rest of his collection is made up of various antiques, primarily vintage English, American and San Francisco silver.

Open Tues.-Sun. 11:30 a.m.-5:30 p.m.

PARIS 1925

1954 Union St., Cow Hollow - 567-1925

There are more reproductions and art deco–inspired furniture and objects than vintage pieces here. Only the watches would be of any interest to the serious deco collector.

Open Mon.-Sat. 11 a.m.-7 p.m., Sun. 11 a.m.-6 p.m.

BILL PEARSON PRIMITIVE ART

3499 Sacramento St., Presidio Heights - 931-2712

Although the emphasis in Bill Pearson's collection is pre-Columbian, Oceanic and African, there's no telling what else you'll spy in this crowded, treasure-filled shop. After admiring the Colima dogs and Gold Coast statuary, we were stopped dead in front of a stunning Regency screen positioned next to a couple of Amish quilts. And there are a few worthy examples of vintage religious objects. Everything here has been chosen with an eye for quality, authenticity and curiosity.

Open Wed.-Fri. 12 noon-5 p.m.

ROYAL CHELSEA ANTIQUES

66 DeHaro St., South of Market - 552-7410

In this large store crammed with good examples of nineteenth-century English pine, from armoires to hutches to coffee tables—ideal pieces for creating a country-cottage look—prices are neither outlandish nor bargain-basement. There's also a less interesting collection of oak and mahogany furniture.

Open Mon.-Sat. 9 a.m.-5:30 p.m.

SEVEN SEAS LTD.

1909 Union St., Cow Hollow - 921-7090

This unprepossessing shop boasts a noteworthy assortment of folk art, textiles and kimonos from Indonesia, Thailand and Japan, respectively. The kimonos, all silk, are 30 to 40 years old, in good condition and range in price from $90 to $300. Among the handicrafts, standouts are the tightly woven baskets from the island of Lombok, just off the coast of Bali, the Indonesian wood carvings and the marvelous wayang, the intricately carved shadow puppets.

Open Mon.-Sat. 10 a.m.-6 p.m., Sun. 12 noon-5 p.m.

THERIEN & COMPANY

534 Sutter St., Union Square - 956-8850

411 Vermont St., South of Market - 956-8850

Therien's two serene, civilized shops, one in Union Square and one in the shadow of the 101 Freeway, feature old Sheffield plate and antique porcelain, much of which is beautifully displayed on seventeenth- and eighteenth-century furniture. There are some especially lovely silver pieces, including a few contemporary tea services and serving utensils.

Open Mon.-Fri. 9:30 a.m.-5 p.m., Sat. 10 a.m.-4 p.m.

TREASURE OF AFRICA
1842 Union St., Cow Hollow - 346-3526

One large skylit room up a flight of stairs, this recently opened gallery deals in the antique and contemporary handicrafts and ceremonial sculpture of primarily the Gold and Ivory coasts of West Africa, along with a few odd Oceanic pieces. The selection is large and the prices affordable.

Open daily 10 a.m.-10 p.m.

WEST OF THE MOON
3464 Sacramento St., Presidio Heights - 922-4650

Established fifteen years ago as a folk-art gallery, West of the Moon is now actually three separate concerns at the same address: Lost Art, which deals in artifacts of Africa, the Americas and Oceania; New World Antiquities, which features pre-Columbian and especially Mayan pieces; and West of the Moon, which now focuses on native North American work.

Open Wed.-Sat. 12 noon-6 p.m., or by appt.

Beauty

BEAUTY PRODUCTS

AGRARIA
1156 Taylor St., Nob Hill - 771-5922

Agraria's house blend of potpourri, redolent of roses and Provence, is as appealing as the romantic shop. Your sense of smell will be agreeably assaulted by the sachets, potpourris, candles and Floris of London soaps, oils and fragrances.

Open Mon.-Sat. 10 a.m.-5 p.m.

THE BODY SHOP
2072 Union St., Cow Hollow - 922-4076

Seventeen years ago in Berkeley the Body Shop made its mark in the world of toiletries by opening a small shop selling quality handmade soaps—in all sorts of traditional and exotic fragrances—that were cut, wrapped and labeled right there. They also initiated the practice of recycling containers and customizing scents. Consistent high quality and an interesting variety of products ensured its success; there are now five shops in the Bay Area, one in New York and a mail-order business. The long, narrow Union Street shop is filled with temptations for self-indulgence—the entire Body Shop line of bath oils, bubble baths, lotions, soaps, shampoos, masks, creams, cleansers and those intoxicating essential perfume oils that range from Canton rose to frankincense to muguet. A few imported toiletries are also stocked, along with Mason Pearson and Altesse brushes, Karina combs, perfume bottles, soap dishes, natural sponges and so much more.

Open Mon.-Sat. 10:30 a.m.-6 p.m., Sun. 11 a.m.-5 p.m.

CRABTREE & EVELYN

50 Post St. (Crocker Center Galleria), Financial District - 392-6111

Whimsy and nostalgic romance are the watchwords of this renowned English fragrance company. We are especially fond of the Alice in Wonderland and Babar soaps and tins, as well as the sweet little baskets, which make wonderful hostess gifts. Also noteworthy are Crabtree's scented bath oils, sculpted soaps, rosewood brushes and attractively packaged teas and jams. There's another branch in the Embarcadero Center (781-7926).

Open Mon.-Fri. 9:30 a.m.-6 p.m., Sat. 10 a.m.-5 p.m.

L'HERBIER DE PROVENCE

1728 Union St., Cow Hollow - 928-4483

Take three steps down from the sidewalk, close your eyes and breathe. You'll either start sneezing violently or think you've been transported to a linen closet somewhere in the south of France. The walls in this lovely, wood-paneled shop are festooned with romantic bunches of dried flowers, and there are baskets, wooden boxes and glass vases replete with handmade scented soaps and potpourri of various blends from Provence. Also stocked in abundance are spices and teas.

Open Mon.-Sat. 10:30 a.m.-7 p.m., Sun. 10:30 a.m.-6 p.m.

SUTRO BATH COSMETICS

1980 Union St., Cow Hollow - 563-7624

Like the Body Shop, Sutro Bath carries its own, but not as extensive, line of toiletries. It also stocks the complete lines of English toiletries made by Potter & Moore and Taylor of London, along with a variety of bath accessories.

Open Mon.-Sat. 10 a.m.-6 p.m., Sun. 11 a.m.-5 p.m.

BODY SHOPS

ELIZABETH ARDEN
230 Post St., Union Square - 982-3755

There's nothing like walking through this famous red door for a steam and a facial to make you forget your cares—and a couple of years, too. The rich and the severely stressed should try the five-hour, head-to-toe beauty treatment, which runs $200 and includes a light lunch; two other package deals, both of which cost $150, combine facials, hair styling, manicures, eyebrow shaping and makeup application. Arden's complete line of makeup and skin- and hair-care products are also sold here (at full retail price).

Open Mon.-Sat. 8:30 a.m.-5:30 p.m.

THE BEAUTY TERRACE
150 Stockton St. (Neiman-Marcus), Union Square - 362-3900

Urban life got you down? Then visit Neiman's for a "Day of Pampering." You'll decompress via an hour-long body massage, an hour-long facial, a hair cut and styling, a light lunch (wine included) in the lovely Rotunda restaurant, a manicure, a pedicure and a makeup job. You'll emerge $150 poorer, but you'll certainly feel like a queen for a day. For those with less time and money, The Beauty Terrace offers each service separately. Its technicians are skilled and friendly.

Open Mon.-Wed. & Sat. 10 a.m.-6 p.m., Thurs.-Fri. 10 a.m.-8 p.m.

MARY OEI'S ABOUT FACE
629 Taylor St., Union Square - 775-9452

Mary Oei and her staff are patient, thorough facial experts who see each client's face as a new and different challenge. Depending on your skin type and your specific problems, they will use one of seven different lines of professional European skin-care products. A one-and-a-half-hour facial, which mainly consists of a deep pore cleaning and peeling, costs $60 with Mary or $48 with one of her associates. The salon also offers waxing, manicures and pedicures.

Open Mon.-Sat. 9 a.m.-7 p.m.

CHRISTINE VALMY
166 Grant Ave. (Transitions Hair Salon), Union Square - 433-7174

Valmy recently closed its Maiden Lane shop and joined forces with Transitions, a prestigious downtown hair salon. All the same services, including the acclaimed seven-day, deep-peel skin-renewal treatment, are still being offered, as are Valmy's Byogenic skin-care products, which are well regarded for their all-natural ingredients and effectiveness. Manicures, pedicures, waxing and makeup are also available.

Open Mon.-Wed. & Fri.-Sat. 10 a.m.-6 p.m., Thurs. 10 a.m.-7 p.m.

HAIR SALONS

CONFETTI

334 Presidio Ave., Presidio Heights - 921-2164

A very small (just two stylists and one barber) but very good salon that will give you a handsome, natural haircut. The staff is willing to take clients in the evening. Haircuts are in the $25-to-$30 range.

Open Mon.-Sat. 9:30 a.m.-5:30 p.m. (hours flexible).

CUTTING CORNER

Stockton St. & Geary St. (I. Magnin), Union Square - 362-2100

A good, basic hair salon for men and women on I. Magnin's sixth floor. Don't come here for the latest haircut that's making the SOMA nightclub rounds, but do make an appointment if you want a cut that is stylish but won't draw too much attention to yourself. Men's cuts are a reasonable $16, and women's are $28; weaving, perms and the like are also offered.

Open Mon. & Thurs.-Fri. 9:30 a.m.-8 p.m., Tues.-Wed. & Sat. 9:30 a.m.-6 p.m., Sun. 12 noon-5 p.m.

MASA'S HAIR SALON

2536 California St., Presidio Heights - 921-4033

The six stylists at Masa's are adept at chic but not overly trendy haircuts. A basic cut and style for men or women ranges from $25 to $35, with extra charges for coloring, special moisturizing treatments and so on. Most of the stylists will stay late to give you an after-work cut. There is neither a manicurist nor a makeup person on staff.

Open Mon.-Sat. 9:30 a.m.-5 p.m. (hours flexible).

TRANSITIONS

166 Grant Ave., Union Square - 433-7174

This longtime downtown salon has about twenty stylists, all of whom can provide you with a fashionable cut that suits your face and lifestyle. Cuts range from $30 to $45, depending on the stylist. Every conceivable hair service is provided, along with complete facial and beauty treatments at Christine Valmy, which shares Transitions's large space.

Open Mon.-Wed. & Fri.-Sat. 10 a.m.-6 p.m., Thurs. 10 a.m.-7 p.m.

Books & Stationery

BOOKS

ARGONAUT BOOK SHOP
786 Sutter St., Union Square - 474-9067

A simple, uncluttered, quiet shop stocked with rare and out-of-print books, prints, maps and manuscripts. Owner Robert Haines has an especially fine collection of books and maps of early California, including the Gold Rush days, along with some lovely prints of old San Francisco. A must for the California history buff.

Open Mon.-Fri. 9 a.m.-5 p.m., Sat. 9 a.m.-4 p.m.

THE BOOKPLATE
2080 Chestnut St., Marina District - 563-0888

The book selection is small and unexceptional. But the Bookplate is worth knowing about anyway for its quiet, attractive art deco café in the back. One could spend a very happy afternoon sipping a Chardonnay or cappuccino in the café while losing oneself in a new murder mystery or gossipy bestseller.

Open Mon.-Fri. 8:45 a.m.-10:30 p.m., Sat. 9 a.m.-10:30 p.m., Sun. 9 a.m.-9:30 p.m.

BOOKS INC./TRO HARPER
140 Powell St., Union Square - 397-1555

This large, well-stocked general bookstore has something for everyone. Especially noteworthy are the cookbooks. Its weeknight hours make Books Inc. a good spot for nocturnal bookworms.

Open Mon.-Fri. 9:30 a.m.-11:30 p.m., Sat. 9:30 a.m.-7 p.m., Sun. 10 a.m.-6 p.m.

THE BOOKSMITH
1644 Haight St., Haight-Ashbury - 863-8688

Haight Street's newest bookshop is a sign of the neighborhood's gentrification. The store is spacious, attractive, organized and stocked with a well-rounded selection of new books. The collections of fiction (especially oversized paperbacks), mysteries, cookbooks and photography and architecture books is commendable.

Open Mon.-Fri. 10 a.m.-9 p.m., Sat.-Sun. 10 a.m.-6 p.m.

Browser Books

2239 Fillmore St., Upper Fillmore - 567-8027

An appealing rabbit-warren in which you can happily lose yourself for hours. Don't let the small storefront fool you—one room leads to another, and all are crammed with books of every kind; we particularly like the large collection of contemporary and classic fiction, the unusual travel books and the used books. If you aren't sure about that newest sensation, take it in the back reading room, pour yourself a cup of coffee, plop down on one of the chairs and see if the first chapter grabs you.

Open Mon.-Sat. 10 a.m.-10 p.m., Sun. 9 a.m.-10 p.m.

Charing Cross Road

1687 Haight St., Haight-Ashbury - 552-4122

You're sure to walk out with a couple of finds after visiting this clean, well-organized shop, which boasts an intriguing collection of used hardcover and paperback books. Prices are very fair, and the friendly owners will be happy to try to fill any special requests for hard-to-find books.

Open daily 11 a.m.-6 p.m.

City Lights Books

261 Columbus Ave., North Beach - 362-8193

A cultural mecca since 1953, City Lights is synonymous with the literary life of the city. Through its door have passed the movers and shakers in every branch of the arts from the Beat Era to the present. Still going strong, the bookstore has expanded—a former Italian travel agency next door is now a room devoted entirely to poetry—and boasts possibly the best selection of periodicals and books in town. Each member of the staff has a particular area of expertise, be it film or music or nineteenth-century French poetry, and keeps the inventory in that area up to date. Stop here to while away an hour or two checking out the latest small press publications, then buy the latest novel by that 23-year-old literary prodigy and saunter down the street for an espresso at the Puccini.

Open daily 10 a.m.-11:30 p.m.

Cookbook Corner

620 Sutter St., Union Square - 673-6281

Tucked away in the YMCA building is this fine collection of new, used and out-of-print cookbooks from all over the world, including wine books and regional charity cookbooks. Its location a few doors away from Williams-Sonoma makes this block a mecca for cooks.

Open Mon.-Sat. 9:30 a.m.-6 p.m.

FANNING'S BOOKSTORE

900 North Point St. (Ghirardelli Square), San Francisco - 775-2067

Tiny though it may be, this bookshop is notable for two things: a fine collection of both famous and little-known books by Northern California writers (dead and living) and a very large selection of travel books. Owners Phil and Linda Fanning can almost always be found in their friendly and neat little shop.

Open Mon.-Sat. 10 a.m.-9 p.m., Sun. 10 a.m.-7 p.m.

GOURMET GUIDES

1767 Stockton St., North Beach - 391-5903

A cramped, wonderful shop just around the corner from Washington Square, Gourmet Guides sells virtually every travel guide, cookbook and wine book in print. If they don't have it, they'll get it for you. A must-visit for armchair travelers, amateur cooks and dedicated gourmets. Be sure to get on their mailing list—they ship all over the country.

Open Mon.-Wed. & Fri. 12 noon-5 p.m., Thurs. 12 noon-7 p.m., Sat. 12 noon-3 p.m.

HUNTER'S BARGAIN BOOKSTORE

151 Powell St., Union Square - 397-5955

An offshoot of Books Inc., Hunter's is a large, cluttered outlet for discount books, primarily publishers' closeouts. Most tend to be underwhelming specialty books, but you can almost always find at least one worthwhile bargain.

Open Mon.-Fri. 9:30 a.m.-9:30 p.m., Sat. 9:30 a.m.-7:30 p.m., Sun. 10 a.m.-6 p.m.

KUL'CHA

2162 Union St., Cow Hollow - 567-3945

You'll find all the latest coffee-table books in this attractive bookstore, with an emphasis on art, photography and cooking. There's an intriguing selection of used books and a small but serious collection of out-of-print and rare books on photography.

Open Mon.-Sat. 10 a.m.-10 p.m., Sun. 11 a.m.-6 p.m.

SIERRA CLUB BOOKSTORE

730 Polk St., Civic Center - 923-5600

Naturalists, environmentalists and outdoors enthusiasts should hike over to this small, friendly bookstore stocked with books and maps on the Bay Area, the Sierra, Alaska and the wild West. Hunters, real estate developers and hopeless urbanites won't feel at home here.

Open Mon.-Fri. 10 a.m.-5:30 p.m.

WILLIAM STOUT ARCHITECTURAL BOOKS

Unlike at the Sierra Club Bookstore, man-made structures are the things of beauty here. An outstanding collection of new and rare architectural books for both the scholar and the layman is well displayed on shelves and tables. A must for the

804 Montgomery St.,
Financial District -
391-6757

architect, designer, landscaper and dedicated homeowner.

Open Mon.-Wed. & Fri.-Sat. 10 a.m.-5:30 p.m., Thurs. 10 a.m.-9 p.m.

STATIONERY

DESK SET

3252 Sacramento St.,
Presidio Heights - 921-9575

One of life's little pleasures is good stationery and desk accessories. This is well understood at Desk Set, which stocks elegant stationery and cards that can be imprinted with whatever you want right there on the premises. Tempting knickknacks include picture frames, blank books bound in leather and cloth, letter openers, metal seals with sealing wax, stacks of agendas and smart address books, French Elysée fountain pens and even personalized computer paper.

Open Mon.-Fri. 10 a.m.-6 p.m., Sat. 12 noon-5 p.m.

GUMP'S

250 Post St., Union
Square - 982-1616

When young women from wealthy San Francisco families become engaged, they hurry over to Gump's to order impeccable engraved invitations on Crane paper. (While there, they also register for china and crystal.) The stationery department in this San Francisco shopping landmark is nonpareil, with exquisite stationery, striking desk accessories and antique and contemporary silver letter openers and picture frames. The level of service is as high as the prices.

Open Mon.-Sat. 9:30 a.m.-5:30 p.m.

OGGETTI

1846 Union St., Cow
Hollow - 346-0631

Oggetti's hand-marbled stationery from Florence is perfect for billets doux, thoughtful thank-yous and wonderful gifts. Marbling is clearly a major industry in Florence, since virtually everything in this charming eighteenth-century-style shop—from the notebooks to the bookmarks to the pencils—is covered in it, which robs it of some of its cachet. Out of the context of the shop, however, these items are perfectly lovely and romantic. We would be pleased as punch to receive a gift of the stationery with illuminated and gilded initials at the top.

Open Mon.-Thurs. & Sat. 10 a.m.-6 p.m., Fri. 10 a.m.-8 p.m., Sun. 11 a.m.-6 p.m.

QUANTITY POSTCARDS
1441 Grant Ave., North Beach - 986-8866

Not only does Quantity Postcards sell thousands of strange, outlandish and hilarious postcards, it publishes them, too. You'll find all its wacky cards here, along with boxes of vintage postcards and some put out by other publishers. Bring your sense of humor and plenty of stamps.

Open daily 12 noon-10 p.m. (hours may vary; call first).

UNION STREET PAPERY
2162 Union St., Cow Hollow - 563-0200

High-quality announcements, invitations and personal stationery are the specialty here, and the selection will occupy you for a while. The large assortment of greeting cards in this split-level shop includes some one-of-a-kind cards of handmade paper folded into fanciful shapes, and among the wrapping papers are some beautiful examples of hand marbling.

Open Mon.-Sat. 10 a.m.-6 p.m., Sun. 11 a.m.-5 p.m.

Children

BOOKS

LAND OF COUNTERPANE
3610A Sacramento St., Presidio Heights - 346-4047

This fine bookstore speaks to children and parents alike. An incomparable selection of books, cassettes and records for infants to sixteen-year-olds is invitingly displayed and can be intelligently discussed and recommended by the staff members, who know and love the merchandise. Storytellings are frequently held on Saturdays, along with occasional guest appearances by the country's best children's-book authors and illustrators.

Open Mon.-Sat. 10:30 a.m.-5:30 p.m.

CLOTHES

ARLEQUIN

Cheerful, attractive and expensive, Arlequin sells designer clothing for infants and small children. There is also a small but very well-chosen selection of well-made educational toys from such makers as Ambi, as well as stuffed animals from

900 North Point St. (Ghirardelli Square), Fisherman's Wharf - 776-0428

Gund. The quality throughout is high. Two other branches are located in the Embarcadero Center (788-6393) and the Crocker Center Galleria (989-8011).

Open Mon.-Fri. 10 a.m.-9 p.m., Sat.-Sun. 10 a.m.-6 p.m.

BENETTON 012

450 Powell St., Union Square - 391-4146

The very same wool and cotton sweaters and cotton shirts and pants that adorn seemingly every teenager in the western world are now made to fit children under the age of twelve. If your third-grader is fashion conscious, he'll talk you into spending far more than you should (even though the prices are not unreasonable).

Open Mon.-Sat. 10 a.m.-7 p.m., Sun. 12 noon-5 p.m.

KIDS ONLY

1415 Haight St., Haight-Ashbury - 552-5445

If you can't abide clutter, stay out of this shop. But if you're looking for attractive, practical, fairly priced clothing for infants and children, you will have come to the right place. No $150 designer playsuits here, just fun, well-wearing clothes, with a particular emphasis on OshKosh. Kids Only is also a must-visit for clothing historians and lifelong hippies—it stocks tiny tie-dyed T-shirts in psychedelic colors.

Open Mon.-Sat. 10 a.m.-7 p.m., Sun. 11 a.m.-7 p.m.

LILLIPUT

2040 Union St., Cow Hollow - 929-1983

After you've decked out your little darling in designer diapers, come here to find the appropriate shoes. Elefanten from Germany, Primigi from Italy and Baby Bottle from France are just a few of the makers you'll find, with their charming creations in patent leather, kid and canvas, along with a selection of socks that will guarantee your baby the smartest little tootsies in town. Once you tear yourself away from the shoes, you'll notice the few mildly interesting items of clothing.

Open Mon.-Sat. 10 a.m.-5:30 p.m., Sun. 12 noon-5 p.m.

MUDPIE

1699 Union St., Cow Hollow - 771-9262

Running the gamut from OshKosh to Jean Bourget and Dior, this moderately upscale shop has a few surprises. How can you resist red watermelon rompers with little black seeds, complete with a hat fashioned to resemble half a watermelon to crown your little tot?

Open Mon.-Sat. 10:30 a.m.-6 p.m., Sun. 12 noon-5 p.m.

SHERIDAN-FLYNN

*3462 Sacramento St.,
Presidio Heights - 921-5961*

Any shop that bills itself as an "infant clothier" is most likely going to involve a major fiscal and cultural experience. And, yes, this place is not only expensive, but the help is pretty darn huffy. Our innocent note-taking goaded one tight-lipped matron into asking us to leave. To be fair, however, we must admit that this "clothier" does carry some very smart imported duds—Tartine de Chocolat is just one of the standouts—and the most darling pair of tiny suede shoes from Germany caught our eye as we were being ushered out.

Open Mon.-Sat. 10 a.m.-6 p.m.

THURSDAY'S CHILD

*1980 Union St., Cow
Hollow - 346-1666*

Why are so many childrens' clothing shops, even expensive ones, such pandemonium? Is the clothing too small to organize? There are some great finds in this packed basement shop, such as Monkey Wear—imaginative, pricey, all-cotton playclothes—if you have the patience to sort through the stacks on tables and shelves and all the merchandise hanging from the ceiling and walls.

Open Mon.-Sat. 9:30 a.m.-6 p.m., Sun. 11 a.m-4 p.m.

STELLA VOLO KIDS

*2056 Chestnut St., Marina
District - 346-6722*

This boutique, an offshoot of the Stella Volo womenswear shop nearby, has a small but exceptionally wonderful collection of children's clothing. Our favorites are the old-fashioned cowboy hats (either straw or felt, just like we had as kids), the brightly colored cotton playclothes from such makers as Berlingot, the socks and the tiny designer eyeglass frames, including rhinestone-studded cat's-eye models.

Open Mon.-Sat. 10:30 a.m.-6:30 p.m., Sun. 11 a.m-6 p.m.

YOUNTVILLE

*2416 Fillmore St., Upper
Fillmore - 922-5050*

If the unpleasant mothball aroma doesn't scare you off, you'll discover a well-rounded selection of clothes for newborns to five-year-olds, with a few things for older children. Fabrics are cotton, and the makers range from Absorba to such trendy-tot outfitters as Malima, Baby Guess and Ton Sur Ton. There are also a few Brio and Ambi toys.

Open Mon.-Sat. 10 a.m.-6 p.m., Sun. 12 noon-5 p.m.

FURNITURE

JONATHAN-KAYE

Literally spilling out the door onto the sidewalk, unfinished pine furniture for children is the principal merchandise here.

3485 Sacramento St.,
Presidio Heights - 563-0773

There are bunk beds and dressers, chairs and desks, all well made, reasonably priced and just waiting for the stroke of the paintbrush. Jammed in with the furniture are some high-quality toys by Brio and Gund, a respectable selection of Paddington bears and a good selection of books.

Open Mon. 12 noon-6 p.m., Tues.-Fri. 10:30 a.m.-6 p.m., Sat. 10 a.m.-5:30 p.m.

TOYS

FAO SCHWARZ

180 Post St., Union
Square - 391-0100

Though nationally famous, this acclaimed toy store from New York seems unremarkable now that fine children's stores are proliferating. True, there are captivating train sets, Steiff and Trupa stuffed animals and extravagant child-size race cars, but most of the merchandise can be found at any decent toy store, in many cases for less money. Still, no child will object to an FAO Schwarz outing.

Open Mon.-Sat. 10 a.m.-6 p.m.

HEFFALUMP

1694 Union St., Cow
Hollow - 928-4300

This sunny, Victorian shop is an orderly cornucopia of educational toys and books—and it even has a lot of things that kids really go for, like the fluorescent-blue rubberish, creepy rope-thing that can be stretched to unbelievable lengths only to snap back to its original size—as the kids say, gnarly. This makes an interesting contrast to the veritable menagerie of Steiff stuffed animals and oversized, hand-carved and -painted Pinocchios mounted on the walls, slated for heirloomdom. You might have some trouble dragging your child out of here; ten minutes past closing time we were asked politely to please leave.

Open Mon.-Wed. & Fri. 10 a.m.-6 p.m., Thurs. 10 a.m.-7 p.m., Sun. 11 a.m.-5 p.m.

JEFFREY'S

445 Sutter St., Union
Square - 982-3320

An all-purpose toy store with a representative collection of contemporary kids' toys. Dolls range from Madame Alexanders to Barbies, and you can find everything from Care Bears to Laser Tag to intelligent educational toys. Two other shops can be found in the Embarcadero Center (397-3320) and Ghirardelli Square (776-6780).

Open Mon.-Sat. 9:30 a.m.-6 p.m.

THE LITTLEST MOUSE

3480 Sacramento St.,
Presidio Heights - 567-5121

Can't afford the down payment on that Victorian dream house? Then work out some of your frustration in a small way, by having the skilled and accommodating staff here build you (or even your child) a doll-house replica, correct down to the Chippendale dining set, the chintz curtains and the (electrically wired) chandelier. They understand obsession here—it goes with the territory. They'll copy any house, or build one for you from their selection of kits, or sell you a kit to build your own. You can then fill it with furniture made to order or from the selection of miniature accoutrements available here, which is both sizable and choice (ask to see the hooked rugs painstakingly rendered in needlepoint). There's a wide range of options and prices, and this is one house-building experience that won't end in a life-and-death struggle with a contractor.

Open Mon.-Sat. 11 a.m.-5:30 p.m., or by appt.

STELLA VOLO KIDS

2056 Chestnut St., Marina
District - 346-6722

From $2 pinwheels to $110 pedal-powered Porsche 911s, Stella Volo has a fanciful and creative toy selection. There are only a few items, but each is a delight: Oreo cookie watches, inflatable globes, unusual crayons, sleek sailing ships and more. The clothing is also a joy.

Open Mon.-Sat. 10:30 a.m.-6:30 p.m., Sun. 11 a.m.-6 p.m.

Clothes

ACCESSORIES

BRAVA STRADA

3247 Sacramento St.,
Presidio Heights - 657-5757

All roughened concrete and smooth, cool marble, Brava Strada offers an eclectic sampling of Italian leather handbags, art jewelry and various accessories in an oh-so-postmodern environment. From the spare, bleached first floor, where art jewelry by both local and East Coast designers is displayed in long glass cases, and attractive leather goods by Italian designer Pibra slouch against the rough walls, you ascend a brief flight of marble steps (handed up by the attractive, well-turned-out Italian salesman in lieu of a bannister) to the mezzanine, where a large transparent case holding drawers of sweaters, sunglasses, gloves and belts awaits. Although the emphasis is on accessories, the store also carries three lines of knitwear: Kay Cosserat from Britain, Franco Guare from Los Angeles and Braeda & Huran from the Bay Area. Wardrobe consultation and personal shopping services are also available.

Open Mon.-Thurs. & Sat. 11 a.m.-6:30 p.m., Fri. 11 a.m.-8 p.m., Sun. 12 noon-5 p.m.

HOUSE OF HERMÈS

Stockton St. & Geary St. (I. Magnin), Union Square - 986-6184

A small boutique showcasing the accessories of this fine French firm is tucked away in I. Magnin. The leather belts and bags, silk scarves and ties, and silver and leather watches are all very well made and are, for the most part, exceptionally handsome—both chic and classic at the same time. They're also expensive. As we go to press, the House of Hermès is opening a separate boutique in Union Square.

Open Mon. & Thurs.-Fri. 9:30 a.m.-8 p.m., Tues.-Wed. & Sat. 9:30 a.m.-6 p.m., Sun. 12 noon-5 p.m.

SWAINE ADENEY

434 Post St., Union Square - 781-4949

Before you toddle over to the club for a spot of sherry, pop by Swaine Adeney with your valet and have him pick out a few trifles for you. While he selects some valises for your next big-game jaunt to the colonies, visit the room stocked with jolly fine rifles, all handmade in England by Westley Richards. Then have him choose a silk umbrella and a few pairs of leather gloves that will complement your tweeds on city strolls. It's no wonder Swaine Adeney is the umbrella maker to the Queen Mother—the umbrellas are beautifully made and proportioned, constructed of the finest woods, leathers, silks and nylons in a riot of colors and patterns, all supremely tasteful. The leather products—belts, briefcases, wallets, luggage—are equally well made and discreetly handsome. The prices limit the clientele to the landed gentry.

Open Mon.-Sat. 9:30 a.m.-6 p.m.

CASUAL

ACA JOE

295 Geary St., Union Square - 788-8780

Like The Gap and The Limited, Aca Joe stores are spreading like wildfire. And also like The Gap and The Limited, Aca Joe sells fun, colorful sportswear made of sturdy cottons, at prices that are more than fair. The unisex line is limited to T-shirts, sweatshirts, cotton sweaters, cotton jackets, striped shirts, chinos and elastic-waist shorts and trousers, many of which feature Aca Joe's logo. The logos we could live without, but we do like the simple styles and loose, comfortable cuts. There are several other branches, including one in Ghirardelli Square (474-6960).

Open Mon.-Thurs. 9:30 a.m.-8 p.m., Fri.-Sat. 9:30 a.m.-9 p.m., Sun. 10:30 a.m.-7 p.m.

BANANA REPUBLIC
224 Grant Ave., Union Square - 788-3087

Although there's no disputing the high quality and good cut of these khaki and natural-tone cotton ensembles, we wouldn't be caught dead wearing them abroad, especially in Africa or India. There's nothing like a logo-printed Banana Republic T-shirt to advertise your tourist status. But we cannot fault the chinos, mesh T-shirts, unadorned polo shirts, military-style shorts, bomber jackets and striped cotton shirts for stateside casual wearing, and we would gladly take the overpriced but well-designed and rugged luggage around the world. Visiting these safari-crazy stores is as fun as going on the Jungleland Cruise at Disneyland. Devotees should make the trek up to Mill Valley (59 Throckmorton Street, 383-4900), where the Banana Republic craze started. There's another city branch at 2253 Polk Street (474-9711).

Open Mon.-Fri. 10 a.m.-8 p.m., Sat. 10 a.m.-6:30 p.m., Sun. 12 noon-5 p.m.

BENETTON
457 Powell St., Union Square - 989-2609

These bright Italian boutiques are becoming as common as McDonald's in American (and European) cities, San Francisco among them. Benetton's forte is the sweater; its wool and cotton pullovers and cardigans are almost always great looking and are reasonably priced. There are also some unisex cotton shirts, wool and cotton trousers and a few jackets. Despite being a chain, Benetton has managed to stay fashionable and young—though its ubiquitousness means your chic outfits will hardly be one of a kind. You'll find other Benettons in the Embarcadero Center (982-2609) and at 1969 Union Street in Cow Hollow (931-4347).

Open Mon.-Sat. 10 a.m.-6 p.m., Sun. 12 noon-5 p.m.

BOLLA
1903 Fillmore St., Upper Fillmore - 346-3131

Contemporary, casual sportswear for young-in-spirit men and women from such makers as Girbaud and Basic Elements. T-shirts, cotton trousers, slouchy linen jackets and chic miniskirts make up Bolla's fashionable (but not terribly cutting-edge) look. The selection is small but quite reasonably priced.

Open Mon.-Fri. 11 a.m.-6:30 p.m., Sat. 10:30 a.m.-6:30 p.m., Sun. 12 noon-5 p.m.

CP SHADES
2121 Fillmore St., Upper Fillmore - 923-544

Comfort is the statement here, not high fashion. CP Shades's baggy cotton-jersey T-shirts, cardigans, sweaters and elastic-waist skirts, pants and shorts for women are so comfortable that they'd make fine pajamas. The look is rumpled, beachy and oh-so-California, and the prices are within reach, if a bit high given the clothing's simplicity. The line is starting to show up in department stores, but come here for the full range.

Open Mon.-Fri. 11 a.m.-7 p.m., Sat. 11 a.m.-6 p.m., Sun. 12 noon-6 p.m.

FLYING COLORS COTTON COMPANY
1872 Union St., Cow Hollow - 563-0440

T-shirt clothing for men and women in a riot of colors and styles is the main attraction. You can mix and match these mostly cotton, inexpensive separates to wear for aerobics, jogging, going to a go-go or just hanging out. A small investment in bright socks, black leggings or a red sweatshirt is a thrifty way to add panache to a tired wardrobe—and not just for the under-30 crowd.

Open Mon.-Fri. 9:30 a.m.-8 p.m., Sat. 9:30 a.m.-10 p.m., Sun. 9:30 a.m.-6 p.m.

THE GAP
1485 Haight St., Haight-Ashbury - 431-6336

934 Market St., Union Square - 397-2266

The Gap offers the best bargains in attractive American casual wear today, especially for men. The cotton shirts, trousers, polo shirts, denim jackets and jeans are similar in design and quality to the classic sportswear made by Ralph Lauren and Calvin Klein, at half the price: $30 for pleated cotton chinos, $28 for a colorful button-down shirt, $36 for an oversized cotton sweater. The women's line (cotton trousers, skirts, blouses, shorts and sweaters) is also fun, well fitting and low priced. And, of course, there are Levi's of every size and style. The Haight store is a sign of how times have changed—it sells its bright, very-'80s clothing on the acclaimed corner of Haight and Ashbury, where patched jeans and tie-dye once reigned supreme. There are many other stores, including one on Polk, one on Chestnut and one on Market in the Castro.

Open Mon.-Fri. 10 a.m.-8 p.m., Sat. 11 a.m.-7 p.m., Sun. 11 a.m.-6 p.m.

MAC
814 Post St., Union Square - 775-2473

Who says you shouldn't judge a book by its cover? That's precisely why one shops here. Not only does this clothing imply what one is about, some of it literally spells it out, like Katharine Hamnet's eccentric T-shirt couture, boldly lettered with political slogans. Or make your statement with avant-garde clothing by Texan Todd Oldham and Betsy Jackson's sleazette designs. Just making any purchase here will make a statement—about your financial status.

Open Mon.-Sat. 11 a.m.-7 p.m.

Z CLOTHING
1858 Union St., Cow Hollow - 567-0290

Across the Street from Z Gallerie, purveyor of the trendy objet, sits Z Clothing, its counterpart in clothing for men and women. For the young (or for those who still operate in that territory) are the cutting-edge creations of KitKit, Inwear/Matinique, A.K.A. and Café, with prices that reflect their degree of chic. The bright, uncluttered shop is run by a youthful staff who can give you a few pointers on how to assemble the correct look.

Open Mon.-Sat. 10:30 a.m.-6:30 p.m., Sun. 11 a.m.-6:30 p.m.

JEWELRY

CARTIER
231 Post St., Union Square - 397-3180

This large branch of the acclaimed Parisian jeweler and watchmaker is an opulently serene establishment, with glass cases glowing from the wealth inside. Naturally, you'll want to inspect the justly famous watches and the extravagant jewels, but don't neglect the fabulous—and not terribly overpriced—displays of silver. The staff is content to let you browse.

Open Mon.-Sat. 10 a.m.-5:30 p.m.

DI LELIO'S
1739A Union St., Cow Hollow - 771-8445

Not only is the antique silver and gold jewelry here worth a visit, but the vintage costume jewelry is some of the best we've found. Inspired abstract brooches from the '40s and chunky link bracelets from the '50s compose part of this choice, reasonably priced selection. And, as in every notable shop like this, the owner's enthusiasm for the merchandise overrides her interest in making a sale. A good place to visit periodically to see what new marvels have appeared.

Open Mon.-Tues. & Thurs.-Sat. 12 noon-5:30 p.m.

GUMP'S

250 Post St., Union Square - 982-1616

The choicest pearls and jade and the finest gold and silver are crafted into exquisitely simple pieces with price tags that will send you reeling. Equally attractive are the necklaces, earrings, brooches and rings made of such stones as tourmaline and lapis lazuli. Because Gump's combs the world for the finest raw materials and designs and manufactures these pieces itself, you can be assured of their quality. But you'll pay dearly for that assurance.

Open Mon.-Sat. 9:30 a.m.-5:30 p.m.

JEST JEWELS

2049 Union St., Cow Hollow - 563-8839

An adult version of the five-and-dime. You could walk out of here with a jewelry collection to rival the late Duchess of Windsor's in style if not in cost. The selection runs the gamut from faux baroque pearls to bits of anodized engine parts, and what an assortment of watches!—cheap tickers to handsome quartz knockoffs of serious timepieces.

Open Mon.-Sat. 10 a.m.-7 p.m., Sun. 12 noon-6 p.m.

LAYKIN ET CIE

Stockton St. & Geary St. (I. Magnin), Union Square - 362-2100

You can be assured that these baubles, while made of impeccable emeralds, rubies, diamonds and sapphires, will not make *too* much of a statement. As befits its longstanding relationship with I. Magnin, San Francisco's oldest old-money merchant, Laykin et Cie sells refined, elegant but not too ostentatious jewelry at appropriately high prices. The watch collection is lovely.

Open Mon. & Thurs.-Fri. 9:30 a.m.-8 p.m., Tues.-Wed. & Sat. 9:30 a.m.-6 p.m., Sun. 12 noon-5 p.m.

PERL HOUSE

2189 Union St., Cow Hollow - 922-9129

The hundreds of glass jars of beads and charms are enough to make your head spin—jumbo fake pearls, silver and gold plated baubles, carved and painted little animals, humorous charms, all in orderly rows in this bright little shop. The expert staff will sell you everything you need to create your own masterpieces or will custom-make your heart's desire. Repair services are also available.

Open Mon.-Sat. 11 a.m.-6:30 p.m., Sun. 11 a.m.-6 p.m.

ST. ELIGIUS

*1748 Union St., Cow
Hollow - 771-2282*

Reminiscent in spirit of the work of Tiffany's famous designer, Jean Schlumberger, precious stones are used as clever accents in the gold jewelry made here. The eye of the pheasant is a ruby; the dewdrops on the leaf are diamonds. A marked art deco influence is expressed in many of the pieces, but most of it is interesting in its own right. Along with gem appraisal and brokerage, St. Eligius is linked to a computer network that can locate that flawless, marquise-cut emerald you've been searching for.

Open Tues.-Sat. 10 a.m.-6 p.m.

SHREVE & COMPANY

*200 Post St., Union
Square - 421-2600*

An old San Francisco jeweler in an old building that survived the great earthquake, Shreve & Company is a bastion of conservative good taste. The window displays are always a treat, and the silver pieces are especially lovely. There's also a full range of crystal and fine gifts.

Open Mon.-Fri. 9:30 a.m.-5:30 p.m.

TIFFANY & COMPANY

*252 Grant Ave., Union
Square - 781-7000*

Even the least materialistic among us delights in receiving one of these famous little blue boxes—for inside will surely be something wonderful. Whether exorbitant or modest, a gift from Tiffany is almost always beautiful. We especially like Elsa Peretti's modern silver pieces, Jean Schlumberger's classic designs for gold and gems, and the timeless silver gift items, from teething rings to picture frames. Elegant brides register here for Tiffany's own sterling and china. Service is friendly, if slow, and the ambience is conducive to browsing.

Open Mon.-Sat. 10 a.m.-5:15 p.m.

TOM WING & SONS

*190 Post St., Union
Square - 956-4700*

Gump's isn't the only place in town for jade. Fans of the beloved gem of the Orient should visit Wing's elegant shop to inspect the unusual collection of striking lavender, apple-green and emerald-green jade. Asian antiques complement the jade, and diamonds, pearls and watches round out the jewelry selection.

Open Mon.-Fri. 9:30 a.m.-5:30 p.m., Sat. 9:30 a.m.-5 p.m.

UNION STREET GOLDSMITH

*1763 Union St., Cow
Hollow - 776-8048*

Specializing in gold jewelry and custom design, Union Street Goldsmith handles the work of a few well-known artisans whose designs are contemporary. Some pearls and silver jewelry are also showcased.

Open Mon.-Sat. 11 a.m.-5:45 p.m., Sun. 12 noon-4:45 p.m.

MENSWEAR

ARISTON
349 Sutter St., Union Square - 421-2830

This open, attractive store sells the clothing of just three designers: Armani, Ungaro and Hugo Boss. You'll cut a European figure in these slick, well-cut suits and separates. Service can be less than helpful.

Open Mon.-Sat. 9:30 a.m.-6 p.m.

BEBE
1977A Union St., Cow Hollow - 563-2777

Fine European menswear that is casual and trendy for the most part, featuring such brands as KitKit.

Open Mon.-Wed. & Sat. 11 a.m.-7 p.m., Thurs.-Fri. 11 a.m.-8 p.m., Sun. 11 a.m.-6 p.m.

BROOKS BROTHERS
201 Post St., Union Square - 397-4500

You won't turn any heads in these square duds, but neither will you find yourself next year with a closet full of dated clothes. Designed for the man who likes to be part of the crowd—and doesn't like to part with too much money—Brooks Brothers' clothes are well made of mostly natural fabrics, with cuts that are impervious to fashion's passing fancies. We find the suits, ties and shoes dreadfully dull, though they work well as Financial District uniforms. The cotton button-down shirts, invented by Brooks several decades back, are very good buys, and some of the sportswear does have a hint of flair.

Open Mon.-Sat. 9:30 a.m.-5:30 p.m.

BULLOCK & JONES
340 Post St., Union Square - 392-4243

This 135-year-old San Francisco institution is a bastion of maleness, a favorite of the conservatively dressed businessman. Inside the handsome, three-story building you'll find Hickey-Freeman and Oxxford suits, Cole Haan, Church's and Bally shoes, Pringle cashmere sweaters and Bullock & Jones's own shirts, ties, pajamas, sportswear and undergarments. Some of the more bold attempts at fashion—the checked silk sportcoats, polka-dot sport shirts, matching beach sets and pseudo-suede jackets—are dismal failures, but the classic pima cotton dress shirts, paisley ties, linen and wool trousers, Cole Haan loafers and cotton sweatsuits are all eminently wearable.

Open Mon.-Fri. 9:30 a.m.-5:30 p.m.

CASANOVA

1977B Union St., Cow Hollow - 929-7600

For men who like to look seriously turned-out, Casanova purveys mostly French and Italian menswear, highly tailored in fine wools and linens. Its clientele probably thinks Brooks Brothers is an investment firm.

Open Mon.-Sat. 10:30 a.m.-7 p.m.

COMME DES GARÇONS

70 Geary St., Union Square - 362-6400

Rei Kawakubo's clothing requires commitments on the part of the wearer—both a considerable financial commitment and a commitment to setting yourself apart from the ordinary buttoned-down hordes. If you have the wherewithal to spend $100 on a T-shirt and $1,000 on a sportcoat, venture into this stark, urban-chic boutique and let the hip staff give you a look that'll suit a SOMA nightclub or downtown art opening. Women can also get outfitted here.

Open Mon.-Sat. 10:30 a.m.-6:30 p.m.

MILANO VICE

2030 Union St., Cow Hollow - 923-9000

Well, the name of this shop does give one pause. Rumpled pastel jackets with football shoulders thrown artlessly over sleeveless T-shirts, the ensemble completed by a pair of white woven loafers sans socks, come immediately to mind. Unfortunate name aside, this shop carries strictly Italian suits, shirts and trousers executed in the same fabrics that Armani, Coveri, Valentino et al. use, for considerably smaller price tags. But then there's the cut . . .

Open Mon.-Fri. 10 a.m.-7:30 p.m., Sat. 10 a.m.-7 p.m., Sun. 12 noon-5 p.m.

POLO/RALPH LAUREN

90 Post St., Financial District - 567-7656

Ralph Lauren's old-rich clothing strikes a perfect balance between high fashion and conservative good taste—his dress and casual lines are infinitely more interesting than Brooks Brothers', though they'll still look at home on Wall Street or a world-class yacht. The suits, sportcoats and shirts have an American cut, and the sportswear has an American sense of color and preppiness, yet all the clothing has a touch of European sophistication. Though the fabrics and construction are very good, we still find the prices a bit excessive.

Open Mon.-Fri. 10 a.m.-6 p.m.

THE PRODUCER

The clothes displayed in this open, airy, low-pressure shop are stylish and young in spirit, though not overly trendy.

175

2133 Fillmore St., Upper Fillmore - 931-5000

Such makers as Mondo and Axis are represented in this collection of well-cut linen and wool sportcoats and trousers and cotton casual wear.

Open Mon.-Sat. 10 a.m.-6 p.m., Sun. 12 noon-5 p.m.

SWAINE ADENEY

434 Post St., Union Square - 781-4949

Along with a marvelous array of fine umbrellas and leather goods, Swaine Adeney sells properly stodgy business suits and tweeds, all sturdily made in Britain. Of note are the shoes, leather belts and gloves and discreet ties.

Open Mon.-Sat. 9:30 a.m.-6 p.m.

SYAAL

1864 Union St., Cow Hollow - 929-1864

We're not sure what "men's fashions with a woman's point of view" means (unless it's clothing a woman would like her husband or boyfriend to buy so he'll look right standing next to her), but that's the motto here. Given the merchandise displayed, which is mostly fine Italian sweaters and shirts and an amazing stock of socks, we don't think many men would object. But then we may be expressing a woman's point of view.

Open Mon.-Fri. 11 a.m.-7 p.m., Sat. 11 a.m.-6 p.m., Sun. 12 noon-5 p.m.

CALE THOMAS

900 North Point St. (Ghirardelli Square), Fisherman's Wharf - 885-5388

A small but well-chosen collection of classic (but not stuffy) clothing for young professional men and women. The offerings are pretty much limited to oxford-cloth and broad-cloth dress shirts, knit polo shirts, pleated wool and linen trousers, casual jackets and a few sweaters, with a small choice of handsome ties, suspenders and accessories. Prices are very reasonable.

Open Mon.-Sat. 10 a.m.-9 p.m., Sun. 10 a.m.-6 p.m.

GIANNI VERSACE

50 Post St. (Crocker Center Galleria), Financial District - 956-7957

Very chic, very Italian and very expensive. The line changes with each season; at our last visit to this minimalist shop (in spring), we admired a small collection of mostly black and white suits, sportcoats, trousers and shirts in linen and cotton. One particular black linen jacket that caught our eye was $795. The Italian salespeople will try to pounce on you, but with one well-timed withering look, they'll let you browse in peace.

Open Mon.-Fri. 9:30 a.m.-6 p.m., Sat. 10 a.m.-5:30 p.m.

WILKES BASHFORD

375 Sutter St., Union Square - 986-4380

A veritable supermarket of clothing for the fashionable man. Wilkes Bashford recently moved across the street to an even larger space; it now has six floors of suits, sportcoats, tuxedoes, shoes, shirts, overcoats and accessories—cutting-edge fashion for men who want more than a basic button-down. Valentino, Brioni, Matsuda, Armani—it's all here, and it's all expensive. The third floor (men's suits and jackets) keeps shoppers' spirits up with a bar, and the selection and quality of the clothing are exceptional. We especially like Wilkes Bashford's own line of shoes. Womenswear and jewelry are also sold.

Open Mon.-Sat. 10 a.m.-6 p.m.

LARGE & SMALL SIZES

ROCHESTER FOR THE SPECIAL MAN

Mission St. & 3rd St., South of Market - 982-6455

Rochester is a lifesaver for the fashion-conscious large or small man. The well-established store has an especially good selection of business wear—suits, sportcoats and trousers from the likes of Chaps, Hickey-Freeman, Lanvin and Hart, Schaffner & Marx—along with Cole Haan and Bally shoes up to size 16, and sportswear from a variety of makers.

Open Mon.-Sat. 9 a.m.-6 p.m., or by appt.

RECYCLED CLOTHING

AAARDVARK'S ODD ARK

1501 Haight St., Haight-Asbury - 621-3141

This musty shop, one of a chain of six scattered about the West, isn't as good as it once was; perhaps the competition has become more fierce for old military uniforms, '50s party dresses and vintage tweed sportcoats. But the selection of antique Hawaiian shirts remains good.

Open Mon.-Sat. 11 a.m.-7 p.m., Sun. 12 noon-6 p.m.

MASQUERADE

2237 Union St., Cow Hollow - 567-5677

Although the selection is small, the vintage clothing and jewelry sold here were chosen with a discerning eye. Everything is interesting and in good condition, but it's also fairly expensive, with Hawaiian shirts going for around $100. The bias-cut silk chiffon dresses, however, are worthy of Daisy Buchanan, and the rayon shirts could have been found in Kate Hepburn's or Gary Cooper's closet. Unusual gifts can be found among the accessories, like the handpainted ties, and good bargains sometimes show up on the sale rack (we found a beautiful red gabardine coat from the '40s for $35!). Definitely worth a visit.

Open daily 12 noon-7 p.m.

OLD VOGUE

1412 Grant Ave., North Beach - 392-1522

The previously worn leather jackets, tuxedoes, shirts, khaki trousers, Hawaiian shirts and party dresses in this cheerful shop are clean, moderately priced and in good condition. No priceless classics, but a better-than-average selection of popular recycled clothing.

Open Mon.-Thurs. 11 a.m.-10 p.m., Fri.-Sat. 11 a.m.-11 p.m., Sun. 12 noon-6 p.m.

LA ROSA

1711 Haight St., Haight-Ashbury - 668-3744

An unusual store that both rents new tuxedoes and sells used clothing, La Rosa has an excellent selection of near-perfect used overcoats, sportcoats, leather jackets and vintage tuxedoes and dinner jackets. Prices aren't rock-bottom, but they're justified by the quality.

Open Mon.-Sat. 11 a.m.-7 p.m., Sun. 11 a.m.-6 p.m.

THE WAY WE WORE

2238 Fillmore St., Upper Fillmore - 346-1386

No recycled junk here: The Way We Wore is home to a lovely collection of clothing from the last 100 years. Come here for a one-of-a-kind formal dress in perfect condition, with period shoes, gloves and jewelry to match; marvelous hats from the '20s, '30s and '40s; fluffy party frocks; and exceptionally beautiful white tuxedo shirts, many from the days of detached collars and some with fine detailing. Owner Doris Raymond loves her merchandise and will steer you to the best buys. Our favorite vintage clothing store in the city.

Open daily 11 a.m.-7 p.m.

SHOES

BALLY OF SWITZERLAND

238 Stockton St., Union Square - 398-7463

Supple leathers and skilled craftsmanship combine to make shoes that are boring and, in some cases, downright ugly. We don't object too strenuously to the sensible women's models, and the men's tie dress shoes are quite wearable, but the famous loafers, many with little gold doodads on the vamp, remind us of leisure suits. Nonetheless, their quality is legendary and their prices are high.

Open Mon.-Fri. 9:30 a.m.-6:30 p.m., Sat. 10 a.m.-5:30 p.m., Sun. 12 noon-5 p.m.

WALTER CHASE

222 Sutter St., Union Square - 362-5800

Walter Chase's own line of men's and women's shoes are the focus here, though a few other brands are sold—mainly Ralph Lauren's Polo shoes, which are actually manufactured by Chase. The shoes are classically handsome and carefully made, with quality price tags to match.

Open Mon.-Fri. 10 a.m.-6 p.m.

KENNETH COLE

2078 Union St., Cow Hollow - 346-2161

We certainly like Kenneth Cole's politics, but we're getting a little tired of his shoes. How much stamped leather and crepe soles can one work into a wardrobe? He's made some of our favorite shoes in the past and will, we hope, surprise us again. In addition to men's and women's shoes in this minimal, hip space are a few groovy accessories—socks, belts and sunglasses.

Open Mon.-Thurs. 10:30 a.m.-7:30 p.m., Fri.-Sat. 10:30 a.m.-8 p.m., Sun. 11 a.m.-7 p.m.

MAUD FRIZON

249 Grant Ave., Union Square - 398-1311

Frizon's fanciful, extravagant shoes, especially the women's, are among our very favorites, though our net worth is not yet sufficient to allow us to actually purchase a pair. Anyone interested in shoe fashion must visit this ultracool gallery dedicated to the shoe as an objet d'art.

Open Mon.-Sat. 10 a.m.-6 p.m.

GIMME SHOES

868 Post St., Union Square - 928-6677

After you've picked out a new ensemble at MAC (see "Casual" section) for a party at the hottest of the SOMA clubs, stop into this tragically hip store for a pair of the latest shoe sensations from Europe. Gimme's men's and women's shoes are le dernier cri in shoe design for the moneyed nightclub set.

Open Mon.-Sat. 11 a.m.-7 p.m.

MACY'S

Stockton St. & O'Farrell St., Union Square - 397-3333

Macy's boasts the most astounding shoe collection we've ever seen. From Sperry Topsiders to Pfister pumps, Keds tennies to Polo loafers, every shoe imaginable can be found somewhere in this madhouse. Highlights include a Charles Jourdan boutique stocked with a rainbow of its classic pumps in every heel size, and Macy's own Charter Club line of stylish, reasonably priced women's shoes for wide, narrow and large sizes. Cole Haan, Anne Klein, Ferragamo, Reebok, Van Eli, Timberland, Amalfi . . . you name it, it's here.

Open Mon.-Fri. 9:30 a.m.-9 p.m., Sat. 9:30 a.m.-6:30 p.m., Sun. 11 a.m.-6 p.m.

BRUNO MAGLI

285 Geary St., Union Square - 421-0356

Magli attracts an older, conservative crowd who can afford the prices and appreciate classic lines and quality Italian construction. Investment dressers put their money into these reassuringly classic shoes. Some of the men's models are especially handsome.

Open Mon.-Sat. 10 a.m.-6 p.m.

SHAW

2001 Union St., Cow Hollow - 922-5676

Shoe fetishists have their own map of the city, and Shaw's two shops are on it. The boot selection is ample, and the women's shoes range from Via Spiga to Anne Klein to Shaw's own good-looking line. The second shop is at 140 Grant Avenue near Union Square (433-6030).

Open Mon.-Sat. 11 a.m.-7 p.m., Sun. 12:30 p.m.-5:30 p.m.

ENZO VALENTI

249 Grant Ave., Union Square - 398-1141

If only Imelda could get a U.S. visa! Surely she'd make a beeline for this boutique, which offers the imaginative footwear of Maude Frizon, Andrea Carrera and, of course, Enzo Valenti, among others. There are also a few items of clothing by comparable designers at comparable prices. And don't worry, Ferdinand, there's also a large selection of men's shoes. Valenti has a second shop at 2117 Union Street in Cow Hollow (346-5111).

Open Mon.-Sat. 10 a.m.-6 p.m.

WOMENSWEAR

ALCOTT & ANDREWS

124 Geary St., Union Square - 981-2121

A conservative haven for well-bred women of all ages, from young stockbrokers to old–San Francisco matrons. The clothing in this huge, multilevel store is cleverly organized by color, making it easy to coordinate your new suits, blouses, dresses, shoes, sweaters and weekend wear. Its office wear, mostly of its own design, is properly sober, especially the dull suits; the casual wear is more lively, if on the preppy side. Within the store is a Ralph Lauren boutique, and scattered around it are tasteful accessories, from Coach bags to Cole Haan shoes. You won't turn the fashion world on end by appearing in these well-made clothes, but you can be assured of being correct and comfortable. The saleswomen are exceptionally agreeable.

Open Mon.-Fri. 10 a.m.-8 p.m., Sat. 10 a.m.-6 p.m., Sun. 12 noon-5 p.m.

AMBIANCE
1458 Haight St., Haight-Ashbury - 552-5095

One of our favorite women's boutiques in town, Ambiance is a sign of the Haight's changing times. The split-level shop houses an unusually attractive array of young-in-spirit sportswear, dresses, costume jewelry and accessories—some trendy, some discreet, most falling somewhere in between. We love the Betsey Johnson party dresses, the separates by Rabbit and Michel, the WASPy Jane Singer dresses, the jewelry and the leather bags. We also love the very fair prices.

Open Mon.-Fri. 10 a.m.-6 p.m., Sat. 10 a.m.-7 p.m., Sun. 12 noon-6 p.m.

LAURA ASHLEY
563 Sutter St., Union Square - 788-0190

Now a virtual emporium for the English country look, Laura Ashley can provide you with the wherewithal to dress yourself up like Little Bo Peep, then fling yourself down on a matching settee in a room wallpapered in the same little print. As with Ralph Lauren, there's a Laura Ashley product for just about every aspect of life, except paper towels, which we expect are in the works. Within the confines of the original concept, the clothing, linens and housewares are well designed and well made. The sallies into more contemporary-looking clothing, however, are ill conceived. There's another store at 1827 Union Street in Cow Hollow (922-7200).

Open Mon.-Sat. 10 a.m.-6 p.m.

ATTITUDE
2191 Union St., Cow Hollow - 567-9031

This place is aptly named; when we asked the salesman at the desk, his gold chains bobbing to the beat of the deafening disco music, what time they closed, he said eight or nine, depending on how they felt. Cool. We still can't tell if this is a discount designer clothing store or *what*, and the salespeople are reluctant to declare themselves. Randomly situated on the racks is an odd assortment of both day and evening frocks by the likes of Laura Bagiotti, Chanel, Claude Montana and Krizia at prices that look a bit low for this class of merchandise. The same goes for the belts and handbags hanging here and there. With a little patience and ear plugs, you could possibly come up with some great bargains.

Open Mon.-Sat. 11:30 a.m.-8 p.m., Sun. 12 noon-8 p.m.

BEBE
1954 Union St., Cow Hollow - 563-6661

A women's annex to the men's shop of the same name, Bebe caters to the European taste for tight leather skirts, large leather jackets and sweaters with leather worked into the designs.

Open Mon.-Wed. & Sat. 10:30 a.m.-7 p.m., Thurs.-Fri. 10:30 a.m.-8 p.m., Sun. 11 a.m.-6 p.m.

CACHET
3350 Sacramento St., Presidio Heights - 929-1141

No wandering in off the street at this shop. Every customer is buzzed in and greeted by either Ari or Brenda, who will show you fairly serious haute-bourgeois silk and linen creations by the likes of Emanuelle Khanh, Flora Kung and Levante. Stop in here before your next evening on the town—the cocktail dresses are worth checking out, though pricey.

Open Mon.-Sat. 11 a.m.-5:30 p.m.

DONNA EAST/WEST
1424 Grant Ave., North Beach - 397-4447

The setting is unimpressive, but there are some nice things to be found here. Donna's look is loose, unconstructed and natural, with linens, cottons and knits in attractive earth tones. Though very costly, the sweaters are worthwhile; more affordable are the Code Bleu jeans, Zanella separates and Joan & David shoes.

Open Mon.-Sat. 11 a.m.-7 p.m., Sun. 12 noon-5 p.m.

EARTHLY GOODS
1918 Union St., Cow Hollow - 922-0606

The racks and racks of natural-fiber clothing almost cause gridlock in this busy and very popular shop. At earthly prices, it offers a staggering choice of mostly cotton items by Esprit, Axis, Cotton Cruise, Metropole and Shadows, a line of beautifully cut, slightly faded separates. As if this weren't enough, there are racks of sale clothing in the back room. A few lines of moderately priced shoes are sold here, too: Zodiac, 9 West, Nina and Unisa. There's also a branch in Berkeley.

Open Mon.-Sat. 10:30 a.m.-6:30 p.m., Sun. 12 noon-6 p.m.

FUTUR ANCIEN
1801 Union St., Cow Hollow - 921-0140

Helmut Newton's models could stop here to outfit themselves on the way to a photo session. The starkly chic creations of Kansai and the eveningwear by Christopher Morganstern, Patricia Kline, Joan Vass and Michele Lamy are featured in this glittery little boutique. It's all very Eurostyle and very costly, down to the ultracool shades by Alain Mikli.

Open daily 11:30 a.m.-6:30 p.m.

JIMELLE

2237 Fillmore St., Upper Fillmore - 567-9500

"Clothes for the fashion confident" is Jimelle's motto, and if you're confident enough to shell out several hundred bucks for an Issey Miyake outfit, you'll fall in love with the place. It's all crisply modern and tasteful, and not everything is expensive. Don't miss the belt collection.

Open Mon.-Sat. 11 a.m.-7 p.m., Sun. 12 noon-6 p.m.

KHYBER CROSSING

2259 Fillmore St., Upper Fillmore - 563-2933

If you've seen *Out of Africa* six times, hie yourself to Khyber Crossing, a wonderfully romantic store that will have you looking like an English noblewoman in no time at all. The range is complete, from hardy khakis to fine linen blouses to lacy dresses perfect for bridesmaids or garden parties, by such designers as Ralph Lauren, Jessica McClintock, Ruff Hewn and Nancy Johnson. Completing the picture are discreetly helpful saleswomen and a spacious, uncluttered store accented with steamer trunks and British colonial touches.

Open Mon.-Fri. 10 a.m.-7 p.m., Sat. 11 a.m.-6 p.m., Sun. 12 noon-5 p.m.

KNITZ

1429 Grant Ave., North Beach - 391-3480

A minuscule, one-of-a-kind shop that's a must for any woman who loves knits. Anna Martin and Anna Katharina, a shy but friendly mother-and-daughter team, design and knit these sweaters and outfits themselves. A few ready-to-wear sweaters are available, but most of the outfits are custom-made—you pick from the selection of beautiful yarns and classic styles, and your ensemble is knitted to fit. The prices are fair given the quality and hand work.

Open Mon.-Sat. 10 a.m.-6 p.m.

TED LAPIDUS

156 Geary St., Union Square - 362-2660

The styles are ho-hum, the prices are frightening, and the slimy salesmen ooze phoniness. You can do much better elsewhere in Union Square.

Open Mon.-Sat. 10 a.m.-6 p.m.

JANICE LEE

Janice Lee's own sophisticated, fairly classic designs and a smattering of some Joanie Char creations fill the racks in this

1998 Union St., Cow
Hollow - 922-0253

sizable boutique, catering to the woman who can afford it. Belts, scarves and costume jewelry are within easy reach to correctly accessorize her look.

Open Mon.-Sat. 11 a.m.-8 p.m., Sun. 11 a.m.-6 p.m.

THE LIMITED

259 Post St., Union
Square - 398-8504

This spacious store is the nicest Limited we've been in—a handsome showcase for the mass-market clothes, with a pianist to keep the mood serene. It's not mere kismet that The Limited is one of Wall Street's biggest success stories—these people know how to design, price and market clothes. You won't be the only woman on your block wearing Forenza's youthful sweaters and jeans, Krizia's chic black-and-white ensembles and Outback Red's urban-farmgirl khakis and chambrays, but you'll find the price-to-quality ratio hard to resist. The socks, overcoats, watches and belts are also great buys. Other branches are located in the Crocker Center Galleria (788-3201) and the Embarcadero Center (398-1890).

Open Mon.-Sat. 10 a.m.-6 p.m., Sun. 1 p.m.-5 p.m.

MADRIGAL

590 Sutter St., Union
Square - 989-3478

Classic clothes for the traditional woman. Madrigal's own line of bright, preppy sportswear and cruisewear is only mildly overpriced and is guaranteed to keep you looking solidly Republican. There's also some sportswear by Ruff Hewn and shoes by Cole Haan.

Open Mon.-Sat. 10 a.m.-6 p.m.

JESSICA MCCLINTOCK

353 Sutter St., Union
Square - 397-0987

Upstairs are a few racks of hyper-romantic "designer" silk and lace dresses, some of which make lovely wedding dresses and elegant eveningwear. Downstairs are a few racks of "off-the-rack" silk and lace dresses, which make just as lovely wedding or evening dresses and cost half as much, along with less formal cotton dresses. All of Jessica McClin-tock's dresses are ultrafeminine and most are old-fashioned in spirit. Don't judge them on the hanger—they'll look better on you.

Open Mon.-Sat. 10 a.m.-6 p.m.

MONDI

50 Post St. (Crocker Center
Galleria), Financial
District - 781-4604

Mondi's chic, colorful, moderately expensive sportswear is European in tone and is neither dully traditional nor annoy-ingly trendy. The sweaters and knit ensembles are particular-ly winning.

Open Mon.-Fri. 9:30 a.m.-6 p.m., Sat. 10 a.m.-5 p.m.

NEW YORK WEST
2100 Union St., Cow Hollow - 567-8130

If you're what *W* calls a P.Y.T. (pretty young thing), you'll look pretty fetching in one of the Biondi (of London) stretchy, pleated party dresses sold here. Or you might want to drape yourself in one of the metal-mesh halters for a change. It's all a little too bright and sexy in a clichéd manner. We were particularly fascinated by a two-piece bathing suit that had no sides on the nether half—just a sort of clamplike thing. The saleslady assured us they were selling like hotcakes, which gave us a good idea of the clientele.

Open Mon.-Sat. 10:30 a.m.-6:30 p.m., Sun. 12 noon-5:30 p.m.

Q'S
3349 Sacramento St., Presidio Heights - 346-7481

Q's emphasis is on designer sportswear. Silk Club, Dorthée Bis, Marithé Girbaud and others of that ilk are all represented with their various renditions in silk and distressed denim.

Open Mon.-Fri. 10:30 a.m.-6:30 p.m., Sat. 10 a.m.-6 p.m., Sun. 12 noon-4 p.m.

PHILIPPE SALVET
2163 Union St., Cow Hollow - 563-4453

Truly a boutique in both size and selection, this shop's three predominant lines are Philippe Salvet, Michelle Lamy and Adrienne Vittadini. The prices are what you would expect, and the merchandise is not particularly exciting.

Open Mon.-Sat. 11 a.m.-6 p.m., Sun. 12 noon-5 p.m.

TALBOTS
2 Embarcadero Center, Financial District - 781-2128

We've always suspected that Diane Feinstein sends a personal shopper here. Silk bows at the throats of suit-clad women bound for success while clasping smart briefcases come immediately to mind upon entering this shop. The clothing is well made and moderate to expensive in price, and its rapid expansion from a mail-order business to a burgeoning chain verifies its strong following. Talbots's tailored, no-nonsense style may be in for some modification, however, now that the store has been brought under the same management as Ann Taylor.

Open Mon.-Fri. 10 a.m.-6 p.m., Sat. 10 a.m.-5 p.m.

ANN TAYLOR
441 Sutter St., Union Square - 989-5381

Although in the last year or so the clothing seems to have lost just a little of its sophistication, we still love Ann Taylor and always find several items worth buying. As the years have

185

passed, more of the clothing has become Ann Taylor's own label, which is designed for young-in-spirit urban women who may have just graduated from Esprit's hip-student look. Always worthy are the leather jackets and belts, pleated trousers in seasonal linens or wools, white silk and cotton blouses, Girbaud-style cotton pants, beautiful Joan & David shoes and city-slicker dresses that can go from the office to the evening. Prices vary wildly—one little cotton blouse may be $90 and another may be $35. In back are a couple of permanent sale racks that frequently include something of interest. Other Ann Taylors can be found in Ghirardelli Square (775-2872) and the Embarcadero Center (989-5355).

Open Mon.-Wed. & Fri.-Sat. 10 a.m.-6 p.m., Thurs. 10 a.m.-8 p.m.

THREE BAGS FULL

2181 Union St., Cow Hollow - 567-5753

Known for its high-quality wool sweaters, many of which are handknit, for women, men and children, Three Bags Full also stocks special soaps for wool and an astounding variety of socks. Occasionally it'll have a few Italian linen separates to complement the sweaters, as well as a few wonderful Il Bisonte handbags.

Open Mon.-Sat. 11 a.m.-6 p.m., Sun. 12 noon-5 p.m.

TREND

3 Embarcadero Center, Financial District - 362-0799

Not everything here is wonderful—in fact, some of the clothing is cheap looking—but generally there are good buys. At our last visit, we spotted Anne Klein knits, E. J. Harper linens and Jane Singer dresses, all at prices that bordered on the discount. Worth a look.

Open Mon.-Thurs. 10 a.m.-6 p.m., Fri. 10 a.m.-6:30 p.m., Sat. 10 a.m.-5:30 p.m., Sun. 12 noon-5 p.m.

UKO

2166 Union St., Cow Hollow - 563-0330

Just getting to the threshold of Uko is an accomplishment; first you steal through a plant-lined alley, then trudge up a very steep (45-degree grade?) black ramp to the second-floor shop. (This must make for great spectator sport when it rains.) Once inside you are treated to a small, select array of Japanese designer wear: wonderful, very tailored white cotton shirts for men and women, and linen trousers, skirts, jackets and dresses, most of them by Emico, a designer who has a chain of shops in Japan. Although expensive, the prices won't bring on the cardiac arrest you expect from most

Japanese designer clothing. (What will bring on cardiac arrest is that ramp.) The shop itself is spare, elegant and nicely lit, and the sales personnel are pleasant; unfortunately, not everyone will be fit enough to make it inside.

Open Mon.-Sat. 11 a.m.-6 p.m., Sun. 12 noon-6 p.m.

GIANNI VERSACE
70 Post St., Financial District - 956-7977

Attractive, dramatic haute couture for women who like to make a statement and like to make it in black. The shockingly costly black party frocks are especially lovely. Bring your man along to pick out an ensemble at the men's boutique next door—the two of you will make a terribly chic matched set.

Open Mon.-Fri. 10 a.m.-6 p.m., Sun. 10 a.m.-5 p.m.

STELLA VOLO
2224 Chestnut St., Marina District - 346-6727

This white shop is as clean-lined as the clothing it displays. Owner Linda Armistead sells her own handsome, modern designs, along with a few select items from international designers, including some very nice Italian jeans. The natural fabrics are high in quality, the designs are intelligent and sophisticated, and the prices are rather daunting. Shoes, accessories and dramatic jewelry are well chosen to complement the clothing. Don't miss the children's annex up the street.

Open Mon.-Sat. 10:30 a.m.-6:30 p.m., Sun. 11:30 a.m.-6:30 p.m.

EILEEN WEST
90 Grant Ave., Union Square - 982-7737

Eileen West's trademark is the pretty cotton-linen-lace dress that seems especially well suited to sorority girls and young society matrons. The fabrics are feminine but not as annoyingly ditsy as Laura Ashley's, and the cuts are stylish in a restrained manner; the drop waist has been particularly popular here these last couple of years. Less interesting than the dresses are the separates, but we are fond of the cotton nightgowns and robes, which make good gifts.

Open Mon.-Sat. 10 a.m.-6 p.m., Sun. 12 noon-5 p.m.

WHITE DUCK
517 Sutter St., Union Square - 433-6249

If Talbots is too square and MAC too strange, and you don't want to look like everyone who shops at the middle-of-the-road chain stores, come to White Duck. It sells only clothing of its own design—classic pieces in linen, cotton, silk and wool that will appeal to the woman who has a sense of style but who doesn't live on the sartorial edge. The knits are especially attractive, and all the pieces coordinate beautifully and travel well.

Open Mon.-Sat. 10 a.m.-6 p.m.

ZOE

2400 Fillmore St., Upper Fillmore - 929-0441

There isn't much to this spare, chic shop, but what is there is pretty nice. The collection changes with the season, but expect to see a lot of Adrienne Vittadini and, in the spring and summer, some smart linens. There are a very few choice accessories, mainly belts.

Open Mon.-Tues. & Sat. 11 a.m.-6 p.m., Wed.-Fri. 11 a.m.-7 p.m., Sun. 12 noon-5 p.m.

DISCOUNT

ESPRIT FACTORY STORE

501 Bryant St., South of Market - 495-5940

A chic warehouse but a warehouse nonetheless, with an immense, constantly changing array of Esprit clothing, shoes and accessories at 30 to 50 percent off. Grab a supermarket-style shopping cart and load up on Esprit's lively, youthful sportswear, dresses and hip-young-professional separates. You'll have to do a little digging, but there are almost always good bargains. Esprit's corporate headquarters are just a few blocks away.

Open Mon.-Sat. 10 a.m.-5 p.m.

LARGE & SMALL SIZES

CLASSIC WOMAN

3359 Sacramento St., Presidio Heights - 346-2666

No more stretch pants and polyester blouses for women size 12 to 20—instead, Classic Woman has assembled a winning collection of stylish, natural-fiber clothing in large sizes from such designers as Nancy Heller, Weathervane and Harve Bernard. The range encompasses casual wear and feminine evening ensembles.

Open daily 10 a.m.-6 p.m.

THE COMPANY STORE

1913 Fillmore St., Upper Fillmore - 921-0365

Fashionable sportswear and dressy dresses for women size 8 to 24 are poorly displayed on cluttered racks. But there are some large-size finds that make digging through the mess worthwhile.

Open Mon.-Fri. 11 a.m.-7 p.m., Sat. 10 a.m.-6 p.m., Sun. 12 noon-5 p.m.

ESPECIALLY PETITES

50 Post St. (Crocker Center Galleria), Financial District - 421-5657

We have a hard time mustering sympathy for the size 2 who complains of a shortage of clothing that fits, but we will admit that her plight is a real one. For small women who are sick of sleeves that go to their fingertips and suit jackets that go to their knees, Especially Petites stocks a solid, middle-of-the-road selection of small-size professional clothing and sportswear.

Open Mon.-Fri. 9:30 a.m.-6 p.m., Sat. 10 a.m.-5 p.m.

LINGERIE

ARICIE

50 Post St. (Crocker Center Galleria), Financial District - 989-0261

Such European makers as Gemma, Ronsard, Valentino, Arrete and Adagio are well represented here, as well as Wacoal from Japan and such American standards as Poiret and Jezebel. There are tons of frilly foundations and drop-dead loungewear, including some handpainted silk gowns. Not only is the merchandise expensive, tasteful and seriously sexy, but there are always a lot of well-heeled gentlemen buying it. They must be either loving husbands or big-spending philanderers, or maybe they're parading around in it under their pin-striped suits.

Open Mon.-Fri. 9:30 a.m.-6 p.m., Sat. 10 a.m.-6 p.m.

SUBROSA

3375 Sacramento St., Presidio Heights - 921-7955

For all you ladies who like pretty lingerie but want it in cotton, this is the place for you. There are large drawers full of cotton bras and panties by the likes of Pluto, Pastunette and LeJaby, along with racks of slinky silk negligees and teddies and bins of the socks you've been looking everywhere for.

Open Tues.-Sat. 10 a.m.-6 p.m.

TOUJOURS

2484 Sacramento St., Presidio Heights - 346-3988

Everywhere you turn in this tiny lavender-scented shop your eye is greeted with pastel silks, fragile lace and fine cottons. The shop is run by Beverly Weinkauf, who has collected the prettiest natural-fiber lingerie made by various European and Bay Area designers. From Europe there are Calida, Hanro and Valentina; from the Bay Area, Treesha, Cinzia and Underwriters, with their witty cotton nighties and under-things. The pièces des résistance, however, are the finely woven straw hats—by local designer Laura Fenenga—that collapse so prettily on one's head.

Open Mon.-Sat. 11 a.m.-7 p.m., Sun. 1 p.m.-5 p.m.

VICTORIA'S SECRET

*395 Sutter St., Union
Square - 397-0521*

Anyone who's ever ordered from the Victoria's Secret catalog has probably already received about 25 issues this year
and, consequently, has little interest in actually setting foot
in the shops—but they're worth a visit, since the merchandise is almost completely different from what's offered by
mail. It's nice to see that these stores carry something other
than lace garter belts and push-up bras. There are more
cotton items, menswear-styled underthings, such as silk
boxers and cotton T-shirts (it also carries these for men),
sachets and cuddly chenille robes. There's another branch at
2245 Union Street in Cow Hollow (921-5444).

Open Mon.-Sat. 10 a.m.-6 p.m.

Department Stores

EMPORIUM-CAPWELL

*835 Market St., Financial
District - 764-2222*

A solid, functional all-purpose department store whose
merchandise is neither frumpy nor elegant, Emporium-
Capwell's ornate old building dates to before the big earthquake. It stocks major mass-market brands of clothing,
housewares, furniture, shoes and accessories—the standard
lines from Liz Claiborne, Calvin Klein, Evan Picone, Gener-
ra and the like. The basement level is occupied by Market on
Market, a large gourmet department with a pleasant espresso
bar and gelato bar, along with a decent deli, wine shop and
sweet shop.

*Open Mon.-Fri. 9:30 a.m.-8 p.m., Sat. 9:30 a.m.-6 p.m.,
Sun. 12 noon-6 p.m.*

MACY'S

*Stockton St. & O'Farrell
St., Union Square -
397-3333*

What Bloomingdale's is to New York, Macy's is to San
Francisco. It's a jangling, chaotic, big-city department store,
with everything from discount racks to haute couture, along
with a continual crush of tourists, locals and shoppers from
the suburbs. The main building takes up almost an entire
city block, and there's a huge five-floor annex just for
menswear and children's clothing. We find Macy's
headache-inducing, though we do love the fabulous wom-
en's shoe department, with shoes from seemingly every
designer on earth and plenty of styles for the hard-to-fit
woman. Otherwise, expect a larger-than-usual range of
department-store housewares, clothing, cosmetics and so on.

Open Mon.-Fri. 9:30 a.m.-9 p.m., Sat. 9:30 a.m.-6:30 p.m., Sun. 11 a.m.-6 p.m.

I. MAGNIN

Stockton St.and Geary St., Union Square - 362-2100

Elegant, refined and a tad stuffy, I. Magnin caters to the San Francisco woman who wants well-made, stylish (but not too trendy) clothing. Though womenswear is the focus, there's more: an exceptionally well-rounded gourmet store, a good beauty salon, a superb collection of baby and children's clothing, a very fine stationery department and a branch of Laykin et Cie that is well stocked with conservatively dazzling gems. Magnin began as a lingerie merchant, and it still carries some exquisite handmade lingerie. The cosmetics department is also notable, both for its selection and service. Old money will feel right at home in this old-line store, founded right here in San Francisco in 1876.

Open Mon. & Thurs.-Fri. 9:30 a.m.-8 p.m., Tues.-Wed. & Sat. 9:30 a.m.-6 p.m., Sun. 12 noon-6 p.m.

NEIMAN-MARCUS

150 Stockton St., Union Square - 362-3900

Neiman's Texas nouveau-riche roots are disguised under San Francisco's old City of Paris dome, but the merchandise selection still betrays a certain flash and ostentatiousness. Not all, however, is overdone; there are some wonderfully luxurious departments, especially lingerie, gourmet foods, women's and men's couture, and cosmetics. And one of our very favorite downtown lunch spots is the Rotunda restaurant on the top floor under the beautiful dome—the setting is fabulous, the sophisticated salads and light entrees are delicious, and the service is exemplary.

Open Mon.-Fri. 10 a.m.-8 p.m., Sat. 10 a.m.-6 p.m., Sun. 12 noon-5 p.m.

SAKS FIFTH AVENUE

384 Post St., Union Square - 986-4300

This lovely West Coast sister of the classic New York society department store has a well-rounded selection of upscale merchandise. The sales are perhaps the best in town; other strong suits include a good beauty salon, exceptional furs at Revillon and sophisticated careerwear for women. Solitary shoppers should note the restaurant and cappuccino bar on the top floor, a good lunch spot for those dining alone.

Open Mon. & Thurs.-Fri. 10 a.m.-8 p.m., Tues.-Wed. & Sat. 10 a.m.-6 p.m., Sun. 12 noon-5 p.m.

Flowers

BED OF ROSES

2274 Union St., Cow Hollow - 922-5150

The smell of damp earth and cut greens will lure you into this lovely, darkish little shop. In addition to a healthy array of cut flowers, the store boasts walls lined with interesting old—and just old-looking—baskets and vases, along with wonderful reproductions of antique garden ornaments, including the heads of pouting putti. You can even bring in your favorite vase or pickle jar, and the very agreeable staff will creatively fill it.

Open Mon.-Sat. 10 a.m.-6 p.m.

FLEURTATIONS

1880 Fillmore St., Upper Fillmore - 923-1070

A small but choice selection of fresh flowers, including some you don't see at most florists. Stacks of baskets greet you on the sidewalk; inside, even more baskets hang from the ceiling and walls and sit on the floor, many filled with a panoply of beautiful silk and dried flowers. The pleasant staff and piped-in classical music keep the mood mellow.

Open Tues.-Fri. 11 a.m.-7 p.m., Sat. 10 a.m.-6 p.m., Sun 12 noon-5 p.m.

PODESTA BALDOCCHI

2525 California St., Pacific Heights - 346-1300

This long-established San Francisco mega-florist does it all: small bouquets, huge parties, balloon bouquets, plant rentals, plant maintenance, fruit baskets, you name it. The selection of fresh stems and indoor plants is complete, and the designs can be stunning. Podesta Baldocchi also delivers.

Open Mon.-Fri. 8 a.m.-5:30 p.m., Sat. 8 a.m.-5 p.m.

Food

BAKERIES

ACME BREAD COMPANY

Steve Sullivan worked as the bread baker at Chez Panisse for three years before leaving to open Acme Bread Company.

*1601 San Pablo Ave.,
Berkeley - 524-1327*

He still supplies breads to Chez Panisse and a slew of other Bay Area restaurants, but you can also buy his breads at the bakery. Displayed in baskets beneath a vintage poster from Marcel Pagnol's film *La Femme du Boulanger* are sweet-and-sour baguettes; smaller bâtards made from the same dough; the ladder-shaped fougasse of Provence, flavored with rosemary and olive oil—sometimes with walnut or mint and olive oil; smooth ovals of country-style sourdough rye made with beer; and rounds of rustic sourdough pain du levain. Each of the sourdough breads has its own unique starter. For instance, to develop the starter for the pain du levain, Sullivan allowed grapes from his father's vineyard (with the wild yeasts present on the grape skins) to ferment with whole wheat flour. The same starter is replenished and used repeatedly to make just that particular bread. You'll also find a lighter mixed-grain loaf dubbed "upstairs bread" after Chez Panisse's upstairs café, where it is served, and a whole wheat sourdough with walnuts. Most days, breads are sold out by midafternoon, so plan an early trip—and include a late morning café au lait next door at Alice Waters's Café Fanny, which features toast and sandwiches made from Acme bread. Acme bread is also available at the Singer & Foy wine store in North Beach.

Open Mon.-Sat. 10 a.m.-3 p.m. or 4 p.m., depending on bread availability.

THE BAGELRY

2134 Polk St., Polk Gulch - 441-3003

The Bagelry bakes more than a dozen varieties of bagels, as well as bialys, which are made from the same dough but without the initial water boil. Weekends, try the streusel made with brown sugar, fresh apples and sweet butter.

Open Mon.-Tues. & Thurs.-Sat. 7 a.m.-6 p.m., Wed. 8 a.m.-12 noon, Sun. 7 a.m.-4 p.m.

BOUDIN BAKERY AT THE WHARF

*156 Jefferson St.,
Fisherman's Wharf -
928-1849*

The San Francisco sourdough here is made only from sourdough starter (no yeast, no preservatives). And any day from 8 a.m. to 2 p.m. you can watch the entire process through a window that looks into the baking room. Boudin will also ship loaves out of state on request.

Open Mon.-Fri. 8 a.m.-8 p.m., Sat.-Sun. 8 a.m.-9 p.m.

CASA SANCHEZ

Fresh corn and flour tortillas are made all morning long.

*2778 24th St., Mission
District - 282-2400*

They've got every size, from miniature Mexico City–style rounds to giant fourteen-inch flour tortillas to wrap a substantial Americano burrito.

Open Mon.-Sat. 8 a.m.-6 p.m.

THE CHEESE BOARD

*1504 Shattuck Ave.,
Berkeley - 549-3183*

Bob Waks and the other members of this worker-owned cheese shop produce baguettes—white or whole wheat rye—that are indisputably the best in town for both texture and flavor. Leavened entirely with a lively sourdough "mother" that's kept in a big earthenware crock, the bread is made in small batches in the kitchen at the back of this excellent cheese store. The dark breads are wonderfully solid, moist loaves: sourdough beer rye, made with cracked rye and dark beer and sesame multigrain buckwheat. A tasty buttermilk corn cheddar bread is made with both cornmeal and corn kernels. On Fridays they bake tender braided loaves of challah, and on weekends, Sunday bread, a honeyed sweet bread with raisins and nuts. (See also "Cheese" entry.)

Open Tues.-Sat. 10 a.m.-6 p.m.

COCOLAT

*2119 Fillmore St., Upper
Fillmore - 567-1223*

*655 Montgomery St.,
Financial District -
788-5778*

Alice Medrich is best known for introducing chocolate truffles to the Bay Area. Her chocolate cakes, made with the same care and assurance, are just as divine. They're always elegant, never overdecorated, and sold by the slice as well as whole, so you can buy an assortment for a dinner party. They include a masterful rendition of reine de saba; the gâteau royale, which alternates layers of marzipan and raspberry preserves with chocolate cake; and the gâteau des îles, drenched in Curaçao and layered with apricot jam and coffee buttercream. Holidays are marked by the appearance of such inspired offerings as Medrich's Christmas pudding, special Easter cakes and heart-shaped sweets for Valentine's Day. Baking chocolate and a few distinguished dessert wines are also available. The original store, at 1481 Shattuck Avenue in Berkeley (843-3265), is still there, and there are additional stores in Oakland, Corte Madera, on 24th Street in Noe Valley and at the Stanford Court Shopping Center on Nob Hill. (See also "Confections" entry.)

*Open Mon.-Thurs. 10 a.m.-7 p.m., Fri.-Sat. 10 a.m.-8 p.m.,
Sun. 12 noon-5 p.m.*

Open Mon.-Fri. 9 a.m.-6:30 p.m.

DANILO

516 Green St., North Beach - 989-1806

The display of baked goods in this North Beach bakery changes throughout the day, as fresh batches of Italian bread, big, country-style loaves and thin sticks of grissini (hand-rolled breadsticks) emerge from the oven. Danilo also has cialde (lacy anise-flavored cookies) and Genovese-style panettone.

Open daily 6:30 a.m.-6 p.m.

DIANDA ITALIAN AMERICAN PASTRY

2883 Mission St., Mission District - 647-5469

Green St. & Columbus Ave., North Beach - 989-7745

Elio Dianda, once pastry chef at Salza in Lucca, Italy, developed all the recipes for the Italian pastries at Dianda; his three sons carry on the tradition. They bake moist amaretti, delicate allumette and other cookies, along with a classic torta de mandorle and a bevy of other sweets. The zabaglione that goes into the torta de zabaglione e rum and the zuppa inglese is still whisked by hand in a big copper bowl. The Diandas's chewy, subtly spiced panforte is dense with nuts and covered with a delicate wafer, and their tall panettone is a classic.

Open Mon.-Sat. 6:30 a.m.-6:30 p.m., Sun. 6:30 a.m.-5 p.m.

Open daily 8 a.m.-7 p.m.

DOMINGUEZ BAKERY: FLOR DE JALISCO

2951 24th St., Mission District - 821-1717

These panes (Hispanic breads) are very good and always fresh, baked several times a day. You'll find fresh egg bread, sweet crescent rolls and large, leaf-shaped hojaldre, along with panes dulces in dozens of fanciful shapes and various flavorings—anise, vanilla, lemon, pineapple—and miniature Central American pastries.

Open daily 9 a.m.-10 p.m.

THE ENGLISH TEA SHOPPE: A CRUMPET BAKERY

511 Irving St., Sunset District - 564-2255

Honeycombed with holes to catch sweet butter, the fresh crumpets made here are a sumptuous morning or tea-time treat. Have one here with cream cheese, lemon curd, bitter orange marmalade or any of a dozen or so toppings; take them home in packages of six.

Open Mon. 9 a.m.-5 p.m., Tues.-Fri. 8 a.m.-5:30 p.m., Sat. 9 a.m.-5 p.m.

FANTASIA BAKERY
3465 California St.,
Presidio Heights - 752-0825

German-born Ernst Weil trained at the Cordon Bleu before founding this European bakery years ago. Today, a small army of bakers in South San Francisco are kept busy producing cakes and pastries on a grand—perhaps too grand—scale. Small batches they're not, but many of the bakers are European-trained, and the quality is consistent despite the volume of production. Some of the desserts are too sweet for today's palate, but if you want napoleons, petits fours, Black Forest cake or Sachertorte, Fantasia may be the place. At Christmas, in addition to all sorts of German holiday cookies, they make Baumkuchen, a cake of Gypsy origin cooked on a spit over an open fire. The batter is poured onto the rotating spit and cooked layer by layer to resemble the rings of a tree, then glazed with sugar or chocolate.

Open Tues.-Sat. 8 a.m.-6:45 p.m., Sun.-Mon. 8 a.m.-6 p.m.

IL FORNAIO
2298 Union St., Cow
Hollow - 563-3400
1255 Battery St., North
Beach - 391-4622

These attractive bakeries are related to the Il Fornaio chain in Italy, where each shop is a living museum of Italian regional breads and pastries. When the first shop opened on Union Street, bakers from Italy came over to train the staff. Though not always perfect translations, the breads and pastries were high in quality and fantastic in variety. Customer demand edited down the number of breads and, particularly, pastries that were baked daily. Still, almost everything turns up in the repertory once in a while: gnarled loaves of raisin bread; great wheels of pane pugliese; breads with peppers, potatoes, dates or even tomatoes worked into the dough; breads in whimsical shapes; and handy grissini (breadsticks). All are sold by the kilo, just as in Italy, so you can buy just part of a loaf if you like. Other branches can be found on West Portal and on Shattuck in Berkeley.

Open Mon.-Fri. 7:30 a.m.-7 p.m., Sat. 8 a.m.-7 p.m., Sun. 8 a.m.-5 p.m.

Hours vary.

FRAN GAGE
PÂTISSERIE FRANÇAISE
4690 18th St., Castro
District - 864-8428

The French flag flies in front of this blue and white gem of a bakery. To one side is an appealing baking room with scrubbed wooden tables and ovens at the back; to the other is a tiny retail shop with Fran Gage's beautiful bread arranged on trays behind the counter: torpedo-shaped French country sourdough dusted with flour; round loaves of pain de seigle, a rye sourdough; and dainty mounds of her superlative walnut bread. Also on display are examples of ornate breads decorated with grape bunches or sheaves of wheat that she'll make on request. And in the pastry case are individual desserts, such as genoise layered with buttercream, rum-soaked chocolate hazelnut cake, tartlets and white chocolate mousse.

Open Mon.-Sat. 7:30 a.m.-7 p.m., Sun. 9 a.m.-5 p.m.

HOUSE OF BAGELS

5030 Geary Blvd., Richmond District - 752-6000

Eight kinds of bagels are sold here, plus half a dozen Eastern European breads, including egg twist, rye corn and pumpernickel. There's another store at 2427 Noriega Street in the Sunset (661-2865).

Open daily 7 a.m.-5:30 p.m.

JUST DESSERTS

248 Church St., Castro District - 626-5774

836 Irving St., Sunset District - 681-1277

3735 Buchanan St., Marina District - 922-8675

Just Desserts is both a large wholesale bakery and a chain of pastry shops throughout the city. All of them are comfy, low-key cafés where people come in to have a slice of cake or pie with their tea or coffee. Pastries are all homey and American, from the New York–style cheesecake that launched the business to black-bottom cupcakes, blueberry muffins, Danishes and even that relic of the '60s, carrot cake with a cream-cheese frosting. It bakes dozens of lemon buttermilk and poppy-seed cakes, Southern pecan and apple crumb pies, plus fudge brownies, generous cookies and shortbread. There's another branch in the Embarcadero Center (421-1609).

Open Mon.-Fri. 8 a.m.-11 p.m., Sat.-Sun. 9 a.m.-11 p.m.

Open Mon.-Thurs. 7:30 a.m.-11 p.m., Fri. 7:30 a.m.-midnight, Sat. 8 a.m.-midnight, Sun. 8 a.m.-11 p.m.

Open Mon., Wed., Thurs. 7:30 a.m.-11 p.m., Tues. 2 p.m.-11 p.m., Fri. 7:30 a.m.-midnight, Sat. 8 a.m.-midnight, Sun. 8 a.m.-11 p.m.

LIGURIA BAKERY

1700 Stockton St., North Beach - 421-3786

This venerable North Beach bakery is best known for its delicious focaccia, Ligurian pizza bread. Baked all morning long in the old brick-floored oven, it comes plain, seasoned with olive oil and salt or topped with scallions or tomato sauce. Also tempting are the panettone and thick, toasted biscotti made from dark anise bread.

Open Mon.-Sat. 8 a.m.-5 p.m., Sun. 7 a.m.-12 noon

OLYMPIC GREEK AMERICAN PASTRIES

3719 Mission St., Bernal Heights - 647-6363

Teta Panagiotides is from Mykonos, but the recipes for her cookies, pastries and breads come from all over Greece. Her phyllo pastries are lavished with sweet butter, honey and almonds or pistachios, and her buttery kourabiethes and koulouraika cookies are snatched up as fast as she can turn them out. Every Friday she bakes big crunchy loaves of bread covered with sesame seeds. For Easter she makes the traditional braided wreaths of bread decorated with red hard-boiled eggs, and for Christmas, round anise-scented loaves of Greek Christmas bread, baked with a good luck coin inside.

Open Mon.-Sat. 7 a.m.-7 p.m., Sun. 12 noon-7 p.m.

LA PALMA MEXICATESSEN

2884 24th St., Mission District - 647-1500

A fine source of delicious, freshly made corn and flour tortillas. Don't miss La Palma's tour de force, the thick hand-patted tortillas made by the skilled ladies in back. You can also stock up on bundles of dried chiles, beans, searing hot sauce and corn husks for tamales.

Open Mon.-Sat. 8 a.m.-6 p.m., Sun. 8 a.m.-5 p.m.

LA PÂTISSERIE

397 Arguello Blvd., Richmond District - 386-6633

Good croissants, but most of all, lovely cakes, such as the framboise, a genoise soaked in framboise liqueur, layered with raspberry jam and iced in pale pink.

Open Sun.-Thurs. 8 a.m.-6 p.m., Fri. 8. a.m.-7 p.m.

SHEHERAZADE BAKERY

1935 Lawton St., Sunset District - 681-8439

The Middle Eastern pastries sold here are all made with phyllo dough that is hand-stretched on the premises. Fresh and not preservative-adulterated, the phyllo is as supple and tender as a bolt of silk and can be easily folded into complex shapes. Take home some honey-sweetened baklava, or buy a roll of the phyllo to make your own.

Open Mon.-Sat. 9 a.m.-5 p.m.

SWEET THINGS

1 Blackfield Dr., Tiburon - 435-8583

Since Sharon Leach and Marsha Workman closed their Fillmore Street shop, customers have had to drive over the Golden Gate to the original bakery in Tiburon for the rich chocolate-mousse torte, which boasts a pound of bittersweet chocolate in every cake. You can also get wonderful coffee cakes in several varieties; the most sought after is the Hungarian sour-cream coffee cake swirled with cocoa, brown sugar, cinnamon and walnuts. And they've got such old-fashioned treats as snickerdoodles, sand tarts, homemade fudge, peanut butter cookies and chocolate-chocolate-chip cookies.

Open Mon.-Fri. 8 a.m.-7 p.m., Sat.-Sun. 9:30 a.m.-6 p.m.

TASSAJARA BREAD BAKERY

1000 Cole St., Haight-Ashbury - 664-8947

Building A (Green's), Fort Mason - 771-6330

The Tassajara bakers, mostly students at the Zen Center, make bread with tender care and a sure hand. At least half a dozen kinds are baked every day. Try the stone-ground whole wheat, the tender challah or the substantial sourdough corn rye—and never pass up a loaf of the excellent potato bread, moist with freshly grated potatoes. At Christmas they make panettone and stollen, both rich with glacéed fruits and nuts. And they have tempting brownies, macaroons and chocolate cake year round. Tassajara bread is also sold at Green Gulch Greengrocer on Page Street in the Haight.

Open Mon.-Thurs. 7 a.m.-7 p.m., Fri.-Sat. 7 a.m.-10 p.m., Sun. 8 a.m.-5 p.m.

Open Tues.-Sat. 10 a.m.-4:30 p.m.

TRUE CONFECTIONS

17 Madrona St., Mill Valley - 383-3832

Morning pastries—croissants, pain au chocolat, scones and buttery apple turnovers—are the strong suit here. But the Black Forest cake and the classic tortes have passionate fans all over the Bay Area. During the summer glittering wheels of fresh-fruit tarts, silky lemon mousse and its strawberry cake—a light genoise soaked in kirsch, layered with meringue and filled with fresh berries and cream—are added to the list. Best of all are the pies: strawberry, rhubarb, blueberry and peach. And at the holidays, look for sugar-dusted kugelhopf, wreaths of sweet Christmas bread and moist loaves of French pain d'épice (spice bread).

Open Mon.-Fri. 7 a.m.-6 p.m., Sat. 8 a.m.-6 p.m.

LA VICTORIA

2937 24th St., Mission District - 550-9292

The windows are filled with dozens of kinds of Mexican cookies and panes dulces. Go in, grab a tray and tongs, and help yourself to a heap of these sweet treats. There's a wonderful Mexican restaurant in back.

Open daily 10:30 a.m.-10 p.m.

VICTORIA PASTRY

1362 Stockton St., North Beach - 781-2015

The cornetti made here are better than most you'll find in Italy. These large, plump crescents made from a tender brioche-like dough are perfect for dunking in your morning cappuccino. Round loaves of panettone are baked here year round.

Open Mon.-Sat. 7 a.m.-6 p.m., Sun. 8 a.m.-5 p.m.

LA VIENNOISE

5940 College Ave., Oakland - 655-3209

Karen Shapiro's tiny North Oakland bakery is a wonderland of majestic old-world tortes and exquisite miniature desserts. You'll also find Scotch shortbread and Dutch honey gingerbread. For Valentine's Day, she makes all kinds of heart-shaped pastries, and for the holidays she goes all out with beribboned rounds of fruitcake, linzer tortes decorated with pastry holly, and edible gingerbread Christmas cards.

Open Mon.-Fri. 11 a.m.-7 p.m., Sat. 10 a.m.-6 p.m.

YAMADA SEIKA CONFECTIONERY

1955 Sutter St., Japantown - 922-3848

This tiny shop features traditional Japanese pastries made in elaborate shapes, such as manju (a sweet bean pastry) and yokan (candies jelled with agar-agar, a seaweed derivative).

Open Tues.-Sat. 9 a.m.-6 p.m., Sun. 9 a.m.-5:30 p.m.

BOOKS

COOKBOOK CORNER

620 Sutter St., Union Square - 673-6281

Next time you're shopping at Williams-Sonoma, stroll up Sutter to this sunny shop (inside the YMCA) completely devoted to cookbooks. It's easy to spend the entire afternoon here browsing through Taya Monfried's collection of English-language and foreign cookbooks, which includes just about everything currently in print, plus old and out-of-print books, wine books and regional charity cookbooks. Search service available.

Open Mon.-Sat. 9:30 a.m.-6 p.m.

GOURMET GUIDES

1767 Stockton St., North Beach - 391-5903

Jean Bullock has two passionate interests, cooking and travel, and her charming bookstore is stocked with books on these two subjects. The exuberant cookbook section includes books for novices, scholars and working chefs, including professional textbooks on cookery and pastry making. There's also a large collection of charity and Junior League cookbooks that contain regional recipes from all over the country. And armchair travelers can stock up on travel journals, all sorts of guidebooks, and maps to track down that restaurant you've been reading about. A mail-order service is also available; just ask to be put on the mailing list.

Open Mon.-Wed. & Fri. 12 noon-5 p.m., Thurs. 12 noon-7 p.m., Sat. 12 noon-3 p.m.

HOUSEHOLD WORDS (KAY CAUGHRAN)

P.O. Box 7231, Berkeley, CA 97407 - 524-8859

Former Berkeley librarian Kay Caughran deals in one-of-a-kind, out-of-print and hard-to-find books on cooking, eating, drinking and kindred subjects. Her annotated catalogs ($2), which list all the books she's collected in her wide-ranging searches, make interesting bedtime reading. Mail order only.

WINE APPRECIATION GUILD

155 Connecticut St., Potrero Hill - 864-1202

Although most of the business is wholesale, the guild's showroom is also open to the public. Along with corkscrews, wine buckets, wine racks, wine glasses and all kinds of wine accessories, it stocks an extensive collection of wine books (ask for the catalog), including many from British publishers. Mail order is available, too.

Open Mon.-Fri. 9 a.m.-5 p.m.

CHEESE

THE CHEESE BOARD

1504 Shattuck Ave., Berkeley - 549-3183

One of the first and still the very best of the Bay Area's cheese shops, The Cheese Board has several great advantages. Because it is worker-owned, the people who wait on you really know the cheeses and may have been selling them for ten years or more. They're all experienced buyers, and they can describe each of the 300 or more cheeses like they were friends of the family. Just as important: They take care of their cheeses. The store boasts a very good Italian cheese selection, including mozzarella di bufala and locally made mozzarella and ricotta. There's a strong showing of both French and California cheeses, plus several different feta cheeses, marvelous goat cheeses from all provenances and The Cheese Board's own hearty fresh-baked breads, including the best baguette in the Bay Area. (See also "Bakery" entry).

Open Tues.-Sat. 10 a.m.-6 p.m.

CHESHIRE CHEESE

2213 Fillmore St., Upper Fillmore - 567-4580

Cheshire stocks more than 450 kinds of cheese, it's true, but most are precut, wrapped in plastic and crowded haphazardly onto the shelves. Cheddar, Grùyere and harder cheeses don't suffer, but you might want to buy more delicate cheeses elsewhere, or ask to taste before making a purchase.

Open Mon.-Fri. 7:30 a.m.-6:30 p.m., Sat. 8 a.m.-6:30 p.m., Sun. 10 a.m.-5 p.m.

COUNTRY CHEESE
415 Divisadero, Castro District - 621-8130

You'll find good prices here on both imported and domestic cheeses, sold by the piece (usually not less than a pound), with 200 cheeses in all. Watch for specials of Reggiano and other pricey cheeses used in cooking. And the store has Ferrante Cheese Company's locally made mozzarella, too. While you're there, you can stock up on flours, grains and nuts in bulk. There's a Country Cheese in Berkeley, too.

Open Mon.-Sat. 10 a.m.-6 p.m.

CREIGHTON'S CHEESE & FINE FOODS
673 Portola Dr., Twin Peaks - 753-0750

Creighton's has the same owners as the Sixth Avenue Cheese Shop, but with a much larger retail space, it stocks many more gourmet items and a broader range of bakery goods.

Open. Mon.-Fri. 10 a.m.-7 p.m., Sat. 9:30 a.m.-7:30 p.m., Sun. 10 a.m.-6 p.m.

LAUREL WINE & CHEESE CENTER
3415 California St. (Laurel Village), Presidio Heights - 751-4242

Laurel may not have the city's biggest selection of cheeses, but everything it does have is top quality and in good condition: good Parmigiano, Romano, Cheddar, Stilton and Brie, for example, plus handsome pâtés, pasta from Fettuccine Brothers and a well-edited wine selection. Laurel has a sister store, the Wine Cheese Center, at 205 Jackson Street in the Financial District.

Open Mon.-Fri. 9 a.m.-6:30 p.m., Sat. 10 a.m.-5 p.m.

SAY CHEESE
856 Cole St., Haight-Ashbury - 665-5020

There are new owners at this store, where much of San Francisco learned about cheese after Bob Wiskotzil and George Kovatch opened it in 1976. These days, depending on the season, the store stocks 150 to 200 cheeses.

Open Mon.-Fri. 10 a.m.-7 p.m., Sat. 10 a.m.-6 p.m., Sun. 10 a.m.-5 p.m.

SIXTH AVENUE CHEESE SHOP

The walls are covered with blackboards listing the 200 to 300 cheeses sold here during any given week. Where they are kept in this immaculate shop is anybody's guess. But the clerks know their cheese (for once), and you can find Marcel

311 6th Ave., Richmond District - 387-4192

et Henri pâtés, Boudin bread, caviar, a small selection of wines, and special olive oils, vinegars and mustards.

Open Mon.-Sat. 10 a.m.-6:30 p.m., Sun. 12 noon-5 p.m.

COFFEE

GRAFFEO COFFEE ROASTING COMPANY

735 Columbus Ave., North Beach - 986-2420

The seductive smell of coffee roasting will lead you straight to the door of Graffeo in North Beach. A fixture in the neighborhood for 50 years, Graffeo has been tops in San Francisco for Italian-style—read espresso—coffee through three generations of the Repetto family. The Rube Goldberg–like roaster and rough burlap bags labeled Costa Rica, New Guinea, Java and Colombia take up most of the floor space. Just as in Italy, they keep it simple with just one Graffeo blend, roasted light or dark, and a single water-processed, 100-percent Colombian decaf. That means the coffee you buy is roasted that morning; by late afternoon, they're sometimes sold out. Mail order available. There's another store on 4th Street in San Rafael.

Open Mon.-Fri. 9 a.m.-6 p.m., Sat. 9 a.m.-5 p.m.

MR. ESPRESSO

1902 Encinal Ave., Alameda - 865-3944

Carlo di Ruocco—otherwise known as Mr. Espresso—believes in roasting his beans over an oak fire. "Because the heat has some moisture in it," he explains, "it penetrates the bean evenly and roasts slower. That means more flavor." He's managed to convince Café Fanny, Square One, Modesto Lanzone and a slew of other restaurants that his espresso roast is the best in town. His stylish Viennese, dark French roast and straightforward mocha java are excellent, too, but it is the Neapolitan espresso that is winning fans among dedicated espresso drinkers. The selection of cappuccino machines is also terrific. Mr. Espresso is sold in some coffee stores, markets and bakeries around the Bay Area as well, and it can be purchased by mail order.

Open Tues.-Sat. 11 a.m-5 p.m.

PEET'S COFFEE

1156 Chestnut St., Russian Hill - 931-8302

Alfred Peet became the first to bring gourmet coffee to the Bay Area when he opened the first Peet's Coffee in Walnut Square in Berkeley in 1966. He grew up in the tea and coffee business in Holland and was an expert buyer and roaster. Unfortunately, since he left the business some years ago, the firm's penchant for very dark roasts has become even more pronounced, and many of the 30 or so coffees have a decidedly burnt taste. Best bets are the Garuda, Sulawesi-Kalossie and Major Dickason's blends. The tea selection continues to be superb. And Peet's has an outstanding selection (often at very good prices) of coffee grinders, espresso makers, coffee makers, tea pots and the like. You can buy Peet's coffees and teas at several branches in Berkeley, Menlo Park and Oakland, or through mail order.

Open Mon.-Sat. 9 a.m.-6 p.m.

CONFECTIONS

THE CANDY JAR

210 Grant Ave., Union Square - 391-5508

A Hungarian with a strong bent for perfectionism, Maria Stacho spent an entire year developing the recipe for the basic truffle she sells in her charming, minuscule Grant Avenue shop. Then she created dozens of variations on the theme, all of which appear in her repertoire from time to time. Best bets: the truffles filled with haunting fruit-flavored creams. Try the Grand Marnier truffle, too, with its center steeped in orange and then dipped in darkest chocolate. Bring in a silver basket from Tiffany's, an antique tin, or even a plain paper bag, and The Candy Jar will fill it with an assortment of truffles and candies. You can also purchase Godiva chocolates here.

Open Mon.-Sat. 9:30 a.m.-6 p.m.

CHOCOLATES FROM CHOCOLATES

218 Church St., Castro District - 431-3640

The heady scent of chocolate fills this band box of a shop that produces competent chocolate truffles in a dozen or so flavors, along with chocolate-covered graham crackers, Oreo cookies and even pretzels.

Open Mon.-Fri. 11:30 a.m.-7 p.m., Sat. 10 a.m.-6 p.m.

COCOLAT

2119 Fillmore St., Upper Fillmore - 567-1223

655 Montgomery St., Financial District - 788-5778

4106 24th St., Noe Valley - 647-3855

When Alice Medrich started fooling around with her Paris landlady's chocolate truffle recipe, one truffle led to another, and soon she was the undisputed truffle queen of California, if not the entire country. Her romantic Cocolat shops, with their nostalgic French decor and ravishing truffles and chocolate gâteaux, are responsible for turning countless chocolate lovers into fanatics. Nobody makes better truffles maison. These are very dark, not too sweet and rolled in unsweetened cocoa to resemble Perigord's famous black truffle. Her dipped chocolate truffles are endlessly inventive (at last count her repertoire included more than 30), and you can count on any of them—hazelnut, chestnut, Grand Marnier, framboise, pistachio—to be remarkably good. Somehow you always end up buying far more than you intend—a few for a friend, a few for enjoying with your murder mystery, a few more for the movies. Life without Cocolat would be grim. The original store is at 1481 Shattuck Avenue in Berkeley (843-3265). Additional stores are in Oakland, Corte Madera and at the Stanford Court Shopping Center. (See also "Bakery" entry.)

Open Mon.-Thurs. 10 a.m.-7 p.m., Fri.-Sat. 10 a.m.-8 p.m., Sun. 12 noon-5 p.m.

Open Mon.-Fri. 9 a.m.-6:30 p.m.

Open Mon.-Sat. 10 a.m.-7 p.m., Sun. 12 noon-5 p.m.

CONFETTI LE CHOCOLATIER

4 Embarcadero Center, Financial District - 362-1706

One of the prettiest chocolate stores ever, Confetti features Moreau chocolates from Switzerland. Made in a small family-owned factory with more than a hundred years experience in making fine chocolates, the Moreau chocolate "collection" comprises dozens of molded and filled confections, all shipped to San Francisco on the night flight from Geneva so they arrive as fresh as possible. Another Confetti is located at 2801 Leavenworth Street in Fisherman's Wharf (474-7377).

Open Mon.-Fri. 8 a.m.-6 p.m., Sat. 10 a.m.-5 p.m.

FINDLEY'S FABULOUS FUDGE

1035 Geary St., Polk Gulch - 673-6655

There are times when a chocolate truffle, however sophisticated, just doesn't do it. What you crave is fudge. Remember old-fashioned fudge—gooey, full of nuts, irresistible? Findley's has been turning out batch after 25-pound batch for decades now. Your best bets are the bags filled with one piece of each of the twelve fudges made here. Then you can taste the classic walnut-studded fudge, the Chicago Cream (no nuts), the almond fudge (with almonds instead of walnuts) and the Rum du Café, spiked with rum and dark coffee. You'll want to go on and on.

Open Mon.-Fri. 10 a.m.-6 p.m., Sat. 11 a.m.-5 p.m.

GODIVA CHOCOLATIER

As you would expect, here you'll find luxurious, sculpted chocolates from the renowned Belgium firm. Although we

50 Post St. (Crocker Center Galleria), Financial District - 982-6798

find homegrown Cocolat to be better, Godiva nonetheless sells lovely chocolates, and receiving one of those little gold boxes is something akin to receiving one of Tiffany's little blue boxes.

Open Mon.-Fri. 9:30 a.m.-6 p.m., Sat. 10 a.m.-5 p.m.

NOB HILL CHOCOLATES

1386 Pacific Ave., Nob Hill - 474-6335

This small chocolate workshop will appeal to the child in everyone. You'll want to buy everything as soon as you breathe in the aroma of chocolate and candy making in the traditional Swiss style. The ingredients all come from Europe and are blended to make the chocolate right on the premises, including chocolate bars in six to ten flavors that are wrapped and labeled by hand. The dark-chocolate espresso bar and the cappuccino bar with milk chocolate walk out the door as fast as they are made. Much of the production of molded chocolates and truffles goes to restaurants. The candy makers here also design such popular gifts as chocolate Champagne bottles filled with an assortment of chocolates.

Open Mon.-Fri. 9 a.m.-5 p.m. (by appt. only).

JOSEPH SCHMIDT CONFECTIONS

3489 16th St., Mission District - 861-8682

This is the most enchanting chocolate shop in the city, especially at Easter, when it practically bursts with chocolate bunnies, huge speckled white chocolate eggs and demure little baskets filled with very realistic eggs and maybe a woodsy mushroom or two. Swiss-trained Joseph Schmidt is a master chocolatier, sufficiently confident of his craft to step outside tradition and come up with such wonderful, goofy creations as his chocolate spiny cactus and his dark-and-white chocolate saddle shoe. Schmidt's beautifully crafted truffles can be found not only here but in several specialty and chocolate shops in the Bay Area. The more than two dozen flavors include such knockouts as chocolate decadence, Hawaiian coconut, English walnut and white kirsch. He does a witty "cherry bomb" and a white chocolate mushroom, too. And those miniature tennis balls, baseballs and golf balls with nougat fillings are really something—not to mention the white chocolate swan boats or the free-form chocolate bowls swirled with color (fill them with mousse or sorbet for an elegant dinner party). He also makes individual petal-shaped cups.

Open Mon.-Sat. 11 a.m.-6:30 p.m.

TEUSCHER CHOCOLATES OF SWITZERLAND

255 Grant Ave., Union Square - 398-2700

This 50-year-old Swiss firm is best known to chocolate fanciers for its seductive Champagne truffle. That's all the more reason to try a small sampling of the other flavors, about a dozen in all, made with the same care and craftsmanship. Though all the truffles and molded chocolates are made in Switzerland, they're just as fresh as the locally made candies because they're flown in once a week from Zurich.

Open Mon.-Fri. 10 a.m.-5:30 p.m., Sat. 11 a.m.-5 p.m.

VALENTINE'S COSMOPOLITAN CONFECTIONS

1112 4th St., San Rafael - 456-3262

Darin Baranoff grew up surrounded by European chocolate in Japan, where her Russian grandfather had a chocolate and candy shop. At her own store in San Rafael, she dips fresh and dried fruit in the velvety chocolate that her father, Valentine Morozoff, refines at the family's Cosmopolitan Confections in Kobe, Japan. The rest of her chocolates— exquisite fruit-sweetened Russian caramels, satiny pralines in tiny pleated foil cups—come from the Japanese confectionery. Try the liqueur-soaked prunes glazed with dark chocolate and the subtle homemade truffles rolled in cocoa. Summers, Darin dips strawberries and other fruit in white or dark chocolate, and year round she offers three kinds of fudge.

Open Mon.-Sat. 10 a.m.-5:30 p.m.

ICE CREAM

BRAVO FONO

99 Stanford Shopping Center, Palo Alto - 322-4664

Now that the small Fono ice cream shop on Fillmore is closed, it's back to Palo Alto for the gelato many aficionados consider tops in San Francisco. Paulette and Lazlo Fono didn't just amble into the ice cream business. They traveled extensively in Italy, stopping to work with master gelato makers, then returned to California, where they built each recipe from scratch, using American ingredients and Italian machines. Theirs is the definitive mocha and nocciola (hazelnut). The amaretti is gritty with crushed almonds, while the chocolate has an extraordinary balance of sweet and bitter. Don't miss the sorbetti or ices, especially if you have the time to savor them under the big white umbrellas outside.

Open Mon.-Sat. 11 a.m.-9 p.m., Sun. 12 noon-5 p.m.

DOUBLE RAINBOW

407 Castro St., Castro District - 621-2350

As kids, Steve Sachar and Mike Fisk spent their summers scooping ice cream on Coney Island. In 1977 they moved to San Francisco and opened their first ice cream parlor on Castro Street. Now they have their own line of superpremium ice cream and shops in many locations all over the Bay Area (and California). This is American-style ice cream, as rich and creamy as it comes. If you need to be convinced, taste the ultra-chocolate or the pistachio studded with whole nuts. Other locations at 3933 24th Street in Noe Valley (621-3420) and 1653 Polk Street in Polk Gulch (775-3220).

Open Mon.-Thurs. & Sun. 11 a.m.-12 midnight, Fri.-Sat. 11 a.m.-1 a.m.

GELATO CLASSICO ITALIAN ICE CREAM

2223 Chestnut St., Marina District - 931-7251

The first of the new wave gelateries to charm San Francisco, Gelato Classico is still riding the gelato crest while other shops have closed their doors. Its ingredient for success? American flavors made in Italian machines, which gives the ice cream a dense, seductive texture without an overly exotic taste. There are many other locations, including Clement Street in the Richmond District, Post Street in Union Square, Union Street in North Beach and Parnassus Avenue near the Haight.

Open Mon.-Thurs. & Sun 12 noon-11 p.m., Fri.-Sat. 12 noon-12 midnight.

HÄAGEN-DAZS ICE CREAM SHOPPE

504 Castro St., Castro District - 861-8198

The old standard is still surprisingly good. There's lots of competition now, but Häagen-Dazs's flavors hold their own. Nobody makes better coffee chip or chocolate chocolate chip. The new Key lime sorbet swirled with classic vanilla ice cream is a winner. And the Häagen-Dazs bars have quickly become staples in home freezers all over town. Two other branches can be found at 1406 Polk Street in Polk Gulch (474-6414) and 663 Union Street in North Beach (982-4451).

Open Mon.-Thurs. & Sun. 12 noon-11 p.m., Fri.-Sat. 12 noon-12 midnight.

LATIN FREEZE

3338 24th St., Mission District - 282-5033

Paletas are frozen fruit bars made of puréed fresh fruits. Here they make them in such tropical flavors as mango, papaya, strawberry and watermelon. There's Jamaica (hibiscus flower), cacahuete (peanut) and fresh coconut, too. Have one or two on the spot and take home an assorted dozen for your freezer.

Open Mon.-Sat. 12 noon-6 p.m.

MARKETS

ETHNIC MARKETS

AMERICAN FISH MARKET
1790 Sutter St.,
Japantown - 921-5154

You can expect any market that caters to the Japanese community to have high standards for fresh seafood. That's true here, where customers line up to buy fresh tuna, squid and spiny sea urchins, along with all sorts of Japanese foodstuffs: tender, fresh tofu, soba or buckwheat noodles, pickled ginger and other Japanese pickles, Japanese condiments, seaweed and a large selection of fresh produce.

Open Mon.-Fri. 9 a.m.-6:30 p.m., Sat. 9 a.m.-6 p.m.

BOMBAY BAZAAR
548 Valencia St., Mission
District - 621-1717

It's hard to walk into this enticing Indian grocery and not buy enough ingredients to cook Indian food for two years straight. It has unusual dals, special flours for making Indian bread and all the spices that are so hard to find elsewhere. You'll even find tikka spice paste for grilled meats and poultry and, of course, an arsenal of pickles, chilis and chutneys, plus edible gold- and silver-leaf and Indian cooking implements.

Open Tues.-Sat. 10 a.m.-6 p.m., Sun. 10 a.m.-5:30 p.m.

CASA LUCAS MARKET
2934 24th St., Mission
District - 826-4334

This is the place to get the ingredients you'll need to cook Caribbean, Central American and Latin American dishes. Hundreds of specialty items are stocked on the crowded shelves—everything from Brazilian palm oil and dried hominy to salt cod, Andean dried potatoes and tins of chorizo imported from Spain. The produce department displays fresh tamarind, coconuts in the husk, mangoes, papayas and cherimoyas.

Open daily 8 a.m.-7 p.m.

HAIG'S DELICACIES
642 Clement St., Richmond
District - 752-6283

Haig's carries a full line of Middle Eastern groceries, as well as spices and ingredients for Indian and Indonesian cooking. Stop here for wine-dark Kalamata olives, Greek olive oil, feta cheese in brine, phyllo dough from the Sheherazade bakery, soujouk (spicy beef sausages) and basturma (the Armenian-style dried beef cloaked in a ruddy spice paste), plus green beans to roast for your Arabian-style coffee.

Open Mon.-Sat. 10 a.m.-6 p.m.

HOUSE OF COFFEE

1618 Noriega St., Sunset District - 681-9369

Buy finely ground beans for Turkish-style coffee here, along with such Middle Eastern staples as pistachios, lavosh cracker bread, olives and dried fava beans.

Open Tues.-Sat. 9 a.m.-6 p.m.

LUCCA DELICATESSEN

2131 Chestnut St., Marina District - 921-7873

After 56 years of roasting chickens, making salads and baking zucchini frittatas, the folks at Lucca Delicatessen have got it down. This is the most authentic of the neighborhood Italian delis, and a necessity for cooks in search of anchovies under salt, well-aged Parmesan, pancetta and polenta flour. Early every morning, they make their own ravioli, stuffed with finely chopped meat, Swiss chard and cheese. No machine here—the cooks use one of those old-fashioned wooden ravioli pins, then cut the plump little squares apart with a pastry wheel.

Open Mon. 10 a.m.-6:30 p.m., Tues.-Sat. 9 a.m.-6:30 p.m., Sun. 9 a.m.-6 p.m.

MAY WAH TRADING COMPANY

1265 Stockton St., Chinatown - 397-1527

In the midst of Chinatown, May Wah does a landmark business in Southeast Asian ingredients. The produce outside is exceptional: stalks of fresh lemon grass, tiny crimson chilis, young coconuts and fragrant Southeast Asian herbs grown locally. Inside, look for all the requisite fish sauces, chili sauces and pastes, rice papers, peanuts and more. Check the refrigerator case for Vietnamese pâtés wrapped in foil, rolls of rice noodle dough studded with scallions and dried shrimp, and French baguettes.

Open daily 7 a.m.-6 p.m.

METRO FOOD COMPANY

641 Broadway, Chinatown - 982-1874

An emporium of Shanghai foodstuffs, Metro Foods has a grand selection of ingredients for Chinese cooking: several grades of jellyfish in big crocks, dried Chinese mushrooms and other fungi, packaged spices, Szechwan vegetables and so forth. The refrigerator cases harbor fresh egg and rice noodles, dumplings, fish cakes and rice cakes, as well as fresh bean curd skin and fermented sweet rice pudding.

Open daily 9:30 a.m.-6 p.m.

MI RANCHO MARKET

464 7th St., Oakland - 451-2393

Mi Rancho in downtown Oakland is both a tortilleria and a Mexican market. You can buy handmade corn and blue-corn tortillas still warm from the griddle, plus papery husked tomatillos, tortilla chips in bulk, myriad dried chiles and chile powders and hot sauces in a range of firepower.

Open Mon.-Sat. 8 a.m.-6 p.m.

MOLINARI DELICATESSEN
373 Columbus Ave., North Beach - 421-2337

Heroic Italian sandwiches, dull Italian-American salads, a respectable array of cold cuts and cheeses and a mixed bag of Italian wines are the basic fare at this North Beach deli. But Italian cooks also can find baccala and stock fish, musky porcini mushrooms, semolina, arborio rice, Tuscan olive oils and other imported goodies.

Open Mon.-Sat. 8 a.m.-5 p.m.

K. SAKAI COMPANY
1656 Post St., Japantown - 921-0514

K. Sakai is a bustling Japantown supermarket with a well-groomed produce department and a busy fish counter. The meat counter stocks barbecued pork for your noodle dishes and paper-thin beef for sukiyaki and shabu shabu. One refrigerator holds all the distinctly shaped fish cakes, another just the pickles. You'll find even the most esoteric Japanese ingredients somewhere on K. Sakai's shelves.

Open Mon.-Sat. 9 a.m.-6 p.m.

HANS SPECKMAN
1550 Church St., Noe Valley - 282-6850

A splendid array of wurstwaren awaits at this German deli, everything from bratwurst and liverwurst to paprika sausage and Westphalian ham, along with Swiss bundenfleisch (air-dried beef) and the house leberkase (a pork and veal meatloaf). You can buy German-style horseradish, plus the pumpernickel and rye breads the deli has collected from local Eastern European bakeries. And there are more than twenty German beers.

Open Mon.-Thurs. 11 a.m.-6:30 p.m., Fri. 11 a.m.-7 p.m., Sat. 10 a.m.-7 p.m., Sun. 12 noon-6 p.m.

WEE WAH TRADING COMPANY
1248 Stockton St., Chinatown - 434-2553

Across the street from the May Wah Trading Company is Wee Wah, which stocks a similar array of Southeast Asian spices and condiments, plus such produce as taro root, sugar cane and baby bok choy.

Open daily 7 a.m.-6:30 p.m.

GOURMET MARKETS

EDIBLES

Belgian chocolates, dainty crackers, imported shortbread and all the usual trappings of a department-store gourmet shop

Stockton St. & Geary St. (I. Magnin), Union Square - 362-2100

are here. But Edibles has Narsai's pâtisserie, charcuterie and boulangerie at the back, where you can buy the TV cooking personality's signature pâtés, smoked fish and caviar, as well as freshly baked breads, croissants, miniature brioches and pastries. There's also a wonderful collection of jams, vinegars, relishes and other condiments under Narsai's label, including a fabulous hot fudge sauce, plus a number of other top-quality lines to round out the selection. And be sure to check out the superb collection of single-malt Scotches and fine Armagnacs from the respected négociant Francis Darroze.

Open Tues.-Wed. & Sat. 9:30 a.m.-6 p.m., Mon. & Thurs.-Fri. 9:30 a.m.-8 p.m., Sun. 12 noon-5 p.m.

EPICURE

150 Stockton St. (Neiman-Marcus), Union Square - 362-3900

The best thing about Neiman-Marcus's gourmet department is the Petrossian boutique tucked discreetly in one corner—and painted the same blue as the caviar purveyor's famous store on the Boulevard de Latour-Maubourg in Paris. If you want to splurge and splurge big, this is the place to buy sevruga and beluga caviar, smoked eel, smoked salmon and cod roe. The truly exceptional quality justifies the high prices. Epicure's other strong points are the cart of biscotti and cookies from the DiCamillo bakery in Niagara Falls and the display of biscotti (almond or hazelnut, chocolate-dipped or plain) from the local La Tempesta bakery. You'll also find a few fashionable cheeses and cold cuts, some decent pâtés and rare roast beef. And if you really feel the need to have Neiman-Marcus's own brand of West Texas mesquite, go right ahead.

Open Mon.-Wed. & Fri.-Sat. 10 a.m.-6 p.m., Thurs. 10 a.m.-9 p.m., Sun. 12 noon-5 p.m.

THE OAKVILLE GROCERY

7856 St. Helena Hwy., Oakville - (707) 944-8802

Those of us who remember and miss San Francisco's Oakville Grocery can't resist paying a visit now and again to its country cousin, the original store in the Napa Valley. It's still lavishly stocked with Smithfield hams, country pâtés and terrines, olives in every hue and top-quality herbs and spices. If you're visiting the wine country, this is picnic heaven. Throw a baguette, some local goat cheese and whatever else appeals to you into a basket. You can buy the wine here, or purchase directly from one of the wineries up the road.

Open daily 10 a.m.-6 p.m.

G. B. RATTO, INTERNATIONAL GROCERS

821 Washington St., Oakland - 832-6503

An unpretentious international grocer in the midst of downtown Oakland, G. B. Ratto stocks hard-to-find ingredients for a wide range of cuisines at very low prices. You can find the requisite dried beef and black beans for your feijoada, palm oil for your West Indian and African dishes, gumbo filé and andouille sausages for your gumbos, cracked green olives for your Moroccan tajine and leathery dried chiles for a chicken mole. Shop here for blue-corn polenta meal, dried fava and cannelli beans, top-quality basmati rice, cracked wheat and couscous in bulk. The bulk herb selection is one of the best in the Bay Area, and the cheese counter is no slouch, either. Look for Acme bread, Smithfield hams and bacon, Graffeo coffee and bulk baking chocolate. No matter how esoteric the ingredient, they'll know what it is and will probably have stocked it at one time or another. Just twenty minutes across the Bay Bridge, Ratto makes a great rainy-day excursion—and it opens at 8 a.m., which is when you'll find caterers and professional cooks roaming the crowded aisles.

Open Mon.-Sat. 8 a.m.-5 p.m.

VASILIO'S KITCHEN

2655 Telegraph Ave. (Andronico's Park & Shop), Berkeley - 845-1062

1850 Solano Ave. (Andronico's Park & Shop), Berkeley - 524-1673

Vasilio's is the high-tech gourmet delicatessen at the two Andronico's Park & Shop supermarkets in the East Bay. Daniel Strongin, former executive chef at the Claremont Resort Hotel and chef at the Ritz Boston, runs the kitchen, supervising the salads and takeout items, made here every day. Turnover is brisk, so everything looks well-groomed and fresh—from the mozzarella sold in its brine, the locally made ricotta and the slew of imported and domestic cheeses to the unusual sausages made by Bruce Aidell and the broad selection of cold cuts, prosciutto and salami. There are breads from Acme, truffles from Joseph Schmidt, milk in glass bottles with the cream on top from Peninsula Creamery, Mr. Espresso coffees and an impressive meat counter with real butchers.

Open daily 8 a.m.-11 p.m.

Open daily 8 a.m.-9 p.m.

VIVANDE PORTA VIA

2125 Fillmore St., Upper Fillmore - 346-4430

Hands down the most beautiful food store in the city, Vivande celebrates Carlo Middione's love affair with Italian cooking. Author of several books on the subject, he's stocked his Fillmore Street salumeria with the best possible ingredients for cooking Italian, and he cooks antipasti and other dishes for taking home or taking out on a picnic (or eating in the café in back). The assembled goodies include prosciutto, pâtés, terrines, galantines, Italian cheeses, fresh sausages flavored with fennel and pepper, a profusion of fried sausages, various antipasti and salads, including one of pale green fagioli with caviar, and homemade pastries and biscotti. Best bets are the pizza rustica and the torta Milanese, a tall layering of spinach, cheese and red and yellow peperonata in a pastry crust. Anything from the rotisserie is great, especially the chicken roasted to a lovely mahogany color with rosemary and garlic or with lemon; on occasion there's quail, duck or pork loin. Sometimes there are charming little round loaves of panini di noce with walnuts and black pepper, and a simple but delicious version of focaccia topped with a bright marinara sauce and scattered with green onions. And for dessert, try the homemade amaretti or the terremoto (earthquake) cake. Shop for distinguished Italian wines, Tuscan olive oils, arborio rice, dried porcini mushrooms and all manner of special Italian ingredients. (See also "Quick Bites" entry.)

Open Mon.-Fri. 10 a.m.-7 p.m., Sat. 10 a.m.-6 p.m., Sun. 10 a.m.-5 p.m.

MEAT, POULTRY & GAME

ANDRONICO'S PARK & SHOP

1200 Irving St., Sunset District - 661-3220

This is one supermarket with good quality meat, a remarkable selection of cuts, good specials and, what's more, real butchers behind the counter until closing—at the Telegraph Avenue store in Berkeley, that's 11 p.m. You want just half of a smoked shank or your veal liver sliced especially thin? No problem. Plus they've got great-looking veal, free-range chickens, fresh Cornish hens and freshly made sausages. This is where you'll meet late-night cooks buying pancetta, Bruce Aidell's New Orleans–style andouille sausages, a little mascarpone and whatever else they need to whip up a late supper. The Berkeley markets are at 1850 Solano Avenue (524-1673) and 2655 Telegraph Avenue (845-1062).

Open daily 7 a.m.-9 p.m.

ANTONELLI & SONS

3585 California St. (Cal Mart Super), Presidio Heights - 752-7413

This small counter offers the very freshest poultry. The staff will gladly bone your chicken breasts or order fresh game birds or poussin for a special dinner. The ranch eggs sold here are laid one day and sold the next. Also in Cal Mart Super: Bryan's Quality Meats (see below).

Open Mon.-Sat. 8 a.m.-6:30 p.m.

BRYAN'S QUALITY MEATS

3585 California St. (Cal Mart Super), Presidio Heights - 752-3430

The meat here is beautifully displayed in modest quantities, which means they cut it just as they need it. Steaks are labeled "prime" and "choice"—prime when they can get it, otherwise choice. But both are sold at the same price. The roasts are good looking, too, and you'll see such old-fashioned cuts as flat-iron pot roast and cross-rib roast, plus handsome corned beef briskets, pale veal and corn-fed Eastern pork. Bryan senior no longer mans the counter, but he still buys the meat directly from the slaughterhouse, then brings it back to the store for aging.

Open Mon.-Sat. 8 a.m.-6 p.m.

HARRIS'

2100 Van Ness Ave., Van Ness - 673-1888

This highly regarded steakhouse serves only prime beef from Nebraska, aged 21 days before it hits the grill. You can buy the same meat served in the restaurant at the small counter just inside the entrance. (See also "Restaurant" entry.)

Open Mon.-Fri. 11:30 a.m.-11 p.m., Sat.-Sun. 8 a.m.-6 p.m.

R. IACOPI

1642 Grant Ave., North Beach - 421-0757

This North Beach butcher shop dates from before the earthquake—1896 to be precise, and it's still busy every morning making fresh and dried sausages for the Italian community. Iacopi turns out all kinds of regional sausages: hot Calabrese, sweet (not hot) Sicilian and garlicky Toscana, flavored with cloves, nutmeg and cinnamon. It makes its own pancetta and, even more unusual, cures its own prosciutto crudo. You can buy it sliced by the pound or whole (fifteen pounds) at considerable savings.

Open Mon.-Fri. 9 a.m.-7 p.m., Sat. 9 a.m.-6:30 p.m.

ISRAEL & COHEN KOSHER MEAT AND POULTRY

5621 Geary Blvd., Richmond District - 752-3064

You'll find a good selection of kosher meat and poultry here, as well as canned and packaged Jewish foodstuffs.

Open Sun.-Fri. 7 a.m.-7 p.m.

ITALIAN MARKET

This is the Chinatown source for whole chickens and ducks, as well as plump squabs and all kinds of chicken parts. The

1107 Stockton St.,
Chinatown - 982-6414

small deli section sells roasted birds by the whole and the half.

Open daily 8 a.m.-5:30 p.m.

JUNMAE GUEY
1222 Stockton St.,
Chinatown - 433-3981

Junmae Guey is an informal Chinese restaurant with Formica tables and a small deli where you can buy what many Chinese cooks consider to be the best roast pig in Chinatown. The roast duck and barbecued pork are also excellent. While you wait for your takeout order, sit down and order a bowl of congee (Chinese rice gruel) to fortify you after braving the Chinatown crowds.

Open daily 8:30 a.m.-6 p.m.

KWONG JOW SAUSAGE MANUFACTURING COMPANY
1157 Grant Ave.,
Chinatown - 397-2562

The things to buy in this tiny Chinese sausage shop are hunks of chewy, dried lop cheong sausage, twists of bacon rind and slices of barbecued pork. The sausages are good sliced and steamed with rice for a quick, satisfying meal.

Open Mon.-Fri. 9 a.m.-5 p.m.

LITTLE CITY MEATS
1400 Stockton St., North
Beach - 986-2601

This longtime North Beach butcher shop specializes in locally raised veal, weighing in at just 60 to 70 pounds. Look for thick-cut veal chops, scaloppines, veal shoulder for stews and meaty veal shanks for osso buco. Sometimes the store has veal fillet, and it always has breast of veal ready to stuff. Don't worry if you don't have a recipe—they're plastered all over the walls.

Open Mon.-Fri. 9 a.m.-6 p.m., Sat. 9 a.m.-5:30 p.m.

MAGNANI POULTRY
6317 College Ave.,
Oakland - 428-9496

1586 Hopkins St.,
Berkeley - 528-6370

Magnani is a well-run store with top-quality, very fresh poultry. Look for roasters, small broilers and free-range chickens, as well as fresh Cornish game hens, chicken livers and as many backs as you can carry home for your stockpot. Or you can pick up one of the barbecued chickens. Duck livers and all sorts of fresh game birds are available by special request. This is also one of the few sources outside Chinatown for fresh, locally raised Peking duck, with head and feet intact.

Open Mon.-Sat. 9:30 a.m.-6:30 p.m.

NIGHT BIRD GAME & POULTRY COMPANY

650 San Mateo Ave., San Bruno - 543-1099

Night Bird is an enormously successful wholesaler of game and game poultry to restaurants and hotels. Home cooks can buy here, too, but since it takes about 45 minutes to process an invoice, it's a good idea to call your order in and pick it up later that day or the next. Tell them what you're looking for, and they'll tell you if they have it or can get it for you. This includes local quail, partridge, pheasant and squab, plus grouse, hare and red deer from Scotland. At one time they had caribou from Lapland, elk from Sweden and wild boar from Australia. A ranch in Texas raises elk and antelope for the firm. Founder Gerald Prolman has established a network of sources all over the world.

Open Mon.-Fri. 9 a.m.-3 p.m.

POULET

1685 Shattuck Ave., Berkeley - 845-5932

Poulet, an inspired delicatessen with chicken prepared in all sorts of delightful ways, recently added a poultry counter to the store. Shop here for freshly killed chickens, either free-range or organic, and Peking ducks. Game birds and poussin can be special-ordered.

Open Mon.-Fri. 10:30 a.m.-6 p.m., Sat. 10 a.m.-5 p.m.

SHEW WO MEAT COMPANY

1151 Stockton St., Chinatown - 982-7234

One of the many good Chinatown butcher shops, Shew Wo is the place for all manner of pork, impeccably fresh innards and such hard-to-find cuts as pigs' feet (fore or back), fresh pork belly (bacon) and pigs' ears and snouts. Prices are always very good, whether you're buying big slabs of ribs or a few pork chops for a barbecue.

Open daily 8:30 a.m.-6:30 p.m.

SUNG SANG MARKET

1205 Stockton St., Chinatown - 989-3060

Roasted foods are Sung Sang's strong suit: the main attractions are good roast pig, ducks roasted with anise and fresh coriander, and roast chickens and squab.

Open Mon.-Sat. 8:30 a.m.-5:30 p.m., Sun. 8 a.m.-5:30 p.m.

PASTA

AUNTIE PASTA

1501 Waller St., Haight-Ashbury - 681-4242

From a single store in 1981, Auntie Pasta has become a Bay Area chain, successful because it has kept the concept simple: good, fresh pasta, sauces made every day and just a few other essentials for preparing a pasta-based meal—olive oil, imported plum tomatoes, wine and great bread (in San Francis-

741 Diamond St., Noe Valley - 282-0738

co from Fran Gage's Pâtisserie Française, and in the East Bay from Acme Bread Company). Expect to find half-a-dozen different pastas, flavored with roasted peppers, fresh garlic, red chile, beets or lemon. To top them, pick one of nine sauces, including a tomato-basil, a sweet red pepper and, for garlic lovers, a cream sauce with roasted garlic and porcini mushrooms. Other locations include stores on 7th Avenue, on McAllister near the Civic Center, 3101 Fillmore near the Marina and several in the East Bay.

Open daily 12 noon-9 p.m.

Open daily 11 a.m.-7 p.m.

FETTUCCINE BROTHERS

2100 Larkin St., Russian Hill - 441-2281

The fresh pasta here, made daily from durum and semolina flours, whole fresh eggs and filtered water, comes in either plain egg or spinach versions. They'll cut it to whatever width you want and sell you some sauce if you don't have time to make your own. The basics are marinara, a traditional bolognese sauce, a vongole (baby clam) sauce made with white wine, and a well-made pesto. But do try the northern Italian walnut sauce and, in warm weather, the primavera, lavished with the season's best fresh vegetables. The tortelloni stuffed with ricotta, Parmesan and spinach is a good bet, too. This pasta is also available in some markets and delis.

Open Mon.-Thurs. 11 a.m.-7 p.m., Fri.-Sat. 11 a.m.-6 p.m., Sun. 12 noon-5 p.m.

NEW HONG KONG NOODLE COMPANY

874 Pacific Ave., Chinatown - 982-2715

Twenty-five sizes and types of Chinese noodles are produced by this Chinatown noodle company, including Shanghai-style noodles, very thick Hong Kong–style noodles and wide noodles. You'll also find several types of skins for won tons, potstickers and other dumplings. Prices are only slightly above wholesale.

Open Mon.-Sat. 8 a.m.-6 p.m., Sun. 10 a.m.-4 p.m.

THE PASTA SHOP

5655 College Ave. (Rockridge Market Hall), Oakland - 547-4005

This Oakland shop makes some of the best pasta in the Bay Area (as quite a few restaurateurs will testify). Not only is the dough supple and fine, but it can be cut to any of six different widths—from angel hair up to pappardelle—or can be purchased by the sheet. The flavors are wonderful, too. Basics are egg, spinach, garlic and herb, whole wheat, and tomato; specials include black pepper, buckwheat and saffron. The spa marinara sauce (no oil) and winter pesto (with arugula and Italian parsley) vie with the puttanesca sauce as customer favorites. Try the homemade ravioli with the squash, prosciutto and sage filling. The Pasta Shop also makes its own sausages and has a marvelous array of charcuterie and cheeses and a complete stock of Mediterranean groceries—olives and olive oils; flours for making your own pasta; imported dried pasta; vinegars; and herbs from Lhasa Karnak.

Open Mon.-Fri. 10 a.m.-8 p.m., Sat. 10 a.m.-7 p.m., Sun. 10:30 a.m.-5 p.m.

PRODUCE

GREEN GULCH GREENGROCER

297 Page St., Haight Ashbury - 431-7250

Green Gulch is the name of both this greengrocer and the farm in Marin where the Zen Center grows produce for its acclaimed vegetarian restaurant, Green's. In summer the shop may get some of the farm's overflow, but normally the mostly organic produce is purchased directly from truck farmers and farmer friends of the Zen Center. Breads from the Tassajara Bakery are also sold here.

Open Mon.-Sat. 8 a.m.-7 p.m., Sun. 9 a.m.-2 p.m.

LIVING FOODS

149 Throckmorton Ave., Mill Valley - 383-7121

This is a model natural-foods store with good-looking organic produce shrewdly supplemented by commercial produce when necessary. It stocks flavorful lettuces, wild mushrooms, blood oranges, lavender gem grapefruit and more, plus bulk nuts, grains, beans and flours, and spices and herbs sold by the ounce. Berkeley has its own Living Foods, at 1581 University Avenue (549-1714).

Open Mon.-Fri. 9 a.m.-8 p.m., Sat. 9 a.m.-7 p.m., Sun. 9 a.m.-6 p.m.

MONTEREY FOODS

1550 Hopkins St., Berkeley - 526-6042

Monterey Foods is simply the best produce store in the Bay Area, if not in all of California. Whatever the season, there's always at least one New Yorker stopped dead in the aisles gasping at the low prices and all that gorgeous produce. There may be a few Southeast Asian herbs or vegetables you won't find, but Monterey has just about every other exotic item: fresh galangal and turmeric root, chiles in umpteen varieties, tamarind pods, Key limes, Spanish garlic, special pie apples and spectacular organic baby lettuces. Out front are bins overflowing with top-quality bargain produce, from mandarin oranges to sweet red pimentos, ripe avocados to slender young asparagus. In summer, look for giant strawberries with the stems intact and berries from small local growers. Always worth every bit of the trip.

Open Mon.-Sat. 9 a.m.-6 p.m.

REAL FOOD COMPANY
*1023 Stanyan St.,
Haight-Ashbury -
564-2800*

The produce here is both organic and commercial, but there's never any confusion since everything is clearly marked and displayed in shallow baskets. The range of products is quite a bit broader than you'll find at other organic-produce stores. While you're here you can stock up on organic flours, polenta and whole grains. Other Real Food stores are located on Polk Street, 24th Street, Sutter Street and in Sausalito and San Rafael.

Open daily 9 a.m.-8 p.m.

SAN FRANCISCO FARMER'S MARKET
*100 Alemany Blvd., City
South - (no phone)*

This outdoor farmer's market is such an old San Francisco tradition that it's just about as crowded on drizzly winter days as on sunny summer and spring mornings. Small truck farmers come in from outlying counties to set up their stalls and weigh out sweet oranges, fresh almonds and exotic greens. One stand sells garlands of chile peppers and garlic; another, baskets of beautiful berries. It's friendly, has pretty good bargains and is a fun place to shop, but come early—some of the stalls close by early afternoon.

Open Sat. 6 a.m.-late afternoon.

WO SOON PRODUCE COMPANY
*1210 Stockton St.,
Chinatown - 989-2350*

Wo Soon is the best place in Chinatown for Chinese produce: fresh water chestnuts, baby bok choy, Chinese mustard and broccoli, handsome cabbage and watercress.

Open daily 7 a.m.-6 p.m.

SEAFOOD

AMERICAN FISH MARKET

See entry under "Ethnic Markets."

ANTONELLI & SONS

3585 California St. (Cal Mart Super), Presidio Heights - 752-7413

The Antonelli family has decades of experience with local seafood. They do their buying at the wharf in the early morning and bring everything back to the store for cleaning, scaling and cutting. It's great for thick, freshly cut steaks— halibut, swordfish and salmon—plus lots of whole fish, fresh fillets and some shellfish. Live lobsters are available by request. (See also "Meat, Poultry & Game" entry.)

Open Mon.-Sat. 8 a.m.-6:30 p.m.

CANTON MARKET

1135 Stockton St., Chinatown - 982-8600

Canton is one of Chinatown's best poultry and fish markets, and its fish counter is popular with Chinese customers. Look for pristine scallops, giant squid, shrimp and whole fish. Sometimes they'll even tell you the name of the fish, but don't count on it.

Open daily 8 a.m.-6 p.m.

DELTA CRAYFISH

608 Hwy. 12, Rio Vista - (707) 374-6654

It's fun on the weekend to make an excursion to Delta Crayfish for enough of the little blue creatures to put on a real crayfish boil. Delta sells them to you live, just as it does to restaurants all over California. It's only open during crayfish season, and it's a good idea to call first.

May-Nov.: open daily 10 a.m.-5 p.m.

GULF SPRAY

609 Cole St., Haight-Ashbury - 751-0473

Dale Sims (a former chef at the Hayes Street Grill and other local restaurants) is at the wharf almost every morning choosing the best of the day's catch for Gulf Spray's retail and wholesale business. Shellfish include locally raised Pacific oysters and mussels, Portuguese and Gulf oysters, fresh East Coast bay and sea scallops and blue crabs in season. They're generous with cooking advice, but buy only what looks freshest.

Open Mon.-Sat. 11 a.m.-7 p.m.

MONTEREY FISH MARKET

1582 Hopkins St., Berkeley - 525-5600

Much of fishmonger Paul Johnson's business is supplying seafood restaurants with the best of what's available. A former chef and one of the authors of *The California Seafood Cookbook*, Johnson is an expert buyer; his small retail store is stocked with the same select fish he sells to restaurants— only what's fresh and in season—plus shellfish and some unusual specialties.

Open Tues.-Sat. 10 a.m.-6 p.m.

LA ROCCA'S OYSTER BAR

3519 California St.,
Presidio Heights - 387-4100

The window in front displays seafood to be cooked on-site or to take home and cook yourself. The selection is small enough and business brisk enough to assure you it's very fresh.

Open Mon.-Sat. 9 a.m.-7:30 p.m., Sun. 11 a.m.-6 p.m.

SANG SANG MARKET

1143 Stockton St.,
Chinatown - 433-0403

Another popular Chinatown fish market, Sang Sang is a good place to find the requisite redfish for Cajun cooking, as well as loads of squid, clams and mussels and a great selection of whole fish. The store is long and narrow, and always impossibly crowded. Take a deep breath and plunge right in, waving like everybody else for the attention of the men behind the counter.

Open daily 8:30 a.m.-5:45 p.m.

SWAN OYSTER DEPOT

1517 Polk St., Polk
Gulch - 673-1101

The friendly staff at this decades-old café and fishmarket will sell you whatever oysters they're shucking for café customers that day, plus any of the fish they're serving: steelhead salmon, swordfish, ling cod, red snapper . . . whatever's available and fresh.

Open Mon.-Sat. 8:30 a.m.-5:30 p.m.

WAH FAT FISH MARKET

821 Pacific Ave.,
Chinatown - 392-3837

This relatively new Chinatown fish market boasts five enormous tanks of live fish and crab. In front, you'll see boxes of live frogs and some very big turtles, which would crawl right out of their boxes if they could. The quality of the seafood at the counter is high. Most of the fish is sold in the round, but you can ask the vendors to scale and clean whatever you buy, and if you like, they'll quickly fillet it.

Open daily 8 a.m.-6 p.m.

SPICES & HERBS

BOMBAY BAZAAR

548 Valencia St., Mission
District - 621-1717

Stock up on all kinds of exotic flours, lentils and basmati rice before checking out the exceptional spice selection. You serve yourself from the rows of jars filled with everything from familiar coriander, mustard seed and turmeric to green or black cardamom in the pod—even the harder-to-find white variety. There's a wide range of spice mixes and spice pastes, too. (See also "Ethnic Markets" entry.)

Open Mon.-Sat. 10 a.m.-6 p.m., Sun. 10 a.m.-5:30 p.m.

BUFFALO WHOLE FOOD & GRAIN COMPANY

1058 Hyde St., Nob Hill - 474-3053

Shop here for organic grains and flours milled at Giusto's in South San Francisco, and also for herbs and spices in bulk. Lined up alphabetically, the 180 jars of herbs, spices and teas make a study in color and texture. And at these prices, even the largest treasure trove of spices won't cost you all that much.

Open Mon.-Sat. 9 a.m.-9 p.m., Sun. 10 a.m.-8 p.m.

HAIG'S DELICACIES

642 Clement St., Richmond District - 752-6283

The best-known Middle Eastern food store in the city, Haig's is a great place for the innumerable spices used not only in Middle Eastern cooking but in Indian and Southeast Asian cooking as well. It buys in bulk and repackages in four-ounce quantities under its own label.
(See also "Ethnic Markets" entry.)

Open Mon.-Sat. 10 a.m.-6 p.m.

THE LHASA KARNAK HERB COMPANY

2513 Telegraph Ave., Berkeley - 548-0380

Specialists in herbs and spices, Lhasa Karnak is a romanticist's idea of an herb store. Small and impeccably neat, the shop has dozens of gallon glass jars filled with herbs, spices, roots and seeds in all the colors of autumn and earth. The emphasis is medicinal, but the cook will find much of interest, too. Another branch at 1938 Shattuck Avenue in Berkeley (548-0380).

Open Mon.-Sat. 10 a.m.-6:30 p.m., Sun. 12 noon-6 p.m.

NATURE'S HERB COMPANY

281 Ellis St., Union Square - 474-2756

Since 1915, Nature's Herb Company has been dispensing all manner of herbal remedies, custom tonics and culinary herbs and spices to generations of health-conscious San Franciscans. The old-fashioned store has hundreds of varieties of herbs, roots and seeds filed away in cabinets. For cooks, it has all the basics, plus such hard-to-find items as chicory root, galangal, mugwort, turmeric root and fragrant whole vanilla bean. All herbs are sold in leaf form, which maintains flavor longer than when ground or powdered. And there's no real minimum—clerks will sell you four ounces of this and that, if you like.

Open Mon.-Sat. 7 a.m.-3:30 p.m.

G. B. RATTO, INTERNATIONAL GROCERS

This old-fashioned store in the midst of downtown Oakland's Victoriana boasts an extensive serve-yourself spice section. Not only does it have dozens of familiar herbs and spices to scoop from gallon jars, but it also has the best sweet

223

821 Washington St.,
Oakland - 832-6503

and hot paprika around, ground chile labeled by variety, white poppy seeds and cream of tartar for grandma's recipes. The scent of the Greek hills pulls at you from bundles of wild oregano and thyme. Burlap sacks of dried red peppers and black peppercorns add their note, and the glorious mix of pink, green, black and white peppercorns belongs in everyone's arsenal of spices.

Open Mon.-Sat. 8 a.m.-5 p.m.

THE SPICE HOUSE

2343 Birch St., Palo Alto -
326-8811

A wonderful resource for everything exotic, The Spice House stocks spices you've never even heard of, like cubeb pepper, used in classical recipes, and melagueta pepper, a relative of cardamom that is listed in some medieval recipes. Kalajeera, black cumin seed and zubrovka, a grass used to flavor vodka, are also in stock. This has to be the best herb and spice selection for ethnic cuisines in the Bay Area. And whenever possible, The Spice House stocks both the dried herb for your pantry and the healthy plant for your kitchen garden.

Open Mon.-Sat. 9:30 a.m.-5:30 p.m.

STAPLES

THE FOOD MILL

3033 MacArthur Blvd.,
Oakland - 482-3848

A favorite with cooks and bakers for the consistently high quality of flours, grains and cooking oils, The Food Mill sells almost all of its goods in bulk. To assure maximum freshness, they grind all the whole-grain flours themselves; you'll notice the difference immediately. Check here also for nut butters, cereals, dried fruit and nuts.

Open Mon.-Sat. 8:30 a.m.-6 p.m.

OHS FINE FOODS

2651 Mission St., Mission
District - (no phone)

Ohs has no telephone. That may be a bit eccentric, but never mind—the store is a good source for flours, grains, beans, nuts, dried fruits and spices, all displayed in open sacks in a store about as wide as your hand. At the front there's even birdseed for your parrot. You'll find very good prices on coffee, too, which Mr. Ohs roasts and distributes. Ohs is also known as the California Direct Importing Company.

Open Mon.-Sat. 9 a.m.-6 p.m.

WINE

BELTRAMO'S

1540 El Camino Real, Menlo Park - 325-2806

A mecca for aficionados from all over the Bay Area, Beltramo's boasts a formidable collection of wines from every wine-growing region in the world. You can spend hours browsing through buyer Tony Wood's eclectic finds.

Open Mon.-Thurs. 9 a.m.-9 p.m., Fri.-Sat. 9 a.m.-9:30 p.m., Sun. 9 a.m.-7:30 p.m.

CALIFORNIA WINE MERCHANT

3237 Pierce St., Marina District - 567-0646

This tidy shop has what may be the widest selection of California wines in the city. That means a stash of older California vintages, too.

Open Mon.-Sat. 11 a.m.-7 p.m., Sun. 12 noon-6 p.m.

COIT LIQUORS

585 Columbus Ave., North Beach - 986-4036

Tony Giovanzana has managed to fit a remarkable selection of Italian, French and California wines into his corner liquor store in North Beach, along with a lot of good Champagne at some of the best prices in town. Customers buy steadily all day long, yet the shelves are always fully stocked. How does he do it? He has a huge cellar beneath the store. Be sure to check the grappa selection, too, for such respected products as Gaja, Ceretto and Castello di Barbaresco.

Open daily 9 a.m.-12 midnight.

CONNOISSEUR WINE IMPORTS

462 Bryant St., South of Market - 433-0825

Its warehouse space a maze of stacked wine crates, Connoisseur is the place to bone up on German wines and their intricate classification system. Connoisseur has fine examples of them all, from Spätlese to Trockenbeerenauslese, along with a staff that genuinely enjoys discussing these wines or any others in stock. It also has great old Bordeaux, a splendid collection of Sauternes of both recent and older vintages, fine Burgundies and gentlemanly vintage Ports, plus a well-edited selection of California wines, many from wineries with limited production. The store is a good source for British wine books as well.

Open Tues.-Fri. 10 a.m.-6:30 p.m., Sat. 10 a.m.-5 p.m.

DRAPER & ESQUIN

655 Davis St., Financial District - 397-3797

When Draper & Esquin moved from the Vintner's Building on Sutter Street a few years ago, it lost a bit of its scholarly, decidedly old-world aura. No matter, it has kept its remarkable collection of old Bordeaux, quite good Burgundies, Champagnes, Sauternes and wonderful Italian wines. This is also one of the few stores in town with a stock of older California vintages as well as top-notch current releases. The annual catalog with snapshots of producers and notes on visits to the wine country makes for great bedtime reading. Another plus is free Bay Area delivery.

Open Mon.-Fri. 9 a.m.-6 p.m., Sat. 9 a.m.-5 p.m.

ENOTECA MASTRO

933 San Pablo Ave., Albany - 524-4822

A small enoteca, or "wine library," devoted entirely to Italian wines from Tuscany, Piedmont, Friuli, the Alto Adige and the Veneto. Show a little interest and owner Mark Anthony Mastro will take you on a tour around the shop, describing the characteristics of each wine. And you can taste any of six different wines at the bar before you buy.

Open Tues.-Wed. 11 a.m.-6 p.m., Thurs.-Sat. 11 a.m.-6:30 p.m.

LIQUOR BARN

201 Bayshore Blvd., City South - 282-0532

If you know your wines, you can find some extraordinary bargains here, mostly on imported wines. The California wine prices are competitive, but you can sometimes match or better them at other wine stores. But if you're up on wines from Tuscany, Piedmont, Alsace, the Rhône and Germany's Rheingau, stop in often for a quick browse. Wines appear and disappear with unseemly haste—and each Liquor Barn seems to have a slightly different stock of imported wines. Other stores are located in Alameda, Albany, Colma and San Mateo.

Open Mon.-Fri. 10 a.m.-8 p.m., Sat. 9 a.m.-8 p.m., Sun. 10 a.m.-7 p.m.

KERMIT LYNCH WINE MERCHANT

1605 San Pablo Ave., Berkeley - 524-1524

Anyone who loves French wines, but must love them on a modest budget, is well acquainted with the wines of Kermit Lynch, wine merchant extraordinaire. Every wine he sells, he has imported himself. He makes several months-long trips to Europe each year, revisiting his wine makers, tracking down properties he's heard about and discovering new producers. He has built his considerable reputation on what are known in Europe as "petits vins." But when he does buy from Bordeaux or Burgundy, he favors traditionally made wines at good prices. He has a special love, too, for the wines of the Côtes du Rhône and the Loire Valley. Look here for distinguished wines from Alsace, along with vintage Chiantis and other interesting Italian wines. Also tempting are the olive oils, jams and lavender honeys from wine producers. And you can taste a few of his wines at Alice Waters's Café Fanny next door.

Open Tues.-Sat. 11 a.m.-6:30 p.m.

PACIFIC WINE COMPANY

2999 Washington St., Pacific Heights - 922-8600

The majority of the wines stocked in this Pacific Heights shop are personally selected in France by the buyer, Mike Lynch. You'll find wines from the Côtes du Rhône, the Loire and other wine regions, but the store's strength lies in its selection of Burgundies and Bordeaux. He's got Champagnes (more than 30), sumptuous dessert wines and a fine collection of Cognac, Armagnac and Calvados, plus 36 single-malt Scotches.

Open Mon.-Fri. 10 a.m.-8 p.m., Sat. 10 a.m.-6 p.m.

SINGER & FOY

1821 Powell St., North Beach - 989-0396

A lovely sign hung from twined wrought-iron grape leaves marks this stylish North Beach wine bar and retail store. You'll find wines imported by Kermit Lynch, along with an astutely edited selection of older Bordeaux and Burgundies, some fabled California wines and the best of Oregon's Pinot Noirs. You can taste wines at the bar every day; special tastings are held on Friday and Saturday. And on Wednesday, Friday and Saturday, stop in for marvelous breads from the Acme Bread Company in Berkeley.

Open Mon.-Sat. 11 a.m.-7 p.m.

JOHN WALKER & COMPANY

175 Sutter St., Union Square - 986-2707

If you have a taste for legendary Bordeaux vintages or fine old Burgundies, you can find more than enough to keep you happy at John Walker. Surprisingly, even in this high-rent district, prices are sometimes just a touch lower than you might pay elsewhere. John Walker has kept some of these wines maturing in his warehouse for years—he didn't pay a fortune for them when they were young; he may charge you only a small one now.

Open Mon.-Sat. 9 a.m.-6 p.m.

THE WINE HOUSE

535 Bryant St., South of Market - 495-8486

John Carpenter is an importer who specializes in the wines of Bordeaux and Burgundy, although he has digressed into other, lesser-known French wine areas. Since his customers

227

want to get a sense for older wines before they invest heavily in new ones, a good portion of his business is in older wines, both from Europe and California. Look here for rare California vintages, noble Italian wines and vintage Ports, Sauternes and Champagnes.

Open Mon.-Fri. 10 a.m.-6 p.m., Sat. 10 a.m.-4 p.m.

Gifts

AUSTRALIA FAIR
700 Sutter St., Union Square - 441-5319

A cheery spot for rarely seen products from down under, many of which make good gifts. For children and animal lovers, there are stuffed koalas; for rakish outdoorsmen, ranch coats and bush hats; for skiers, wool underblankets and lambskin rugs to decorate the cabin; and for gourmands, tins of Vegemite.

Open Mon.-Sat. 9:30 a.m.-5:30 p.m.

H. P. CORWITH LTD.
1833 Union St., Cow Hollow - 567-7252

There's a cool, art-gallery tone to this shop, with its white walls and glass cases, that quickly dissipates the minute you focus on the wacky stuff displayed. Along with some of the most winsome cloth vegetables we've ever seen are humorous dishes of fake food, miniatures of all kinds and handsome antique tools. Even people who have everything don't have most of the things sold here.

Open Mon.-Sat. 10 a.m.-6 p.m., Sun. 12 noon-5 p.m.

FABULOUS THINGS LTD.
1974 Union St., Cow Hollow - 346-0346

Some of the "fabulous things" in this Asian-curio-turned-American-folk-art shop are the genuine antique quilts, priced accordingly. The not-so-fabulous things, and there are a lot, are the ersatz works of folk art—carved wooden pigs, cows and farm couples that are crudely rendered and painted. Some of the leftover Asian objects are more attractive and definitely more authentic.

Open Mon.-Sat. 10:30 a.m.-5:30 p.m., Sun. 12 noon-5 p.m.

FOLK ART INTERNATIONAL GALLERY

900 North Point St. (Ghirardelli Square), Fisherman's Wharf - 441-6100

Take the time to seek out this spacious gallery tucked away in a little-seen corner of Ghirardelli Square. The showroom for the nonprofit Folk Art International group, it offers a well-balanced selection of folk arts and crafts from around the world: masks from Mexico, South America and the Philippines; handwoven baskets from Africa; paintings from China, Ecuador and France; sculptures and artworks from as close as the Appalachians and as far as Sri Lanka; and antique bronzes, porcelains and ivory carvings from the Orient. You'll also find winsome toys, unusual furniture and colorful clothing and textiles. Next door is the affiliated Xanadu Gallery, which specializes in tribal art.

Open Mon.-Thurs. 10 a.m.-6 p.m., Fri.-Sat. 10 a.m.-9 p.m., Sun. 11 a.m.-6 p.m.

FORMA

1715 Haight St., Haight-Ashbury - 751-0545

Forma sells gifts and objects for those who appreciate the bizarre side of life. In a stark faux-stone room are such modern-day necessities as troll dolls, Sea Monkeys, a statue of Bob Hope golfing, the Elvis Love Her Tender hair-care line, jars of human teeth and dishes festooned with black cats.

Open Mon.-Sat. 10 a.m.-7 p.m., Sun. 10 a.m.-6 p.m.

FUMAKI

1894 Union St., Cow Hollow - 922-0573

An eclectic array of antique and contemporary art objects and fine jewelry from Japan, China and Korea, including elegant silk obi (the sashes for kimonos) and a noteworthy group of ivory and wooden netsuke (the intricately carved toggles used to fasten small containers and obi).

Open Mon.-Sat. 10 a.m.-6 p.m.

GOOSEBUMPS

900 North Point St. (Ghirardelli Square), Fisherman's Wharf - 928-2112

Trendy, wacky and sometimes tacky, Goosebumps is also great fun. While TV theme songs play over the sound system, you can browse through the diverse selection of gifts, none of which is practical or essential: six-foot inflatable Bozo the Clown dolls, moronic joke books, outlandish T-shirts, plastic dinosaurs, liquid crystal jewelry, windup toys, see-through barbecue aprons and much, much more.

Open daily 10 a.m.-9 p.m.

GUMP'S

250 Post St., Union Square - 982-1616

Like anything in one of those little blue boxes from Tiffany's, a gift from Gump's is always welcome. It helps to have a hefty net worth, though—the jade and pearl jewelry, crystal vases, silver frames, handsome desk accessories and exquisite

Oriental antiques are breathtakingly expensive. Even if you don't want to buy, come here for a browse. (See also "Home" entry.)

Open Mon.-Sat. 9:30 a.m.-5:30 p.m.

KITES AND DELIGHTS

2801 Leavenworth St. (The Cannery), Fisherman's Wharf - 775-5483

A small shop with a good collection of kites—from simple little backyard models to huge, elaborate ones—all in bright colors. There are also wind socks of every size, Chinese-style kites and windup plastic birds. If there's a breeze (a good bet in San Francisco), take your new kite to the waterfront across the street for a trial run.

Open Sun.-Fri. 10 a.m.-7 p.m., Sat. 10 a.m.-8 p.m.

MADE IN U.S.A.

1749 Union St., Cow Hollow - 885-4333

The cow, specifically the Hereford cow (the white one with black spots), is the dominant leitmotif in this contemporary handicrafts store. There are three-legged cow stools with udders, large, flat, freestanding wooden cows, cow stationery and many more bovine vendibles. Noncow items include a free-spirited collection of handmade plastic and ceramic jewelery, cute greeting cards and eccentric ties (some of which are white with large black spots).

Open Mon.-Fri. 10:30 a.m.-7 p.m., Sat. 10:30 a.m.-6:30 p.m., Sun. 12 noon-5 p.m.

MARGAR'S

1957 Union St., Cow Hollow - 346-2719

Stashed in a little alley off Union Street, Margar's is basically a nice knickknack shop with a large candle selection, lots of marvelous ornamental mirrors in wood, brass and plaster, and an equal number of ornamental frames, which make the perfect gift for someone who'd like a nicely framed picture of you.

Open Mon.-Sat. 10 a.m.-6 p.m.

THE NATURE COMPANY

900 North Point St. (Ghirardelli Square), Fisherman's Wharf - 776-0724

If you, like most good consumers, are regularly deluged with catalogs, chances are you're already familiar with the Nature Company. These very clever people sell an unusual collection of nature-related gifts for adults and children: animal posters, handsome moon-phase watches, geodes, wind chimes, stegosaurus T-shirts, globes (both inflatable and permanent), clever scientific toys and games, new age records, tapes and compact discs, beautiful books, and posters featuring the work of such artists as Ansel Adams. A must-visit in Ghirardelli Square.

Open daily 10 a.m.-9 p.m.

Sfo

1837 Union St., Cow Hollow - 567-5913

Another T-shirt, sunglasses and plastic dinosaur store with a trendy edge. Definitely teenage-oriented.

Open daily 10 a.m.-7 p.m.

The Sharper Image

532 Market St., Financial District - 398-6472

The famous catalog come to life, with all kinds of fashionably useless items for the spoiled rich executive: household remote controls, space-age briefcases, suits of armor, radar detectors, miniature TVs, crossbows, air purifiers, elaborate exercise equipment, high-tech telephones and some incredibly boring jewelry.

Open Mon.-Sat. 10 a.m.-7 p.m., Sun. 12 noon-5 p.m.

Techsis

50 Post St. (Crocker Center Galleria), Financial District - 362-2777

Granted, these hologram watches won't put Cartier out of business, but they are unusual. Aside from the watches, Techsis sells similarly high-tech gifts, some of which are quite clever (the folding bikes and the games) and some of which are dreadful (the hologram jewelry).

Open Mon.-Fri. 9:30 a.m.-6 p.m., Sat. 10 a.m.-5 p.m.

Xanadu

900 North Point St. (Ghirardelli Square), Fisherman's Wharf - 441-5211

Next door to the Folk Art International Gallery, with which it is affiliated, Xanadu is a showcase for some remarkable tribal art and artifacts from Africa, Asia, Oceania and the Americas. From elaborate, expensive masks and sculptures to moderately priced weavings to inexpensive elephant-hair jewelry (which brings the wearer good luck), the collection is chosen with a fine eye.

Open Mon.-Thurs. 10 a.m.-6 p.m., Fri.-Sat. 10 a.m.-9 p.m., Sun. 11 a.m.-6 p.m.

Z Gallerie

1861 Union St., Cow Hollow - 346-9000

High in design and low in price, Z Gallerie exhibits a strong predilection for high-tech—black calculators, black watches, black chairs and black tables set with black dishes and napkins. The merchandise is well selected, however, and will make the necessary statement without bankrupting you. At the back of the store are equally modern and attractive housewares. The "gallerie" moniker is justified by the large stock of bathetic framed posters. There's another Z Gallerie in the Haight at 1465 Haight Street (863-5331).

Open Mon.-Thurs. 10 a.m.-7 p.m., Fri.-Sat. 10 a.m.-11 p.m., Sun. 11 a.m.-7 p.m.

Home

CHINA & CRYSTAL

BIONDI ART IMPORTS

412 Columbus Ave., North Beach - 392-8096

A one-of-a-kind store filled with dazzlingly colorful Italian ceramics. The remarkable handpainted dinnerware, vases, platters and objets d'art from several Italian manufacturers are Biondi's main draw, both in the store and through its large mail-order business, but there is more: espresso and cappuccino machines, authentic Italian cookware, pasta rollers and ornate Capodimonte china.

Open Tues.-Sat. 9:30 a.m.-6 p.m.

GUMP'S

250 Post St., Union Square - 982-1616

No trip to San Francisco is complete without a visit to Gump's, the fabulous china/stationery/jewelry/gift store that opened its first downtown doors in 1862. Its stationery is refined and its jewelry is timeless, but the china and crystal departments are unequaled. There are more than 400 patterns from every fine maker in the world, including Waterford, Baccarat, Steuben, Limoges, Fitz & Floyd and Spode. As one would expect with such merchandise, the bridal registry, gift wrapping and shipping services are outstanding. (See also "Gifts" entry.)

Open Mon.-Sat. 9:30 a.m.-5:30 p.m.

WEDGWOOD SAN FRANCISCO

304 Stockton St., Union Square - 391-5610

The entire range of Wedgwood's bone china and stoneware are available at this spacious store, which also stocks most Waterford crystal patterns. Our favorites from the Wedgwood line are the adorable Peter Rabbit china and the colorful Jasperware. Service is good.

Open Mon.-Sat. 9:30 a.m.-5:30 p.m.

FABRIC

LAURA ASHLEY

563 Sutter St., Union Square - 788-0190

Behind the racks of flouncy dresses, corduroy jumpers and cuter-than-cute little-girl clothes are shelves filled with Laura Ashley's English-country fabrics. If used in moderation, these cotton prints can help create a lovely nursery or charming country cottage. If used excessively, the flowery patterns will make one long for the Bauhaus look. There's another store at 1827 Union Street in Cow Hollow (922-7200).

Open Mon.-Sat. 10 a.m.-6 p.m.

BRITEX FABRICS
146 Geary St., Union Square - 392-2910

Traveling tailors and seamstresses head straight for Britex when they get into town—they know that few places in the world have such an extensive collection of fine fabrics, leathers, buttons and notions. From sea-island cotton to cashmere, couture knits to crêpe de chine, Britex has every kind of fabric imaginable. Get on the mailing list and you'll receive regular swatch samples of the newest offerings. Though there's almost always a crowd, the staff is cheery and helpful.

Open Mon. & Thurs. 9 a.m.-8 p.m., Tues.-Wed. & Fri.-Sat. 9 a.m.-6 p.m.

MARIMEKKO
50 Post St. (Crocker Center Galleria), Financial District - 392-1742

Many a child's room has been brightened with these bold, colorful fabrics from Finland. Along with the cheerful, contemporary cottons, there's a small selection of simple cotton and wool clothing for men, women and children.

Open Mon.-Fri. 10 a.m.-6 p.m., Sat. 10 a.m.-5 p.m.

PIERRE DEUX
532 Sutter St., Union Square - 788-6380

The front of this handsome French country store is filled with purses, cosmetic cases, pillows and notebooks covered with Pierre Deux's trademark fussy cotton prints. Those same fabrics—which we find attractive only in very small doses—are sold by the yard in the back.

Open Mon.-Sat. 9:30 a.m.-5:30 p.m.

FURNISHINGS

BAY COMMERCIAL LIGHTING CENTER

Bay Lighting sells high-style and Eurostyle lighting fixtures —floor lamps, walls sconces, table lamps, hanging fixtures— from European and American designers. The selection of

1140 Folsom St., South of Market - 552-4110

cutting-edge contemporary fixtures is exceptional. It's also a good place for well-made track and recessed lighting. The emphasis is on design and quality, not budget.

Open Mon.-Fri. 8 a.m.-5 p.m., Sat. 10 a.m.-2 p.m.

CRATE & BARREL

125 Grant Ave., Union Square - 986-4000

Just try to walk out of this huge, cheerful store without buying something—unless you have an iron will, you'll leave toting a Crate & Barrel bag filled with some intelligently designed, practical, inexpensive household item. Crate & Barrel's first West Coast store is a merchandising marvel, with three floors of great-looking household basics, from Adirondack chairs to terra cotta dishes, storage systems to Champagne flutes—everything a fledgling yuppie needs to set up a first big-city apartment.

Open Mon.-Sat. 10 a.m.-6 p.m., Sun. 12 noon-5 p.m.

FILLAMENTO

2185 Fillmore St., Upper Fillmore - 931-2224

Young, modern and somewhat Eurostyle, Fillamento's merchandise is reminiscent of Conran's, the British home-furnishings giant. This is a good place for reasonably priced, attractive dhurrie rugs, glassware, terra cotta dishes, dining room tables, folding chairs and clever storage systems. The staff is quite friendly.

Open Mon.-Wed. & Fri.-Sat. 10 a.m.-6 p.m., Thurs. 10 a.m.-8 p.m., Sun. 12 noon-5 p.m.

HEARTLAND

1801A Fillmore St., Upper Fillmore - 931-7622

Though quilts are Heartland's focus, they are mediocre in quality. But the fairly priced wreaths, baskets, rugs and knickknacks are attractive homey accents for a country decor.

Open Mon.-Fri. 11 a.m.-6 p.m., Sat. 11 a.m.-5 p.m., Sun. 12 noon-5 p.m.

SUSAN HOWELL TEXTILES

1900A Fillmore St., Upper Fillmore - 567-3093

Her store no bigger than a closet, Susan Howell carries some quite lovely rugs—some of her own making and some from the Navajo and the Orient. She also does a fine job of restoring worn or damaged rugs.

Hours vary; call for appt.

JAPONESQUE

50 Post St. (Crocker Center Galleria), Financial District - 398-8577

There's a timeless quality to the handicrafts, lan? furniture displayed in this quiet, modern shop. Some ... are antiques, others new, but there is no break in continuity. Cases display small treasures, such as carved wooden "stones," eyeglass frames and netsuke. There are ukeoye, the woodblock prints from the turn of the century, and contemporary sculpture in stone and wood. Not hard-edged like many trendy Japanese designer shops.

Open Mon.-Sat. 10:30 a.m.-5:30 p.m.

JUST CLOSETS

460 Post St., Union Square - 989-0748

One of the better and more reasonably priced of the closet-organization companies that have sprung up in the last few years. Closets can be custom designed and installed, or you can create your own from the modular systems, baskets, shoe organizers and special hangers in the boutique. Some of these organizational systems are also great for home offices.

Open Mon.-Fri. 10 a.m.-6 p.m., Sat. 10 a.m.-5 p.m.

POLO/RALPH LAUREN

90 Post St., Financial District - 567-7656

All it takes is many thousands of dollars and a few well-placed antique picture frames and, *voilà*, your entire house can instantly reek of old money. Ralph Lauren has tapped deep into America's new-found desire not to be crass and nouveau riche, first with his expensive classic clothing and now with his expensive classic furniture. These beds, linens, chairs, dressers, sofas, pillows and fabrics are elegant, tasteful, understated and well made, with designs that draw on the past instead of looking toward the future. Some of the fabrics—such as the plaids and hunting motifs—are tiresome, but most of Lauren's line is quite handsome in a solid, conservative way.

Open Mon.-Sat. 10 a.m.-6 p.m.

REVIVAL OF THE FITTEST

1701 Haight St., Haight-Ashbury - 751-8857

Want a phone like the one Humphrey Bogart barked into in the old Sam Spade movies? How about a set of Fiestaware, or a streamlined Mixmaster that would have made Harriet Nelson proud? Then get on over to Revival of the Fittest, a cheerful store with well-displayed vintage and contemporary home and kitchen accessories. There's a small selection of choice furniture, along with great mantel and wall clocks, glassware, old-fashioned toasters, art deco lamps and antique jewelry.

Open daily 10 a.m.-6 p.m.

UNION STREET FURNITURE

1775 Union St., Cow Hollow - 771-6565

Contemporary Finnish and Italian furniture with clean lines, realized in first-class materials. Try out the Finnish bed with a futon-like mattress supported by bentwood slats held together by leather. The very attentive staff members are happy to point out the virtues of the merchandise.

Open Mon.-Sat. 10:30 a.m.-6:30 p.m., Sun. 12 noon-5 p.m.

LA VILLE DU SOLEIL

556 Sutter St., Union Square - 434-0657

We love this store. One could spend a whole afternoon here, roaming through the several rooms thick with antique country French furniture (marble bistro tables, huge pine dining tables, marvelous armoires and chests), fine linens, handpainted china, unusual dolls, old signs from French bakeries, bars and cafés, French kitchenware and much, much more. La Ville du Soleil is an extremely romantic world unto itself, a kind of French country paradise. In one room, a life-size Alice and her friends are having a tea party on a lavishly set table; in another, you half expect a white-aproned waiter to come take your order for a tarte tatin and espresso. Upstairs are some remarkable new and antique linens, from christening gowns to Irish linen pillow-cases. A must in any Union Square shopping trip.

Open Mon.-Sat. 9:30 a.m.-5:30 p.m.

HOUSEWARES & KITCHEN

FIGONI HARDWARE COMPANY

1351 Grant Ave., North Beach - 392-4765

A North Beach classic from another era. Friendly salesmen who've been here since the good old days bring down bulk nails, pipe fittings, wire, you name it from the old wooden shelves that climb all the way to the fifteen-foot ceiling. Figoni is worth a visit just for a look, since these old hardware stores are an almost-extinct breed. But it's also worth a visit if you're looking for sturdy, well-designed, inexpensive restaurant-quality glassware, dishes and cook-ware; simple home linens; stove-top espresso makers and kitchen gadgets; and even some sporting goods, including bocci balls and fishing tackle. It's like a visit to Lake

Wobegon by way of Little Italy. (See also "Where to Find . . ." entry.)

Open Mon.-Sat. 8 a.m.-5 p.m.

FORREST JONES, INC.

3274 Sacramento St., Presidio Heights - 982-1577

151 Jackson St., Financial District - 567-2483

There's something very traditional and familiar about Forrest Jones; it reminds one of those turn-of-the-century French shops photographed by Atget, with its wares hanging round the door and lining the entrance. Once you get past the baskets and leather shopping bags festooning this doorway, you can lose yourself in the maze of shelves filled with glasses, candles, napkins, napkin rings, travel accessories, cooking utensils and handpainted Italian and French dishes. The staff is helpful, there are bargains to be found, and there's a great selection of Panama hats.

Open Mon.-Sat. 10 a.m.-6 p.m., Sun. 11 a.m.-5 p.m.

RUSH CUTTERS

2505 Sacramento St., Presidio Heights - 922-5100

Striking a happy balance between high-tech and traditional, Rush Cutters sells very high-quality kitchen products, including Italian splatterware and kitchen gadgets, Michael Graves teapots, artists' ceramics, attractive cutlery and linens. It's a little more au courant than Williams-Sonoma and is not overpriced.

Open Mon.-Fri. 10:30 a.m.-6:30 p.m., Sat. 10:30 a.m.-6 p.m., Sun. 12 noon-5 p.m.

WHOLE EARTH ACCESS

401 Bayshore Blvd., City South - 285-5244

This relatively new store is an offshoot of the very popular Marin and Berkeley stores, which are offshoots of the old Whole Earth Access catalog, a bible for the socially conscious early-'70s consumer. Today, Whole Earth is an appealing warehouse with unbeatable prices on high-quality computers, televisions, large and small appliances, cookware, dishes, kitchen supplies and some furniture. Don't buy without checking here first. (See also "Image & Sound" entry.)

Open daily 10 a.m.-6 p.m.

WILLIAMS-SONOMA

576 Sutter St., Union Square - 982-0295

Thousands of customers have made the Williams-Sonoma catalog immensely successful, and now residents of many American cities have a Williams-Sonoma of their very own. But this branch, the company's headquarters, is the best of the Williams-Sonoma bunch—several spacious rooms, done in white and green, filled but not crammed with the best kitchen products available. Dishes range from white classics to Italian charmers, cookware from copper to Calphalon, and appliances from cappuccino machines to Cuisinarts. We especially like the cotton table linens, colorful dishrags, Taylor Woodcraft chairs and tables, cookbooks and gadgets. Prices are on the high side of reasonable, though there are usually good special buys.

Open Mon.-Sat. 9:30 a.m.-5:30 p.m.

LINENS

O'PLUME

1764 Union St., Cow Hollow - 771-6100

Absolutely deluxe. With Italian silk sheets, Battenburg lace, plump goose-down comforters covered in fine Egyptian cotton and antique hand-embroidered pillowcases, table-cloths and handkerchiefs, this narrow street-level shop boasts the most exquisite linens imaginable. Its chubby down-filled pillows are guaranteed for ten years, and the store will custom-cover pillows and comforters. We had to fight the impulse to dive headlong into the snowy eiderdown displayed on an antique bed.

Open Mon.-Sat. 10 a.m.-6 p.m., Sun. 12 noon-5 p.m.

REGINA LINENS

3369 Sacramento St., Presidio Heights - 563-8158

Stacks of tablecloths, napkins, placemats, sheets and pillow-cases surround you in this curious shop. The handiwork of China, Portugal and Belgium is represented in these stacks and on the walls. Prices are fair; at $3.95 the hand-embroidered linen handkerchiefs make charming gifts. One wall is devoted to an odd assortment of children's clothes.

Open Mon.-Sat. 11 a.m.-5:30 p.m.

SCANDIA DOWN SHOPS

1546 California St., Nob Hill - 928-5111

3 Embarcadero Center, Financial District - 392-0522

Credit Scandia Down with bringing European-style down-comforter bedding to the American masses. These small shops sell good comforters, from the less-expensive feather down to the more expensive pure goose down, along with down pillows, comforter covers and stylish cotton and cotton-blend sheets. Prices are fair.

Open Mon.-Fri. 10 a.m.-6 p.m., Sat. 10 a.m.-5 p.m.

Image & Sound

PHOTOGRAPHY

BROOKS CAMERAS

45 Kearny St., Union Square - 392-1900

Professionals and amateurs alike shop at Brooks, a large, solid, all-purpose camera store that sells cameras, accessories, film and darkroom supplies. It also rents and repairs cameras and has a good-quality overnight developing service. Prices are middle-of-the-road.

Open Mon.-Fri. 9 a.m.-6 p.m., Sat. 9 a.m.-5:30 p.m.

ADOLPH GASSER

181 2nd St., South of Market - 495-3852

With a complete range of cameras, including the world's finest, Adolph Gasser caters to a professional clientele. You can also buy and rent video and movie cameras. The staff know their stuff.

Open Mon.-Fri. 8:30 a.m.-5:30 p.m., Sat. 9 a.m.-5 p.m.

OSAKA-YA CAMERA

1581 Webster St., Japantown - 567-1160

Steel yourself for impatient, almost rude service, and don't expect expert advice. But if you come to Osaka-ya knowing exactly which camera you want, Mr. Kim will sell it to you at the best price in town. Call first to see if he stocks the model you want.

Open Mon.-Sat. 10 a.m.-6 p.m., Sun. 12 noon-5 p.m.

RECORDED MUSIC

BOSTON COMPACT DISC

3027C Fillmore St., Cow Hollow - 567-9595

An intelligent, idiosyncratic store with a sense of humor and a great selection of hard-to-find CDs. Check out the flyers stacked on the counter listing all the CDs newly available worldwide (even ones BCD can't get), which profile BCD's eclectic list of "must-buys" for the month with wit and taste (of "The Renaissance Christmas" by Boston Camerata: "Terribly Protestant in approach . . . a must if you're a Calvinist"; of "A Lie of the Wind" by the Red Clay Ramblers: "Tighter than a croc on an Everglades poacher").

Open Mon.-Wed. 10 a.m.-9 p.m., Thurs.-Sat. 10 a.m.-10 p.m., Sun. 12 noon-6 p.m.

RECKLESS RECORDS

*1401 Haight St.,
Haight-Ashbury -
989-8999*

Carefully graded used rock records are sorted by artist instead of stacked willy-nilly in bins, as is usually the practice at used record stores. Reckless guarantees its grades; if you buy a B-plus used copy of "Heartbreak Hotel" and find it to be a D-minus, you'll get your money back. Some new domestic and imported rock, too.

Open Mon.-Sat. 10 a.m.-11 p.m., Sun. 10 a.m.-8 p.m.

RECYCLED RECORDS

*1377 Haight St.,
Haight-Ashbury -
626-4075*

This crowded store recycles rock, jazz, blues and classical records, from recent releases to rarities. The records are well organized and fairly priced.

Open daily 11 a.m.-7 p.m.

STREETLIGHT RECORDS

*3979 24th St., Noe Valley -
282-3550*

*2350 Market St., Castro
District - 282-8000*

Two very good all-purpose record stores. Along with a complete range of new records in every category, Streetlight sells used, vintage, rare and out-of-print records. If you don't see it, ask for it.

Open Mon.-Sat. 10 a.m.-10 p.m., Sun. 11 a.m.-8 p.m.

TOWER RECORDS

*Columbus Ave. & Bay St.,
North Beach - 885-0500*

The best new-record store in the city, with virtually every new rock, pop, country, soul, jazz, blues and classical release on record, tape and compact disc. There's also a great collection of old rock and pop singles and classic rock and R & B. Hot new records are usually discounted. Tower puts such ordinary chains as Music Plus to shame.

Open daily 9 a.m.-12 midnight.

VILLAGE MUSIC

*9 E. Blithedale St., Mill
Valley - 388-7400*

It may not have a big-city address, but Village Music is indubitably the best record store in the Bay Area—indeed, the best in the state. A veritable museum of music history, it boasts walls crammed with a priceless collection of gold records, photographs, autographs and memorabilia, and bins chock-a-block with a comprehensive collection of new, used, rare and obscure discs from every musical field, from rock and blues to soundtracks and opera. Every music fan should make a Marin pilgrimage to this outstanding store.

Open Mon.-Sat. 10 a.m.-6 p.m., Sun. 12 noon-5 p.m.

STEREO & VIDEO

AUDIO EXCELLENCE
425 Washington St., Financial District - 433-1335

When that workhorse Sony doesn't do it for you anymore, have a talk with one of the audiophile salesmen at this store. They'll have you listen to some of the finest sound components money can buy (and you need lots of money to buy here), from such makers as Thorens, Audio Research, Michell and Kyocera. Naturally, you'll need a state-of-the-art video system to go along with your new stereo, so Audio Excellence carries the best from Proton, Thomson and NEC.

Open Mon.-Sat. 10:30 a.m.-5:30 p.m.

HOUSE OF MUSIC
1718 Union St., Cow Hollow - 771-1962

Stereo components are treated as works of art here, with devoted, unusually knowledgeable salesmen singing the praises of exemplary but costly equipment from Mark Levenson, Bang & Olufsen, McIntosh and the like. The salesmen will steer you to the right pieces for your home, ear and budget without being pushy or pretentious. House of Music will also properly install, set up, maintain and fix your new equipment.

Open Tues.-Sat. 11 a.m.-6 p.m.

WHOLE EARTH ACCESS
401 Bayshore Blvd., City South - 285-5244

If you're looking for good midrange stereo and video equipment, look no further than Whole Earth. Friendly, reasonably well-informed salesmen will sell you Sony (including the entire ES line), Aiwa, JVC, Harman-Kardon, Onkyo, Infinity, Mission and Boston Acoustics components at the lowest prices in town. (See also "Home" entry.)

Open daily 10 a.m.-6 p.m.

Leather

BOTTEGA VENETA
120 Geary St., Union Square - 981-1700

A marvelous array of Italian leather goods are displayed on three floors in this fabled shop. The staff is friendly and unpretentious, and the luggage, briefcases, purses, belts and wallets are supple, handsome and unspoiled by logos or initials. But, of course, the prices are shocking (small, modest bags made of the signature woven leather *start* at $275).

Open Mon.-Sat. 10 a.m.-6 p.m.

THE COACH STORE

164 Grant Ave., Union Square - 392-1772

The styles may not be the most au courant, but the quality is undisputed. Many a woman is still carrying the Coach bag she bought five (or ten) years ago, a bit dirty perhaps, but still going strong. Since the hearty leather is crafted to last, the bags, belts, wallets and accessories are styled so they won't look foolishly dated in the years to come. But that's not to say the merchandise is stodgy—many of these bags, especially the briefcases and drawstring purses—are beautiful.

Open Mon.-Sat. 10 a.m.-6 p.m.

MARK CROSS

170 Post St., Union Square - 391-7770

These finely crafted leather products are worth their high price tags. Along with the supplest of calfskins and pigskins, the wallets, briefcases, purses and so on are handmade from such exotic hides as ostrich, alligator and lizard. Both the shop and the styles are elegant, timeless and refreshingly discreet.

Open Mon.-Sat. 10 a.m.-5:30 p.m.

GUCCI

253 Post St., Union Square - 772-2522

Snooty and touristy, Gucci appeals to those who like to advertise their supposed good taste. While it's true that these leather shoes and belts and coated-canvas-and-leather bags and wallets are well made (especially the comfortable shoes), in our opinion the styles leave much to be desired. But if a bag plastered with double Gs spells success to you, by all means hurry over.

Open Mon.-Sat. 10 a.m.-5:30 p.m.

MALM LUGGAGE

222 Grant Ave., Union Square - 392-0417

Exceptionally handsome luggage from fine manufacturers—Ghurka, Ralph Lauren, French, Hartmann—are sold here at prices that match the quality. Malm also carries Gold-Pfeil's purses, briefcases, wallets and leather accessories, which we find dowdy and overpriced. Malm has a branch in the Crocker Center Galleria (391-5222).

Open Mon.-Fri. 9:30 a.m.-6 p.m., Sat. 10 a.m.-6 p.m.

LOUIS VUITTON

317 Sutter St., Union Square - 391-6200

Although many consider Louis Vuitton's pieces major status symbols, we can't abide most of the line—specifically, the boring coated canvas bags and luggage covered in pretentious LVs. However, we are fond of the old steamer trunks and the initial-free all-leather pieces, especially the briefcases. Needless to say, if you have to ask, you can't afford it.

Open Mon.-Fri. 10 a.m.-5:30 p.m., Sat. 10 a.m.-5 p.m.

Sporting Goods

AVENUE CYCLERY

756 Stanyan St., Haight-Ashbury - 387-3155

Just across the street from Golden Gate Park, Avenue Cyclery sells impressive machines for the serious cyclist, including racing and mountain bikes from Klein, Cannondale, Biandi and Panasonic. But it also caters to the occasional park cruiser and rents three-speed, ten-speed and mountain bikes from Friday through Sunday for $2 to $4 an hour. There's also an in-house repair shop that is well stocked with parts.

Open daily 9:30 a.m.-5:30 p.m.

EDDIE BAUER

220 Post St., Union Square - 986-7600

Eddie Bauer caters to the rugged outdoorsman and outdoorswoman—even those who like to keep their activity limited to sitting in front of a roaring fire wearing a handsome flannel shirt. Most of the cotton and wool clothing for hiking, running, cycling and skiing carries the Eddie Bauer label, which ensures durability and fair prices; the same goes for the camping, fishing and other sports equipment sold here. The down jackets are especially good values. On the lower floor of this immense three-story shop are well-made shoes for walking, hiking and running.

Open Mon. & Thurs. 10 a.m.-7 p.m., Tues.-Wed. & Fri.-Sat. 10 a.m.-6 p.m., Sun. 12 noon-5 p.m.

BODY OPTIONS

1951 Union St., Cow Hollow - 563-4003

These shops stock enough aerobic wear to raise your pulse just looking through it all, not to mention wriggling in and out of it in the dressing rooms. You'll find leagues of swimsuits, leggings and leotards in lycra and cotton by all the best makers: Gilda Marx, Dance France, Sexotard, Baryshnikov (to name a few), along with socks in every hue and

243

attractive, simple cotton separates by Shadows. Reasonably priced. There are several other locations, including in Embarcadero Center, on Upper Fillmore and on Chestnut in the Marina.

Open Mon.-Sat. 10:30 a.m.-7 p.m., Sun. 11 a.m.-6 p.m.

CITY CYCLE

3001 Steiner St., Cow Hollow - 346-2242

For serious cyclists, the bicycles sold here are all hand built and custom-made, using high-quality frames by Italian makers Inelli and Masi, Bertrand from Canada, Washington State's Gary Klein, and Fat Chance, an American trail-bike maker. The owners/operators are all experienced cyclists who will custom-build and -tailor your bike and keep it in perfect repair. The only assembled bikes sold here, made by Georgena Terry, are designed especially for women. Desiente apparel and some cycling accessories are also available.

Open Mon.-Tues. & Thurs.-Fri. 11 a.m.-7 p.m., Sat.-Sun. 10 a.m.-4 p.m., and by appt.

COPELAND'S SPORTS

901 Market St., Union Square - 495-0928

This large, two-story paean to the active life sells just about everything for the athlete. The clothing selection is pedestrian, but the equipment—rowing machines, baseball bats, weights, camping gear—is first-rate. Service is friendly and informed.

Open Mon.-Sat. 10 a.m.-7 p.m., Sun. 10 a.m.-6 p.m.

ELLESSE

355 Sutter St., Union Square - 421-6853

At these prices, you may not want to break a sweat, but you'll cut a good-looking figure on the tennis court or ski slope in your boldly colored matching ensembles. The active sportswear is limited to tennis and ski wear, and there's an equally expensive line of casual weekend wear.

Open Mon.-Sat. 9 a.m.-6 p.m., Sun. 11 a.m.-5 p.m.

FILA

239 Grant Ave., Union Square - 956-4170

There's no doubting that these tennis whites and ski colors are handsome and well made. You'll pay dearly, however, for the distinctive Fila logo splattered all over the tennis shirts, sweatsuits, headbands, socks and ski sweaters.

Open Mon.-Sat. 9 a.m.-6 p.m.

FIRST STEP

216 Powell St., Union Square - 989-9989

Athletic shoes of every size, color and logo are on display here: running shoes from New Balance, basketball shoes from Converse, tennis shoes from Nike, aerobics shoes from

Reebok, walking shoes from Timberland and boat shoes from Sperry. Prices are neither high nor low.

Open Mon.-Sat. 10 a.m.-7 p.m.

HOY'S SPORTS
1860 Fillmore St., Upper Fillmore - 921-3677

A small general-purpose sporting goods store run by a gregarious and athletic young woman. The swimsuits, swim accessories, T-shirts, balls and weights are high in quality and reasonably priced.

Open Mon.-Fri. 11 a.m.-6 p.m., Sat. 10 a.m.-6 p.m., Sun. 11 a.m.-4 p.m.

MOUNTAIN AVENUE
1865 Haight St., Haight-Ashbury - 221-6630

Mountain bikes are the passion in this tiny Haight store. Fine bikes from such makers as Fisher, Klein and Cunningham are sold by a staff made up of mountain-bike enthusiasts.

Open daily 10 a.m.-6 p.m.

NEVADA BOB'S
214 California St., Financial District - 362-7737

Everything for the golfer—from the finest clubs to the loudest plaid pants. Prices are fair; at sale time, they're exceptional. There's an indoor range for trying out your dream clubs.

Open Mon.-Fri. 9 a.m.-6 p.m., Sat. 9 a.m.-5 p.m.

SWISS SKI SPORTS
559 Clay St., Financial District - 434-0322

An exceptionally friendly store devoted to all things ski. The selection of skis, boots, accessories and handsome clothing is broad and fairly priced, and there's also a good collection of tennis equipment and clothing. Snow reports and Tahoe ski information are always available.

Open Mon.-Fri. 10 a.m.-7 p.m., Sat. 10 a.m.-5 p.m.

TENNIS LADY/TENNIS MAN
170 Geary St., Union Square - 982-1049

The racquet and shoe collections are rather limited, given that this store sells nothing but tennis gear. But there's a good range of clothing, from costly Fila and Ellesse to more frugal (and just as handsome) Nike and Head. Salespeople can be overly helpful.

Open Mon.-Sat. 10 a.m.-6 p.m.

Tobacconists

GRANT'S TOBACCONISTS
562 Market St., Financial District - 981-1000

An aromatic shop with a well-rounded (but not inexpensive) selection of pipes, cigars, tobaccos, humidors and smoking accessories.

Open Mon.-Fri. 9 a.m.-5:30 p.m., Sat. 10 a.m.-5:30 p.m.

JIM MATE PIPE & TOBACCO SHOP
575 Geary St., Union Square - 775-6634

This well-known tobacconist sells fine pipes from the likes of Sasieni, Dunhill and GBD, along with the world's finest cigars and tobaccos. Mate's house-blend tobacco is exceptional; also quite respectable are the five different house-brand cigars. The staff's love of the merchandise is evident.

Open Mon.-Sat. 9 a.m.-5:30 p.m.

Where to Find . . .

A BABYSITTER

BAY AREA BABY SITTERS AGENCY
991-7474

A state-licensed, extremely reliable agency that has been supplying San Francisco with mature babysitters for 40 years. Rates are $4 an hour with a four-hour minimum, plus an extra charge for transportation.

A CLEANERS

BRENTWOOD CLEANERS
1919 Fillmore St., Upper Fillmore - 346-1919

This careful, full-service dry cleaner will pick up and deliver. It also offers good laundry and leather-cleaning services (neither of which is on the premises).

Open Mon.-Fri. 7:30 a.m.-6:30 p.m., Sat. 8 a.m.-5 p.m.

SAGAN LAUNDRY & CLEANERS

989 Post St., Union Square - 775-8000

A large, well-located cleaners that also launders shirts on the premises. Laundry and shirts can be turned around in one day, and Sagan picks up and delivers to several downtown hotels.

Open Mon.-Fri. 7:30 a.m.-6:30 p.m., Sat. 8 a.m.-4 p.m.

A DATE

GREAT EXPECTATIONS

2330 Marinship Way, Sausalito - 332-2353

Of the plethora of dating services that have arisen in these lonely times, Great Expectations is probably the most successful. This branch has 2,700 members of all ages and from many Bay Area locations—from Daly City to Santa Rosa, with a great many in the city. When you join, you are videotaped and a profile is kept on file; you then come in to inspect the videos and files of prospective mates (or at least, dates), and they will in turn study yours before a meeting is arranged. The staff is sales-oriented but friendly and unintimidating.

Open Mon.-Fri. 10 a.m.-8 p.m., Sat.-Sun. 10 a.m.-5 p.m.

A DRUGSTORE

MANDARIN PHARMACY

895 Washington St., Chinatown - 989-9292

This well-stocked pharmacy is notable for its friendly service and, most important, its free delivery.

Open Mon.-Fri. 10 a.m.-6:30 p.m., Sat. 10 a.m.-6 p.m.

WALGREEN DRUGSTORE

135 Powell St., Union Square - 391-4433

Though chaotic and rather drab, this Bay Area chain has everything a drugstore should have and is convenient for the downtown visitor.

Open Mon.-Sat. 8 a.m.-10 p.m., Sun. 9 a.m.-8 p.m.

A FIVE-AND-DIME

F. W. WOOLWORTH COMPANY

A classic example of the classic American five-and-dime chain, complete with lunch counter. Socks, notions, candy, frying pans, greeting cards, wrapping paper . . . all the little

*898 Market St., Union
Square - 986-2164*

necessities of everyday life are here. You might have to push past a few mumbling street people to gain entrance.

Open Mon. & Thurs.-Fri. 8:30 a.m.-8 p.m., Tues.-Wed. & Sat. 8:30 a.m.-6:30 p.m., Sun. 12 noon-5 p.m.

A HARDWARE STORE

FIGONI HARDWARE COMPANY

1351 Grant Ave., North Beach - 392-4765

This store-out-of-time is a blast from North Beach's old Italian past. Worn wooden shelves stacked up to the high ceiling are filled with bulk nails, screws, chain and so on; the cheerful old-timers who work here will climb a classic rolling ladder to get the supplies you need. These men also make keys, dispense advice and sell you inexpensive restaurant-quality dishes, glassware and kitchen supplies. (See also "Home" entry.)

Open Mon.-Sat. 8 a.m.-5 p.m.

A LIMOUSINE

P & F CUSTOM LIMOUSINE SERVICE

824-6767

This established firm rents Lincoln and Cadillac limousines, complete with professional drivers, for $38.50 to $50 an hour with a three-hour minimum.

A MESSENGER

NUMBER 1 SPECIAL DELIVERY

974 Harrison St., South of Market - 543-4285

Along with the usual letters and small packages, Number 1 will deliver unusually large objects—anything they can fit in their vans (up to 1,500 pounds). Consequently, Number 1 is the favorite delivery company of artists and galleries. They'll also deliver nights and weekends if arranged in advance. Rates are competitive.

Open Mon.-Fri. 8 a.m.-6 p.m.

A NEWSSTAND

UPTOWN NEWS

Unfortunately, this all-purpose newsstand has limited hours. Fortunately, it has a good stock of out-of-town newspapers

248

14 Trinity Pl., Financial
District - 398-1641

and foreign and unusual magazines, along with cigarettes, cigars and candy.

Open Mon.-Fri. 8 a.m.-5 p.m.

A PET HOTEL

PET EXPRESS

Triple A Shipyard,
Bayview - 822-7111

This popular kennel boards dogs and cats at reasonable rates ($9 a day for a retriever-size dog). And for an extra $5 each way, Pet Express will pick up and deliver your pooch. Book your pet as far in advance as possible to ensure a space, especially for the holidays. Grooming services are also available.

A PHOTO LAB

CUSTOM HOUR PHOTO

123 Powell St., Union
Square - 956-2374

Bring your color shots of the cable cars here and they'll be ready for you to take home in an hour.

Open Mon.-Fri. 8:30 a.m.-6:30 p.m., Sat.-Sun. 9:30 a.m.-6 p.m.

GAMMA PHOTOGRAPHIC LABS

351 9th St., South of
Market - 864-8155

A good lab for careful developing and printing of black-and-white film. Though it'll cost you extra, Gamma will rush jobs.

Open Mon.-Fri. 9 a.m.-5 p.m.

A SECRETARY

KELLY SERVICES

1 Post St., Financial
District - 982-2200

A large, long-established temp chain that will supply skilled typists, word processors, receptionists and general-purpose secretaries on an hourly, daily or monthly basis.

Open Mon.-Fri. 8 a.m.-6 p.m.

PRO-TEMPS

130 Bush St. (4th Floor),
Financial District -
788-3623

Along with your garden-variety temporary secretary, Pro-temps provides qualified word processors, data processors and even computer programmers. A word processor goes for about $20 an hour.

Open Mon.-Fri. 8 a.m.-6 p.m.

A TAILOR

WALTER FONG

459 Geary St., Union Square - 397-7777

This longtime San Francisco tailor does good work for a reasonable price. The service and attitude are accommodating.

Open Mon.-Sat. 9:30 a.m.-6 p.m.

THE TAILORED MAN

324 Stockton St., Union Square - 397-6906

Given The Tailored Man's location facing onto Union Square, it's not surprising that its prices are high (just having a pair of pants taken in costs $15). But the quality of the tailoring, including the custom-made suits, is equally high. There's a large selection of ready-to-wear clothing as well.

Open Mon.-Fri. 9:30 a.m.-6 p.m., Sat. 9 a.m.-5:30 p.m., Sun. 12 noon-5 p.m.

A TRANSLATOR

BERLITZ TRANSLATION SERVICE

660 Market St. (4th Floor), Financial District - 986-6474

Berlitz can provide you with someone to translate almost every language imaginable, from French to Farsi. Oral translation fees are about $50 an hour, with a two-hour minimum; written translators are paid by the word.

Open Mon.-Sat. 8 a.m.-9 p.m.

A TUXEDO

LA ROSA FORMAL WEAR

1780 Haight St., Haight-Ashbury - 668-3746

Not only can you rent new designer tuxedoes in this Haight shop, but you can also buy clean, well-preserved vintage tuxes, dinner jackets and formal gowns at reasonable prices.

Open Mon.-Sat. 11 a.m.-7 p.m., Sun. 11 a.m.-6 p.m.

SELIX FORMAL WEAR

123 Kearny St., Union Square - 362-1133

A full line of contemporary tuxedoes, tails, morning suits and dinner jackets rent for $50 to $70 a day. Selix can also fit women in some of the models.

Open Mon.-Fri. 9 a.m.-6 p.m., Sat. 8:30 a.m.-5 p.m.

A VETERINARIAN

PETS UNLIMITED

2343 Fillmore St., Upper Fillmore - 563-6700

A well-established, always-busy veterinary hospital with four skilled, compassionate vets on staff. Unfortunately, Pets Unlimited does not board animals (see Pet Express under "A Pet Hotel").

Open Mon.-Wed. 9 a.m.-7 p.m., Thurs.-Fri. 9 a.m.-6 p.m., Sat. 9 a.m.-5 p.m., Sun. 10 a.m.-4 p.m.

SIGHTS

Beaches & Parks

BEACHES

It may be surrounded by water, but San Francisco is not known for its beaches. The fog is always rolling in, the waves are always crashing against rocky cliffs, and the whole scene seems suitable only for sea lions and squawking gulls. But while most surfers and sun worshippers head south to Santa Cruz or north to such Marin beaches as Stinson, San Francisco does have a few choice spots, and the weather is warm and sunny more often than you might suppose.

BAKER BEACH

Gibson Rd. off Bowley St., Presidio - 556-0560

A part of the Golden Gate National Recreation Area, this mile-long stretch of clean, sandy beach attracts fishermen, family picnickers and nude sunbathers (tolerated north of the "High Tide" sign). Overnight camping is not allowed, but picnic and barbecue facilities, restrooms and drinking water are all provided by the park service. Although Baker is often warmer than other local beaches, its waves are hazardous and swimming is discouraged.

LAND'S END BEACH

Land's End Trail off Merrie Way, near Geary Blvd. & Great Hwy., Richmond District - 556-0560

Swimming is not allowed at this small but picturesque beach, but since the 1960s it has been a favorite of the clothing-optional crowd. Getting there, down a steep trail, is difficult, but protected as it is by the high cliffs, Land's End is private and affords a grand view back on the San Francisco harbor. The crowd at the moment is largely gay, although this has shifted like the tides over the years.

OCEAN BEACH

Great Hwy. south of the Cliff House, Richmond District - 556-0560

Where Golden Gate Park ends its long stretch toward the sea, San Francisco's most accessible beach begins. When most city dwellers head for the beach, this is where they come. The long strip of sand is often heavily populated with joggers, Frisbee throwers, sunbathers and beachcombers. But because of the rough tides and dangerous undertow, wading and swimming are frequently unsafe.

PHELAN BEACH

Seacliff Ave. off El Camino del Mar, Richmond District - 558-3706

At last a beach where you can swim! Nestled into a small cove, Phelan, once known as China Beach, is sufficiently protected from the tides and undertows so that swimming is feasible during the warmest periods of the summer months. Lifeguards are on duty from April to October, but you should call ahead to check on the conditions.

PARKS

AQUATIC PARK

Next to Ghirardelli Square (900 North Point), Fisherman's Wharf - 556-0560

When the sun breaks through the ubiquitous "morning and evening low clouds and fog," this small bayside park fills up with picnickers and sunbathers. Its tiered layout affords a splendid view of the Bay, out to Alcatraz and across the Golden Gate to Sausalito and Angel Island. There is a large lawn and a small beach for wading, and joggers are a regular part of the landscape.

DOLORES PARK

Dolores St. & 18th St., Mission District - 558-3706

Just two blocks away from Mission Dolores, this small oasis of greenery in the densely populated Mission District is a frequent rallying point for political demonstrations and marches. On most days its quiet setting affords a panoramic view of San Francisco, from downtown to the southern waterfront.

GOLDEN GATE PARK

Bounded by Fulton St., Stanyan St., Great Hwy. & Lincoln Blvd. - 558-3706

Inspired by Frederick Law Olmstead's pioneering work with Central Park in New York City, Golden Gate Park is a masterwork of creative urban transformation. In the 1860s, when Olmstead visited the city, this four-and-a-half-mile-long, nine-block-wide expanse was simply dry, sandy land brutalized by rough winds from the Pacific Ocean. Olmstead may have been intimidated, but engineer William Hammond Hall, the park's first superintendent, along with John McLaren, the tireless landscape gardener who took over as superintendent in 1876 and served for the next 55 years, designed, planted, nurtured and tended the 1,000 acres until they flourished with lush, green foliage and over one million trees. The narrow Panhandle, the jogger-filled peninsula between Fell and Oak streets on the park's east side, leads into a dazzling maze of wooded drives. The Hall of Flowers, the spectacular Conservatory of Flowers, the Strybing Arboretum, the Rhododendron Dell, the California Academy of Sciences, the De Young Museum, the Children's Playground, the peaceful Japanese Tea Garden, several lakes (including Stow and Spreckels), a buffalo paddock, a nine-hole golf course, tennis courts, baseball diamonds, handball courts and designated roller skating areas are all brilliantly tucked into their own green havens within the park. The entire realm is a supreme example of man tempering a harsh urban landscape with natural wonders. The park headquarters are in McLaren Lodge, the romanesque house at Fell and Stanyan streets that served as John McLaren's home during his tenure.

SIGMUND STERN MEMORIAL GROVE

19th Ave. & Sloat Blvd., Sunset District - 398-6551

For the past 50 years, this 63-acre park has hosted a summer festival of afternoon concerts in its natural tree-lined amphitheater. The music programs feature classical, popular and jazz artists performing in the sylvan setting of redwoods and eucalyptus. The Grove is also a gorgeous place for barbecues and picnics.

Excursions

ALCATRAZ ISLAND

Pier 41 (Red & White Fleet), Powell St. at the waterfront, Fisherman's Wharf - 546-2805

The Rock, one of the most notorious prisons in America, has been closed as a penitentiary since 1963. Named Isla de los Alcatraces in 1775 for the pelicans roosting there, the island's isolation made it a prime location for detention facilities. Although the fate of the island is a perennial subject for debate, for the moment it is open to tourists. The Red & White Fleet will ferry you there and provide an optional recorded tour; on the island, rangers from the Golden Gate National Recreation Area conduct guided tours, or you can just wander. Bring a jacket, plan on a two-hour trip, and buy your ferry tickets at least two days in advance, especially in summer (advance tickets available through Ticketron).

Open daily 8:15 a.m.-4:40 p.m. Ferries depart hourly from 8:15 a.m.-4:15 p.m.; last ferry returns 4:40 p.m. Adults $4.50 for self-guided tour & $6.50 for recorded tour, children 5-11 $2.75 for self-guided tour and $4.25 for recorded tour, children under 5 free. Ranger-led guided tours free.

BALCLUTHA

Pier 43, Powell St. & the Embarcadero, Fisherman's Wharf - 982-1886

With its three masts reaching skyward and its classic square rigging, this century-old sailing ship is a favorite attraction along the waterfront. Built in Scotland in 1883, the *Balclutha* has been a cargo ship, a lumber ship, a salmon cannery in Alaska, a carnival ship and a Hollywood prop. Full of memorabilia, she conjures up images of old sailing days and offers a grand view along the Embarcadero. The *Balclutha* is part of the Maritime Museum (see "Museums").

Open daily 10 a.m.-6 p.m. Adults $2, children & seniors 25 cents-$1.50, children under six free.

FILBERT STEPS

Filbert St., Telegraph Hill

To walk down the breathtakingly steep east slope of Telegraph Hill, follow Filbert Street until it turns into a neatly landscaped walkway. From the platforms along the path that snakes down the hillside you can look from side to side at a rich array of eclectic architecture or out across the redeveloped Embarcadero warehouses to the Bay.

FISHERMAN'S WHARF

Jefferson St. & Hyde St., northern waterfront

Although now overshadowed by the immense shopping complexes of the Cannery and Ghirardelli Square, Fisherman's Wharf is not without its tacky charm. This quaint relic of tourism boasts such crowd-pleasers as the Wax Museum, Ripley's Believe It or Not! Museum and the Enchanted World of San Francisco mini–cable car ride, all of which we find dismally dull. Once the city's center of commercial fishing, the wharf still harbors fishing vessels, whose crews can be seen around the docks—though they are far outnumbered by tourists wearing loud T-shirts and toting bags of sourdough bread. Skip the mostly dreadful seafood restaurants in the area and opt instead for the street food, especially the wonderfully fresh sourdough bread and the decent "walkaway" cocktails of shrimp or Dungeness crab from the open fish markets. Souvenir trinkets abound.

FORT MASON

Under the supervision of the Golden Gate National Recreation Area, the pier-situated buildings of this former

*Franklin St. & Bay St.,
northern waterfront -
441-5705*

nineteenth-century army post have been transformed into a fine array of workshops, galleries, museums, theaters and restaurants. Greens, run by the Zen Center, is a nationally acclaimed showcase of health-oriented nouvelle cuisine. Two warehouse buildings are used for annual crafts fairs, and the Great Meadow is home to the rousing San Francisco Blues Festival every September. Just to the west, extending to the yacht harbor, is the Marina Green, a vast bayside lawn typically dotted with kite-fliers, joggers and sunbathers.

FORT POINT

*Long Ave. off Lincoln Blvd.,
Presidio - 556-1693*

Tucked under the southern anchorage of the Golden Gate Bridge, the area surrounding this 1853 fort will be familiar to fans of Alfred Hitchcock's *Vertigo*. The point where James Stewart meets Kim Novak is perfectly located for an awe-inspiring view of the bridge from underneath. The fort itself, built to protect the city from naval attack, houses a museum of Civil War–era military memorabilia.

GHIRARDELLI SQUARE & THE CANNERY

*North Point St. &
Leavenworth St.,
Fisherman's Wharf*

Just west of Fisherman's Wharf, these two renovated factory complexes house scores of shops, galleries and restaurants. Ghirardelli Square, originally a woolen mill in the mid-1800s and later the Ghirardelli chocolate factory, was converted to its present commercial state in the early 1960s. It boasts a lively outdoor scene, including street vendors and sidewalk performers, a lovely central plaza and some fine upscale chain shops. The Cannery, so called because it was the home of Del Monte's peach-canning operation, was remodeled in 1968 and is another early example of San Francisco's clever commercial redevelopment of old buildings. The mix of shops is less interesting than at Ghirardelli, but both centers are usually packed shoulder-to-shoulder with tourists.

LOMBARD STREET

*Lombard St. between Hyde
St. & Leavenworth St.,
Russian Hill*

The residents on the legendary "crookedest street in the world" have grown impatient with rude tourists jamming bumper-to-bumper down the serpentine maze that they call home. Designed in the 1920s to conquer the steep hill with a switchback scheme, the lovely brick-paved and richly landscaped boulevard allows one-way traffic down the hill. But while it is an irresistible magnet for tourists, Lombard Street may eventually be closed to all but residents if the burdensome traffic and minor accidents finally spark action from City Hall.

MOUNT DAVIDSON

Rex Ave. & Portola Dr.,
City South

In the city of hills, Mount Davidson soars above the rest, climbing to all of 938 feet. Once part of Adolph Sutro's magnificent 12,000-acre estate, the mountain was surveyed in 1852 by George Davidson, who called it Blue Mountain, and is now a city park. Since 1923 Easter sunrise services have been held at the base of the 103-foot cross that rises above the summit.

PIER 39

Northern waterfront near
Beach St. & Powell St.,
Fisherman's Wharf -
981-PIER

Almost exclusively a tourist attraction, this two-level shopping area took over an old cargo pier in 1978, replacing the authentic waterfront buildings with a developer's fantasy of a Barbary Coast village. Other than the architecture, little here is turn-of-the-century, what with the hundreds of tourist-oriented specialty shops, fast-food joints and restaurants. There are, however, a few quaint and crafty respites from the schlock and tack. For the kids, a small-scale amusement park has bumper cars and other rides.

SAN FRANCISCO ZOO

Sloat Blvd. & Great Hwy.,
Sunset District - 661-4844

Gradually catching up to the new consciousness in the housing and display of wild creatures, this 70-acre animal park has developed such popular features as Monkey Island, Gorilla World, the Seal Pool, Wolf Woods and other environmentally "natural" showcases for its more than 1,000 exotic wards. There's also a popular children's zoo.

Open daily 10 a.m.-5 p.m. Adults $3.50, children under 15 free, seniors $1 (for a quarterly pass).

TREASURE ISLAND

Midway across the Bay
Bridge (I-80 Fwy.)

Although this man-made island in the middle of the Bay Bridge, off Yerba Buena Island, is reputed to be slowly sinking into the Bay, it is still home to a large Navy base. Built as a setting for the 1939 Golden Gate International Exposition, most of Treasure Island's 400 acres are off limits to the public, but a quick stop when crossing the Bay Bridge affords beautiful views of the city and its bridges.

TWIN PEAKS

Twin Peaks Blvd. south of
Clarendon Ave., between
Noe Valley & the Sunset
District

They may not be the highest points in San Francisco, but on clear days and nights these chilly, windswept peaks offer the grandest view of the city. You can look across the panorama that inspired Adolph Sutro to conjure up a rebuilding plan for the city after it had been devastated by the great earthquake.

UNION SQUARE

Geary St., Powell St., Post St. & Stockton St.

Crowding the streets surrounding this one-block oasis of downtown greenery are many of San Francisco's most elite shops and hotels. Union Square is always thick with people, especially during summer tourist season and the holidays, when Christmas shoppers are drawn to such magnets as Neiman-Marcus, Saks, Gump's and Macy's—not to mention countless smaller shops and boutiques, ranging from Eddie Bauer and Crate & Barrel to Ralph Lauren and Louis Vuitton. Scattered throughout the square and the streets are street musicians, street vendors and street people. When you've charged your cards to the limit, recover in the soothing lounge of the classic St. Francis Hotel facing Union Square.

The Great Outdoors

San Francisco has so thoroughly spread its civilization over its hills and valleys that its outdoor sports are confined to an occasional oasis of green or blue, often where man has deigned to install a touch of nature amid the dense development. Most of the Bay Area's best outdoor activities are focused on points north, south or east of the city. But if walking the hills, window shopping and bending an elbow in a neighborhood tavern don't provide you with enough exercise, and you don't want to leave the city limits, there are some fine places to skate, bicycle, golf, jog and sail.

BICYCLING

GOLDEN GATE PARK

South Dr. off Fell St. entrance - 558-3706

Although downtown's fast and furious bicycle messengers are legendary, we don't recommend imitating their dangerous weaving through autos and pedestrians. Instead, ride the relaxed way along the seven-and-a-half-mile bike path from Golden Gate Park to Lake Merced. Start on the Fell Street side of the Panhandle and, after entering the park, follow South Drive to Sunset Boulevard, which leads to Lake Merced and a pleasant five-mile loop. Or take South Drive to Great Highway and ride along the beach for a few miles.

Several shops along the Stanyan Street side of the park rent bikes of every kind.

FISHING

LAKE MERCED

Skyline Blvd. & Harding Rd. (Harding Park), City South - 753-1101

Along with the many charter fishing boats that depart from Fisherman's Wharf in search of such deep-sea denizens as rock cod, San Francisco actually has its own large, freshwater fishing hole where you can row out and cast for trout during fishing season. Lake Merced, a backup reservoir just south of the zoo, has a boathouse that rents rowboats and pedal boats; a bar and restaurant; and plenty of picnic areas complete with barbecues for cooking up your catch.

Open daily 6 a.m.-7:30 p.m. Boats rent for $5-$7.

GOLFING

GLENEAGLE'S GOLF COURSE

Sunnydale Ave. & Hahn St. (McLaren Park), City South - 587-2425

A tough, hilly nine-hole course, Gleneagle's makes up for the frustrations it imparts with the southern Bay view it allows from the clubhouse. Though on McLaren Park property, the course is privately operated.

Open daily 7 a.m.-8 p.m. Admission $6 weekdays, $7 weekends.

GOLDEN GATE PARK GOLF COURSE

47th Ave. between Fulton St. & John F. Kennedy Dr., Golden Gate Park - 751-8987

Once you've been tested by the short but tight fairways, tricky turns, ample hills and surrounding trees, not to mention the wisps of fog that blow in from the nearby Pacific, you might be glad this course is only nine holes.

Open daily 7 a.m.-8 p.m. Admission $2 weekdays, $4 weekends.

HARDING PARK GOLF COURSE

Harding Rd. near Skyline Blvd. (Harding Park), City South - 664-4690

Formerly the site of the Lucky Open on the PGA tour, the eighteen-hole, 6,637-yard Harding course, beautifully set in lush forest surroundings, is a challenge from hole to hole. Harding Park is also home to the nine-hole Fleming Golf Course.

Open daily 6:30 a.m.-dusk. Admission $8 weekdays, $15 weekends.

LINCOLN PARK GOLF COURSE

34th Ave. & Clement St. (Lincoln Park), Richmond District - 221-9911

San Francisco's oldest eighteen-hole golf course is 5,081 yards of rough but scenic terrain. Some holes boast views of the Golden Gate Bridge.

Open daily 6 a.m.-8 p.m. Admission $8 weekdays, $12 weekends.

HORSEBACK RIDING

GOLDEN GATE PARK STABLES

John F. Kennedy Dr. & 34th Ave., Golden Gate Park - 668-7360

Unfortunately, these stables do not rent out horses for unescorted riding. But you can take riding lessons, either alone or with a group, and enjoy Golden Gate Park on horseback. Reservations are required.

Open Tues.-Sun. 10:30 a.m.-4 p.m. Group lessons $12-$17 an hour per person, private lessons $30 an hour.

ROLLER SKATING

GOLDEN GATE PARK

John F. Kennedy Dr. between Kezar Dr. & Transverse Dr. - 558-3706

While the hills of central San Francisco would be death-defying folly on any wheels other than those belonging to autos and cable cars, Golden Gate Park has a designated area for skaters on Sundays. A good stretch of John F. Kennedy Drive is closed to cars, allowing plenty of open space for trick skating and casual rolling. Skate rentals are available from several shops around the park.

ROWING AND SAILING

LAKE MERCED BOATHOUSE

Harding Rd. & Skyline Blvd. (Harding Park), City South - 753-1101

You can explore this long, narrow lake in Harding Park via a rowboat, canoe or pedal boat, all of which are rented (for a mere $5 to $7 an hour) at the park's boathouse.

Open daily 6 a.m.-7:30 p.m.

STOW LAKE BOATHOUSE

Lake Dr. off John F. Kennedy Dr., Golden Gate Park - 752-0347

The largest body of water in Golden Gate Park has a boathouse that rents rowboats, pedal boats and motorboats. Take your loved one and a picnic basket and row over to Strawberry Hill island in the middle of the lake for a romantic picnic.

Open Tues.-Sun. 9 a.m.-4 p.m.

RUNNING

CITYWIDE

Most runners make their own trails where they find them, including the hilly streets of San Francisco. And the city is known for its annual Marathon and Bay to Breakers footraces. But some routes are better than others. Our favorites are Lake Merced in Harding Park, with five flat miles of asphalt and dirt; the Marina Green, a very popular one-mile stretch of grass with spectacular views of the Golden Gate, Alcatraz and the Bay; the Polo Field, just off Middle Drive in the center of Golden Gate Park, with its pleasant tracks and trails; and Stow Lake, a short, scenic course around the water with the option of more difficult dirt trails on Strawberry Hill.

TENNIS

SAN FRANCISCO RECREATION & PARKS DEPARTMENT

Fell St. & Stanyan St. (McLaren Lodge), Golden Gate Park - 558-3706

One call to the Parks Department will give you the location of more than 100 city tennis courts, most of which are free to use. The most popular courts, located on the east end of Golden Gate Park, cost $2 after 5 p.m. and close at dark. They can be reserved on the weekends by calling 478-9500 from Wednesday through Friday.

Landmarks

We can't begin to cover the breadth of architectural and historical gems in San Francisco—there are far too many. But we can present you with a somewhat idiosyncratic list of our very favorites.

BANK OF AMERICA BUILDING

California St. & Kearny St., Financial District

A 52-story block dwarfing everything but the Transamerica Pyramid, this early '60s giant escapes the monotonous monolithic look through faceted walls and windows, an odd-shaped top and glazing that reflects light differently throughout the day. For the city's best view, ride the elevator up to the penthouse Carnelian Room for a before- or after-dinner drink.

BAY BRIDGE

I-80 Fwy. between San Francisco & Oakland

Actually two bridges—a double suspension bridge on the San Francisco side and a cantilever bridge on the Oakland side—connected by a tunnel through Yerba Buena Island, this 50-year-old span was brilliantly engineered by Charles H. Purcell. The entire structure is more than eight miles long, on-ramps included, and the bridge spans four-and-a-half miles of water. The longest steel high-level bridge in the world, it has two one-way decks for traffic (the lower deck originally ran trucks and electric trains) and requires a 75-cent toll westbound into the city.

130 BUSH STREET BUILDING

130 Bush St., Financial District

Only twenty feet wide but ten stories high, this George Applegarth Gothic creation is remarkably (and gracefully) slim.

CHILDREN'S CAROUSEL

Kezar Dr. & Martin Luther King Jr. Dr. (Children's Playground), Golden Gate Park - 558-3706

Constructed in New York around 1912, and arriving in San Francisco after the 1939 World's Fair, these 62 animals, two chariots, one tub and one rocker on a turning platform have been lovingly restored and are housed in a turn-of-the-century Greek temple.

June-Sept.: open daily 10 a.m.-4:45 p.m.; Oct.-May: open Wed.-Sun. 10 a.m.-4:45 p.m. Adults $1, children under 12 25 cents, children under 39 inches free with paying adult.

CHINA BASIN BUILDING

Berry St. between 3rd St. & 4th St., China Basin

With a horizontal measurement of 850 feet, this chunky former warehouse, built in 1922, is longer than any San Francisco skyscraper is high. Repainted bright blue in streamline ocean-liner style in 1973, its warehouse-to-office conversion prefigured the current SOMA rehabilitation mania.

CIRCLE GALLERY

140 Maiden Ln., Union Square - 989-2100

This 1949 Frank Lloyd Wright building, with a brick facing and fine archway opening, features an interior spiral ramp that was the prototype for Wright's famous design for the Guggenheim Museum in New York. It currently houses a gallery stocked with questionable art.

Open Mon.-Wed. & Sat. 10 a.m.-6 p.m., Thurs.-Fri. 10 a.m.-7 p.m.

CIVIC CENTER
Polk St. to Franklin St. & Grove St. to McAllister St.

A masterful complex of Beaux Arts buildings, the Civic Center was the brainchild of architect Daniel Burnham, the creation of the some of the country's finest architects and the pride of Mayor Sunny Jim Rolph. The first building was completed in 1913, with original construction continuing into the 1930s. The center includes the domed and beautifully detailed City Hall; the War Memorial Opera House, which houses a remarkable foyer with a stunning gilt ceiling; the San Francisco Public Library, which boasts exceptional interior murals; and many other beauties, including the Civic Auditorium, the State Office Building and the Federal Office Building. One of the Civic Center's latest additions (built in 1980) is the Louise M. Davies Symphony Hall, designed by Skidmore, Owings & Merrill to fit with integrity into the Beaux Arts scheme.

CLIFF HOUSE
109 Point Lobos Ave., Richmond District - 982-2648 (restaurant & bar), 386-1170 (museum)

Perched on the cliffs near Point Lobos, the westernmost tip of San Francisco, this 1909 relic (which followed several previous resorts that burned down on the same spot) houses a popular restaurant and a museum that showcases one of the world's largest collections of coin-operated automatic musical instruments. The building, a typical turn-of-the-century, Newport-style beach house, is upstaged by the spectacular setting, especially the view from the bar.

Restaurant open daily 11 a.m.-10:30 p.m.; bar open daily 11 a.m.-1:30 a.m.; museum open daily 10 a.m.-8 p.m. Admission to museum free.

COIT TOWER
Telegraph Hill Blvd., Telegraph Hill - 982-2648

Built in 1934 by Lillie Coit, in memory of her late husband and in honor of the city's firefighters, this example of '30s moderne architecture also contains a series of significant and once-controversial WPA murals depicting scenes from the immigrant and working-class side of California history. Elevator rides can be taken to the top of the tower, and there's a gift shop selling the expected tourist trinkets.

Open daily 10 a.m.-5:30 p.m.

COLUMBUS TOWER

A classic Victorian office building on the edge of North Beach, the Columbus Tower was owned for several years by

Columbus Ave., Kearny St. & Pacific Ave., North Beach — director Francis Ford Coppola, who had his offices there. The weathered green building has an unusual triangular design and is wonderfully ornate.

FERRY BUILDING

The Embarcadero & Market St., Lower Market

This grand clock tower with dramatic arcades and galleries, built in 1896 and modeled after the cathedral tower in Seville, Spain, was once the gateway to San Francisco, receiving millions of ferry boat passengers before the bridges were built.

450 SUTTER BUILDING

450 Sutter St., Financial District

A quintessential art deco skyscraper designed by Timothy Pflueger. Finished just as the Depression took hold, this was the last skyscraper to be built in San Francisco for twenty years. The deco/pre-Columbian detailing is fabulous.

GOLDEN GATE BRIDGE

101 Fwy. between San Francisco & Marin County

One of the longest suspension bridges in the world (with a 4,200-foot clear span), this 50-year-old masterpiece by Joseph Strauss is also one of the most beautiful. Its orange paint flashes brilliantly against the blue of the sky and water, and its grand scale is rendered human and graceful through fine moderne styling. A toll is required southbound into the city.

GRACE CATHEDRAL

1051 Taylor St., Nob Hill - 776-6611

This poured-in-place concrete Gothic Episcopal cathedral was begun in 1914 but not completed until 1965. It's as grand as most European cathedrals, with twin towers rising some 170 feet high (the North Tower is stocked with 44 working bells). After inspecting the doors cast from a mold of the famous doors on the Baptistry of Florence, walk inside for a look at the impressive marble and stained glass, including the lovely rose window. The cathedral's most recent addition is a mammoth pipe organ.

HAAS-LILIENTHAL HOUSE

2007 Franklin St., Pacific Heights - 441-3000

A spectacular Victorian stick-style house from 1886, this creatively gabled and towered Queen Anne building is open to the public, with guided tours every half hour on Wednesday and Sunday afternoons.

Open Wed. 12 noon-4 p.m., Sun. 12:30 p.m.-4:30 p.m. Admission $3.

HALLIDIE BUILDING

Built by Willis Polk and Company in 1917 for the University of California, and named in honor of Andrew Hallidie,

130 Sutter St., Financial District

the U.C. regent who invented the cable car, this historic building was reputed to have the first curtain-wall glass façade. This ahead-of-its-time façade is curiously adorned with of-the-era wrought iron ornamentation and fire escapes.

HALLIDIE PLAZA

Market St. & Powell St., Union Square

This modern, terraced, amphitheater-style plaza was created in 1973 as part of the Bay Area Rapid Transit/Market Street Renewal Program. At lunchtime it attracts hundreds of brown-bagging downtown workers who enjoy the open-air seating and the frequent music—an occasional organized concert or, more commonly, performances by itinerant musicians.

HIBERNIA BANK

Jones St., McAllister St. & Market St., Civic Center

Constructed in 1892, this Beaux Arts bank was called "the most beautiful building in San Francisco" when it was built. It is notable on the outside for its gilt copper dome; go inside to see the lovely ceilings and the vaulted glass dome.

HYATT REGENCY SAN FRANCISCO

5 Embarcadero Center, Financial District - 788-1234

Even if you can't afford to rent one of the expensive rooms, at least stroll into the stunning atrium lobby, which rushes upward into twenty stories of space filled with plants, trees, birds and overhanging balconies. One of John Portman & Associates' most distinctive hotel designs, the Hyatt also boasts a gimmicky rotating bar on top.

KAHN HOUSE

66 Calhoun Ter., Telegraph Hill

A bit of contemporary Los Angeles planted on the Telegraph Hill slope, this Richard Neutra work, a private residence, is similar to his famous Lovell House in the Hollywood Hills.

MANSION HOTEL

2220 Sacramento St., Pacific Heights - 929-9444

Built in 1887 by Utah Senator Richard C. Chambers, this magnificent twin-towered Queen Anne mansion has a garden with the world's largest collection of Benjamino Bufano statues.

MILLS BUILDING

220 Montgomery St., Financial District

A downtown survivor of the great earthquake, refurbished in 1907 by Willis Polk, this unusual ten-story Chicago School building features a beautifully detailed Romanesque archway and a dramatic lobby replete with black marble and large friezes of San Francisco.

MISSION DOLORES

Dolores Ave. near 16th St., Mission District - 621-8203

Having survived three major earthquakes, this simple Mexican church, built by the Indians of sun-dried adobe between 1782 and 1791 as one of the string of Junipero Serra's California missions, is San Francisco's oldest building. Its three original bells are still in place but are rung only during Holy Week.

OCTAGON HOUSE

2645 Gough St., Union Square - 441-7512

Eight-sided houses were once considered lucky. The luck is still holding for this unusual structure, now the home of the National Society of Colonial Dames—it has endured since 1861. Call for information about tours.

OLD CHINESE TELEPHONE EXCHANGE

743 Washington St., Chinatown

This colorful, three-tiered pagoda building, now the Bank of Canton, once housed the operators for the Chinatown phone system, and stands on the site of the long-gone *California Star*, San Francisco's first newspaper, which announced the discovery of gold in 1849.

OLD METROPOLITAN LIFE BUILDING

Pine St. & Stockton St., Union Square

This white, terra-cotta-tiled Roman Revival building, consonant with the grand hotels on Nob Hill, was built in 1909 and remodeled in 1930 by Timothy Pflueger.

OLD MINT BUILDING

5th St. & Mission St., South of Market - 974-0788

A classical revival building built in the post–Civil War years (1869-1874), the Old Mint is the oldest stone building in San Francisco and was for many years the country's largest mint. Its solid stone construction saved the Mint when all its neighbors burned in the great fire after the 1906 earthquake. The on-site museum offers free tours on the hour and shows a movie about the building called *The Granite Lady*.

Museum open Mon.-Fri. 10 a.m.-4 p.m. Admission free.

PACIFIC STOCK EXCHANGE

301 Pine St., Financial District

The pulse of the Financial District beats in this offbeat blending of art deco and classical styles. Its main façade is adorned with a row of grand pillars, which are flanked by a pair of 21-foot high moderne statues that are worth a look.

PACIFIC TELEPHONE BUILDING

130 New Montgomery St., South of Market

If all of San Francisco's skyscrapers had been built with the grace and proportion of this 1925 giant by Miller & Pflueger and A. A. Cantin Architects, the skyline might today be a thing of beauty instead of a postmodern mass. The moderne lobby has striking Chinese ceilings.

PACIFIC UNION CLUB
1000 California St., Nob Hill

Built for railroad baron James C. Flood in 1886, this baroque Italianate brownstone was remodeled by Willis Polk in 1910 and now houses a private club for modern-day business barons. The imposing 42-room mansion was the only Nob Hill home left standing after the great quake.

PALACE OF FINE ARTS
Baker St. between Bay St. & Marina Blvd., Marina District - 563-7337

Constructed in 1915 for the Panama-Pacific Exposition, the Palace stands next to a beautiful lagoon and represents a pinnacle of architect Bernard Maybeck's career. One of the most popular buildings in the city, with its magnificently curving colonnades and classical Roman rotunda, it was completely restored in 1962 and now houses a theater and the Exploratorium, a wonderful hands-on science and technology museum.

PALACE OF THE LEGION OF HONOR
Clement St. & 34th Ave. (Lincoln Park), Richmond District - 221-4811

Designed by George Applegarth after the Palace of the Legion d'Honneur in Paris, this majestic gray stone museum was a gift from the Spreckels family in 1924. It sits atop a hill and overlooks a breathtaking vista of the city.

Open Wed.-Sun. 10 a.m.-5 p.m.

ROOS HOUSE
3500 Jackson St., Presidio Heights

Bernard Maybeck's detailing, especially the windows and eaves, highlights the handsome English Tudor styling of this 1909 house, now a private residence.

RUSS BUILDING
235 Montgomery St., Financial District

Until the "Manhattanization" building boom of the early 1960s, this Gothic Depression-era high-rise, modeled after the Chicago Tribune Tower, was San Francisco's tallest building, rising to a dazzling 31 stories.

ST. MARY'S CATHEDRAL
Geary Blvd. & Gough St., Cathedral Hill

An ultramodern cathedral built in 1971, this simply flamboyant church is distinguished by its 190-foot roof formed by four deeply sloping concave sides that meet in a cross at the top. Inside is a breathtaking altar canopy made of fourteen tiers of brilliant aluminum rods.

ST. PAUL'S LUTHERAN CHURCH
994 Eddy St., Civic Center

Inspired by the frontal design of the Gothic cathedral at Chartres, A. J. Kraft's 1894 church is one of the city's grandest.

SAN FRANCISCO GAS LIGHT COMPANY BULDING

3600 Buchanan St., Marina District

Completed in 1893, this small Queen Anne–style brick building is a simply detailed jewel. Recently remodeled, it is now an office building.

STEINER STREET HOUSES

700 block of Steiner St., Western Addition

One of the most photographed blocks in the city, this row features six identical houses—each a Victorian gem—that were built by Matthew Kavanaugh in 1894 and 1895. They have been handsomely restored.

SPRECKELS MANSION

737 Buena Vista St. (Buena Vista Park), Haight-Ashbury - 861-3008

A grand, square Victorian built in 1887 and known to have numbered Ambrose Bierce and Jack London among its guests. Today the Spreckels Mansion is a quiet, discreet bed-and-breakfast inn.

SUTRO BATHS

Point Lobos Ave. (Sutro Heights Park), Richmond District

Here lie the ruins (mostly just the old foundation) of Adolph Sutro's ambitious re-creation of Roman-style baths. A three-acre spa with six saltwater pools of varying temperatures sat under a roof of colored glass. The building burned in 1966.

TRANSAMERICA PYRAMID

Montgomery St. & Columbus Ave., Financial District

Designed by the Los Angeles firm of William Pereira & Associates, this narrow white pyramid drew much criticism when it was completed in 1972; its many detractors considered it ugly and weird and denounced it for overly dominating the skyline. Today, however, it has been adopted, with either a certain fondness or simple resignation, as a novel landmark in a city of incredibly diverse architecture. It's the city's tallest structure, towering 853 feet over the Financial District.

Museums

ART MUSEUMS

ASIAN ART MUSEUM

When Avery Brundage donated his incomparable collection of Asian art to San Francisco in 1966, the city cleared out the

8th Ave. & Kennedy Dr.
(M. H. De Young Memorial
Museum), Golden Gate
Park - 668-8921

West Wing of the De Young Museum to make room for the almost 10,000 pieces. Only a portion of the paintings, ceramics, sculptures, jades, bronzes and textiles can be exhibited at one time. Don't miss the breathtaking blue-and-white porcelains or the Jade Room, where some objects date back more than 3,000 years.

Open Tues.-Sun. 10 a.m.-5 p.m., Wed. 10 a.m.-8:45 p.m. (winter hours may be shorter). Adults $4, seniors $2, children under 18 free. Admission free Sat. morning, Wed. evening and the first Wed. of the month.

CALIFORNIA HISTORICAL SOCIETY

Pacific St. & Laguna St.,
Pacific Heights - 567-1848

A library in the grand old style of large chairs, broad tables, deathly stillness and meticulous librarians who know the collection inside out, the CHS is a primary holder of books, documents, photographs and periodicals on Western history. Its 25,000 volumes and sizable art collection are a vast resource for California historians, and the sandstone mansion, built for paint magnate William Whittier in the 1890s, is an appropriate period setting.

Open Wed.-Sat. 1 p.m.-5 p.m. Admission free.

CHINESE HISTORICAL SOCIETY OF AMERICA

17 Adler Pl. (near Grant
Ave.), Chinatown -
391-1188

The history of the Chinese in the Americas is woefully underwritten, but this small museum houses changing displays of photographs, documents, artifacts and memorabilia that shed light on the heritage of a major segment of the city's population.

Open Tues.-Sat. 1 p.m.-5 p.m. Admission free.

M. H. DE YOUNG MEMORIAL MUSEUM

8th Ave. & Kennedy Dr.,
Golden Gate Park -
221-4811

Reflecting its age and the character of its benefactors, the De Young Museum houses the most eclectic permanent collection in San Francisco. Although its genesis was the 1894 California Midwinter International Exposition, the building expanded dramatically after 1917, when newspaper baron Michael De Young sparked new construction. The permanent collection could form the basis for a history course on western civilization, from ancient Egypt, Greece and Rome through the Renaissance to the present. This collection includes works by Rubens, seventeenth- and eighteenth-century Italian paintings and an extensive American collection bolstered by paintings donated by John D. Rockefeller III. Another gallery contains traditional arts of Africa, Oceania and the Americas. Such blockbuster traveling exhibitions as the King Tut show pitch their tents here.

Open Wed. 10 a.m.-8:45 p.m., Thurs.-Sun. 10 a.m.-5 p.m.

(winter hours may be shorter). Adults $4, seniors $2, children under 17 free. Admission free Sat. morning, Wed. evening & the first Wed. of the month.

THE MEXICAN MUSEUM

Marina Blvd. & Laguna St. (Fort Mason Center), Building D, Fort Mason - 441-0404

So many immigrant cultures have been laid over one another in California's history that the state's Mexican heritage is often associated only with the Spanish missionary era and the wars for territory. This museum, the first of its kind outside Mexico, pays tribute to the considerable Mexican contribution to California's past. The collection of Mexican and Mexican-American art is displayed in five thematic settings—Hispanic, Colonial, folk, Mexican fine arts and Mexican-American fine arts. Special exhibitions honor such holidays as Cinco de Mayo (May 5) and the Day of the Dead (November 1).

Open Wed.-Sun. 12 noon-5 p.m. (first Thurs. of the month to 8 p.m.). Adults $3, seniors & students $2, members & children under 10 free. Admission free Wed.

MUSEO ITALO AMERICANO

Marina Blvd. & Laguna St. (Fort Mason Center), Building C, Fort Mason - 673-2200

Although the Italian influence in San Francisco is still felt in present-day North Beach, its impact has greatly diminished over the years. Thankfully, this museum, the first in the U.S. to collect the work of contemporary Italian-American artists, preserves an authentic touch of Italy in the Bay Area.

Open Wed.-Sun. 12 noon-5 p.m. Admission free.

MUSEUM OF MODERN MYTHOLOGY

693 Mission St., South of Market - 546-0202

You may think our consumer culture is producing artifacts faster than any curator could keep up with. You may think we are living in a disposable world. But in this marvelous museum Mr. Peanut and the Poppin' Fresh Doughboy are the heroes, and they are surrounded by thousands of advertising signs and symbols. This is the raw material of Andy Warhol's vision.

Open Thurs.-Sat. 12 noon-5 p.m. Adults $2, children 50 cents.

PALACE OF THE LEGION OF HONOR

Clement St. & 34th Ave. (Lincoln Park), Richmond District - 221-4811

People visit this spectacularly located museum almost as much for the view as for the art. Beautifully situated atop a hill in Lincoln Park, it commands a sweeping view eastward across the city and the Bay. Built in 1924, the Palace was a gift of the Spreckels family and was designed by George Applegarth after the Palace of the Legion d'Honneur in Paris. Its permanent collection includes Rodin sculptures, eighteenth- and nineteenth-century French paintings (including Impressionist works by Monet, Renoir and Degas), decorative arts and tapestries. Downstairs, the Achenbach Foundation for Graphic Arts houses more than 100,000 works of art on paper, the largest collection of its kind in the West. Pipe organ concerts are presented every Saturday and Sunday at 4 p.m.

Open Wed.-Sun. 10 a.m.-5 p.m. Adults $4, children under 18 free. Admission free Sat. 10 a.m.-12 noon & the first Wed. of the month.

SAN FRANCISCO ART INSTITUTE

800 Chestnut St., Russian Hill - 771-7020

An important focus of the contemporary art scene in the Bay Area and Northern California, the Art Institute, founded in 1871, is the oldest art school in the western U.S. Its four galleries—the Diego Rivera, the Emmanuel Walter, the Atholl McBean and the Still Lights—show the work of both students and professionals.

Open Sept.-June: Tues.-Sat. 10 a.m.-5 p.m. Admission free.

SAN FRANCISCO MUSEUM OF MODERN ART

Van Ness Ave. & McAllister St. (Veterans' Memorial Building), Civic Center - 863-8800

Located in the Veterans' Building, one of Brown and Landsburgh's 1932 architectural contributions to the grand Beaux Arts Civic Center complex, the SFMMA was the first modern art museum in California. It is especially strong in Abstract Impressionism (with a large Clyfford Still collection), photography and works by twentieth-century California artists. Works by Picasso, Matisse and Kandinsky are included in the ever-expanding permanent collection. Lectures, films, poetry readings and the occasional "Jazz in the Galleries" evenings add to the vitality the museum brings to the Civic Center, which is also home to the Opera, Symphony Hall and City Hall. There is an interesting café, and the fine museum bookshop is accessible without admission to the galleries.

Open Tues.-Wed. & Fri. 10 a.m.-5 p.m., Thurs. 10 a.m.-9 p.m., Sat.-Sun. 11 a.m.-5 p.m. Adults $3.50, seniors & children under 16 $1.50. Admission free Tues. & reduced Thurs. night.

OTHER MUSEUMS

CABLE CAR MUSEUM

After two years of inaction and $60 million worth of repairs and renovations, the city's famous cable car system reopened

Washington St. & Mason St., Nob Hill - 474-1887

in 1984 with new cables, tracks, brakes, seats and shiny coats of paint. In this refurbished cable car barn, built in 1887 and rebuilt after the 1906 earthquake, you can not only peruse historical photographs and memorabilia, but from an underground viewing room you can watch the giant gears, pulleys and spinning cables that operate the novel urban transit system.

April-Oct.: open daily 10 a.m.-6 p.m.; Nov.-March: open daily 10 a.m.-5 p.m. Admission free.

CALIFORNIA ACADEMY OF SCIENCES

Music Concourse, Golden Gate Park - 750-7145

Gorgeously situated near the middle of Golden Gate Park stands this endlessly fascinating complex of museums. Across the neatly tree-dotted Music Concourse from the De Young Museum, and bordered by the splendid Rhododendron Dell and the lovely Shakespeare Garden, the Academy of Sciences houses a museum of natural history, a planetarium and an aquarium.

Morrison Planetarium. In addition to the enthralling and spectacular star shows that one comes to expect of a major planetarium with a 65-foot dome, the Morrison hosts dazzling laser light shows with contemporary high-tech and rock soundtracks. There's a separate admission charge for the specially scheduled "Laserium" shows. Call 387-6300 for times and prices.

The Museum of Natural History. From Cowell Hall, where an enormous geophysical globe and a 27-foot-long allosaurus skeleton stand, proceed through the Wattis Hall of Man and see life-size models of humans throughout the ages. If you can get past the absorbing, perpetual rhythm of the huge Foucault Pendulum, marking the earth's rotation by knocking down one peg at a time on a circle, there are more visual treasures to behold. The Simson African Hall and the North American Hall include lifelike dioramas of animal and plant life from the two continents. Children can get closer to nature in the Discovery Room.

Steinhart Aquarium. If something seems fishy here, it must be the nearly 15,000 species of aquatic plants and animals housed in glass-front tanks and nature-imitating environments. In the Roundabout, you proceed up a spiral ramp, surrounded by an enormous ring-shaped tank where sharks, tuna, yellowtail, rays and other large ocean fish swim around you in an endless current. The immersion effect is astounding. The Swamp houses lazy-looking alligators and crocodiles that seem to know more than they let on. A simulated tide pool allows you to reach in (with guidance from the monitors) and handle certain rock-dwelling creatures. Dolphins and seals put on amusing shows at feeding time, which is every two hours. And there are nearly 190 other tanks containing all manner of large and small fish.

Open daily 10 a.m.-7 p.m. (winter hours may be shorter). Adults $3, seniors & children 12-17 $1.50, children 6-11 75 cents, children under 6 free. Admission free first Wed. of the month.

EXPLORATORIUM

Baker St. between Bay St. & Marina Blvd. (Palace of Fine Arts), Marina District - 563-7337

The masterpiece hands-on learning center designed by scientist/educator Frank Oppenheimer, the Exploratorium opened in 1969 and has delighted, fascinated and astounded visitors ever since. Over 500 exhibits allow the child in everyone to explore the principles of physics, chemistry, geometry, math, botany, biology, geology, astronomy and more. Lasers, sound rooms, mirrors, video screens, magnets and fantastically rigged contraptions challenge you to figure out how the world works by getting physically involved. The Tactile Dome is so popular that it requires reservations and separate admission. If this isn't the best science museum in the world, it's certainly the most fun.

Open for group tours Wed.-Sun. morning; open to the public Wed. 11 a.m.-9:30 p.m., Thurs.-Fri. 11 a.m.-5 p.m., Sat.-Sun. 10 a.m.-5 p.m. (hours may vary during winter months). Adults $4 (good for 6 months), children under 18 free.

NATIONAL MARITIME MUSEUM AND HISTORICAL PARK

Hyde Street Pier, Hyde St. at the waterfront, Fisherman's Wharf - 556-6435

When commuting across the Bay to San Francisco was a more romantic venture, the Hyde Street Pier was the docking point for the Golden Gate ferries. Today five antique ships, including the *Eureka*, the last of the side-wheel ferries to run in the U.S., are docked here. Guided tours twice daily.

Open daily 10 a.m.-6 p.m. Admission free.

PRESIDIO ARMY MUSEUM

Lincoln Blvd. & Funston Ave., Presidio - 561-4115

Originally the northernmost military post of the Spanish when they ruled Mexico, the 1,400-acre Presidio has a fascinating and varied history, much of which is documented in this museum. The oldest building in the Presidio, the museum began life in 1857 as the Old Station Hospital.

Open Tues.-Sun. 10 a.m.-4 p.m. Admission free.

TATTOO ART MUSEUM
30 7th St., South of Market - 552-1215

Lyle Tuttle's body is legendary. Covered virtually head to toe with tattoos, his decorated torso and limbs are a walking museum of this needle-meets-flesh art. But since Lyle can't live his life on display, he has assembled the world's largest collection of tools, photos and arcana from his trade. There is a tattoo studio on the premises.

Open daily 12 noon-6 p.m. Admission free.

Neighborhoods

Want to discover the *real* San Francisco, not the tourist-shop approximations? Then wander through the picturesque neighborhoods that are often as colorful as their names. Reflecting the ethnic, cultural and economic diversity of the city, many of these neighborhoods are self-sustaining communities with their own unique sights, sounds, smells, architecture and lifestyles.

The Castro District, spilling out from Castro and Market streets, is the gay capital of the world: proud, close-knit and bustling with foot traffic and a lively café scene. The charming Victorian architecture and the rather insular small-town completeness give the Castro the air of an independent city.

Chinatown, a maze of streets and alleys between North Beach and the Financial District, is home to the largest Chinese community outside the old country and is in some ways a city unto itself. Bordered roughly by Broadway, Bush, Stockton and Kearny streets, Chinatown has been burgeoning since the 1850s and now houses over 80,000 residents, including many new residents from Southeast Asia. It bustles with the daily activities of any overcrowded urban neighborhood. Throw in thousands of tourists, browsers, shoppers and diners and you have a magnificent (if sometimes stifling) swarm of humanity. In addition to countless restaurants (of every quality and price range), tea shops (where dim sum prevails), jade stores, curio shops and souvenir bazaars, Chinatown highlights include old-world architecture, a Chinese wax museum and exotic food and herb shops.

The Haight-Ashbury, just south of the Golden Gate Park Panhandle, still contains a few remnants of the Summer of Love, when tour buses used to bring gawking Midwesterners to stare at authentic hippies. But the gentrification of the Haight has resulted in trendier stores, restaurants and bars and a population that is overwhelmingly affluent and baby-boomer, both gay and straight. A few hippie holdouts (and burnouts) still roam Haight Street, and a few counterculture shops hang in there.

Japantown, or Nihonmachi, is a concentrated community of businesses around Geary and Fillmore streets. The focus is Japan Center, a five-acre mercantile complex featuring gift, jewelry and electronics shops; restaurants, teahouses and sushi bars; the Japanese Consulate; the Miyako Hotel; and the Japanese Trade Center. A new movie theater multiplex is now bringing in even more people from around the city.

The Mission District, south of Market Street and east of the Castro, is practically a separate city. Largely Latin, its fascinating mix includes Mexican, Central and South American, Filipino and Southeast Asian populations, along with low-income artists and musicians of every ethnic heritage. Several walls boast elaborate murals depicting the area's culture and history, and the choice of good ethnic restaurants is staggering.

Noe Valley, west of the Mission and protected from the foggy breezes by Twin Peaks, is a long-standing enclave of beautifully refurbished row houses. The population is a mix of old-time families, upwardly mobile professionals and somewhat bohemian artists. The shops, restaurants, coffeehouses and bookstores along 24th Street preserve the small-town atmosphere that has prevailed since this was farming territory.

North Beach, bounded by Broadway, Columbus and the Embarcadero, is at once the city's most beloved and most rapidly disappearing ethnic neighborhood. The old Italian merchants and family restaurants are gradually yielding to franchise businesses and fast-food outlets. But amid the rampant development, many charms endure: cafés and bookstores from the Beat era; picturesquely peopled Washington Square and the Church of St. Peter and St. Paul (prominently featured in *Dirty Harry*); dozens of fine restaurants; the old shops, saloons and Italian cafés along Columbus Avenue; and foot traffic as varied and intriguing as anywhere in the city.

Polk Gulch, along Polk Street near California Street just west of Nob Hill, is a vibrantly gentrified but somewhat less expensive shopping area than Union Street. It is also known for its variety of good restaurants and its gay bar scene.

South of Market, or SOMA, is a developer's dream come true. The industrial area between Market Street and China Basin has been undergoing a phenomenal renaissance. Warehouses have become Gallerias and Showplace Squares, hosting trade shows and consumer exhibitions. A motel has been turned into a restaurant and rock club. A sleek jazz club rises up next to a Bay Bridge off-ramp. Hipper-than-hip nightspots crop up at an alarming rate. Galleries and artists' studios multiply faster than you can say "art in the age of mechanical reproduction." Fashion and style are the bywords, and they change with the blink of an aloof and distanced eye. Once the province of biker and leather bars, SOMA (a relatively new and commercially contrived title) is now an entrepreneurial heaven—the place to be and an amusing place to watch.

Union Street, or Cow Hollow, in the upper Marina (or lower Pacific Heights), features scores of upscale boutiques for shopping, galleries and bookstores for browsing, and restaurants and cafés for trendy dining and drinking.

Tours

BLUE & GOLD FLEET
Pier 39, Fisherman's Wharf - 781-7877

The Blue & Gold's basic tour, which lasts a little over an hour, takes you along the waterfront, under both the Golden Gate and Bay bridges and around Alcatraz. It's as touristy as can be, but weather permitting, you will be rewarded with some lovely views. Special dinner cruises are offered on Friday and Saturday evenings.

Spring & summer: open daily 10 a.m.-7 p.m.; fall & winter: hours vary. Adults $10, seniors & children 5-18 $5, children under 5 free.

COMMODORE HELICOPTERS
Pier 43, Fisherman's Wharf - 981-4832

Three different tours are offered in four- and six-seat Bell Jet Ranger helicopters: a seven-mile Bay tour at $20 for adults and $10 for children; a ten-minute Golden Gate tour around the skyline and over the bridge at $20 per person; and a fifteen-minute, $60 skyline tour that takes you over Sausalito, Belvedere and Tiburon in Marin, then out to Ocean Beach and the Cliff House. If the fog stays away, the vistas can be outstanding. Custom tours of the wine country and other areas are also available.

Open daily 9 a.m.-sunset. Tour times and prices vary.

GRAY LINE TOURS

420 Taylor St., Union Square - 771-4000

Gray Line's package bus tours hit all the expected attractions. The three-and-a-half-hour city tour includes the Mission District, Golden Gate Park, the Cliff House, Fisherman's Wharf and a drive across the Golden Gate Bridge, with stops along the way. It can be supplemented with a Bay Cruise package or an Alcatraz walking tour. Tours to Muir Woods, Sausalito and the wine country are also available. Not for the independent or the adventurous.

City tours depart daily 9 a.m., 10 a.m., 11 a.m. & 1:30 p.m. Adults $19.50, children 5-11 $9.25. Times and prices of other tours vary.

HERITAGE WALKING TOURS

2007 Franklin St. (Haas-Lilienthal House), Pacific Heights - 441-3000

These docent-led tours help preserve San Francisco's history and give residents and tourists alike a look at some of the city's finest architecture. There are several tours, including one of the spectacular Victorian-era Haas-Lilienthal House; one through Pacific Heights, a neighborhood rich with Victorian and Edwardian mansions; and one through the old north waterfront. Call for details, directions to starting points and information on special and custom tours. Admission fees benefit the nonprofit conservatory group.

Tour times and locations vary. Admission $3.

LEVI STRAUSS & COMPANY

250 Valencia St., Mission District - 544-6000

A 45-minute guided tour takes you through the cutting and sewing operations of the factory where the world's most famous pants, Levi's blue jeans, are made. Reservations are requested a week in advance.

Tours Wed. 10:30 a.m. Admission free.

MALTESE FALCON TOURS

Meets at 200 Larkin St. (San Francisco Public Library), Civic Center - 564-7021

This four-hour, three-mile walking tour takes you through the San Francisco of writer Dashiell Hammett, creator of the legendary Sam Spade. A Pinkerton detective and ad copywriter before his star rose in the murder-mystery firmament, Hammett set most of his pulp magazine stories and his classic hard-boiled detective novels (most notably *The Maltese Falcon*) in these streets.

May-Oct.: tours Sat. 12 noon. Admission $5.

RED & WHITE FLEET

Pier 41 & Pier 43 1/2, Fisherman's Wharf - 546-2805

The Red & White handles commuter and ferry service to Angel Island, Sausalito, Tiburon, Marine World, Vallejo and Stockton and offers group rates and special charters. Its tours include the round-trip ferry ride to and tour of Alcatraz

Island (see "Excursions") and the 45-minute Golden Gate Bay Cruise, which sails under the Golden Gate Bridge and around Alcatraz.

Golden Gate Bay Cruise departs Pier 43 1/2 every 75 minutes from 10:15 a.m. to 3:45 p.m. Adults $9.95, seniors & children 12-18 $5.95, children 5-11 $3.95, children 5-11 free. Hours & prices of other trips vary depending on the destination & the season.

ENVIRONS

East Bay

RESTAURANTS

AUGUSTA'S

2955 Telegraph Ave.,
Berkeley - 548-3140

American

12/20

Showing up here with a reservation on a weeknight is almost like going to a friend's house for a dinner party. The sunny, comfortable neighborhood restaurant gets its homey feel partly from being in a shambling old house and partly from the familial aura projected by the staff. Ah, home . . . except Augusta's food is better than anything mom ever made (sorry, Mom, it's no disgrace). One reason for its success is that the fish, a special focus here, is impeccably fresh and well chosen (the supplier is the Monterey Fish Market, the top seafood purveyor in the East Bay). Augusta's pescatorial productions are always good, even imaginative; they do great things with shark and swordfish. Soups and pastas are also consistently excellent, and we have had good luck with nonseafood specials (delicious homemade Italian sausage on our last visit). Garlic lovers will quickly become addicted to the roast garlic potatoes, and dessert lovers are cautioned to reserve something from the daily sweets selection when ordering entrees—otherwise the meal could end in disappointment later. Two can eat and drink well for only $40.

Open Tues.-Fri. 11:30 a.m.-2 p.m. & 6 p.m.-10 p.m., Sat. 6 p.m.-10 p.m., Sun. 11 a.m.-2:30 p.m. & 6 p.m.-10 p.m. Cards: MC, V.

BAY WOLF CAFÉ

3853 Piedmont Ave.,
Oakland - 655-6004

California

13

The name has always appealed to us, with its echoes of *Beowulf* and the famous *Sea Wolf* of Oakland writer Jack London. The food has echoes, too—of Chez Panisse, James Beard and Provence—though it is also unique. There's a consistency, call it a kitchen flavor, to the inventive and well-produced cuisine that has created a legion of Bay Wolf devotees; as a result the competition for tables, especially on weekends, makes reservations essential. The dining rooms occupy an expanded Victorian house in the Oakland hills, a comfortable place with an appealing touch of hail-fellow-well-met tavern cheer. We recently visited on a Thursday evening to find the place bustling, but not to the detriment of service. We had bluefin tuna sautéed with red and gold tomatoes and lacy, airy onion rings; grilled shrimp on a bed of grilled eggplant; and toothsome fettuccine with two kinds of sausage, one spicy and one mild. Memorable meals past have included a very good mixed grill. Perhaps the best thing about the Bay Wolf is the list of drinkable, as opposed to merely trendy, wines. Call the restaurant to receive copies of upcoming menus, which may determine the night you wish to visit. About $45 for dinner for two, with wine.

Open Mon.-Fri. 11:30 a.m.-2 p.m. & 6 p.m.-9:30 p.m., Sat. 11 a.m.-3 p.m. & 6 p.m.-9:30 p.m., Sun. 10 a.m.-3 p.m. & 6 p.m.-9:30 p.m. Cards: MC, V.

BRIDGE CREEK

1549 Shattuck Ave., Berkeley - 548-1774

American

13

Bridge Creek is the quintessential Berkeley restaurant: calm and laid back, its peaceful dining room fashioned out of the front rooms of an old house, its staff warm and helpful and its food the kind you'd make for yourself at home if you were a great cook. Bridge Creek began life as a breakfast café, with a menu designed by American food guru Marion Cunningham and a kitchen run by owner-chef John Hudspeth. Hudspeth's gingerbread pancakes, herb sausages, huevos con chorizo, johnnycakes and butter-grilled breakfast sandwiches proved irresistible, and in no time there was an hour-long wait on weekends. This led to the creation of a dinner menu, and now regulars return for carefully prepared American classics: buttery corn muffins; lovely cream of tomato soup with fabulous homemade crackers; dry-aged New York steak; large loin lamb chops of the highest quality, perfectly cooked and served only with their juices; grilled or baked fresh fish; rich, comforting scalloped potatoes; and delicious chocolate cake, the kind American moms have been making for years. If you accompany your meal with one of the modest California wines, expect to pay about $80 for a three-course dinner for two; breakfast for two will run about $25. In true Berkeley fashion, Bridge Creek does not allow smoking.

Open Tues.-Fri. 6 p.m.-10 p.m., Sat. 8 a.m.-2:30 p.m. & 6 p.m.-10 p.m., Sun. 8 a.m.-2:30 p.m. No cards (checks accepted).

CAFÉ AT CHEZ PANISSE

1517 Shattuck Ave., Berkeley - 548-5049

A light, airy room with a constant hubbub, superb wines and Alice Waters's wonderful food (she seldom cooks here these days, but it's hers anyway). Why go downstairs? Actually,

California

16

that's not fair. The formal prix-fixe meals downstairs consti-
tute a serious endeavor, a different matter entirely from the
café. The excitement up here is in fine-tuned flavor combinations, especially in the salad and grilled vegetable departments. Aïoli is usually around in one form or another, and
pizza still reigns. Our most recent meal consisted solely of
Hog Island Sweetwater oysters, a goat cheese pizza and a few
glasses of the free-flowing house Zinfandel. It was terrific.
The only problem is that it's hard to get in if you're not a
regular—the hostess and staff definitely play favorites. Still,
even the wait can be fun. But if you hate waiting, come for
lunch, when reservations are accepted. Two will spend about
$40 for the ultimate California café dinner for two, with
wine.

Open Mon.-Sat. 11:30 a.m.-3 p.m. & 5 p.m.-11:30 p.m.
Cards: AE, MC, V.

CHEZ PANISSE

1517 Shattuck Ave.,
Berkeley - 548-5525

California

18

The most significant thing about Chez Panisse, and the
truest measure of Alice Waters's stature as a cultural revolu-
tionary, is that the restaurant is still as good as it ever was.
Sure, the staff can be haughty, but let's face it, the clique
mentality in restaurants wasn't invented in Berkeley. California cuisine was, however—not the ingredients and the
general style, perhaps, but certainly its focused, refined form
as practiced at Chez Panisse. Rather than going on about the
inspiration and deep savvy behind these meals, or the ways in
which they can expand one's culinary horizons, we will
simply say that everyone should dine here at least once. After
all these years, Chez Panisse remains the wellspring of
California cuisine and a guiding light for American contemporary cooking, whether it be rooted in New England or
New Mexico. Both Chez Panisse and its lively, more
informal upstairs café occupy a big old house in an old
Berkeley neighborhood. The main dining room on the first
floor has dark wood paneling, classic furniture and soft
lighting, a basic American setting for the quintessential new
American cuisine. The prix-fixe menu, which changes every
few days, is $45 per person, without wine. Make reservations
three weeks to a month in advance.

Seatings Tues.-Sat. 6 p.m., 6:30 p.m., 8:30 p.m. & 9:15 p.m.
Cards: MC, V.

DAKOTA

Appetizers like grilled squid, fresh from Monterey Bay and
served with jalapeños, cilantro and other goodies, are what

*2086 Allston Way
(Shattuck Hotel), Berkeley -
841-3848*

Southwestern

14

make Dakota successful. Unabashed grilling is the key: grilled fish, grilled poussin stuffed with goat cheese and herbs, succulent mixed grills. They'd probably grill the wine list, if they could figure out how to do it. Dakota opened in 1986 with chef Daniel Malzahn at the helm—a loss for San Francisco, where Malzahn's expertise and imagination made Café Americain a grazer's dream pasture, but a gain for Berkeley, which hadn't had a new grill with a different slant in many months. What distinguishes Dakota from its more established peers is the eclectic regionalism of the cuisine; the seasonal menus amount to a North American travelogue for the palate. The Southwestern motif is enhanced by the restaurant's residence in the old Shattuck Hotel, which wouldn't be out of place in downtown Albuquerque. Two will spend about $50 to $60, with wine.

Open Mon. 11:30 a.m.-2:30 p.m., Tues.-Fri. 11:30 a.m.-2:30 p.m. & 5:30 p.m.-9:30 p.m., Sat.-Sun. 10 a.m.-2 p.m. & 5:30 p.m.-9:30 p.m. Cards: AE, MC, V.

FOURTH STREET GRILL

*1820 4th St., Berkeley -
849-0526*

**California/
Southwestern**

15

No longer a culinary laboratory and showcase, which it was when Mark Miller held court (he has since moved on to Santa Fe), the Fourth Street Grill is now merely an exceptional grill joint. The credo here is the first line of a litany for California (and nouvelle) cuisine: great ingredients, perfectly cooked. The decor is a combination of Berkeley natural and Southwest chic (ceramic cacti and the like). Scratch any given waitperson and you'll find an artist, an actor or an aspiring chef. In our opinion, the twin culinary pillars on which the whole panoply rests are the classic bacon, lettuce and tomato sandwich (each ingredient is its own acme) and the splendid Caesar salad, which we always have with Zinfandel for dessert. We're not kidding. Plan on about $60 for dinner for two, with wine.

Open Mon.-Thurs. 11:30 a.m.-2:30 p.m. & 6 p.m.-10 p.m., Fri. 11:30 a.m.-2:30 p.m. & 5 p.m.-11 p.m., Sat. 5 p.m.-11 p.m., Sun. 5 p.m.-9:30 p.m. Cards: MC, V.

NAKAPAN

*1971 Martin Luther King
Jr. Way, Berkeley -
548-3050*

Thai

11/20

The delicate renditions of Thai favorites here are in direct contrast to the brazen, fire-born dishes served at Siam Cuisine. What is proper Thai, you might ask? We've visited that dreamy country several times and still can't say with certainty whether a given stateside Thai restaurant is true to form. We think it has to do with the philosophy of individual kitchens. Nakapan's philosophy seems to be that flavors should be arranged like blossoms to make a bouquet on the palate. The ingredients assert themselves individually, and they also coalesce. But enough beating around the bush—to be specific, Nakapan's tom ka gai, yam pla muk and som tum are delicious in a delicate way. That doesn't mean they can't blaze, if you so ordain. The decor is handsome, with plenty of wood and indirect lighting, and it's even possible to find a parking space in this transitional neighborhood. Two will spend $45 for dinner with beer.

Open Mon.-Fri. 11 a.m.-3 p.m. & 5 p.m.-10 p.m., Sat.-Sun. 5 p.m.-10 p.m. Cards: MC, V.

OLIVETO

5655 College Ave.,
Oakland - 547-5356

Italian/French

12/20

The cuisine of Southern Europe has a near-universal appeal. Who can resist the homey, sun-drenched cooking—its pastas, risotti and polentas; its tomatoes, garlic, peppers, olives, artichokes and citrus fruits; its aïoli, basil and sage; and its biscotti, flan and zabaglione? We certainly can't, which is why we're so fond of Oliveto, a handsome, rough-plastered, country restaurant in the middle of Oakland's gentrification district. "Rustic cooking of Italy, France and Spain" is how the management describes the offerings on the daily-changing menu, which will tempt you to order more than you should. Pastas and risotti—with Tuscan sausage and arugula, with red and gold beets and pancetta—are especially successful, as are the various calamari preparations and most of the seafood entrees. We won't soon forget the simple joys of the meaty spearfish in a bright citrus vinaigrette, accompanied with roasted potatoes and creamy aïoli. The wine list is modest but appropriate to the cuisine, and service is just fine. There's an inexpensive café and tapas bar downstairs that offers wine by the glass and tastes of this good cooking. Dinner for two, with wine, will run about $70.

Open Tues.-Sat. 6 p.m.-10 p.m., Sun. 5:30 p.m.-9:30 p.m. Cards: MC, V.

PAVILION ROOM

41 Tunnel Rd. (Claremont
Resort Hotel), Berkeley -
843-3000

This is a horizontal version of the view-struck Carnelian Room. From our windowside table one summer evening, we looked over Berkeley and across the Bay to San Francisco, and for once it was the golden city touted in fable and lore. With such a glorious sunset in our laps, the menu took on a heavenly glow, but the reality of the middle-of-the-road California-style grill cuisine fell short of the pearly gates.

California

11/20

Little things made the difference, especially in the appetizers: a leathery tuna carpaccio, an overdressed salad and goat cheese that tasted like cream cheese. A pair of grilled lamb chops had juice and flavor, and an interesting bourbon sauce added a nice dimension, but the accompanying vegetables were soggy. If your eyes happen to stray from the window, they'll settle on a beautiful room: elegant table settings, plenty of cool tones and mirrors, a piano tinkling the likes of "Stardust" and "I Won't Dance," and fresh flowers everywhere; a large abstract painting by Michael Dailey dominates one wall. The wine list is sound but pricey. Two can dine for about $80 or $90, with wine.

Open Mon.-Sat. 11 a.m.-2 p.m. & 6 p.m.-10 p.m., Sun. 10 a.m.-2 p.m. & 6 p.m.-10 p.m. All major cards.

SANTA FE BAR & GRILL

1310 University Ave., Berkeley - 841-4740

California/ Southwestern

14 🍳

Jeremiah Tower needs no introduction, but his former showcase needs to be reintroduced in the wake of Tower's departure (and the messy litigation that followed). The question on everyone's mind, of course, was whether the restaurant would decline in his absence. In our opinion, it hasn't. Ostensibly still under Tower's tutelage, Santa Fe's kitchen staff continues to turn out its hybrid Southwest/ French/California grill cuisine with flair, and service is as good as it ever was. The rambling white adobe building looks like an old train station on the outside (for good reason—it was once the depot for the Atchison, Topeka & Santa Fe) and feels like a hacienda inside. The menu is a primer on the imaginative and deft uses of all the different kinds of chiles. About $60 for two, with wine.

Open Tues.-Sun. 11:30 a.m.-2 p.m. & 5:30 p.m.-10 p.m. Cards: MC, V.

SIAM CUISINE

181 University Ave., Berkeley - 548-3278

Thai

12/20

There's nothing fey or ethereal about this cuisine. The flavors are right there in every bite, and quite welcome at that. If this food were a wine, we'd say it was forward and aggressive. Not that Siam goes for the throat, unless you order the food hot—as we always do. The decor evokes an upscale burger joint more than the Far East, but there's an undeniable wacky charm in eating superb Thai food in a high-backed red vinyl banquette. Perhaps it's for the best that they don't serve martinis. Our very favorite mee krob of all time is served here, and it makes a good foil for such Siam specialties as calamari salad and chicken with sweet basil.

Another good foil is deep-fried tofu, which is served with peanut sauce and makes an exquisite accompaniment to a spicy seafood dish, such as fresh red snapper in curry sauce. Because the pungence of chiles is rounded off by coconut milk, the heat builds slowly—but it does build. Dinner for two, with beer, will be about $30.

Open Sun.-Thurs. 5 p.m.-11 p.m., Fri.-Sat. 5 p.m.-12 midnight. Cards: MC, V.

QUICK BITES

The East Bay is heaven for café-hoppers and low-budget gourmands. From Oakland's barbecue houses to Berkeley's diners, you can find every kind of quick meal for very little money. We can't possibly cover the myriad cafés, coffeehouses and joints in the U.C. Berkeley area, but we can tell you to wander Telegraph Avenue and College Avenue near the campus, where you'll be tempted by espresso bars, pizza-by-the-slice joints, ethnic restaurants and lively pubs, all of which offer low prices and great people-watching. And we can tell you about our very favorite East Bay quick bites.

BETTE'S OCEAN VIEW DINER

1807A 4th St., Berkeley - 644-3230

Using the best ingredients—farm-fresh eggs, smoky black beans, fresh salsa and homemade muffins, scones and tortillas—Bette's takes breakfast classics to new heights. The pancake here is actually a huge but delicate soufflé encasing either apple and brandy or banana and rum. On weekends, eggs, linguiça (Portuguese pork sausage), bell peppers, onions and home fries combine into a bountiful, wondrous dish called the Farmer's Scramble. Bette's huevos rancheros comprise two sunny-side-up eggs topped with melted cheese and salsa and served with black beans and tortillas. Because of these creations, patrons are willing to wait interminable lengths of time to get into this bright, new-wavish diner; the owners have tried to accommodate those who won't wait by opening a takeout shop next door stocked with Bette's excellent baked goods, coffee and espresso. The lunches aren't quite as inspired as the morning meal, but they're still well above average. About $15 for a breakfast feast for two.

Open Sun. 8 a.m.-3 p.m., Mon. 6:30 a.m.-2:30 p.m., Tues.-Sat. 6:30 a.m.-4 p.m. No cards.

CAFÉ FANNY

1603 San Pablo Ave.,
Berkeley - 524-5447

Devotees of California cuisine make regular pilgrimages to Chez Panisse, the restaurant that started it all. If you're such a devotee, but have neither big money to spend nor patience to wait three weeks for a reservation, then hie yourself to Café Fanny, Alice Waters's gem of a café named for her daughter. The tiny food bar has no tables, just one bench inside and a couple of benches outside. But never mind the setting—we'd eat one of Café Fanny's sandwiches on a refuse heap if it came to that. Waters's love of just-picked garden products shows in these sandwiches, which pair meats and cheeses with watercress, radishes, red peppers and the like. Try the baked ham and watercress on foccacia, a thick, savory, pastrylike bread baked with herbs and olive oil. Or come for breakfast and lose yourself in a bowl of steaming cappuccino and outstanding buckwheat crêpes, prosciutto toast or marvelous eggs from free-ranging hens. About $15 for breakfast or lunch for two, with an espresso or a glass of wine.

Open Mon.-Sat. 7:30 a.m.-5 p.m., Sun. 9:30 a.m.-2:30 p.m. No cards (checks accepted).

CAFÉ OLIVETO

5655 College Ave.,
Oakland - 547-5356

That the Rockridge section of Oakland is undergoing rapid gentrification is evidenced by the opening of places like Café Oliveto, a chic tapas bar with a very handsome Mediterranean decor. While patrons at the upstairs restaurant sample large plates of rustic Italian/Spanish food, those at the downstairs café nibble on small, savory dishes from the menu of innovative tapas (essentially glorified appetizers). Everything we've tried has been good: calamari in a tomato-caper sauce, chicken and linguiça (pork sausage), an inspired tart of roasted garlic, mozzarella and basil, delectable little pizzas and more. A few tapas (priced at $2 to $3 each) and a glass of Chardonnay from the small but select list make for a very pleasant lunch or supper. About $26 for two, with wine.

Open Mon.-Thurs. 11:30 a.m.-11 p.m., Fri. 11:30 a.m.-12 midnight, Sat. 12 noon-12 midnight, Sun. 12 noon-10 p.m. Cards: MC, V.

FLINT'S

3814 San Pablo Ave.,
Oakland - 658-9912
6609 Shattuck Ave.,
Oakland - 653-0593

Although upstarts are ever crowding on the horizon, no one has yet managed to usurp Flint's position as the Bay Area's barbecue leader. The sound of surly women hacking away at smoked meats is music to the ears of the fanatic customers who come into the shabby, smoky Flint's outlets to pick up

*6672 E. 14th St.,
Oakland - 569-1312*

ribs, chicken, links or barbecued-beef sandwiches. Flint's barbecue is a match made in heaven: perfectly smoked meat married to an almost mystical hot sauce. And, of course, it wouldn't be authentic barbecue without the slices of Wonder bread and the scoops of overly sweet potato salad. Flint's only failure is with dessert: the sweet potato pie is depressingly gelatinous and smacks of long hours sitting on a shelf. Nonetheless, the barbecue buck stops here. A whole slab of ribs is about $14, a chicken $8.

Open daily 11 a.m.-3 a.m. No cards.

Open Sun.-Thurs. 11 a.m.-2 a.m., Fri.-Sat. 11 a.m.-4 a.m. No cards.

Open Sun. & Tues.-Thurs. 11 a.m.-12 midnight, Fri.-Sat. 11 a.m.-3 a.m. No cards.

PICANTE

1328 6th St., Berkeley - 525-3121

The kind of Mexican food found at the best Mission District taquerias has finally made it to Berkeley. Like all taquerias, Picante has no decor to speak of, looking rather like a college dorm cafeteria, but its tacos, burritos, tostadas and nachos are unimpeachable. The soft-shell taco crammed with exceptionally juicy chorizo is almost a meal in itself, and the nachos—drenched in fine melted jack cheese and crowned with luscious fresh hot salsa—certainly make a meal. The pork, beef and chicken chunks, well grilled and tender, are in no danger of being overwhelmed by runny sauce and tepid refried beans, as is usually the case. And the carnitas, tortas and quesadillas are all superb. About $10 for two, with beer.

Open Mon.-Thurs. 11 a.m.-10 p.m., Fri.-Sat. 11 a.m.-12 midnight. No cards.

SAUL'S RESTAURANT & DELICATESSEN

1475 Shattuck Ave., Berkeley - 848-3354

The jury is not quite in yet, but Saul's just might be the first quality kosher-style deli to grace the East Bay in years. This type of cuisine has been more conspicuously absent than any other in these parts, and Saul's, while not the Carnegie, is successfully filling the gap with its pastrami flown in from New York (it loses a little moisture in transit but is otherwise fine), melt-in-your-mouth lox, real kippered salmon, concentrated chicken soup with matzo balls, sandwiches piled high (though not as high as the Empire State Building), tangy coleslaw and fabulous cheesecake. In all those deli classics, Saul's shines, though there are a few disappointments, especially the excessively doughy blintzes. Moderately dilled pickles and tomatoes are brought to your table gratis, and dinnertime sees such standards as roast chicken and Hungarian beef goulash. About $28 for two, with beer, wine or Dr. Brown's sodas.

Open Sun.-Thurs. 8 a.m.-9 p.m., Fri.-Sat. 8 a.m.-10 p.m. No cards (checks accepted).

THE SWALLOW

2625 Durant Ave.
(University Art Museum),
Berkeley - 841-2409

University cafeterias are usually home to the most shocking food—from mystery "Mexican" casseroles to strange Jell-O salads. But leave it to Berkeley to surprise us with this cafeteria on the lower level of the campus art museum. The chefs here do wondrous things with eggs and cheese, whipping up inspired quiches and frittatas. We took a lean "Roast Beast" sandwich (served on excellent homemade French bread), a buttery shortcake and an espresso outside to the sculpture garden and ate in the glorious sunshine. We couldn't have asked for a more satisfying simple lunch. Between the museum, The Swallow and the wonderful Pacific Film Archive, one could do much worse than spend an entire day in this building. About $15 for lunch for two.

Open Tues.-Sat. 11 a.m.-8 p.m., Sun. 11 a.m.-5 p.m. No cards.

TAQUERIA MORELIA

4481 E. 14th St.,
Oakland - 261-6360

This is not a neck of the woods you're likely to find yourself in, unless it's to visit Taqueria Morelia, which raises the creation of burritos, tacos and tortas (Mexican sandwiches) to a high art. There's no pretense to ambience here, just a loving devotion to good food. As is always the case with a superior taqueria, freshness makes the difference: the meats, beans and salsas really stand out, instead of congealing into a blob. Unlike most taquerias, Morelia offers a full menu of tortas, made with ham, chicken, carnitas and chorizo. If Morelia is crowded, take your food to the adjoining bar, Talk of the Town, which is under the same ownership. About $10 for two, with beer.

Open Mon.-Thurs. 10 a.m.-10 p.m., Fri. 10 a.m.-12 midnight, Sat.-Sun. 10 a.m.-11 p.m. No cards.

TOP DOG

2534 Durant Ave.,
Berkeley - (no phone)

The occasional craving for a hot dog should not be denied, but, unfortunately, the Bay Area has few good hot dog stands. Berkeley's phone-booth-size Top Dog stands, however, have been holding the top-dog spot for many years now,

291

2503 Hearst St., Berkeley -
(no phone)

offering all kinds of dogs, including a kosher New York–style frank (which holds its own against *any* N.Y. deli dog), kielbasa, smoked bratwurst, Italian calabrese and Top Dog's own all-American frank. We found ourselves unable to resist trying six varieties, each flawless on a seeded French bun. Our stomachs paid the price, but it was worth it. A couple of dogs and a soda apiece will cost two $8.

Open Sun.-Thurs. 10 a.m.-2 a.m., Fri.-Sat. 10 a.m.-3 a.m.
No cards.

YORKSHIRE FISH & CHIPS

1984 Shattuck Ave.,
Berkeley - 841-7743

If you demand authenticity in a restaurant, try Yorkshire, a favorite hole-in-the-wall of the collegiate set. The owners went so far as to haul British frying equipment overseas to get the fish and chips just right, which they are. The fish is tender, crisp and delicious, and though the chips are more routine, they respond well to a splash of malt vinegar. The meat pasties are hearty and tasty, but we couldn't bring ourselves to try the bangers, which Yorkshire batters and fries. Bring your own beer, and expect to pay about $10 for two.

Open Mon.-Fri. 11 a.m.-8 p.m. No cards.

ZACHARY'S PIZZA

5801 College Ave.,
Oakland - 655-6385

1853 Solano Ave.,
Berkeley - 525-5950

Zachary's offers both normal and deep-dish pizza, the latter being the Bay Area's closest approximation of the Chicago-style pizza. Crusts are thick and crisp, and the sauce, cheese and toppings are well layered; the end product is more like an Italian bread casserole than a pizza. But even though a lot of care goes into these pizzas, the fresh-tasting tomato sauce lacks zest. Still and all, Zachary's pizzas are among the very best around. Lines form early, and since the pizzas take longer than usual to cook, it's a good idea to order ahead. About $17 for a pizza for two, with beer.

Open Mon.-Thurs. 11 a.m.-10 p.m., Fri.-Sat. 11 a.m.-10:30 p.m., Sun. 11:30 a.m.-9:30 p.m. No cards.

HOTELS

CLAREMONT RESORT HOTEL

Many millions of dollars in restoration have given new life to this grand old lady of the East Bay, and now the great white Claremont, with its tower, cupolas, twenty acres of grounds

41 Tunnel Rd., Berkeley - 843-3000

and 1915 resort-hotel architecture, is almost as attractive on the inside as it is on the outside. Though large, it is quiet and is a perfect romantic hideaway, especially if you request a room with a view of San Francisco. Amenities include an Olympic-size pool, ten tennis courts, a nearby golf course, a bar with a great city view and an equally view-struck stylish restaurant that is a favorite of the Sunday-brunch set. Such details as high ceilings and moldings add period charm to the spacious rooms, which are all comfortably furnished.

Singles: $140-$190; doubles: $160-$210; suites: $240-$600. Weekend and other discount packages available.

HOTEL DURANT

2600 Durant Ave., Berkeley - 845-8981

This modest old hotel is popular with professors, lecturers and parents visiting their U.C. Berkeley students in school just a block away. Though the 140 rooms are plain and rather shabby, the location is perfect for enjoying both the campus and the many restaurants and shops of central Berkeley. The hotel houses a restaurant and a bar, and guests can buy passes to use U.C. Berkeley's pool, gym and tennis courts.

Singles: $68-$82; doubles: $74-$86; suites: $100-$170.

Marin County

RESTAURANTS

CAPRICE

2000 Paradise Dr., Tiburon - 435-3400

French

11/20

This is one of the most romantic restaurants in the Bay Area. The contrast between a spectacular view of San Francisco and the Bay, and the dreamy, intimate dining room creates a creamy sensuality that is ably abetted by deft service. We're not exaggerating. We would be, however, if we said the food was great. It's in the sumptuous vein and is well done, but of an older, stuffier order, not the kind of thing foodies get excited about these days. But who cares? Foodies have no hearts anyway, and hearts are what Caprice is all about. The wine list has some extraordinary French selections at pretty reasonable prices. Two can spend $100 for dinner with wine without trying too hard.

Open daily 11:30 a.m.-2:30 p.m. & 5:30 p.m.-10 p.m. All major cards.

CASA MADRONA

805 Bridgeway, Sausalito - 331-5888
California

12/20

We love this place, especially during crab and salmon seasons. The view of Sausalito's postcard-perfect harbor is just what we want to see while we munch a little fresh salmon with herb sauce, suck down a few crisp oysters on the half shell, or address a delectable Dungeness or soft-shelled crustacean. A spot of Chardonnay doesn't hurt, either. Do the hard-working men on that tugboat down there know how good life can be? The food is heartwarming, though not fantastically delicate, and the California/French menu has an interesting touch of sunny Italy to it, as telegraphed by the liberal use of pancetta and flavorful vine-ripened tomatoes. Service is friendly, but there's often a wait, even with reservations. We finished dinner around midnight on our last visit, and wished we'd booked a room for the night. Next time. About $60 for a romantic dinner for two, with wine.

Open Mon.-Thurs. 11:30 a.m.-2:30 p.m. & 6 p.m.-10 p.m., Fri. 11:30 a.m.-2:30 p.m. & 6 p.m.-11 p.m., Sat. 6 p.m.-11 p.m. All major cards.

MOUNTAIN HOME INN

810 Panoramic Hwy., Mill Valley - 381-9000
American

11/20

The view would be sufficient, but the food is pretty good, too, especially when eaten on the veranda with the sun setting on the pleasure domes of Marin at your feet. This handsome, rustic/modern lodge is perched on the flank of Mount Tamalpais, a peak sacred to Indians of yore and contemporary Marinites alike. The site is historic, but the building itself has been rebuilt from the foundation up, to excellent effect. We have found the outdoor deck to be quite pleasant on a sunny afternoon but chilly at night, even during the summer. That's okay, because the indoor dining room is charming and cozy, with a cheery blaze on the hearth most nights. The rack of lamb has pleased us mightily on more than one occasion. At our last visit, grilled salmon was still quivering from the swells of Point Reyes, but a swordfish steak was dry. The cream of artichoke soup must be the best way yet invented to eat this troublesome but tasty vegetable. The wines are mostly on the young side, but the by-the-glass selection is good. Two will spend about $65 for dinner with wine.

Open Tues.-Sat. 11:30 a.m.-3 p.m. & 5:30 p.m.-9 p.m. Cards: AE, MC, V.

ROYAL THAI

*610 3rd St., San Rafael -
485-1074*

Thai

14 (chef symbol)

A few years ago, fans of Khan Toke Thai House in San Francisco were horrified to learn that certain members of the kitchen crew had defected to Marin. The kitchen closed ranks and everything was fine, and the upshot is that now there's an outstanding Thai restaurant in San Rafael. Royal Thai is small, occupying one wing of a large old house that's been converted into a mini shopping mall. The Thai crêpe is the best we've tried, and the pad Thai has a deep, rich flavor with real tang. Don't be afraid to turn on the heat—the flavors in every dish we've had (and we've pretty much worked through the menu) have been well-balanced even at high-combustion levels. The wine list is unusually fine. Two will spend about $40.

Open Sun.-Thurs. 5 p.m.-9:30 p.m., Fri.-Sat. 5 p.m.-10 p.m. Cards: AE, MC, V.

SAVANNAH GRILL

*55 Tamal Vista Blvd.,
Corte Madera - 924-6774*

American

10/20

It's hard to say what Savannah has to do with this place. If we're talking African plains, perhaps it's the grilled and house-smoked meats (just like the lions eat); if it's the Belle of Georgia, then we're in nebulous territory. There's little evidence of Southern cooking, but there is a nod to trendy Southwestern, especially in the spicy sauces that turn up on some fish dishes. The rest is basic grill 'n' graze, with a well-chosen list of wines by the glass. The location in a shopping mall bodes poorly, but the wood, brass and frosted-glass interior, with comfortable booths and a bar where one may eat solo, are pleasant enough. Better than your average chain theme joint. About $60 for two with wine.

Open daily 11:30 a.m.-4:30 p.m. & 5:30 p.m.-10:30 p.m. Cards: AE, MC, V.

HOTELS

CASA MADRONA

*805 Bridgeway, Sausalito -
332-0502*

Some of the rooms are small and some lack style, but most have wonderful views of the idyllic Sausalito harbor. Though its size—35 rooms—makes it more like a hotel, Casa Madrona considers itself a bed and breakfast, and is set up accordingly: a communal breakfast is served in the morning, and guests gather for wine and cheese in the evening. Amenities include a hot tub and a lovely restaurant with good seafood and a great view.

Singles & doubles: $65-$195.

Wine Country

RESTAURANTS

JOHN ASH & COMPANY
4330 Barnes Rd., Santa Rosa - (707) 527-7687
California

12/20

A relative newcomer to the wine country, young chef John Ash brings a welcome spirit of experimentation to an often-staid French culinary scene. "Fresh and local ingredients" are the bywords of California cuisine (as with nouvelle cuisine), and Ash is a zealous adherent, drawing on the fertile region's gardens and farms. A number of appetizers indicate the credits and debits of the Ash approach. The range-fed chicken and apple sausage, redolent of thyme, is a superb testament to the value of local livestock raised in a healthful environment, but it benefits not a whit from the presence of sun-dried tomatoes. Pairing an Oriental black-bean mayonnaise with prawns is an inspired bit of magic, diminished only by shrimp that can be less than tender. Cold trout with a subtle orange-saffron sauce, dolloped with red caviar, is another taste sensation, but at our last visit the trout was underdone and mealy. Ash can also get too carried away on occasion, as evidenced by a dish of pasta that was overwhelmed by a heap of green beans, baby asparagus tips, whole yellow wax peppers, red pepper rings, avocado, pine nuts and a sauce of crème fraîche and puréed tomatillos. It's enough to make one a strict carnivore, which is a good idea considering the incredibly tender chop of range-raised veal.

As befits the neighborhood, the wine list is vast, with several local vintages available by the glass. The large portions may not leave room for dessert, but try them anyway: you won't soon forget the white-chocolate mousse in a little dark-chocolate boat drifting on a sea of raspberry sauce and zabaglione. All in all, we applaud Ash's experimental verve but urge him to check his more sophomoric urges. Dinner for two, with wine, is a reasonable $75.

Open Tues.-Sun. 11 a.m.-2 p.m. & 6 p.m.-9:30 p.m. All major cards.

AUBERGE DU SOLEIL

180 Rutherford Hill Rd.,
Rutherford -
(707) 963-1211

French

13

From the first impression of rosy adobe, tile, wicker and foliage, this could be the governor's dining room at a French colonial outpost on some subtropical island. It's not, though —it's just an expensive, very good if slightly reactionary restaurant with a wine list to dream about and the best restaurant view in the Napa Valley. To look out over the fabled vineyards at sunset, while sipping a properly aged wine from those very vines, is a heady experience. The menu supports the experience adequately, occasionally with brilliance, though if one were to be rigorously objective, it's clear that in any other location this kitchen would really have to compete. But why get hypothetical? An evening here can easily be the high point of a Napa Valley weekend. We love the grilled farm rabbit with a pungent mustard sauce and the house-made seafood sausage. Desserts are perfectly decadent, especially when peaches are in season (chocolate, of course, is always in season). Service harkens back to the old surf 'n' turf milieu, but it's sincere. The prix-fixe dinner is $42 a head, and the sky's the limit on the wines.

Open daily 11:30 a.m.-2 p.m.; seatings nightly 6 p.m. & 9 p.m. Cards: AE, MC, V.

LA BOUCANE

1778 2nd St., Napa -
(707) 253-1177

French

15

Perhaps because it is located in the *city* of Napa (which is to the wine country what Bakersfield is to California), La Boucane has eluded the attention of the culinary press. That's unfortunate, because this place is a joy. It serves classic French fare, intricately prepared with an occasional ethnic twist, in a sensuous remodeled Victorian house at extremely reasonable prices. The garrulous Algerian chef and owner, Jacques Mokrani, defines Boucane as a kind of smoky, bawdy, seafaring ambience, and the food follows suit. If the appetizer of prawns is offered, choose it—the shrimp are lightly floured, sautéed, deglazed in Cognac and finished with garlic, tomatoes, butter and lemon juice. Standout entrees include the monkfish Bretonne, the lobsterlike fish sautéed in clarified butter, well sauced and served with rice timbales and perfectly finished vegetables; and the medallions of lamb, as tender as can be and well matched with crispy diced potatoes that are both roasted and sautéed. Subtle essences are distinctively combined into the creamed vegetable soups, and a salad snappily dressed in a walnut-Roquefort vinaigrette shows that the chef can be as au courant as anyone. La Boucane breaks with French tradition by not offering pastries for dessert—a shame, though the chocolate and hazelnut mousses will more than suffice. Dinner for two, with wine, will run about $70.

Open Mon.-Sat. 5:30 p.m.-10:30 p.m. Cards: AE, MC, V.

FRENCH LAUNDRY

6640 Washington St., Yountville -
(707) 944-2380
California

14

Tucked away in a nest of bushes on a quaint corner, the French Laundry offers a dining experience that epitomizes the wine country. Ambience is the main attraction, and it is nigh impossible to resist the charms of this old two-story brick French country chalet. Patrons have their table for the entire evening, and avuncular host Don Schmitt invites everyone to roam the premises over the course of the meal. Pick up your glass of Chardonnay and take him up on the offer: wander into a modest yet bountiful vegetable and herb garden before studying the prix-fixe menu, which perpetuates the French country mood. For the most part, the food delivers, taking you far away from California cuisine's trendy excesses and plopping you in the middle of a French village. The basil egg (simply a coddled egg served on a bed of basil mayonnaise with three kinds of basil leaves), the buttery duck liver pâté with shiitake mushrooms, the creamy sorrel soup studded with bacon . . . each of these starters transported us. Sadly, we were brought back to earth with the suprême of chicken with rosemary and orange; the waitress confirmed our suspicion that the remarkably bland bird was *not* range fed. Given the depths to which commercial chicken producers have sunk, and given the French Laundry's reputation and prices, we find that inexcusable. But we were once again transported, this time to Alsace, when we sampled the lovely apple Kuchen with a hot cream sauce. And despite the dismal chicken, we must unabashedly recommend the French Laundry—it's hard to imagine a more pleasant evening. About $115 for two, with wine.

Open Wed.-Sun. 7 p.m.-10:30 p.m. No cards (checks accepted).

THE GRILLE

18149 Sonoma Hwy. 12 (Sonoma Mission Inn), Boyes Hot Springs -
(707) 938-9000
California/French

14

The celebrated spa cuisine originated here, but don't hold that against The Grille. Normal people can eat here, too. We did, and we were glad we did. A perfect salmon fillet was gently steamed and served with a caviar beurre blanc and fresh Sonoma vegetables. A roast Sonoma duck was lovely, dark and deep, and a roast saddle of veal was cooked par excellence. The room itself is handsome, with plenty of white linen to show up your tan, and the pool laughs and shimmers outside the French windows as you dine. The wine list is a Sonoma County showcase. How could anything go wrong in such a place? Well, the service has been known to be lax, and they could run out of dessert . . . Two will spend about $80, with wine.

Open daily 12 noon-2:30 p.m. & 6 p.m.-10 p.m. All major cards.

MADRONA MANOR

*1001 West Side Rd., Healdsburg -
(707) 433-4231*

California

13

As long as you're having dinner in the lovely old house on the Dry Creek Benchland, why not stay overnight? The grounds are lovely, an oasis in the dry madrona-chapparal country hereabouts. Chef Todd Muir, a Chez Panisse graduate, prepares a straightforward regional cuisine, the region being northern coastal California as illuminated by the cuisines of Europe and Asia—that is, California cuisine. The three elegant, Victorian dining rooms in the 1881 mansion overlook lawns and gardens, the source of many of the vegetables, herbs and edible flowers that appear on the table. Muir learned the art of making pizza from Alice Waters, so naturally Madrona Manor has a wood-fired oven for pizza and breads. Goat cheese is glorified in a tangy herbed soufflé, and there are always meats and fishes from the mesquite grill. Dessert embraces such heady delights as prune-Armagnac ice cream. After a romantic meal in these storied rooms, the canopied bed upstairs seems truly inviting, all the more so because breakfast comes with the price of the room. And breakfast on the Madrona Manor veranda is very fine indeed. Dinner, either à la carte or prix fixe, will run about $70 for two, with wine.

Open Mon.-Sat. 6 p.m.-9 p.m., Sun. 10:30 a.m.-2 p.m. & 6 p.m.-9 p.m. Cards: AE, MC, V.

MIRAMONTE HOTEL

1327 Railroad Ave., St. Helena - (707) 963-3970

French

15

French food with a twist: Chef Udo Nechutny, a former student of Paul Bocuse, has spent time in Japan, and his prix-fixe meals (at several cost levels) reflect that influence in their lightness, presentation and inclusion of raw or briefly cooked ingredients to punctuate and offset the grilled and roasted ones. The effect is exhilarating. Coquilles St.-Jacques, perfect scallops in a pale sauce made from clouds of cream, is just one of the many marvelous dishes we've enjoyed here. We've always liked the looks of the old gray stone hotel by the railroad tracks and were pleased to find the dining room and bar complementary, with white walls, high ceilings and enough silverware to arm the French Foreign

299

Legion. The service is impeccable, and the wine list is a catalog of California's best (mostly from Napa Valley), plus some French bottles. Two can easily spend $125, with wine.

Open Wed.-Sun. 6:15 p.m.-9 p.m. No cards.

MOUNT VIEW HOTEL

1457 Lincoln Ave.,
Calistoga -
(707) 942-6877

California

 16

If you're going to eat here, stay here. There's nothing finer than indulging fully in one of these deft, inventive meals—and in the very fine, reasonably priced wine list—and then drifting upstairs to one of the charming art deco rooms, all of them blessedly sans TV. At first glance the menu looks pretty ordinary, but that's because it can't communicate the exceptional quality of ingredients or the subtlety of the kitchen's talent. Chef Brad Mollath, ex of Chez Panisse, recently assumed the toque from former chef Diane Pariseau, who left to open her own place. As he masters his new kitchen he is adding more of himself to the menu, but he has also kept Pariseau's best creations, especially the uninhibited sauces, which he makes in as many flavors as he does sorbet, with as many different fruits and herbs. Sauces of fresh berries may accompany fish, while various stone fruits lend their essences to meat and poultry. The flavor combinations are unfailingly sublime, and the very attentive staff is tuned in well enough to recommend just the right wines, whether by glass or bottle. The menu changes frequently, reflecting the best of what's available, both as close by as the cornucopious Napa and Sonoma valleys and as far away as the rest of the world. Amazingly, the prix-fixe dinner is a mere $28, without wine.

Open daily 8 a.m.-2 p.m. & 6 p.m.-9 p.m. Cards: AE, MC, V.

MUSTARDS

7399 St. Helena Hwy.,
Yountville -
(707) 944-2424

California

14

This was the prototype for such new temples of hedonism (though not necessarily gastronomy) as the Fog City Diner in San Francisco and the Rio Grill in Carmel. Chef Cindy Pawlcyn took her cue from the delights of noshing—she observed that the appetizers were often the best part of a menu and began tampering with such nibble items as tapas, canapés and zakuski. The result has been dubbed, for lack of a better description, grazing cuisine. And there's no question that the grazing cuisine here is a cud above the imitators. The Napa Valley was a perfect birthplace for the concept, what with two-thirds of the clientele ordering food pretty much as an excuse to taste various wines, a pastime that calls for wild flavors in discreet packages: pan-fried green tomatoes with salsa, Sonoma goat cheese with an herb vinaigrette, cold strawberry-nectarine soup, crisp onion rings, rabbit with mustard seeds, strawberry-rhubarb pie. Tables on the screened porch are nice in the evening or for late lunch during spring or autumn rains. Two will spend about $50, with wine.

Open daily 11:30 a.m.-10 p.m. Cards: MC, V.

TRAVIGNE

1050 Charter Oak, St. Helena - (707) 963-4444
Italian/California

10/20

The old St. George Restaurant and bar had been pathetic for years before it went its way. The kids who made such a hit with Mustards, and then went on to open such phenomenally successful grazing joints as the Fog City Diner, bought the St. George in 1987 and turned it into a trompe l'oeil Italian experience. It immediately became a hangout for young post-collegiates and what few swingers are left in these perilous times; the staff hangs out with the best of them. It all comes down to fashion in the end. We could see a heck of an ad campaign being shot in this bleached-brick beauty, with its overlay of industrial tech and honest remnants of the St. George (the fine old bar, for one), but food is another matter. We're not impressed so far, and the word on Travigne is: If you want to make a certain kind of scene, this is your place. If you're hungry, go to Mustards. Dinner will cost two about $65, with wine.

Open daily 11:30 a.m.-10 p.m. Cards: MC, V.

WASHINGTON STREET RESTAURANT

6539 Washington St., Yountville - (707) 944-2406
American

10/20

This is a convenient and amenable place that aims to cash in on a number of popular concepts, and does it pretty well. The menu is American and eclectic and is set up for grazing, with regular changes to take advantage of seasonal foods. Calorie counters will find a friend in the chef, though some of the heartier dishes (and, of course, desserts) will tempt the enemy within. The wine list is pretty good, with a nice selection by the glass. It even looks good: dinerlike, bistrolike, publike, trattorialike and then some. Though you'll have forgotten what you ate mere moments after leaving, you won't have regretted passing your dinner hour away in this pleasant place, especially given the decent price: $40 for two, with wine.

Open Mon.-Thurs. 11:30 a.m.-9:30 p.m., Fri. 11:30 a.m.-10 p.m., Sat. 5:30 p.m.-10 p.m., Sun. 11 a.m.-9:30 p.m. Cards: AE, MC, V.

QUICK BITES

THE DINER

6476 Washington St.,
Yountville -
(707) 944-2626

Before beginning a rigorous day of wine tasting, stop into The Diner for a marvelously fortifying breakfast. Your day will start right with a cup of Graffeo's coffee, continuing with such joys as cornmeal waffles with bits of bacon in the batter, ultrafresh eggs, homemade spicy sausage and great home fries. The plain white interior won't assault your senses before you've had a chance to wake up, though it is given interest with an old-fashioned soda fountain and a few charming touches. The best breakfast in the wine country will cost two about $15.

Open Tues.-Sun. 8 a.m.-3 p.m. No cards.

HOTELS

With its sprawling vineyards, charming towns, lush countryside, brilliant weather, romantic restaurants and excellent wine-tasting opportunities, it's no wonder the wine country is thick with hotels and inns. But that doesn't mean finding a room is always a snap. In the on-season months (April through October), getting a reservation can be difficult, especially on short notice. Two organizations can help, however: Bed & Breakfast Exchange (707-257-7757) and Napa Valley Reservations Unlimited (707-252-1985).

In the winter months, when it rains, it's a different story. Hotels practically beg for you to be their guests, some offering discounted rates and special packages. Sun provided, we find this to be the best time of year in the wine country—it's peaceful, and there are no lines at the wineries.

AUBERGE DU SOLEIL

180 Rutherford Hill Rd.,
Rutherford -
(707) 963-1211

Auberge du Soleil is the crème de la crème of wine country inns, and the staff knows it. Problem is, they can be a little rude in letting *you* know it. Make no mistake, this place caters to the upper crust, and in the busy summer months anyone less than a movie star, multimillionaire or member of the royal family can get short-shrifted. (We know a few people who were shunted from room to room more than once, presumably to make way for more eminent guests.) And Auberge du Soleil is so pretentious that, here in the heart of America's wine country, each of the nine adobe buildings (containing four rooms each) is named after a *French* wine region.

All that said, we must say that in luxury, setting and cuisine, Auberge du Soleil is unparalleled. Each building is gently terraced up the hills of an olive grove overlooking vineyards. No room is without a view and a deck from which to appreciate it, and the interiors include fireplaces, stocked wet bars, tasteful furnishings and baskets of fruit, cheese and pâté. Other amenities include tennis courts, a large pool and the inn's acclaimed restaurant, which may not be quite as ethereal as when Masa Kobayashi was here, but which still serves very good nouvelle cuisine on a lovely outdoor patio.

One-bedroom suites: $195-$300; two-bedroom suites: $450.

INN AT THE TIDES

800 Coast Hwy., Bodega Bay - (707) 875-2751

Staggered up and down the rugged Sonoma Coast hills, the Inn at the Tides is a modern hotel that conforms well to its salty, foggy environs. Warmth is provided by fireplaces (in most rooms) and a heated pool, which has adjoining sauna and massage facilities. The rooms are crisp and immaculate, stocked with fresh flowers, refrigerators filled with snacks, comfortable sofa beds and terrycloth robes. Guests are greeted in the morning with a complimentary breakfast and daily newspaper. The Bay View dining room takes full advantage of the inn's proximity to the ocean and serves a range of fresh seafood; the wine list draws extensively from the wine country communities to the east.

April-Oct.—singles & doubles: $100-$150; suites: $175. Nov.-March—singles & doubles: $85-$125; suites: $150.

MADRONA MANOR

1001 Westside Rd., Healdsburg - (707) 433-4231

Perhaps the best example of the efficacy of converting an old private mansion (in this case circa 1881) into a guest house, the Madrona Manor combines antique opulence with modern luxury. Much of the original furniture remains—ancient dressers with marble tops and beds with carved headboards —in the nine mansion rooms, and eight more rooms in the carriage house behind the mansion are outfitted with furniture purchased in Nepal. All rooms have private baths, some have balconies, and none have phones or television. The magnificent eight-acre grounds, replete with palms and redwoods, complement the picture, as does the superb mesquite-grill-anchored restaurant run by Todd Muir, who learned his California-cuisine craft from Alice Waters and is a whiz with baked goods. Breakfast, included with the accommodations, is quite substantial. With a swimming pool to boot, Madrona Manor is a Napa Valley best bet.

Singles & doubles: $90-$122.

MEADOWOOD RESORT HOTEL

900 Meadowood Ln., St. Helena - (707) 963-3646

The Meadowood is our idea of heaven: total luxury, with just enough rusticity to permit a sense of proportion. The ten lodges are insouciantly scattered around the beautifully forested acreage as if they were backwoods cabins. And though each lodge (containing four suites and a studio) looks stolidly modest from the outside, inside are stunning, spacious nests of opulent seclusion. The architecture is New England in style, so there are exposed beams, peaked roofs and soft whites and grays, and the details are carefully thought-out: brass door and drawer handles, warmed floor tiles in the bathroom, Krups coffee makers, well-stocked wet bars, fireplaces made of Silverado stone, and terrycloth robes in the closet. Though it's hard to imagine wanting for much in this setting, the main lodge, just a stone's throw away, will deliver anything desired, including a masseur or masseuse. And you'll want to leave your room now and then to take advantage of the sports facilities—not such big-city things as aerobics, exercycles and saunas, but such fresh-air sports as golf (on a splendid nine-hole course), tennis, croquet (complete with an Australian pro!), hiking and swimming. The Starmont Restaurant, featuring a standard California-cuisine menu, is not yet on a par with the wine country's best restaurants, but chef Hale Lake is improving steadily, and the food will certainly leave you content.

Singles & doubles: $110-$165; suites: $150-$265.

MOUNT VIEW HOTEL

1457 Lincoln Ave., Calistoga - (707) 942-6877

Get enough of a concentration of hotels and you're sure to find one that uses a gimmick to attract customers; this one employs art deco. The entire 34-unit building is done up in the style of the '30s, with rooms named after Hollywood stars of the period. This might seem like the kind of urban pretension that people would come to Napa Valley to escape, but there's no doubting that the Mount View offers charm, comfortable quarters and full hotel amenities. The atmosphere is lively, and guests come here for fun: to listen to the live swing jazz in the Deco Lounge, to dance in Fender's Lounge and to sip bubbly drinks poolside. Special deals abound; our favorite is the "Wine, Dine and Don't Drive" package, which gets you a night's room, a bottle of wine and dinner and breakfast for two. Given the remarkably high quality of the restaurant, the package's $110 price tag is a gift from the gods.

Singles & doubles: $60-$85; suites: $110-$135.

NAPA VALLEY RAILWAY INN

6503 Washington St.,
Yountville -
(707) 944-2000

The idea of converting turn-of-the-century railroad cars into guest rooms is a cute one, but if these are the conditions rail travelers had to face back then, we're glad to be living in the jet age. With their New Orleans bordello theme, the rooms are as spacious as you'd expect from a large box, but the ventilation is poor, the noise level high and the bathrooms less than pristine. And, to boot, there are no phones. One benefit: It's just a short walk to The Diner, the best breakfast place in the wine country.

Singles & doubles: $82-$110.

RANCHO CAYMUS INN

170 Rutherford Dr.,
Rutherford -
(707) 963-1777

In the shadow of Auberge du Soleil sits the spanking-new Rancho Caymus Inn, another theme house. Here California's Spanish history is evoked, with suites named after such figures as Black Bart and such places as Bella Oaks Mine. Much is made of the artistry behind the construction—furniture hewn of California oak, black walnut and fir, Ecuadoran wrought-iron lamps and the like—but the all-suite Caymus is nonetheless très Best Western. There's a pleasant floral courtyard where you can take your complimentary breakfast, and the fancier rooms have fireplaces and Jacuzzis.

Suites: $95-$250.

SILVERADO COUNTRY CLUB & RESORT

1600 Atlas Peak Rd.,
Napa - (707) 257-0200

Its size alone makes Silverado a wine country anomaly. With 350 condominiums, 280 of which are available for guest lodging, the 1,200-acre spread is reminiscent of a Florida retirement community, with the adjacent city of Napa filling the Miami shoes. The condos are ordinary and furnished unexceptionally, though they are certainly large and comfortable enough. As for the resort, it offers everything one could want except rusticity and seclusion. Golfers love Silverado for its two eighteen-hole golf courses, tennis players have twenty courts at their disposal, and swimmers can choose from nine pools. Rounding out the sports facilities are jogging trails and rental bikes. As for the food, you won't find any of that froufrou nouvelle, spa or California cuisine here, just good old steak and seafood at the Royal

Oak Grill and a mundane Continental menu at the Vintner's Court.

Rooms & studio condos: $95-$155; one-bedroom condos: $180; three-bedroom condos: $345.

SONOMA MISSION INN & SPA

18149 Sonoma Hwy. 12,
Boyes Hot Springs -
(800) 862-4945

The Sonoma Mission Inn is geared toward the sybarite who wants to get in shape—which is, of course, a contradiction. *We* certainly don't come to the wine country for abstinence, preferring instead to sample its rich wines and creative food. Yet the Sonoma Mission Inn is a tremendously popular spa that attempts to combine luxury with a low-calorie intake and a high-calorie expenditure. Celebrities swear by the five-day fitness program ($1,350 to $1,550), an intense, personal-trainer-led regimen of aerobics, weights, swimming and so on, accompanied by spa-cuisine meals. But Tammy Faye Bakker would feel comfortable here, too, getting beauty treatments and consuming more plentiful and traditional fare. For a luxury hotel, the ambience is quite casual; the breezy concierge dresses informally and immediately tries to put stressed-out executives and matrons at ease. No one could object to the accommodations, which are modestly elegant. There are two parts to the inn: the smallish, 60-year-old rooms, in brown and white earth tones with minibars and canvas canopies, and the larger, somewhat sterile new rooms, done in pink pastel and equipped with capacious baths and ample closets. All rooms are near the spa facilities. The inn's Grille, a wellspring of spa cuisine, is well thought of for its Pritikin-influenced California cuisine; in the past we had found the service inattentive and the food disappointing, though it has much improved lately.

April-Oct.—singles & doubles: $120-$225; suites: $300-$475. Nov.-March—singles & doubles: $85-$205; suites: $195-$475.

BASICS

At Your Service

FOREIGN EXCHANGE

When the banks are closed (when aren't they?), you can still change money at a few convenient downtown locations. Amparo's Foreign Exchange, 1 Hallidie Plaza (956-5503) and 233 Sansome St. (362-0462), is open on weekends from 9 a.m. to 2 p.m. Bank of America Foreign Currency Services, in the international terminal at San Francisco International Airport (876-7080), changes money daily from 7 a.m. to 11 p.m. And Foreign Exchange Ltd., 415 Stockton St. (397-4700), stays open Saturday from 8:30 a.m. to 1:30 p.m.

LATE NIGHT

BABYSITTER

Bay Area Baby Sitters Agency, 991-7474. Overnight sitters are provided, though they must be reserved during regular business hours.

CAR REPAIR

Transportation Guarantee Co., 555 1st St., South of Market, 431-4700. Open 24 hours Monday through Friday and until midnight on Saturday and Sunday.

DENTIST

Drs. Ronald Mack and Joseph Keery, 661-5133. One of these children's dentists is on call all night.
Dr. Jeffrey I. Stone, 334-2600. On call 24 hours a day.

DOCTOR

Dr. Eugene Gaenslen, 752-4028. Makes house calls 24 hours a day.

LIMOUSINE

P & F Custom Limousine Service, 824-6767. Lincolns and Cadillacs (stretch or squat) are available 24 hours a day if reserved in advance. Prices range from $38.50 to $50 an hour with a three-hour minimum.

LOCKSMITH

Campbell's, 861-5882. A 24-hour emergency locksmith service.
San Francisco Locksmith & Safe Co., 681-4000. On call 24 hours.

NEWSSTAND

Believe it or not, there is no newsstand in the city open all night. If you must find the latest copy of *Pravda* at 3 a.m., you'll have to venture across the Bay to De Lauer Super Newsstand, 1310 Broadway in Oakland (451-6157), which is open 24 hours.

PHARMACY

Walgreen's, 3201 Divisadero St., Pacific Heights, 931-6415. Open all night, but no delivery (see Pickup & Delivery below).

PHOTOCOPY

The Carbon Alternative, 2336 Market St., Castro District, 431-6725. You can rent a LaserWriter or make a copy 24 hours a day Monday through Thursday.

The Copy Factory, 47 Spear St., Financial District, 641-7555. If you're downtown and need a midnight copy, this place is open 24 hours Monday through Friday and until midnight on weekends.

PICKUP & DELIVERY

It's not a universally known fact, but most cab drivers will act as errand runners for you. If you need something delivered to you, call a cab, prepay the driver for the cost of the item to be purchased, then, after delivery, pay what's on the meter plus a negotiated extra fee (usually a couple of dollars).

RESTAURANTS

San Francisco's cosmopolitanism diminishes significantly when you consider how hard it is to get a decent meal after 10 p.m. True, there's always Zim's, but you might as well dine out at 7-Eleven. Nonetheless, we've found a few good late-night restaurants in town.

Basta Pasta, 1268 Grant Ave., North Beach, 434-2248. The fare is standard North Beach Italian and the clientele is touristy, but at midnight, the pasta and seafood dishes will surely satisfy. Open until 2 a.m.

The Brasserie, 950 Mason St. (Fairmont Hotel), Nob Hill, 772-5199. Decent hotel food—sandwiches, pasta, omelets and some fair Cajun dishes—served 24 hours a day.

Clown Alley, 42 Columbus Ave., North Beach, 421-2540. The best hamburger stand in town, and a welcome sight in the middleof the night. The fries and shakes aren't as good as the burgers. Open until 3 a.m.

David's Delicatessen, 468 Geary St., Union Square, 771-1600. Like all deli in San Francisco, it's ersatz and overpriced, but in the wee hours you might not notice. Open until 1 a.m.

Enrico's, 504 Broadway, North Beach, 392-6220. A San Francisco institution with a huge menu of generally fine food; try the chicken thighs. And if you find yourself on this part of Broadway at 2 a.m., you may want to duck in here for safety. Open until 3 a.m.

Everett & Jones Barbeque, 5130 3rd St., Bayview, 822-7728. Some of the best barbecue in the city. Succulent ribs, chicken and links smoked in a brick oven are served until 2 a.m. Friday and Saturday and midnight during the week. Not the best neighborhood in the middle of the night, but it's worth the trek.

The Grubstake, 1525 Pine St., Polk Gulch, 673-8268. Decorated like a dining car, the Grubstake is one of the best places in town to get a decent burger and fries 22 hours a day (it closes from 5 to 7 a.m. to clean up).

Korea House, 1640 Post St., Japantown, 563-1388. Korea House will take the chill out of any damp midnight with its fiery, delicious fish stews, noodle dishes, steamed fish and do-it-yourself barbecue. It's open every night until 3 a.m.

Hamburger Mary's Organic Grill, 1582 Folsom St., South of Market, 626-5767. Not the best burgers in town, but they're certainly edible, and you can't beat the dark, sawdust-and-oak atmosphere and the bizarre clientele at this SOMA institution. There's a great jukebox, too. Open until 1:15 a.m.

Max's Diner, 311 3rd St., South of Market, 546-6297. The owners of

Max's Opera Café have combined the deli, the fern bar and the neo-American diner in this trendy spot. Buffalo chicken wings, meatloaf and mashed potatoes and Dr. Brown's sodas are served until midnight Sunday through Thursday and 1 a.m. Friday and Saturday.

Max's Opera Café, Opera Plaza, Civic Center, 771-7300. More phony deli, but at least it doesn't pretend to be the Carnegie. The proprietors apparently think opera patrons prefer their pastrami on a croissant. The barbecue, however, is decent. Food is served until 1 a.m. Friday and Saturday.

Mitoya, 1855 Post St., Japantown, 563-2156. A Japantown hot spot. Delicious meats, vegetables and shellfish are masterfully cooked by a robata-yaki chef until 3 a.m. Friday and Saturday.

La Rondalla, 901 Valencia St., Mission District, 647-7474. Excellent Mexican food is served in a noisy, chaotic setting until 4 a.m. every night except Tuesday. After a Mexican beer and an order of great guacamole, you'll join in the fun and sing along with the mariachis.

Sparky's Diner, 240 Church St., Castro District, 621-6001. Why there aren't more 24-hour establishments like Sparky's is a mystery. This ultra-trendy neodiner serves meatloaf and burgers to all-night partiers in the vivacious Castro District.

El Zocalo, 3230 Mission St., Mission District, 282-2572. Above-average Mission District Mexican food served until 3 a.m. during the week and 4 a.m. on Friday and Saturday.

TELEPHONE NUMBERS

Ambulance, 911
Amtrak, 982-8512
Animal Bite Reporting, 558-2926
Bay Area Rapid Transit (BART), 788-BART
Bay Area Seating Services (BASS) Ticketmaster Outlets, 762-BASS
Camping Information, (800) 446-7275
Care Line, 333-3333
Chamber of Commerce, 392-4511
Children's Emergency Services, 665-0757
Coast Guard, 911
Directory Information, 411

Fire & Rescue, 911
Highway Conditions, 557-3755
Highway Patrol, 911
Library Information, 558-3191
Oakland International Airport, 577-4000 (call airlines for flight information and booking)
Paramedics, 911
Poison Control, 911
Police, 911
Postal Information, 550-0100
San Francisco International Airport, 761-0800 (call airlines for flight information and booking)
San Francisco Municipal Railway (MUNI), 673-MUNI
San Francisco Ticket Box Office Services (STBS), 433-7827
Taxis, 626-2345 (Yellow), 673-0333 (De Soto), 282-4141 (Luxor), 552-1300 (Veteran's)
Ticketron, 546-9400
Time, 767-8900
Visitors' Information Bureau, 391-2000
Weather Report, 936-1212

Getting Around

AIRPORT TRANSPORTATION

SAN FRANCISCO INTERNATIONAL AIRPORT

Tenth busiest in the world, San Francisco International Airport (SFO) now has the dubious distinction of harboring some of the country's severest flight delays, though no U.S. airport is immune. That aside, getting in and out of SFO is a fairly painless and civil experience. Located fourteen miles south of the city off Highway 101, the airport is excellently served by a number of transportation companies.

Fierce competition among a profusion of van shuttle services means you can get a quick ride to or from your flight from any part of the city at any time of day for just $7. The shuttles prefer 24-hour advance notice, but they will usually pick up with less warning. At this writing, Bay Area SuperShuttle (558-8500) seems to be the best staffed, and Lorrie's Travel & Tours (626-2113) provides reliable service.

Slightly more economical but slightly less convenient are the SFO Airporter buses (495-8404), which pick up at the major downtown and Fisherman's Wharf hotels every fifteen or twenty minutes; you can also board at the downtown terminal, 301 Ellis St., until 2 a.m. The fare is $6 one way and $11 round-trip.

Taxis, of course, are an easy if less cost-effective way to get to the airport; from downtown, expect to pay about $25 plus tip. And there is a plethora of limousine companies waiting to whisk you to your plane in style. Concierges can steer you to a reliable firm.

OAKLAND INTERNATIONAL AIRPORT

A much smaller sister to SFO, the Oakland airport is nevertheless seeing an increase in business, thanks to the public's aversion to the increasingly long waits and the confusing connections at SFO. But unless you're being driven by a friend, renting a car or leaving your own car in the parking lot, getting to and from the Oakland airport is more of a chore and more of an expense than getting to SFO. Located five miles from downtown Oakland on Highway 880, the airport is about a $30 (plus tip) cab ride from downtown San Francisco. With a day's advance notice, the Downtown Airporter (236-8702), a 24-hour door-to-door van service, will take one or two of you to the airport for $20. Lorrie's Travel & Tours (626-2113) charges $34.75 for up to five passengers and asks for at least two hours notice.

If you're traveling light, consider BART (Bay Area Rapid Transit; 465-BART), which will get you to Oakland from downtown San Francisco in 25 minutes for $1.90. BART trains run every fifteen minutes during the day and every twenty minutes at night; they stop running at midnight. To reach the airport, take a Fremont train to the Coliseum stop, then pay another dollar and take an Air BART bus, which runs every fifteen minutes and takes five minutes to reach the airport. But be prepared to add another half hour to your trip if you take BART after rush hour or on Sunday—Fremont trains don't operate in San Francisco then, so you have to take a train to Oakland and transfer to the Fremont line.

CARS

With public transportation as good as it is and parking as hopeless as it is, a car is the last thing you'll want in the city. But if you plan to venture afield to Marin, the wine country or perhaps Lake Tahoe, you'll need to rent a car. Hertz (771-2200) and Avis (885-5011) both have offices around the city and plenty of standard-issue cars. Somewhat less expensive than the two giants are Budget (775-5800) and Avcar (441-4779), along with a host of agencies along O'Farrell Street near Union Square. If you plan to pick up a car at the airport, Bob Leech's Autorental (583-2727) is highly recommended for its low rates and quality cars, but you'll need to reserve a week in advance. For those seeking something other than a Ford Fiesta, try Rent-a-Wreck (776-8700) for a fun jalopy or Autoexotica (673-4653) for a Rolls or a Lamborghini.

PUBLIC TRANSPORTATION

BART (BAY AREA RAPID TRANSIT)

The underground railway that links San Francisco to the East Bay and Daly City, BART is the best way to travel to Berkeley and Oakland. Trains are remarkably clean and quiet, and fares are reasonable. They vary depending on distance traveled; a round-trip to Berkeley will run about $4, and travel anywhere within San Francisco is 80 cents. The high-tech system is entirely automated: machines dispense magnetic-card tickets valued at anywhere from 80 cents to $20, and these tickets are read by computers at the turnstiles when you enter and exit. The computer will calculate your fare and automatically subtract it from your ticket. Diehard rapid transit buffs may want to purchase a special $2.60 excursion ticket, which allows you to ride the entire 71-mile system in one trip. BART trains run Monday through Saturday 6 a.m. to midnight, Sunday 9 a.m. to midnight. Call 788-BART for more information.

CABLE CARS

San Francisco would not be San Francisco without its treasured cable cars. These old-world, open-air trolleys, driven by gregarious bell-ringing brakemen and powered by a vast underground cable network, transport thousands of tourists and locals a day roller-coaster-style up and down the awesome hills of downtown and the waterfront. The fare is $1.50, or you can get a $5 ticket that is good for the whole day, including rides on MUNI buses (see MUNI, below). Cable car transfers are also accepted on MUNI. Tickets can be purchased from machines at the terminals (Powell and Market downtown, and Hyde and Beach at Fisherman's Wharf) or on the cable cars themselves if you have exact change. One tip: To avoid long lines, skip the terminal points and board midroute. Cable cars run daily from 6 a.m. to 1 a.m.; call 673-MUNI.

MUNI (SAN FRANCISCO MUNICIPAL RAILWAY)

MUNI is, quite simply, one of the best public transportation systems in the world, and a bargain to boot. There's nary a square foot of the city that isn't within spitting range of either a MUNI diesel bus, electric bus, streetcar or cable car. And MUNI vehicles are modern, efficient and clean, though recently they've been the victims of an intense graffiti campaign.

Fares, which are 75 cents (except cable cars, which are $1.50), exact change required, include a transfer good for *two* connections on any line in any direction within a 90-minute period. All lines run until midnight, after which a more limited—but still ample—number of "Night Owl" buses take over, running all night.

The official MUNI map, available at hundreds of stores for $1.25, is comprehensive and clear, and it serves quite well as a general street map of the city. Call 673-MUNI for route information.

OTHER TRANSPORTATION

AC Transit (839-2882) is the East Bay's bus system, with service to San Francisco over the Bay Bridge. Golden Gate Transit (332-6600) transports commuters over the Golden Gate Bridge to Marin and points north. Samtrans (761-7000) offers local bus service to the San Francisco airport and cities on the peninsula. And Caltrain (557-8661) provides commuter rail service to San Jose and points along the way.

TAXIS

Although taxis aren't the cheapest way to get around the city, they can be the most fun (if you get a good driver) and the fastest (if you avoid rush hour). We have had great success with San Francisco's cabbies, finding 90 percent of them to be friendly, amusing, informative and honest. Most of the time, cabs are easy to flag down (look for the lighted sign on the car's roof), but empty ones become almost extinct at rush hour, when cab companies' telephone lines seem hopelessly busy. The best bet during rush hour is to wait for a cab outside a good hotel. Gypsy cabs are increasingly common, especially at the airport, but you're safer in a city-licensed cab; they come in all colors, but all have a city insignia on the front doors.

At this writing, taxi meters start at $1.40 and add 15 cents for every tenth of a mile (or $1.50 a mile). Drivers should be tipped about 15 percent. The major companies are Yellow (626-2345), Luxor (282-4141) and Veteran's (552-1300).

Goings-on

A combination of rich culture and heavy tourism ensures that there is always some sort of celebration going on in San Francisco. We've put together a calendar of the more prominent and or interesting events, providing dates and phone numbers when possible. For up-to-date information on all these events, call the San Francisco Visitors' Information Bureau at 391-2000.

JANUARY

ACT (American Conservatory Theatre) performances (through March 29), Geary Theater, 415 Geary St., Union Square, 673-6440.

San Francisco Performances (through mid-May), Herbst Theater, 401 Van Ness Ave., Civic Center, 392-4400.

San Francisco Symphony (runs year-round), Davies Symphony Hall, Grove St. and Van Ness Ave., Civic Center, 431-5400.

San Francisco Ballet Repertory season (through early May), War Memorial Opera House, 301 Van Ness Ave., Civic Center, 621-3838.

Chinese New Year Celebration and Parade (late Jan.–early Feb.), Chinatown, 982-3000. Colorful, firecracker-punctuated parade through Chinatown's streets.

FEBRUARY

Crab Festival, Pier 39, Fisherman's Wharf, 981-8030. Annual crab cook-off featuring well-known chefs.

American Ballet Theatre (through March), War Memorial Opera House, 301 Van Ness Ave., Civic Center, 621-3838.

MARCH

St. Patrick's Day Celebration, downtown, Civic Center, the city's pubs and the United Irish Cultural Center, 2700 45th Ave., Sunset District. Festive parade, ceremonies and parties on the Sunday closest to St. Patrick's Day (March 17).

San Francisco International Film Festival, AMC Kabuki 8 Cinemas, Japantown, 221-9055 or 931-9800. Acclaimed film festival that has been running for more than 30 years.

Mostly Mozart Festival, Davies Symphony Hall, Grove St. and Van Ness Ave., Civic Center, 431-5400; Herbst Theater, 401 Van Ness Ave., Civic Center, 392-4400.

APRIL

San Francisco Giants season opens, Candlestick Park, 468-3700.

Oakland Athletics season opens, Oakland Coliseum, 430-8020.

Macy's Easter Flower Show, Macy's, Stockton St. and O'Farrell St., Union Square, 954-6000.

Cherry Blossom Festival, Japantown, 922-6776. Parades, performances and tea ceremonies throughout Japantown.

Easter Sunrise Service (Easter Sunday), Mt. Davidson. A San Francisco tradition. Easter services are held at the base of the giant cross atop Mt. Davidson; you'll have to hike to the top.

Yachting season opens, first day of daylight savings time, San Francisco Bay. Floating bands and boats of every kind parade through the water.

MAY

Black & White Ball, Civic Center, 431-5400. The entire Civic Center is taken over by this gala ball, to which the whole city is invited. Several thousand don black and white and cough up $150 apiece to take part in the great fun. The ball benefits the San Francisco Symphony.

Cinco de Mayo celebration and parade (first weekend in May), Potrero del Sol Park, 25th St. and Potrero Ave., Mission District. Mexican celebration and parade through the streets of the Mission.

San Francisco Historic Trolley Festival (runs through October), Market St., Union Square. Vintage trolley cars from around the world run all summer on downtown's train tracks.

Bay to Breakers Race, San Francisco, 777-2424. Famous seven-and-a-half-mile footrace through the city's streets.

Union Street Spring Festival, Union St. from Gough St. to Fillmore St., Cow Hollow, 346-4446. A merchant-sponsored street fair.

JUNE

Ethnic Dance Festival, Herbst Theater, 401 Van Ness Ave., Civic Center, 392-4400. Dancers from around the world perform.

Haight Street Fair, Haight St. between Masonic St. and Stanyan St., Haight-Ashbury, 661-8025. Haight merchants and craftspeople put on this street fair, which attracts a crazy quilt of locals—yuppies, hippies, punks, old-timers—with some tourists thrown in for good measure.

Carnaval, Mission St. and 24th St., Mission District, 826-1401. Lively festival modeled after Rio's Carnaval, with dancing and parades.

Stern Grove Midsummer Music Festival (through August), Sigmund Stern Memorial Grove, 19th Ave. and Sloat Blvd., City South, 398-6551. This acclaimed music festival, which showcases classical artists but also features jazz and pop, has been going strong for more than 50 years.

San Francisco Symphony Beethoven Festival, Davies Symphony Hall, Grove St. and Van Ness Ave., Civic Center, 431-5400, and Herbst Theater, 401 Van Ness Ave., Civic Center, 392-4400.

Lesbian-Gay Freedom Day Parade, Market St. to the Civic Center. A vibrant and outlandish celebration of the city's substantial gay population.

JULY

Fourth of July Celebration and Fireworks (July 4), Crissy Field, Presidio waterfront. Celebration goes all afternoon, with fireworks beginning at 9 p.m.

Midsummer Mozart Festival, Davies Symphony Hall, Grove St. and Van Ness Ave., Civic Center, 431-5400, and Herbst Theater, 401 Van Ness Ave., Civic Center, 392-4400.

San Francisco Marathon, San Francisco, 681-2322. Thousands complete a 26-mile route from Golden Gate Park to the Civic Center.

San Francisco Symphony Pops season (through Aug.), Civic Auditorium, Civic Center, 552-8000.

AUGUST

Nihonmachi Street Fair, Japantown, 563-5626. Merchants and food vendors line the streets of Japantown.

San Francisco Hill Stride, San Francisco, 546-6150. A walker's work-out up and down the hilly city streets. The most recent stride drew 5,000 walkers.

San Francisco Fair and Exposition, Civic Center, 557-8758. A wonder-ful urban version of a county fair, with food and wine tastings, performers of every kind, and such amusements as the Impossible Parking Space Race.

Renaissance Pleasure Faire (through September), Blackpoint Forest, Novato, 892-0937 or 620-0433. Food, crafts, entertainment, clothing and whimsy of the fifteenth and sixteenth centuries.

San Francisco 49ers season opens, Candlestick Park, 468-2249.

SEPTEMBER

San Francisco Opera season (through mid-Dec.), War Memorial Opera House, 301 Van Ness Ave., Civic Center, 864-3330.

Today's Artists Concerts (through April), Masonic Auditorium and Herbst Theater, 401 Van Ness Ave., Civic Center, 392-4400. Chamber orchestras and string quartets are featured in this series of concerts.

San Francisco à la Carte à la Park, Golden Gate Park, 383-9378. Food festival featuring samples from some of the city's best restaurants.

San Francisco Blues Festival, Great Meadow, Fort Mason, 826-6837. A weekend festival that showcases the best blues talents in the Bay Area and the country.

Transamerica Open Tennis Tournament (late Sept.–early Oct.), Cow Palace, Geneva Ave. and Santos St., City South, 469-6000.

OCTOBER

ACT (American Conservatory Theatre) performances, Geary Theater, 415 Geary St., Union Square, 673-6440. After a summer hiatus this repertory theater, one of the country's finest, resumes its performances. Festa Italiana, Pier 45, Fisherman's Wharf. Italian street fair.

San Francisco Video Festival, Video Gallery, 1324 Howard St., and other locations, 824-9122. The works of cutting-edge video artists are showcased.

Columbus Day Celebration and Parade (October 12), North Beach and Aquatic Park, 391-8000. The city's Italian heritage is celebrated with a parade up Columbus Avenue, a bocci ball tournament, general festivities and the blessing of the fishing boats in Aquatic Park near Fisherman's Wharf.

Fleet Week U.S. Navy Celebration, Pier 32, Fisherman's Wharf, 391-8000. The Navy displays its air and sea muscle.

San Francisco Fall Antiques Show (late Oct.–early Nov.), Pier 3, Fort Mason, 921-1411. Antique dealers display their wares.

Halloween Night (Oct. 31), along Castro St. and Polk St. The gay community (and its straight friends) dress up in wild costumes and informally parade along these two streets.

NOVEMBER

El Dia de los Muertos (Day of the Dead) (Nov. 1), Mission St., Mission District, 826-8009. Parades and ceremonies honoring the dead.

San Francisco International Auto Show (late Nov.–early Dec.), Moscone Center, 3rd St. and Howard St., South of Market, 974-4000. Car makers from around the world show off their newest models and their prototypes for cars of the future.

Run to the Far Side Race, Golden Gate Park. Race with cartoonist Gary Larson.

DECEMBER

Nutcracker Suite, San Francisco Ballet, War Memorial Opera House, 301 Van Ness Ave., Civic Center, 621-3838. This Christmas classic is the San Francisco Ballet's money-maker.

A Christmas Carol, ACT (American Conservatory Theatre), Geary Theater, 415 Geary St., Union Square, 673-6440. No Christmas-season trip to San Francisco would be complete without seeing ACT's fine performances of this beloved Dickens play.

San Francisco Symphony New Year's Gala (Dec. 31), Davies Symphony Hall, Grove St. and Van Ness Ave., Civic Center, 431-5400. Culture vultures can welcome the new year in with style.

New Year's Eve Extravaganza, Cow Palace, Geneva Ave. and Santos St., City South, 469-6000. Pop-rock musicians sing in the new year.

MAPS

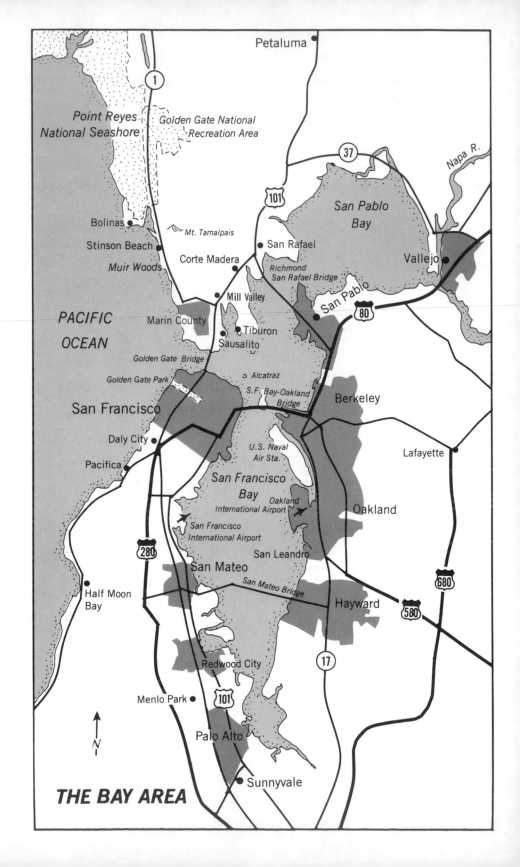

THE BAY AREA

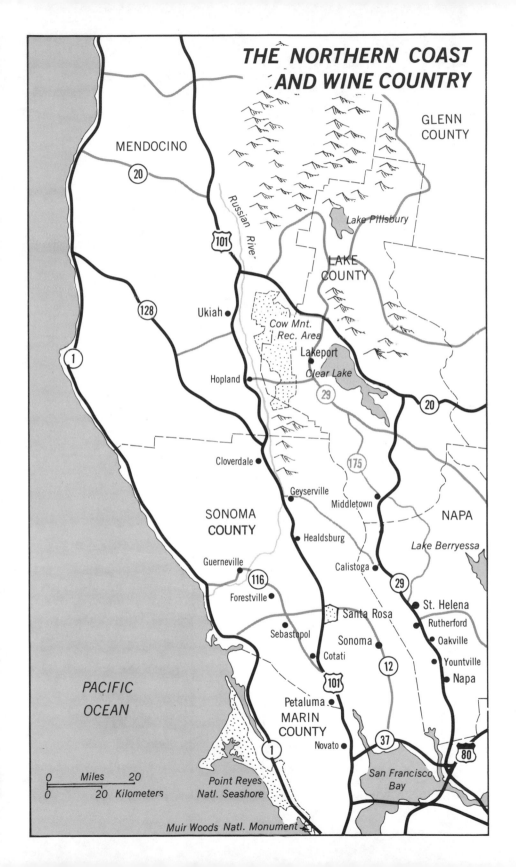

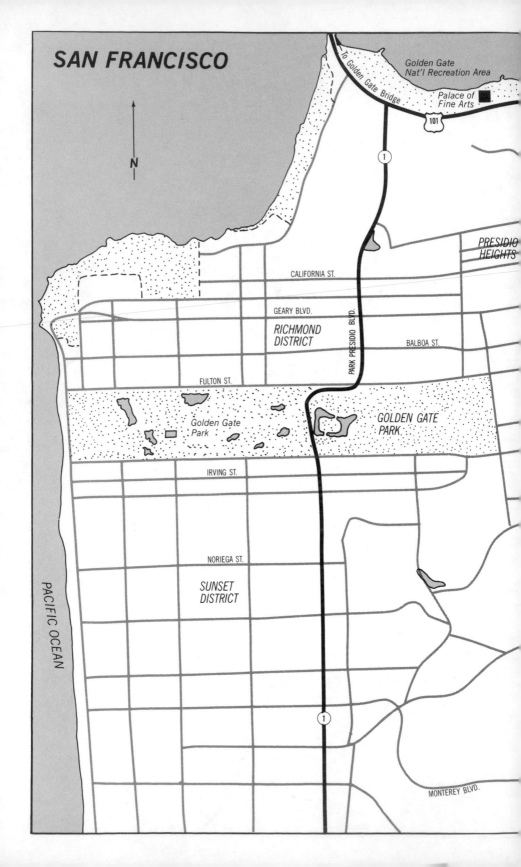

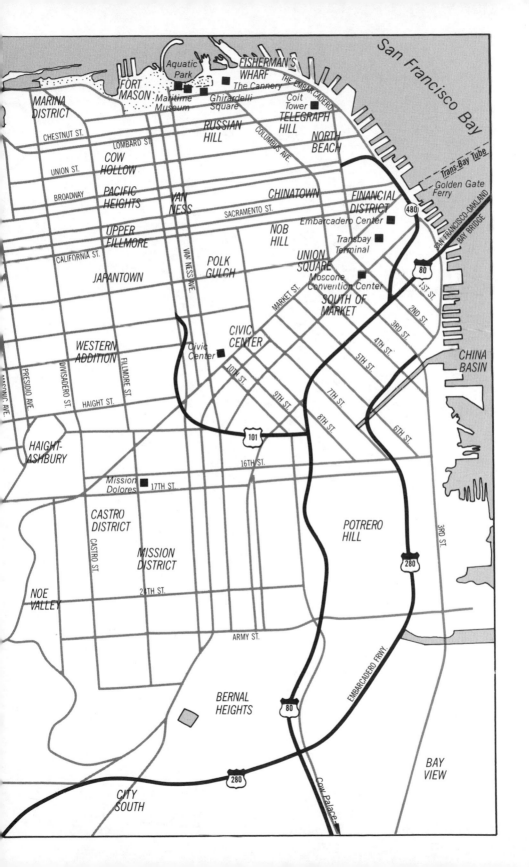

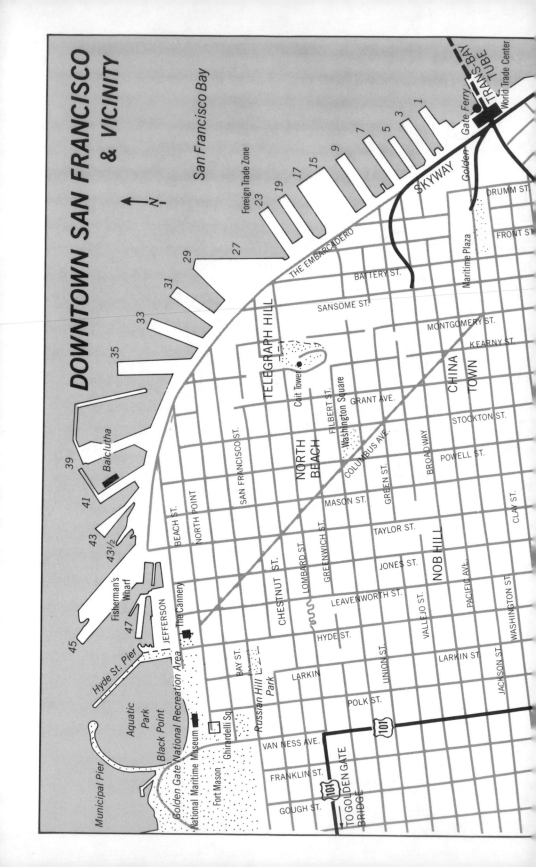

DOWNTOWN SAN FRANCISCO & VICINITY

N →

San Francisco Bay

TRANS-BAY TUBE

World Trade Center

Golden Gate Ferry

SKYWAY

DRUMM ST.

FRONT ST.

Maritime Plaza

THE EMBARCADERO

Foreign Trade Zone

23

19

17

15

9

7

5

3

1

27

29

31

33

35

39

41

43

43½

45

47

BATTERY ST.

SANSOME ST.

MONTGOMERY ST.

KEARNY ST.

CHINA TOWN

STOCKTON ST.

TELEGRAPH HILL

Coit Tower

FILBERT ST.

Washington Square

GRANT AVE.

BROADWAY

POWELL ST.

CLAY ST.

NORTH BEACH

COLUMBUS AVE.

GREEN ST.

MASON ST.

TAYLOR ST.

JONES ST.

NOB HILL

PACIFIC AVE.

WASHINGTON ST.

JACKSON ST.

SAN FRANCISCO ST.

BEACH ST.

NORTH POINT

CHESTNUT ST.

LOMBARD ST.

GREENWICH ST.

LEAVENWORTH ST.

HYDE ST.

VALLEJO ST.

LARKIN ST.

Balclutha

Fisherman's Wharf

Hyde St. Pier

The Cannery

JEFFERSON

BAY ST.

LARKIN

POLK ST.

Russian Hill Park

Aquatic Park

Black Point

Golden Gate National Recreation Area

National Maritime Museum

Fort Mason

Ghirardelli Sq.

VAN NESS AVE.

FRANKLIN ST.

GOUGH ST.

UNION ST.

Municipal Pier

101

101

TO GOLDEN GATE BRIDGE

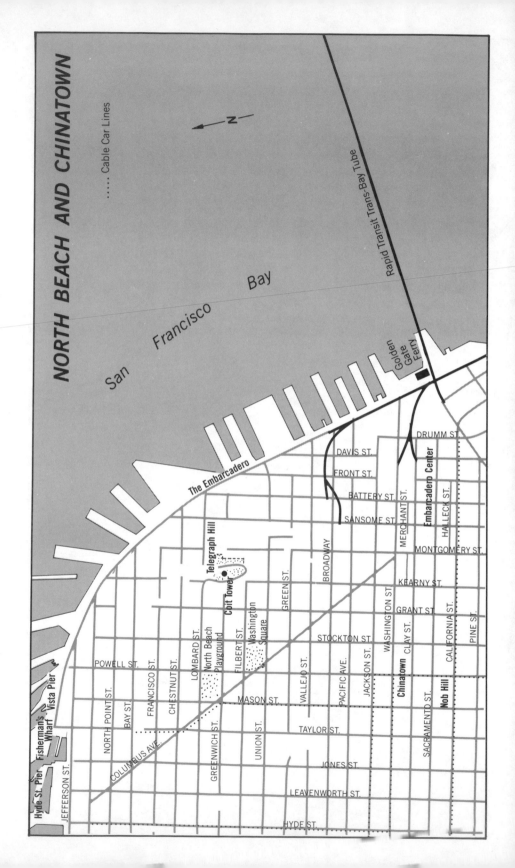

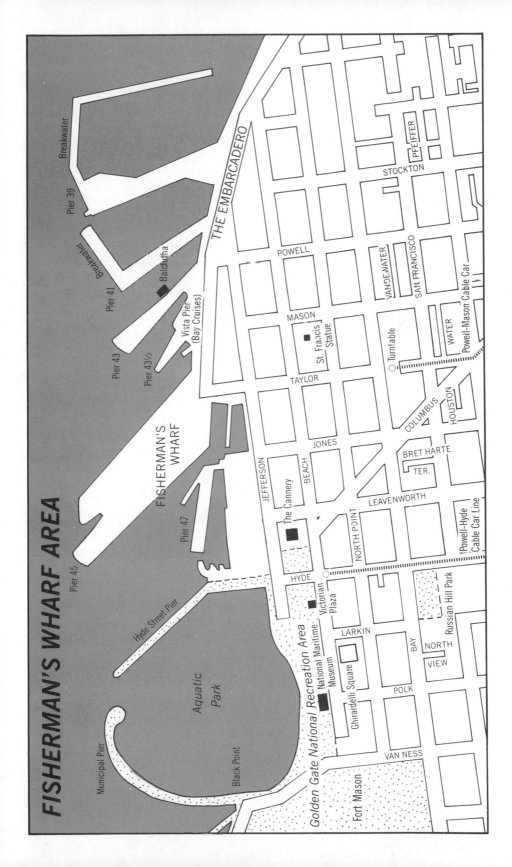

FISHERMAN'S WHARF AREA

INDEX

C

D

MORE GAULT MILLAU "BEST" GUIDES

Now the series known throughout Europe for its wit and savvy reveals the best of four major U.S. cities—New York, Washington, D.C., Los Angeles, and San Francisco. Following the guidelines established by the world-class French food critics Henri Gault and Christian Millau, local teams of writers have gathered inside information about where to stay, what to do, where to shop, and where to dine or catch a quick bite in these key locales. Each volume sparkles with the wit, wisdom, and panache that readers have come to expect from Gault Millau, whose distinctive style makes them favorites among travelers bored with the neutral, impersonal style of other guides. There are full details on the best of everything that makes these cities special places to visit, including restaurants, diversions, nightlife, hotels, shops, the arts—all the unique sights and sounds of each city. These guides also offer practical information on getting around and coping with each city. Filled with provocative, entertaining, and frank reviews, they are helpful as well as fun to read. Perfect for visitors and residents alike.

Please send me the books checked below:

☐ The Best of Los Angeles $14.95

☐ The Best of San Francisco $14.95

☐ The Best of New York $14.95

☐ The Best of Washington, D.C. $14.95

_____

_____

PRENTICE HALL PRESS
Order Department—Travel Books
200 Old Tappan Road
Old Tappan, New Jersey 07675

In U.S. include $1.50 shipping UPS for 1st book, 50¢ each additional book. Outside U.S., $2 and 50¢ respectively.

Enclosed is my check or money order for $ _____

NAME _____

ADDRESS _____

CITY _____ STATE _____ ZIP _____